Sharing Our Worlds

Second edition

Sharing Our Worlds

An Introduction to Cultural and Social Anthropology

Second Edition

Joy Hendry

NEW YORK UNIVERSITY PRESS
Washington Square, New York

First published in the U.S.A. in 2008 by
NEW YORK UNIVERSITY PRESS
Washington Square
New York, NY 10003
www.ny.press.org

Library of Congress Cataloging-in-Publication Data

Hendry, Joy.
Sharing our worlds : an introduction to cultural and social
anthropology / Joy Hendry. – 2nd ed.
p. cm.
Includes bibliographical references and index.
ISBN-13: 978–0–8147–3710–1 (cloth : alk. paper)
ISBN-10: 0–8147–3710–2 (cloth : alk. paper)
ISBN-13: 978–0–8147–3711–8 (pbk. : alk. paper)
ISBN-10: 0–8147–3711–0 (pbk. : alk. paper)
1. Ethnology. I. Title.
GN316.H46 2008
306–dc22
2007041204

Printed and bound in China

In memory of Dennis,
who shared several worlds,
past and present

I thoroughly commend this revised and expanded edition of Joy Hendry's acclaimed book. It is without doubt one of the best introductory texts to social and cultural anthropology that exists. Written in lucid, jargon-free prose and in a style that is both personal and engaging, Hendry once again demonstrates her extraordinary gift for explaining and rendering accessible even the most complex ideas and arguments. This book goes a long way towards bridging the gap between the general public and academic anthropology. It is essential reading for any newcomer to the subject.

Professor Cris Shore, University of Auckland

This is an indispensable text. Hendry conveys key principles in an accessible way without ever losing sight of what it is that makes anthropology such a dynamic and exciting field.

Dr Cathrine Degnen, University of Newcastle

From my own experience I know this book works well with students – and indeed with anyone who is curious about what anthropology is. Hendry deals with a broad range of topics – from what it means to do fieldwork to the classical contributions that have shaped anthropological discourse; from individual symbols to larger constellations of cultural and social organization. The further research sections at the end of each chapter add to the value of the book and the two new chapters, on tourism and on globalization, draw us further into how anthropologists seek to understand contemporary realities. The enlarged new edition of this useful and informative book is easy to recommend.

Professor Leif Manger, University of Bergen

It is very nice to see that my words have been reproduced without editing, without changes, and without interpretation. These are words direct from someone to whom people rarely listen and I appreciate the opportunity to offer something other than romantic nonsense about Travellers' ways.

Mick Ganly, English Traveller, author of one of the
first-hand accounts featured in the book

A lively and accessible introduction to the discipline. Hendry's revised text combines overview and explanation, looking back to anthropology's achievements and forward to the ways in which anthropologists today, and tomorrow, might engage a mobile, connected and globalized world. A very welcome second edition.

Dr Tom Hall, University of Cardiff

A lovely, accessible and engaging introductory book. Hendry's friendly style, together with the clear on-page glossary, personal accounts and useful collections of additional resources, including films and novels, make this an excellent gateway to the world of anthropology.

Gemma Jones, Royal Anthropological Institute

Contents

List of Figures and Maps

List of Photographs

List of First-hand Accounts

Acknowledgements

I must again acknowledge my enormous debt to the people whose worlds I have been privileged to share. These include some who barely receive a mention in the text, for I did not eventually pursue further the study of their worlds, but they undoubtedly influenced my initial discovery of the subject. First, the various people of Morocco amongst whom I lived and travelled in 1966–7, and the French family to whom I became attached on that occasion and who have made me welcome ever since in Paris and les Alpes Maritimes; secondly, the again various people I encountered while living in French Canada in 1967–8, including a Canadian godfather who happened to visit my father, his wartime friend, at the time I was born, and the staff and pupils of Beth Jacob School in Outrement, where I taught for the second two-thirds of an academic year which included the Six Days War in Israel, who introduced me to the (female) world of a highly protected orthodox Jewish community. In Mexico, where I lived and worked from 1968 to 1970 and again in 1972, I discovered the subject of anthropology, which I pursued formally with a period of fieldwork in Texcoco and the formerly Nahuatl community of San Nicolas Tlaminca. Finally, I have shared in many worlds in Japan over the years, but of these I have published: a farming community in Yame, Kyushu, a seaside community in Tateyama, Chiba, and many friends and colleagues in Tokyo and other university cities. To all these and many more casual acquaintances, I record a deep gratitude to them for allowing me to share their lives.

Since the first edition of this book was published I have built up another series of debts to the many Indigenous people with whom I have been working, and who have undoubtedly influenced my thinking about anthropology as well as about their situation. I have tried to name as many as possible of them in my book *Reclaiming Culture*, and as the acknowledgements there are of record length I probably should not repeat the exercise, though my gratitude is none the weaker, and I thank them all again.

The decision to include in this edition first–person accounts of various important issues is also related to my more recent research, and I would like to express a real heartfelt thanks to those people who agreed to write these texts. There was little in it for them – I promised them a copy of the book, that is all – so I thank them warmly for their contributions, which certainly enliven and add authority to the whole book. For help with finding and encouraging some of these people, and proposing others who didn't in the end make it, I would like to thank Gemma Burford, Elizabeth Cory-Pearce, Philippa Deveson, Helen Ganly, David Gellner, Katie Hayne, Gwyneira Isaac, Douglas Johnson, Cees Koelewijn, Howard Morphy, Josephine Reynell, Peter Rivière, John Ryle and Andre Singer.

More people than I can possibly list have influenced my understanding of the social anthropology I present here, and some may anyway feel that I have oversimplified it in an attempt to make the subject accessible to anyone who feels inclined to pick up the book. However, I must at the very least mention my own first supervisor, Peter Rivière, whose words have undoubtedly appeared inadvertently in these pages, so firmly ingrained were some of them in the recesses of my mind, and Rodney Needham, whose work on symbolic classification clearly inspired the whole basis of the original lecture course and therefore the approach of the book. The influence of cultural anthropology came after I published the first edition of this book, when I attended an enlightening course offered by Laura Peers at the Pitt Rivers Museum and, at her introduction, spent a couple of semesters visiting McMaster University in Canada.

For practical help with reading, suggestions and comments on various stages of the whole process, I am indebted to Ross Bowden, Jeremy MacClancy, Howard Morphy and Mike O'Hanlon for help with Chapter 6, Nazia Tenvir and Haroon Sarwar with Chapter 11, and, more generally, to Renate Barber, Genevieve Bicknell, Annabel Black, Paul Collinson, Martin Flatman, Ian Fowler, David Gellner, Clare Hall, Renee Hirschon, William Kay, Tammy Kohn, Chris McDonaugh, Andrew McMullen, Diana Martin, Lola Martinez, Peter Parkes, Bob Parkin, Sue Pennington, Josephine Reynell, Peter Rivière, Alison Shaw, Cris Shore and Felicity Wood. For comments and suggestions on various aspects of the second edition, I would like add Jan Harwell, Garry Marvin and Jacqueline Waldren for Chapter 13, Mitch Sedgwick for Chapter 14, and more generally, Mary Martha Beaton, Mary Louise Bracho, Udi Butler, Hilary Callan, Ericka Chemko, Audrey Colson, Michael Herzfeld, Roger Just, Emiko Ohnuki-Tierney, Laura Rival and Phil Sawkins. Students over the years have also added helpful comments and Peter Momtchiloff at Oxford University Press kindly read and discussed a draft of the first edition when he took on the anthropology list. I must also acknowledge the detailed, helpful and incisive comments and suggestions of the several anonymous readers of the draft of this edition, and thank them for some of the examples I have incorporated into the final text.

Thanks, too, to various friends and colleagues for the generous loan of their photographs, which are credited individually, but especially to the Pitt Rivers Museum for allowing me to publish my snapshot of the totem pole, and also to Michael O'Hanlon, the director, and Jeremy Coote, curator, who have allowed me to use formerly published photographs. For technical support, I would like to thank Bob Pomfret and Lisa Hill for help with the photographs, Gerry Black, who made the original figures and world maps, and Bev Massingham, Kirsten Brown, Maggie Kleszczewska and other Social Sciences staff for general secretarial support.

Specific help with the final stages of the second edition, sometimes quite late in the day, came from Chantal Butchinsky, who responded with amazing calm and speed to requests for help with updating reading lists, films and, particularly, finding websites; Susanne Hammacher, for RAI film lists in the midst of preparing for the annual RAI film festival; Gemma Jones for more helpful websites and a fund of other interesting ideas; and Catherine Travers at Palgrave Macmillan, who offered the most wonderfully cool and organised author support as well as long lists of helpful comments and suggestions on the draft text. To all these, I am especially grateful.

Finally, I would like again to thank my father and mother, whose pleasant but unashamedly chauvinistic bickering about their respective origins in Scotland and Yorkshire made me aware of cultural boundary marking before I had any idea what it was, and helped me to keep at bay the tendency to exoticise anthropology long before it became politically important to do so. Dennis, my husband, and his family made me aware of a special cultural quality that is shared in Liverpool, and James and William, our sons, ensure that I don't forget about it now that he is no longer with us.

Preface

Anthropology is one of those fields that many people have vaguely heard of, but few know how to define. Even students of the subject dread that inevitable party-stopping question: 'Just what is it that you are studying?' and several rather pat answers have been invented to snuff out the interest. Once started on an explanation, however, an enthusiastic student may be hard to stop and, for many, anthropology comes to change their lives in a profound and irreversible way. It may still be difficult to say quite why, but they will share an understanding of life with others who have ventured into the same pastures, an understanding which will also stand them in good stead in all kinds of future endeavours, including when they enter the workplace.

Social and cultural anthropology – the focus of this particular volume – is not an esoteric, difficult subject, however. Quite the contrary, it is concerned with the most mundane aspects of everyday life and it should, up to a fairly advanced point, be relatively easy to understand and absorb. Those who have been brought up bilingual, or in a multicultural school aware of its advantages, or in a society different from that of their parents may have an initial advantage in this respect, for they will have begun to appreciate some of the implications of cultural diversity. Indeed, social anthropology may help them to find a niche of their own in the world. Those who have pondered intriguing differences they encounter during travels abroad may also find they have taken the first steps into the field. For others, novels may have opened the gates.

This book is written to create order out of these initial experiences. It does not aim to be comprehensive, or even to give a broad summary of the basic works in the field. References to the anthropology discussed are provided at the end of each chapter, along with some ideas for further reading, and together these should offer a sound introduction to anyone embarking on the study of the subject. The later chapters also cover several of the traditional sections into which the field is divided. The main aim, however, is to help the initiate over some of the first hurdles they are likely to encounter. My own first professor warned me to expect to be confused for the best part of a year, and some difficulty may be inevitable because of the very nature of the subject, but this book aims to smooth the way.

initiate - a person joining a new stage of life, typically learning in order to be an effective member, sometimes through certain trials and ordeals.

The text is written primarily for students taking up the study of social and/or cultural anthropology, or thinking about taking it up, but it is also written for their mothers, brothers and friends, and for their potential future employers to see how broadly beneficial such a background may be. It is written (I hope) in a style open to any to follow, making no assumptions about prior knowledge or background, and it is written in such a way that one can use it to refer back to the parts one feels unsure about later. Most of all, however, it is written in an effort to make the whole venture enjoyable. It is a subject I discovered almost by chance when, during my youth, I was setting out to enjoy myself. Imagine my delight when I found I could spend the rest of my life doing just that for a career!

This book was inspired by a series of lectures presented annually to first-year students at Oxford Brookes University, lectures that are only part of their learning experience. The students also play games, watch films, read other books and articles, answer short computer-aided tests, and write essays about what they are learning. During the later part of their university career some of the same students go out into the city or further afield to carry out their own investigations, and over the years these have included studies of greyhound racing, public houses, churches, witches' covens and college dinners. In contemporary global society, there are plenty of different 'worlds' to share and to learn about and I am sure that each of you readers will find some interest of your own to follow up, whether it be in your family, among your friends, or in some new world you will discover. I hope that this book will help you to do that in a respectful and egalitarian way.

Preface to the Second Edition

Planning and writing the second edition of this book has been a great opportunity to bring into the text some up-to-date research, some new attitudes to anthropology, and some now quite well-established changes in the approach of potential students. All three of these innovations reflect a rapidly growing aware-ness around the world of the diversity of people who share it with us, whoever we are, and the book seeks to foster a greater knowledge about our common human-ity as well as our continuing cultural differences.

Much anthropological research has moved into a mode which could be described as global, just as there is a wider awareness of its value, and students now often come to the classroom with experience of travel, relocation of their families, and first-hand encounters with worlds that differ from their own. This offers a wealth of experience to bring to discussions, and I have added some end-of-chapter questions to encourage readers to consider how the issues raised may manifest themselves in their own lives. The approach still aims to be directly accessible to those with no prior knowledge, gradually introducing more com-plex issues once the basic building blocks have been laid, but the questions also encourage a deeper consideration of the issues raised. Another innovation for the new edition is the glossary at the end of the book, which defines terms used in the text. These terms appear in bold type at first mention, with an immediate definition to hand in the margin.

A prime aim of the social and cultural anthropology I present here is that we learn to respect and value all peoples equally, an aim that is vitally important in the transnational, global world in which most of us now live and work. A new feature of this second edition about which I am particularly pleased is to be found in the first-hand accounts that have been presented within most of the chapters. These were planned to recognise the essential contributions made by those whose lives anthropologists have described in developing the subject, and to give a few of them a chance to speak directly to the reader without the intervention of the anthropologist along the way. I tried where possible to invite members of groups discussed in the text, and this is particularly valuable when the anthropology is classic, and therefore rather dated, for it allows the reader to get a feel for what has happened to the people since the initial studies were made.

We have also introduced references to new books, articles and films and, of course, generally updated the text to reflect changes in the field. However, we have not interfered with the overall structure of the book, which was and still is designed to form a coherent whole with logical links between chapters building towards an ever-greater understanding of the subject.

Two completely new chapters have been added at the end. Both reflect the place of anthropology in an increasingly globalised world, but they approach it from contrasting angles.

The first of these chapters, 'Tourism and the Intercultural Encounter' (Chapter 13), addresses directly the way in which peoples of different backgrounds are in general much more likely than they were in the past to encounter cultural vari-ety in their worlds. Of course, there have been multicultural regions since time immemorial, and there have for long been those who catered to travellers of one sort or another, but the movement that has become known as tourism has really only burgeoned in the last few decades. This is largely because of technology that has enabled cheap and fast movement around the globe, but the interest in cultural variety is also found at home, as we shall see. This chapter will offer many insights, then, but its base in the new field of Tourism and Anthropology should be of particular interest to those who include a gap year of travel in their lives.

The second new chapter, 'Transnationalism, Globalisation and Beyond' (Chapter 14), examines ways in which social life has been altered since rapidly changing technologies have enabled people in different parts of the world instantly to be in touch on a regular basis. It discusses the consequences, positive and negative, of how people have reorganised or rearranged their lives, and looks at some of the new and often quite interesting situations that have arisen. It also examines how the work of anthropologists has adapted to these new arrangements, and how new roles have emerged for us to play. The playing of some of them is still at an early stage, however, and at the end of this new edition, I merely throw out a few ideas about how a neophyte anthropologist, perhaps like yourself, may take forward the knowledge you will acquire as you tread this path. Undoubtedly, you will think of many others!

Introduction

What Anthropologists Do

Anthropology comes in a variety of different forms, and the Greek basis of the term, which simply means the study of human beings, doesn't really help to narrow things down much, especially when we find that some anthropologists work with monkeys and other non-human primates more than they work with people! The term is used in different ways in different countries, and there are even subtle differences within the same country. You will probably be happy to hear, then, that there is also a broad understanding among anthropologists about how to proceed, and in this opening section, we will focus on the kinds of things that anthropologists do in order to earn that title.

In this book, our prime focus is actually on social and cultural anthropology, and we will therefore not be discussing archaeology, which is a closely related subject that is sometimes included under the term anthropology, but which has its own experts and methods. Nor will we much discuss biological anthropology, which is again quite closely related, but which is concerned with human anatomy and physiology, and, like archaeology, with examining ancient remains and artefacts in order to draw up theories about human evolution. In the United States, linguistics is also regarded as a separate branch of anthropology, and we will touch on this field, but only where it helps us to understand the social and cultural aspects of human life that form *our* main focus.

What social and cultural anthropologists generally share, then, is an interest in different ways people have of looking at the world they live in. These different ways are not individual idiosyncrasies, but different views of the world learned as people grow up in different societies, or within one of the different groups that make up one larger society. It may be the differences between people who live in Birmingham and Brighton, or between those in Bermuda and Bangkok, or even the variety of views across a number of diverse groups within one of those places. There is an almost unlimited variety of world views for us to look at, and each anthropologist tends to specialise, at least for a time, in looking at one of them.

Most social anthropologists gain their specialist knowledge by going to live in a society they have negotiated to work in. They don't just go there for a week or two with an interpreter and a set of questionnaires. They go for a year or more, seek to set up home with the people they are interested in, and try to live as far as possible as those people do – in every respect. The idea is to find out exactly what it is like to be a member of the society in question, and anthropologists operate on the assumption that the best way to do this is to live with those people and seek to share their lives. This form of investigation is called participant observation, because the observer finds out what he or she wants to know by participating in the lives of the people under study.

> **participant observation** – a method used by anthropologists to learn about a people and their activities by observing at the same time as participating in their lives.

Anthropologists participate in the regular routines of everyday life, perhaps trying out the activities of a number of different members of the society, as well as asking permission to take part in their rites, and observe as far as possible their most intimate ceremonies. If the people they are concerned with get up early, they get up early; if they stay up all night, the anthropologist should do the same. If some of the people take hallucinogenic drugs, the anthropologist might legitimately argue that they should do the same, for the activities that are banned in one country may be accepted in another, although a newcomer should always be careful. If the people they choose to work with stand for long periods of the night in a freezing stream, so should the observer (this example may sound far-fetched, but it was part of a study carried out in the Andes on which a book called *The Coming of the Sun* is based [Tayler 1997]). The idea is to experience what it is like to be a member of the world under study, for otherwise one could not begin to understand how it looks and feels.

An important part of this exercise, more technically though rather quaintly known as fieldwork, is to learn the language of the people concerned. This was absolutely vital in the early studies of peoples with whom the outside

> **fieldwork** – carrying out practical investigations necessary to a particular study chosen by an anthropologist.

world had previously had little contact, but it is essential anywhere to gain an understanding of the way the world is seen and described. Anthropologists have found that working with interpreters gives a wholly inadequate view, for first-hand knowledge of a language is the only way to become fully aware of the meanings and implications of the words used, and these might be very different from the straight translations presented in a dictionary.

This concern with language is important even for anthropologists who choose to work in a society where their own idiom is the native tongue, for there are many versions of any particular language. Teenagers who claim that their parents do not understand them, for example, are not merely being adolescent and rebellious. They are also usually quite accurately referring to differences in language (and values) which develop between generations. Within the English language there are also clear regional differences, and differences based on other allegiances such as ethnic origins, class and occupation. An anthropologist working in his or her own mother tongue must be especially careful to look out for these sometimes rather fine distinctions. Consider the difference between American, British and Australian humour, for example.

Anthropologists may experience other difficulties in finding ways to fit into a society of their choice. People may (quite rightly) be very suspicious of a stranger whose main aim in life seems to be to poke their nose into the affairs of those around them, and they are entitled to feel resentful of such interference into their lives. It is important, then, for an anthropologist to consider these feelings, to take care to explain their intentions, and to respect requests from the people they work with not to publish and broadcast all that they learn. It is not only polite, but also ethically essential to discuss with people how the knowledge they share might subsequently be used, and in recent years people generally check back what they write with those who helped them with the work (see Cooper 2007 on this subject, however).

In remote areas, before travellers and television crews became commonplace almost anywhere, a stranger who appeared out of the blue was usually treated to food and accommodation by local people. Anthropologists benefited from this human hospitality, and they learned to carry gifts or medicines to offer thanks, and to make an initial bid for acceptance. In some cases, local people would adopt an anthropologist as a fictitious relative so that others would know how to relate to them, and this helped with their own local learning. Others failed to achieve this kind of trust, and some were even killed. One I know, who went to work in the South American rain forest, claimed he had spent several weeks living off food thrown out for dogs until the local people accepted that he shared human qualities.

Nowadays, it is rare to find a place where people are unaware of the wider world. Communication technologies have penetrated even the most isolated of areas, and outsiders are unfortunately often associated with unwelcome intrusions, such as industrial construction and environmental destruction, into the lives of local people. It is unsurprising then if the old hospitality to strangers has become rare. Anthropologists also work in cities and other places where their business may be confused with that of less welcome visitors, such as tax inspectors, evangelists or political activists. It is important then to devise strategies to gain the trust and confidence of the people with whom they hope to work.

Many anthropologists have found it useful to arrive with their family. This seems less threatening, and helps to overcome problems of crossing local barriers of age and gender. In some parts of the world, men and women lead very separate lives, and a man may find it virtually impossible to investigate the lives of women, and vice-versa. A female anthropologist who worked in Mexico reported that she found it essential to adopt an 'anomalous sexless' role so that women would not be jealous of her talking to men, and men would not misinterpret her intentions. In rural Japan, at gatherings where men and women sat separately, but in age order, I used to be seated between the youngest man and the oldest woman, so my role must have been ambiguous in this respect too. Later, working with my children in Japan opened doors to subjects I had never even anticipated (see Hendry 1999 for examples).

My own experiences were at first relatively easy: in Mexico, where anthropologists are thick on the ground even if the local interpretation of the word (*antropologia*) is closer to archaeology, and then in Japan, where the pursuit of academic inquiry of any kind seems to be regarded with great respect. In both cases, I received much cooperation from the start, but each had its own problems too. In Mexico, people would sometimes express their suspicion of outsiders asking questions by telling quite blatant lies, even in matters as basic as the number of their children. In Japan, people were more likely to tell me things they thought I'd like to hear – a more subtle form of deception. More recently, I have been working with Indigenous people who have sometimes built up a negative view of anthropologists, largely based on their association with the activities of colonial powers.

Indigenous People – a term adopted collectively by those, also called **Aboriginal** or **First Nations**, whose territories have become subsumed into nations built around them, and who are seeking various 'rights' through international bodies like the United Nations.

All of these problems, and indeed many others encountered by anthropologists, are solved at least to some extent by the fact that their initial study at least is carried out over a longish period of time. A year is regarded as a bare minimum in order to see the complete cycle of annual events, seasons and so forth, but many spend much longer, especially if they are starting from scratch with a new language. Thus the initial reservations of the informants (a word that has long been used for members of the society under study) are usually dispelled, and their views become more transparent as they relax and operate in normal everyday life. In recent years, in response to some who complain that their ancestors shared too much of their lives with outsiders,

informants – the word used for members of the society under study by anthropologists.

who then disappeared to publish their knowledge, the word collaborators has been used for those with whom we work, and increased possibilities for return visits and long-distance communication make the practice more collaborative too.

Other aspects of the method of investigation help to smooth relations as well, for it has been common to choose a relatively small group of people to work with so that the anthropologist can get to know everyone well. This allows relationships to be observed first hand, as well as to be described, and differing views may be compared. The group could be a village, a school, perhaps an occupational unit such as a factory, bank or advertising agency, or a large extended family. One of my acquaintances took up the study of a group of criminals, whom he used at first to meet largely in pubs, although later he had to spend a lot of his time in prisons. Another decided to observe an enclosed order of nuns. The authors of two PhD theses I have examined on Japan worked in a bridal parlour (see Goldstein-Gidoni in Chapter 12) and a regional museum.

In all such cases, the anthropologist is observing people in what we call 'face-to-face' relations (though recent technology, and websites like *facebook*, have introduced a new meaning to that phrase, which we discuss in Chapter 14). This is a great advantage, not least because people will talk about each other as well as about themselves, which gives the anthropologist more in-depth, interlocking and complex information than can be gleaned from a few one-to-one interviews. More importantly still, however, members of such groups are likely to share a system of values, and although they might disagree with one another on specific issues, they will draw upon a set of underlying assumptions in their communication with each other. It is this set of shared assumptions which defines in broad terms the language they use and the way they see the world through that language.

The anthropologist learns that language, and the world view it portrays, by living amongst the people. They may start out by asking questions – indeed most do, for there are a lot of practical details to amass. Later, however, they may find they learn more by sitting quietly and listening, by joining in with the work of the day, or even by simply observing the activities of others. In Japan, as elsewhere, much is communicated at a non-verbal level, perhaps in silence, in slight movements of the body, or by exchanging gifts or other material goods such as plates of food. Too much verbosity could blind the investigator to this level of interaction.

Listening also allows one a chance to check the validity of statements made in answer to questions. In Japan, for example, there is something of a controversy about whether love marriages are better than those arranged by elders. One old man told me how much he approved of love marriages, winking and confiding that his own had been such. Later I learned that he had refused to consent when his own daughter wanted to have such a marriage, and, even later, I heard him telling one of his friends how dangerous he thought it was for young people to initiate their own relationships. This man was often sought as a go-between, as it turned out, undoubtedly because of his charm and diplomacy – the same qualities which probably lay behind his initial reaction to my investigations, since he knew love marriages were the norm where I came from.

It is this kind of information which adds an extra dimension to the findings of anthropologists who carry out long-term participant observation, and it goes beyond the more limited fieldwork or statistical surveys of the sociologist or economist. There are of course drawbacks, because much depends on the character and interests of the investigators, and their own cultural background. The depth of understanding anthropologists are able to gain, which enables them to see beyond the cool front of a diplomat, has a value that should not be underestimated, however – especially in the global, multicultural world in which most of us now live. To respond to criticisms about the personal bias involved, anthropologists now usually provide information about their own background and experience when they write up their work. This subject is discussed again in Chapter 1.

Translation is the anthropologists' next task. After learning how to live with the people under study, they must return to their own societies and explain what they have found in their own languages. They must discover ways to analyse and make sense of their findings that are comprehensible to their colleagues and compatriots, which is not as easy as it may sound. Other anthropologists who have parallel experiences provide models in their own work for the subsequent reports from the returned fieldworker. These basic accounts are called ethnography, literally writings about a particular 'ethnic' group of people, though ethnicity has been defined in different ways (see Banks 1996). Groups may also be characterised in other ways, as we saw for the criminals and nuns mentioned above (and see MacClancy 1996, in relation to sport).

translation – for anthropologists, this practice involves much more than finding an equivalent word in a different language; gaining an understanding behind the meaning of words and phrases, is an important part of anthropological work.

ethnography – literally, writings about a particular 'ethnic' group of people, the descriptive part of what anthropologists provide in their reports of fieldwork. The term is also used in other disciplines to describe research methods that resemble those of anthropologists.

Comparisons are usually made with previous work, and much time may be spent trying to assess the extent to which areas of apparent similarity are comparable with phenomena observed elsewhere. Findings that seem to be peculiar to a particular group may be especially interesting, but they may also dissolve into general features of society which are manifested under a different guise in other places. It is beneficial to both sides if anthropologists return to the place of their research after some years have elapsed. On the one hand, the people can see at first hand what they helped to achieve in terms of books, films, articles and so forth, and, on the other, they can comment on its accuracy and help to place the initial findings in a long-term context.

The more accomplished scholars use their material to contribute to or to formulate general theories about social life and human behaviour, and this venture has been one of the most important aims of social and cultural anthropology. We are all interested in difference and diversity in the people with whom we carry out our work, but ultimately we are also keen to identify underlying principles in the way that human beings put together and enact their social, political and ritual life. We may be fascinated by the variety and ingenuity we discover – and this is one of the aspects of the subject that can be shared beyond the field – but to make general theory about the human condition is a bigger aim that is not always so easy to transmit.

It is this part of our work that may irk our informants, or 'collaborators', because the published material will carry 'their' knowledge that they have 'shared' with us into a more esoteric form of analysis that may seem to leave them in an inferior position. (This feeling of inferiority on the part of the collaborators stems from the fact that they may feel excluded by the language of academic anthropology – but in reality, all spheres, academic or otherwise, have their own specialist language and terminology: just as anthropologists may use terms with which their collaborators are not familiar, so archaeologists or biologists may understand different, specialist language which is unfamiliar to the anthropologist.) We will return to this issue several times, for there are also historical reasons for this perception of a power differential. In the meantime, for you, the reader, an important aim of the present book is to introduce some of the specialist language anthropologists share, and some of the theoretical advances that they have made.

It should be emphasised straight away, however, that anthropological theories do not always build upon one another. Indeed, many set out to contradict those of previous scholars; this critical approach is part of an anthropologist's training and we will begin to introduce it here (see Sykes 2005, for another example). There are some classic works, which are accepted by most people in the field, and these will be discussed quite early on in this book. There are also several areas where different interpretations exist side by side, and there is no consensus about which is better. Some of these will be mentioned too. This book is inevitably informed by the British anthropological traditions which exist in Oxford, where I was trained, but it is intended as an introduction to the subject that is accessible and engaging no matter what the reader's background. An important thing to remember, however, is that the study of society is not simply the learning of a body of facts. The study of ourselves and our social worlds is an area of much interpretation and many differing views.

Writing for the general public, on the one hand, or working with them, on the other, is less often the aim of anthropologists, at least at first: rather, they tend to write for and work with colleagues who share much of the same background and have parallel experiences on which to draw. This book is an attempt to bridge the first of those gaps, however. A growing number of anthropologists afterwards bridge the second by putting their new understanding into practical applications in the wider world, an area known as applied anthropology, which we will consider in the last section of Chapter 14 of this book. Some also make, or advise on, television documentaries about the area where they worked, and there is now a superb worldwide collection of visual ethnography (see Banks 2001; Pink 2001). Reference to a selection of films, some of them now classic, is made at the end of each chapter of this book, and some general distributors and anthropological film festivals are listed at the end of this chapter.

applied anthropology – using knowledge gained through the academic study of anthropology out in the public arena, usually to the benefit of people there.

Many students of anthropology go out into the world to do quite unrelated tasks, but always informed by the knowledge that *their* world, *their* way of thinking, is only one of many. They are equipped with the skill to see the other's point of view, whether the other be Chinese, Czech or from Church Hanborough, and it is this skill which can be acquired through the study of social and cultural anthropology. Even without becoming a professional anthropologist, a student of the subject can gain a great deal from at least a smattering of practical experience, carrying out a project in a 'world' different from their own. This book offers only the first key to the first door to this experience, but it is a door that many people fail ever to open.

A Brief History of Social (and Cultural) Anthropology

We have so far made no distinction between the terms 'social' and 'cultural' in qualifying the subject of anthropology, and indeed, there is not a great deal to distinguish the two approaches to the field in the way it is practised today. In this section we will see that they have had rather different histories, reflecting in some ways the locations where they were developed, and in others, the theoretical interests of those who built them up. *Social anthropology* is a more accurate name for the practice I have described so far, as *cultural anthropology* has a greater concern with collecting material objects, and did not always involve such long periods of fieldwork. In practice, the terms 'society' and 'culture' have been much discussed in ways that need not concern us at this stage. Taking a look at the history of the field will give us a basis for a later understanding, however.

The subject as practised today actually developed only within the last hundred-odd years, and some of the stages in its development will be illustrated in the chapters that follow. However, its intellectual foundations go back a little further and it has recently been subjected to considerable critical self-scrutiny, so it is useful before embarking on these chapters to lay out some of this general background. A thorough history of anthropology would form the subject matter of a book in its own right, and indeed, several have been written (an accessible one is *A History of Anthropology* by Eriksen and Nielson, published in 2001). This section seeks only to summarise some of the issues that have been addressed, and to place them in the context of changes that have affected and improved our work.

People have undoubtedly speculated about neighbours they considered strange since time immemorial, and travellers' tales have always been popular, but the European interest in social life became more focused when the tales of explorers and adventurers began to show striking similarities between societies found in different parts of the world. Many such societies fell prey to the destructive European battles for colonisation, largely because their technological resources were inadequate to resist the Europeans who arrived on their shores. The more sympathetic invaders consoled themselves with the thought that they were bringing 'civilisation' to those whose lands they were claiming, and they collected information about the people they met as they realised that their worlds were being irrevocably changed. Theories were also developed about how studies of these so-called 'primitive' people could shed light on the prehistorical past of the investigators' own worlds.

These theories built on the establishment in the eighteenth century of the 'rational' way of thinking of the natural sciences (the period in which this approach developed is described as 'Enlightenment', so important was the understanding scholars felt they were gaining of the world around them). Laws were proposed and tested to explain the physical, chemical and biological worlds, and it came to be thought that society could be regarded as a natural system too. In France, for example, Montesquieu set out to discover the laws of social life by analysing and comparing various types of political institutions, and examining religious beliefs as social phenomena, which he argued were usually suited to the society in which they were found and therefore difficult to transport.

In Scotland, during the same period, David Hume was investigating the origins of religion in human nature, and he posited a development from polytheism through monotheism to the inevitable decline of religion. He was part of the school of Moral Philosophers, which also included Adam Smith, who founded the discipline of economics, and Adam Ferguson, one of the early thinkers to argue that contemporary 'primitive' society could throw light on the past history of 'higher' societies. It was in France, though, that a science of society was seriously proposed. First, Saint-Simon built on an assertion made by Condorcet that social phenomena were just as natural as those of organic and inorganic sciences were, and he suggested therefore that they should be studied by the same methods. The subject was named *sociology* by Comte, who drew up a ranking of sciences ranging from mathematics and astronomy as the most general, through to psychology and sociology at the extreme of greatest complexity. His laws of social life were based on the assumption that all societies evolved through the same stages, and that the human species has a fundamental tendency to ameliorate itself.

polytheism – a belief system that holds that there are multiple gods.

monotheism – a belief system that holds that there is only one God.

This evolutionary approach characterised the wider thinking of the nineteenth century, when several systematic attempts were made to trace the development of social institutions through different stages. J. F. McLennan made a study of marriage, for example, and Henry Maine made one of law. In Britain the most influential theoretical writer of the time was probably Herbert Spencer, whose ideas about the 'survival of the fittest' were later attributed to that other great evolutionist of the nineteenth century, Charles Darwin. Spencer made many biological analogies in his consideration of society as 'superorganic', and he also advocated looking at how the parts of a society related to one another rather than taking them out of context as others were wont to do.

This was later to be the cornerstone of two schools of anthropology known as functionalism and structural functionalism, led by twentieth-century scholars Bronislaw Malinowski and A. R. Radcliffe-Brown, respectively. These approaches, each seeking an explanation of social behaviour within a particular society at a particular time, were something of a reaction to the previous evolutionary method, although they were later criticised for neglecting history. They entailed spending a long time with a particular people and really learning their language in all its complexity, and this came to distinguish *social anthropology* from *sociology*.

functionalism – a word used to describe theories that explain social behaviour in terms of the way it appears to respond to the needs of members of that society, as advocated by Bronislaw Malinowski and his followers.

Malinowski, a Polish-born anthropologist, was the first major proponent of the value of this long-term study in Britain. He had been interned in Australia at the start of the First World War, and spent several years in the Trobriand Islands, where he discovered the great advantages of a long stay for properly understanding the ways of thinking of another people. The functionalist approach he advocated was grounded in the idea that all social and cultural behaviour could be explained as responding to human needs. He taught social anthropology at the London School of Economics (LSE) on his return to Europe, and inspired a whole cohort of anthropological fieldworkers who produced a body of detailed ethnography. Some of Malinowski's work is discussed in Chapters 3 and 7, and that of other members of the continuing LSE department throughout the book.

structural functionalism – a theory of explanation of social behaviour which examines the way that components of a particular society functioned to maintain the **social structure**. It was developed by Radcliffe-Brown and applied for a while by his followers.

Social structure – a way of describing the make-up of the features of a society in order to devise general theories that could be applied to specific cases, but also allow cross-cultural comparison.

Radcliffe-Brown's long-term fieldwork was carried out in the Andaman Islands (Bay of Bengal) from 1906 to 1908, although it was less intensive than that of Malinowski. His interests were in the value of social behaviour for the maintenance and well-being of a network of social relations he called the social structure – hence the phrase structural functionalism. He taught in Sydney, Capetown and Chicago, so his work was very influential around the world. It has remained known as British social anthropology, though it is less often referred to in Britain now than elsewhere, and in the United States, at least, a reaction to the closed nature of his analysis still continues.

We will look at an example of Radcliffe-Brown's work in Chapter 9, and illustrate its inapplicability to the contemporary world in Chapter 14.

In the United States, the emphasis on intensive fieldwork dates back to the earlier work of Franz Boas, a German immigrant of Jewish origin, who argued in 1896 that all cultures were equal but different, and a great deal of work needed to be applied to each one. He spent long periods of time studying with groups of Native Americans, and trained his followers to collect detailed empirical data about their material culture, as well as language and social behaviour. His work became known as *cultural anthropology*, and he introduced the idea of cultural relativism, which argues that because cultures are based on different ideas about the world, they can only be properly understood in terms of their own standards and values, although this does not mean that outsiders cannot learn to decipher those meanings.

cultural relativism – a term devised by Franz Boas to explain that as cultures are based on different ideas about the world, they can only be properly understood in terms of their own standards and values. The phrase has been misunderstood to deny human universals, and to suggest that cultures cannot change.

Ruth Benedict, a student of Boas, continued his efforts to demonstrate the basic equality of different cultural forms, and avidly to collect materials about peoples who were coming under the threat of contradictory assimilation policies that still operated on the assumption of an evolutionary superiority. Like most anthropologists, she opposed war as an expression of this kind of posture, an important stance in the build-up to race-based fascism in Europe. Although she was employed by the United States War Office to study the enemy Japanese during the Second World War, her book (1954[1946]) makes a plea for 'a world made safe for cultural difference'. It was also later described by a Japanese anthropologist as a 'consistently balanced contrast between America and Japan' (Aoki 1994: 5). Almost contemporary with Benedict was the anthropologist Margaret Mead, who brought her writings about Pacific peoples in Samoa and Papua New Guinea so much into the American public domain that she remains famous to this day.

In Europe, a French sociologist who had a profound influence on the evolving subject of social anthropology in the early part of the twentieth century was Emile Durkheim. His concerns were still evolutionary, but he insisted that society must be looked at as more than the sum of individuals who make it up. He advocated the identification of social facts, which exist outside the individual and exercise constraint 'like moulds in which our actions are inevitably shaped'. Examples are legal and moral regulations, religious faiths, financial systems, and taste in art, all of which form part of our socialisation and education in a particular society. He led a group of scholars who were, sadly, largely wiped out in the First World War. Some of the work he wrote with another member, Marcel Mauss, will be discussed in Chapter 1, and Mauss will reappear in Chapter 3.

social facts – the proper materials, which 'exist outside the individual and exercise constraint', to be collected by sociologists and anthropologists, as advocated by Emile Durkheim.

The first chair in anthropology was created in Oxford at the turn of the twentieth century, and it was held by Edward Tylor, who also reacted negatively to the idea that 'savages' were somehow different from 'civilised' people. He had travelled in Mexico as a young man and he continually argued that 'human nature is everywhere similar'. He encouraged the comparison of 'primitive' and 'civilised' practices, but he was still an evolutionist. Another school of thought – the Diffusionists – argued for a cradle of civilisation from which practices had spread or *diffused* around the world, as people influenced and copied one another. Eventually, another influential Oxford professor of anthropology, Edward Evans-Pritchard, pointed to a futility in the speculation about how societies had developed, or evolved, and even rejected the idea of social laws.

He argued that societies are systems only because human beings need to order the world rationally, and anthropologists should study this structural order, and seek *meaning* (rather than *function*) for the elements that make up that order in the context of a particular society. He advocated representing a particular society by establishing sets of related abstractions, which could then be compared with those of other societies. These structures could undergo transformations, which would represent change, an advance on the earlier structural functional explanations, which seemed to ignore history. Some examples of his work are discussed further in Chapter 7 and Chapter 10 of this book.

One of the most influential anthropologists to date has been another Frenchman, Claude Lévi-Strauss, whose name will pop up in several chapters. Among other things, he marvelled at the human capacity to devise, tell and pass on stories, the structure of which he analysed in fine detail. His brand of structuralism was different again from that of Evans-Pritchard and Radcliffe-Brown, however, as he was seeking to explain human behaviour through universal qualities of the human mind. Professors of social anthropology who built on the work of Lévi-Strauss include Mary Douglas in London, Rodney Needham in Oxford, and Edmund Leach in Cambridge, although all three moved on in their own distinctive ways, and we will also see the influence of their thinking in several chapters.

structuralism – a method, originally developed in linguistics, of analysing elements of social phenomena for their meaning in displaying the framework of society as a set of structural relations which express a universal human capacity to classify and construct such systems of thought.

It is hard to know where to draw to a halt in laying out the history of an ongoing field, and much more could have been covered in this brief introduction, but I think that enough background has been presented to give an idea of where social and cultural anthropology has come from. In the academic year that this book goes to press, Mary Douglas and Rodney Needham have passed away, and with them goes a period that will never be repeated. Throughout the subsequent pages of this book the work of many living anthropologists will be discussed, alongside other influential characters from the history of the subject, and towards the end we will look towards the period when these will all become part of history – but for the time being let us examine how the book will be laid out.

The Content of this Book

Because anthropology can be quite complex, and therefore possibly daunting, I have organised the presentation of chapters in a way that will, I hope, start with things that all readers can find familiar and relatively easy to understand. The discussion questions at the end of each chapter are designed to encourage individual readers to consider how the general issues raised apply in your own lives, and these will also offer opportunities for comparison in class, and among friends and fellow students. More complex issues are introduced gradually, once the basic building blocks have been laid, and the material is presented in such a way that theoretical influences we touched upon in the history section should become clearer in the context of specific cases.

The order of the chapters is not entirely chronological, but the material has also been arranged to offer a sense of the way the subject has developed, bringing some of the classic contributions in at the start, and ending with the consequences of recent technological change. It also moves from a consideration of how anthropologists go about their work, to a discussion of various important themes and issues that concern them, and ends with the two new chapters that bring the second edition up to date with various changes in the field. Some of the issues raised are covered only superficially here, partly for lack of space, but also because the aim of the text is to give an overall introduction, and those who wish to can pursue their studies elsewhere. The questions and readings at the end of the chapters are designed to help also with this.

In fact there is much material presented at the end of the chapters, and readers need to take care to evaluate the types of knowledge they will acquire in following up the suggestions. The first section, headed 'References and Further Reading', offers directly the sources of the anthropology discussed in the body of the chapter, as well as other anthropology that pursues the same themes. It is divided into books that present thorough coverage of the various issues, and articles that will give a briefer, though not necessarily easier take on the themes. There then follows a list of novels, which usually do offer easier reading, and which may give a great insight into the aspects of life in question, but which are not anthropology, as such.

The films provide a mixture of the above, but in a different medium. Thus, there are feature films, which offer a level of knowledge that may be compared with the novels, and these can usually be hired in video stores, or downloaded from the internet. Then, there are documentary films, made by professional film-makers, often for release on television, but also sometimes easily available, and these may be quite controversial from an anthropological point of view and, in some cases, we have offered articles discussing such films. There are a few films made by people about themselves (see *Redskins, Tricksters and Puppy Stew*, below, for example), sometimes together with an anthropologist, and then there are films made by anthropologists as part of the work they do. This last is material, like the books and articles listed, that illustrates the work that anthropologists do, in this case known as visual anthropology.

Finally, there are some limited listings of internet sites, and again these are quite varied in quality and content. Some are illustrative of points being made in the text, some go further into the issues, but less authoritatively than the published books, and others provide reading lists and other useful information. These lists of internet sites are only really indicative of the kinds of things that can be found in cyberspace, which actually come and go, and so may not be available for long, but it will be easy enough to find others for yourselves as you go along. Try to ascertain the nature and source of the site before you take the content too seriously. Some are excellent resources, others are less valuable, but there is plenty to choose from out there.

Throughout the body of the text, 'personal accounts' bring first-hand illustrations or modifications of the ideas being presented, mostly from the point of view of people whose forebears have been studied and described by anthropologists, although one or two take a different approach. These are there for three main reasons. First, they make it possible in several cases to see that the people on whose lives anthropologists built their theories, sometimes quite long ago, still exist and still share an identity, though their lives may have changed. Secondly, they add examples of the raw material that anthropologists work with, the real people on whose cooperation we depend. Lastly, and in a way most importantly, they add an authority that no amount of second-hand recounting can do, and I hope that their contributions will help to bring the text alive as you venture into this new field.

References and Further Research

Books

Banks, Marcus (ed.) (1996) *Ethnicity: Anthropological Constructions* (London: Routledge).

Banks, Marcus (2001) *Visual Methods in Social Research* (London: Sage).

Baumann, Gerd (1996) *Contesting Culture: Discourses of Identity in Multi-ethnic London* (Cambridge: Cambridge University Press).

Benedict, Ruth (1954) *The Chrysanthemum and the Sword* (Tokyo: Tuttle).

Davies, Charlotte (1999) *Reflexive Ethnography* (London: Routledge 1999).

Eriksen, Thomas Hylland, with Finn Sivert Nielson (2001) *A History of Anthropology* (London: Pluto Press).

Hendry, Joy (1999) An Anthropologist in Japan (London: Routledge).

MacClancy, Jeremy (ed.) (1996) *Sport, Identity and Ethnicity* (Oxford: Berg).

Pink, Sarah (2001) *Doing Visual Ethnography: Images, Media and Representation in Research* (London: Sage).

Sykes, Karen (2005) *Arguing with Anthropology: An Introduction to Critical Theories of the Gift* (London: Routledge).

Tayler, Donald (1997) *The Coming of the Sun: A Prologue to Ika Sacred Narrative* (Oxford: Pitt Rivers Museum Monograph Series, no.7).

Tuhiwai-Smith, Linda (1999) *Decolonizing Methodologies: Research and Indigenous Peoples* (New York: Zed Books).

Articles

Aoki Tamotsu (1994) 'Anthropology and Japan: Attempts at Writing Culture' *Japan Foundation Newsletter* **XXII** (3): 1–6.

Bourdieu, P. (2003) 'Participant Objectivation', *Journal of the Royal Anthropological Institute* (n.s.) 9: 281–94.

Cooper, M. (2007) 'Sharing Data and Results in Ethnographic Research: Why this Should Not be an Ethical Imperative'. *Journal of Empirical Research on Human Research Ethics*, 2(1): 3–19.

Eriksen, Thomas Hyland (2005) 'Nothing to Lose But our Aitches', *Anthropology Today*. 21(2): 1–2.

Hart, Keith (2004) 'What Anthropologists Really Do', *Anthropology Today*. 20(1): 3–5.

Hendry, Joy 1996 'The Chrysanthemum Continues to Flower: Ruth Benedict and Some Perils of Popular Anthropology', in Jeremy MacClancy and Chris McDonaugh (eds), *Popularising Anthropology* (London: Routledge), pp. 106–21.

Mills, David (2006) 'Trust Me, I'm an Anthropologist', *Anthropology Today*, 22(2): 1–2.

Whisson, Michael G (1986) 'Why Study Anthropology?', *Anthropology Today*, 2(1) 23–4.

Novels

Forster, E. M. (1998 [1924]) *A Passage to India* (London: Penguin,) provides insight into the encounter between Western, colonial values, and Indian society pre-Independence.

Lewycka, Marina (2006) *A Short History of Tractors in Ukrainian* (Harmondsworth: Penguin,) gradually reveals the story of a Ukrainian family and its adjustments to life in Britain.

Lodge, David (1989) *Nice Work* (Harmondsworth: Penguin) is an amusing fictional account of an anthropologist and a businessman who trail each other at work.

Tan, Amy (1994) *The Joy Luck Club* (London: Minerva) is a novel touching on problems of cultural identity in the relationship between Chinese women and their Chinese–American daughters.

Films

The 'Strangers Abroad' series (André Singer, 1985) introduces five of the early anthropologists and their influence on the subject. *Off the Verandah*, about Bronislaw Malinowski, demonstrates the value for British colonists of getting down off their verandahs and living with the people they were describing. *Fieldwork*, about Sir Walter Baldwin Spencer, pursues the theme by illustrating his work with the Arunta and other Australian Aboriginal peoples. There are also films about W. H. R. Rivers (see Chapter 11), Margaret Mead, and Edward Evans-Pritchard. The work of Rivers is introduced in Chapter 1.

Firth on Firth (Rolf Husmann, Peter Loizos, Werner Sperschneider, 1993) a film in which Sir Raymond Firth (see Chapter 5) talks about his life, social anthropology under Malinowski at the London School of Economics, and his fieldwork.

Redskins, Tricksters and Puppy Stew (directed by Drew Hayden Taylor for the National Film Board of Canada, 2000), in which the Ojibwe director presents a humourous account of life in Native Canada.

Good sources of anthropological/ethnographic films include:
Asian Educational Media Services (AMES) www.Ames.uiuc.edu

Documentary Educational Resources (DER) http://www.der.org/
Royal Anthropological Institute (RAI) http://www.therai.org.uk/film/film.html
The National Library of Australia http://www.nla.gov.au/film/
Granada Centre granada.centre@manchester.ac.uk
Life on Lens http://www.lifeonlens.org/ (though not specifically anthropological, this
    charity is dedicated to documenting humanitarian achievements on film and contains
    interesting material.

There are also a number of international ethnographic film festivals:
AA (Screenings of the Visual Anthropology Association at the American Anthropological
    Association congresses, annual) http://www.societyforvisualanthropology.org
Astra Film Festival (Northwest Romania, annual) http://www.astrafilm.ro
Beeld voor Beeld (Amsterdam, annual) http://www.beeldvoorbeeld.nl
Göttingen International Film Festival (Germany, biennial) http://www.iwf.de/giff/
Margaret Mead Film & Video Festival (New York, annual) http://www.amnh.org
Mostra Internacional do Filme Etnográfico (Rio de Janeiro, biennial) http://www.
    mostraetnografica.com.br/
Nordic Anthropological Film Association festival (peripatetic, biennial) www.nafa.uib.no/
International Festival of Ethnographic Film, Royal Anthropological Festival (peripatetic,
    biennial) www.raifilmfest.org.uk
Taiwan International Ethnographic Film Festival (Taipei, biennial) http://www.tieff.sinica.edu.
    tw/

Websites
http://www.anthrobase.com/Browse/Thm/index.html – a limited index of references to
    anthropological works in a variety of European languages.
http://www.as.ua.edu/ant/Faculty/murphy/436/anthros.htm – a site prepared by students for
    students about anthropological theories.
http://www.sas.upenn.edu/~nsalazar/anthropology.html – a site with lots of links useful for
    students of anthropology.

Seeing the World

Souvenirs and Handkerchiefs

Visitors to foreign countries very often return with a selection of objects collectively known as souvenirs. These are items acquired on the journey. They may be received as gifts, purchased in a tourist shop, or even just picked up on the beach. Their economic value is not necessarily important, for these objects are not usually for resale. Instead, they are essentially material reminders of the experience of the traveller. The objects may also be chosen for a variety of other reasons – for some perceived intrinsic beauty, to show off to friends, to give as a gift, or just to stand on the windowsill and bring out one of the colours in the curtains. However, all will be chosen because they are in some way remarkable, and because they stand for the place in which they were acquired.

The same objects, taken individually, will have different meanings to the people for whom they are a part of everyday life. In tourist resorts, local business people become astute at anticipating the interests of visitors, and many secure their living by making available a range of local goods, as we will discuss again in Chapter 13. Some goods may be designed for the purpose, but the best bargains – or business prospects, depending on who notices first – are those goods which are mundane locally, but unusual and appealing to outsiders. Objects that are taken for granted and perhaps readily produced in one place may be rare and charming in another. They may also have quite different uses.

To take a simple example, there are in Japan some light and relatively cheap souvenirs known as *hankachi*. These are neatly finished squares of soft cloth, often individually packed in cellophane, and characteristically printed with a Japanese motif such as an *ukiyoe* print (see Photograph 1.1) or a local view. These *hankachi* are actually named after 'handkerchiefs', but they are often so exquisitely soft and beautiful that it would seem a positive injustice to apply them to a runny nose. Indeed, they may well be inadequate for the task, for in Japan 'handkerchiefs' are for delicately dabbing at a sweaty brow on a hot summer's day. In Japan, the

Photograph 1.1

This Japanese handkerchief makes a good gift or souvenir, but it would hardly serve for blowing the nose (photograph: Lisa Hill)

whole idea of blowing one's nose into a piece of cloth, and storing the subsequent contents in a pocket, is seen as quite disgusting.

This single example illustrates a basic principle underlying the whole subject of anthropology, namely that different people *see* things – or, in anthropological terms, classify things – in different ways. For a foreign visitor to Japan, the *hankachi* is, at least at first, a member of the class of objects known as souvenirs. It may also belong to a *class* known as gifts, which could be shared at least superficially by both Japanese donor and foreign recipient. Once received, however, the same object may be further *classified* together with other similar objects in several different categories, depending on local ideas about usage. Moreover, a possibility amongst one particular people – that of containing nasal mucus and storing it in a pocket – invokes extremely negative reactions in another people.

The handkerchief continues to be a good illustration of principles underlying this subject even within one country, for different segments of the population may well have different ideas about handkerchiefs. A generation ago in Britain, for example, people were brought up to regard 'a clean hankie' as a vital part of their daily dress. Indeed, our mothers (or teachers) would chastise us if we were found to be without one. Thus some older members of the community continue to carry handkerchiefs, as they were trained, while younger people rarely use more than the paper tissue which has come to be a more convenient, if less environmentally friendly, substitute.

These paper tissues – at least the ones known by the brand name Kleenex – were originally designed in America in 1924 for women to use to remove face cream. In the 1930s, when people began also to use them as handkerchiefs, the American company Kimberly-Clark seized upon the idea and created the advertising slogan 'the handkerchiefs you can throw away.' According to an American friend/informant, the replacement of handkerchiefs with paper tissues was fostered by an increasing sensitivity in America to infection. Another tells me they are mostly used by 'older aunts and grandmothers', but an exception is the male gay community, who have a colour-coded use of handkerchiefs 'to indicate their availability and preferences.'

During the heyday of handkerchiefs, there was great variety in the quality, and people would judge one another's taste and affluence according to the type they carried. Perhaps associated with this idea, it used to be part of smart dress among some groups of men to wear a handkerchief peeking out of their top pocket. Others would avoid the custom, seeing it as ostentatious or crude. Some people would carry handkerchiefs made of silk, others would have them embossed with their initial, and some would tie knots in the corners of them and wear them on the beach to keep off the sun. People who thought of themselves as 'ladies' would display the delicate lace edging of their handkerchiefs by wearing them in the front of their low-cut dresses, or by dropping them at strategic moments for passing men to pick up.

Different ideas about these small squares of cloth indicated information about the social allegiances of their owners, and thus provided ways of *classifying* other people according to their upbringing, generation and status. The use of handkerchiefs was thus rather appropriately associated with the *class* system in Britain, and parallel distinctions elsewhere. Nowadays, they are much less used, but beautiful lace hankies are still a popular gift from Venice or Brussels and, in the airport in Beijing, they come in a range of qualities so that they can be given as change in a country which forbids the export of much of its currency. In a 'progressive' kindergarten in Japan, which has done away with the use of uniforms for its charges, the children who go there must nevertheless wear a hankie pinned to their clothes to indicate their membership of a particular *class*.

Learning to Classify

We have see, then, that classification in an anthropological sense is concerned with the way different people *see* the world. This is because people divide up the world into categories of objects and categories of living beings in ways that differ from the ways other people do it. Time and place are classified in a variety of ways, as we shall shortly illustrate in more detail. A system of classification is something that is shared by members of a particular society. It is among the most fundamental characteristics of that society, and it is acquired by children growing up to be members of that society. It is, indeed, the basis of the socialisation of a child, the conversion of a biological being into a social one, who shares a system of communication with those who surround it.

classification – a system of organisation of people, places and things shared by all human beings, but in ways that differ in different societies, which therefore forms a subject of interest to anthropologists.

socialisation – the inculcation into a child of a society's systems of classification and ways of behaving so that it is converted from a biological being into a social one. The term may also be used for adults acquiring a new set of social rules and mores.

As babies learn their first words, they learn simultaneously a range of meaning for the sounds they enunciate. They learn to use the 'label' of each word for a particular 'category' of meaning. Anyone who has spent time with babies will know that this category and its meaning may for some time be rather different from that of the adults around, and parents are usually required to 'translate' the baby's utterances. A classic and potentially embarrassing example is the way some babies learn the word 'Daddy' and then apply it indiscriminately to sundry other men they meet. The baby has learned the label 'Daddy', which applies to a particular man they probably know rather well, but they are not yet aware of any of the further detail about the meaning of the word. They may have in mind a category closer to 'man', or perhaps 'young man with blond or black hair', nothing which they could possibly explain, but some part of the world which they link with that label. Later, they will come to associate much more meaning to the label, and realise to whom it makes an appropriate address. But all this takes time.

In some languages, the label which corresponds to 'Daddy' actually applies to a range of people, as we will discuss in more detail later on, and the baby in that society will eventually learn who those people are and how they are to be distinguished from other people. In both cases, the babies are learning to classify people. They will also learn any number of other terms, together with the characteristics that define them. Just as they learn language, then, they are learning a system of classification shared by other people who use that language. In complex, multicultural societies, like many of those where English is spoken, there will be variations in both the language and the system of classification, and these may be related, rather appropriately again, to class distinctions.

Our first system of classification is usually learnt so early that it becomes deeply ingrained. Until we think about it, it seems as natural as eating and sleeping. We have notions of people, classified as relatives, friends or strangers, with further subdivisions depending on various other characteristics, and we have ideas about the expectations of those categories; we also classify places, again with expectations about them – for example, we may learn to drop our voices or remove shoes when we enter a place of worship, call out a greeting as we enter a house, and perhaps to salivate for popcorn when we enter a cinema. Things of one sort or another are classified as nice or nasty, clean or dirty, safe or dangerous.

Until we travel outside our own society we tend to take for granted that our system of classification is universal. Even then, we may learn differences only rather reluctantly, and some notions are very hard to shift. We may find countries foreign to us, or even just foreign neighbours, 'smelly', 'dirty', or simply 'strange'. For anthropologists to learn the system of classification of another people, they must first learn to stand outside their own system and to reject notions of revulsion or disapproval based on their early upbringing. As a baby learns to classify in its own society, the anthropologist must learn all over again the new system of classification of the people under study.

In the introduction to his translation of a book on the subject of classification, Rodney Needham compares the anthropologist, setting out to study a strange people, with a person blind from birth who is suddenly given sight. In the latter case, the first impression is apparently of a

> painful chaos of forms and colours, a gaudy confusion of visual impressions none of which seem to bear any comprehensible relationship to the others. (Needham in Durkheim and Mauss 1963: vii)

Just as the previously blind person needs to learn to distinguish and classify objects, the 'culturally blind' anthropologist needs to learn to make sense of 'a confusion of foreign impressions, none of which can safely be assumed to be what they appear' (ibid.).

Life, Death and Burial Alive

The task of understanding fully the categories of another society is a very difficult one. Indeed, the whole enterprise is relatively recent, and tended for some time to concentrate on so-called 'primitive' people. In the early twentieth century the French philosopher Lucien Lévy-Bruhl (1910) wrote a book about what he called the mentality of primitive people, which he described as 'pre-logical'. At that time descriptions of people in remote parts of the world were based on limited observation, often without the benefit of language, and their practices sometimes seemed to defy the cherished systems of logic that were held to underpin all 'civilised' thought. As explained in the Introduction, Europeans of the time saw themselves at the pinnacle of development, and they saw people who were technologically less advanced as radically different.

In fact, this 'civilised thought' was actually the thought of Western Europeans. W. H. R. Rivers questioned the idea that there was a fundamental difference between the logic of primitive people and that of their observers. In an essay entitled 'The Primitive Conception of Death' (1926), he suggested that deeper investigation would reveal logic quite recognisable to the Western mind if due consideration was given to the fact that things might be *classified* differently. Drawing on his own experience among Melanesian people in the Solomon Islands, he addressed some apparent contradictions in the use of a local word, *mate*, used to translate 'dead', but also applied to people who by his standards were patently still living.

It might be thought at first sight that the distinction between life and death is rather clear. A person is either alive, or they are dead. Their heart is beating or it is not. This is simply one way in which to classify death as a state, however, and even this has been brought into question since the introduction of life-support machines. A state of 'brain death' might now justify the stopping of a heartbeat sustained by such a machine, and this possibility has brought to the surface a general degree of woolliness in the definition of death. Amongst the Melanesians, Rivers suggested that the category *mate* also included the idea of 'very ill' and 'very old', so that the dividing line between that and the opposite *toa* (*alive*) is drawn in a different way to the distinction between life and death in Europe at the time.

His own distinction was a biological one, based on certain observations of the body perceived through a fairly sophisticated understanding of its component parts. It also involved, more subtly, notions set in a historical and philosophical context about the heart and the soul. Elsewhere, the distinction may be concerned with socioeconomic value, and a scarcity of resources. Japanese folk tales recount a custom of leaving old people up on a mountain once they had reached a certain stage of frailty and inability to contribute to the needs of family life. In Melanesia some people were being buried alive, by a European system of classification, as they were reported to have been in parts of Africa.

Notions of life and death are related to notions of the afterlife, and what becomes of people after they 'die'. Europeans were profoundly shocked in the sixteenth century when they discovered human sacrifice practised among the Aztecs, and they tried immediately to put a stop to it. The Aztec people saw human sacrifice as an essential part of the appeasement of their gods, however, and it was thought to be a noble way to die, which would give one a special, honoured position in the next life. They understood that if they failed to 'feed' their gods in this way, the world would come to an end. As it happened, they were proved right in a way. The Spaniards put a stop to the practice and that particular Aztec world was indeed destroyed. There are people today attempting to recreate Aztec dancing and other practices, but the old Aztec 'civilisation' was indeed destroyed by the arrival of the Europeans.

Prior to the colonisation of the Sudan, when the practice was also prohibited, the Dinka people are said to have preferred to bury members of their priestly class while they were still alive. Godfrey Lienhardt, who did not witness the custom, but analysed it in his immensely readable book *Divinity and Experience*, quotes one of his informants as follows:

> When a master of the fishing-spear has fallen sick and is becoming weak, he will call all his people and tell them to bring his whole camp (tribe or subtribe) to his home to bury him whilst he lives. His people will obey him and quickly come, for if they delay and the master . . . dies before they reach him, they will be most miserable . . .
>
> And he will not be afraid of death; he will be put in the earth while singing his songs. Nobody among his people will wail or cry because their man has died. They will be joyful because their master . . . will give them life so that they shall live untroubled by any evil.   (Lienhardt 1961: 300)

Lienhardt's book contains much information about these masters, and their role in performing myth and ritual, when they are seen to embody the traditions of the Dinka people. He is thus able to interpret this practice as a representation to the Dinka people of a renewal of their own collective life (ibid. 301).

In the case of the Melanesians, Rivers puts the distinction between *mate* and *toa* in the context of different ideas about stages of life, and, again, about what happens to human beings after death. He also suggests that a clearer understanding of a different system of classification in this respect could perhaps explain events which had horrified European travellers and missionaries when they had observed the funerals and burials of people who, for them, were still alive.

He also points out, incidentally, that Melanesians use different systems from Europeans to classify their relatives, applying the term 'father' to the brothers of their fathers, by his reckoning, and also to the husbands of their mother's sisters (systems we will discuss further in Chapter 11). This is related to a wider system, which makes clear distinctions between generations, and between relatives on the mother's and father's side of the family. Rivers makes some amusing speculations about what Melanesians might make of the local system of classifying relatives were they to come and study English people, who, for them, apply words (like cousin, uncle and aunt) indiscriminately across these boundaries. He suggests, not altogether frivolously, a possible native view that 'the hyperdevelopment of material culture has led to an atrophy of the thought processes' – perhaps a 'post-logical mentality' (1926: 45).

Cultural Relativism and the Anthropologists' Bias

Rivers himself betrays a system of classification common amongst writers of the time by describing peoples as 'primitive' or 'savage', as if this in itself allows a degree of generalisation. Although he is arguing against Lévy-Bruhl's ideas of 'pre-logical mentality', he still tends to assume that the Melanesians he describes will share certain forms of classification with other people of 'lower orders'. This broad classification of peoples is related to technological achievements, but it also illustrates the idea of the time that an understanding of earlier stages of development of more 'advanced' peoples could be sought in the practices of the more 'primitive'.

The best-known book which addresses directly the subject of classification, written in French at the turn of the twentieth century, reflects this notion that peoples could be fitted onto a scale of civilisation, with the European scholarly elite (particularly the French) at one end, and the so-called 'primitive' people at the other. Durkheim and Mauss (1963), in their book entitled *Primitive Classification*, turn to 'primitive' society in an attempt to demonstrate their idea that the origins of mental categories are to be found in society. Nowadays social anthropologists are less concerned with origins than they used to be, but they are of necessity concerned with modes of classification, and the book also gives some very good examples of how various these may be.

The first two chapters are concerned in particular with the *classification of other human beings*. They discuss various systems reported from Australian Aboriginal groups, which divide themselves into marriage classes and clans associated with animals. The whole society may also be divided into two major classes described by the observers as *moieties*. The consequences of such a system for the people concerned are multiple, but major ones include a division of all other human beings into those one may and those one may not marry. Some people also have groups into which marriage is preferred. This will have further ramifications as the system operates to produce relatives of one sort or another, and these will fall into indigenous categories quite impossible to translate accurately into the usual English system of names for relatives (see Chapter 6, p. 124, for a first-hand account of Yolngu moieties).

Anyone can approach an understanding of such a system when thinking of which members of their own families would be prohibited to them for marriage, and a reader's own native tongue may more explicitly classify relatives in a parallel way. Regular English terms for relations make few distinctions according to the marriage links involved, however, and these would probably not affect further decisions about marriage with people to whom one can trace no genealogical link, except perhaps for categories such as 'blood brothers'. The Australian groups described, on the other hand, classified everybody within the group as part of the overall marriage system, and all had to fit into the scheme.

Everyone also belonged to one or other of the animal clans, and both of these allegiances may indicate further rules about what in the environment people may or may not eat. A member of the snake clan may be prohibited from eating snake, or they may be the only people allowed to; either way, they are seen as having a special relationship with the snake, just as members of the opossum clan are expected to have a special relationship with opossum. Creatures in the environment may well also be allocated membership of the moieties, as may meteorological phenomena such as wind and rain, and distant objects such as the sun and stars.

The authors then turn to discuss a system they describe as more complex, which also brings into the arrangement the *classification of space*. This is the system observed among the Zuni, a group of Pueblo Indians of North America, whom they describe, with quotations from Cushing, the original ethnographer, as follows:

> ... what we find among the Zuñi [sic] is a veritable arrangement of the universe. All beings and facts in nature, 'the sun, moon, and stars, the sky, earth and sea, in all their phenomena and elements; and all inanimate objects, as well as plants, animals, and men', are classed, labelled, and assigned to fixed places in a unique and integrated 'system' in which all the parts are co-ordinated and subordinated to one to another by 'degrees of resemblance'.
>
> In the form in which we now find it, the principle of this system is a division of space into seven regions: north, south, west, east, zenith, nadir and the centre. Everything in the universe is assigned to one or other of these seven regions. To mention only the seasons and the elements, the wind, breeze or air, and the winter season are attributed to the north; water, the spring and its damp breezes, to the west; fire and the summer, to the south; the earth, seeds, the frosts which bring the seeds to maturity and end the year, to the east. The pelican, crane, grouse, sagecock, the evergreen oak, etc. are things of the north; the bear, coyote, and spring grass are things of the west. With the east are classed the deer, antelope, turkey, etc. Not only things, but social functions are also distributed in this way. The north is the region of force and destruction; war and destruction belong to it; to the west peace ..., and hunting; to the south, the region of heat, agriculture and medicine; to the east, the region of the sun, magic and religion; to the upper world and the lower world are assigned diverse combinations of these functions.   (Durkheim and Mauss 1963: 43–4)

This division of the universe into seven classes is also associated with colours, so that, for example, south is red, the region of summer and fire, the north is yellow, and the east is white. A comprehensive system of classification such as this is again learned very early, and an investigator could not expect members of the society necessarily to be able to explain it in an analytical form. It would nevertheless underlie a lot of communication within that society, and until the ethnographer pieced it together, much communication could be lost. The use of the word 'yellow' could, for example, have connotations based on other associations with north, so that a person described as 'yellow' could be fierce and destructive, rather than cowardly, as is the case in the English language, though again native speakers may not know why.

In fact, colours themselves are classified differently in different societies, and even by different groups within the same society. Newton's classification of bands of the spectrum into the seven 'colours of the rainbow', identified by scientific measurements, is widely accepted now, but there are different indigenous systems still in existence at a colloquial level. For example, the Japanese word *aoi* may be applied to something described in English as 'blue' (a rather light blue), as 'green', (the colour of pine trees, a 'go' traffic light, or a person feeling sick), or as 'pale' (the same person, slightly less sick). The colour blue, even in English, has a huge number of subdivisions, especially for professional artists or designers.

According to a study by Edwin Ardener (1971), the Welsh language used to have only two words for the colours described in English as grey, brown and black, with *du* for a colour covering part of the range described in English as black and part of 'brown', and *llwyd* covering another aspect of 'brown', and part of grey, which also shaded off into *glas*, a colour including hues described as blue and even green in English. Gradually the Welsh have come to adopt the English word 'brown' into their own language, and the shades covered by the modern colloquial Welsh words are much closer to their nearest English equivalents, probably to avoid confusion since Welsh speakers are almost always bilingual (see Figure 1.1).

Durkheim and Mauss (1963) also bring the *classification of time* into consideration in their description of Chinese ideas collectively known as *taoism*. This is a system of classification independent of social organisation, they explain, but it orders and affects many details of daily life. It also comprises a division of space into four cardinal points, again associated with animals and colours, and a division of objects into associations with five elements, namely earth, water, wood, metal and fire, and a further cycle of twelve signs of the Chinese zodiac. There is also a now widely known huge bipartite division of almost everything into *yin* and *yang*, sometimes also described as female and male, negative and positive, younger and older, or passive and active.

The system is used to classify divisions of years, days and even smaller units of two hours within the day, where each is assigned an animal of the zodiac and an element in its *yin* or *yang* form. Taken together with the classification of space into four cardinal points, an immensely complex system of divination (known as geomancy), developed in ancient China, was consulted in all kinds of endeavour and influenced much behaviour, particularly of a ritual kind. The system affected many parts of the Far East and even in today's technological super-states such as Japan and Hong Kong, activities like choosing sites and times for building, arranging weddings and funerals, and investigating unexpected misfortune, will involve consulting almanacs and experts in this ancient lore for advice (see First-hand Account 1 overleaf)

An example quite recognisable to members of Western societies who consult astrological charts is the way people's characters are supposed to be related to the year and time at which they were born. The animal associated with a particular year is said to have an influence, so that a person born in the year of the ox is said to be very patient and to speak little, and one born in the year of the tiger is sensitive, short-tempered and given to deep thinking. Certain pairs of people are also said to be better suited to marriage than others, and a geomancer may advise a change of name to offset a disadvantage of this sort. A Japanese woman born in the year of the horse, which also falls in the active

ENGLISH	STANDARD WELSH	MODERN COLLOQUIAL WELSH
green	gwyrdd	gwyrdd
blue	glas	glas
grey		llwyd
brown	llwyd	brown
black	du	du

Figure 1.1 English and Welsh colour classifications

Source: Edwin Ardener (ed.), Social Anthropology and Language (1971), p. xxi, by permission of Tavistock Publications.

aspect of fire, is still said to be a very bad bet for marriage. A general indication of the seriousness with which these ideas are taken can be found in a sharp drop in the birth rate during those years. On the other hand, this book goes to press in the Chinese year of the 'golden pig', a combination of pig and fire, which is said to be auspicious for babies and therefore a rise in the birth rate is expected.

It is clear, then, that technological advance is not necessarily accompanied by a convergence of ideas about the ordering of space, time and social relations. Some elements of systems of classification may be displaced as societies influence one another, such as the example of the use of 'brown' in Welsh, but others persist, and observers of other societies must try to avoid making assumptions based on their own system of thought. The classic work of Durkheim and Mauss (1963) not only provides us with examples of widely different systems of classification found in societies at that time relatively untouched by outside influence; it also illustrates a system of classification shared by scholars of the period in which it was written.

Anthropologists have recently been much concerned with examining their own preconceptions, and several works published in the last few years illustrate a concern with the way the background, age, gender and theoretical approach of the ethnographer might affect the results of their work. Different ethnographies of the same people were of particular interest, especially where these presented conflicting views, and two studies of the same village in Mexico, by Robert

Like everyone else in Hong Kong and Macau, I have been familiar with the term *Feng Shui* since I was little. Whenever my family moved house, my parents would invite a *Feng Shui* master to come and show us how we should arrange the furniture. When there are big events like weddings and funerals, my family would consult a master to pick an auspicious day and hour. They believe that an auspicious timing for a marriage would make the marriage happy and one for a funeral would make the family happy and prosperous. 2006 was said to be an auspicious year for marriage so the marriage registry offices in both Hong Kong and Macau were filled with bookings from the beginning of the year! During Chinese New Year, I listen to the radio programmes about the Chinese horoscope in order to find out whether I am having a good or bad year and how I can attract more luck and avoid bad fortune.

First-hand account 1:

Wong Si Lam, Chinese from Macao* – on Feng Shui

Feng Shui, which is literally translated as 'wind' and 'water', is about how the *chi*, or the energy of the life force, flows around us and influences our lives. It is a practice used to make adjustments to improve the naturally occurring *chi* of a place. This practice is estimated to be more than four thousand years old by the Chinese. Basically, it is a Taoist practice of positioning and arrangement of space to achieve comfort, balance and harmony with the environment. *Feng Shui* was a guarded secret in ancient China and was not accessible to the public. The teachings were transmitted orally from a master to a limited number of students, and confidentiality was strictly required. In ancient times, *Feng Shui* masters never took women as their students because Confucianism did not promote the transmission of important and sacred knowledge to females, as it was said: 'teach sons, not daughters'. Today, there are many female *Feng Shui* practitioners and masters around the world.

In Hong Kong, *Feng Shui* is everywhere. For example, there are television programmes about *Feng Shui* everyday in the afternoon, teaching people how they should arrange their home

CHINA

Macao

©MAPS IN MINUTES™ 2008

in order to receive the best *chi* and to avoid 'dirty stuff', meaning bad luck, disease, injuries and spirits. These programmes are even more popular during the Chinese New Year period when the *chi* of the year changes. There are also radio programmes hosted by *Feng Shui* masters, who would answer personal questions such as whether the colour and the licence number of one's car are harmonious with the owner. There are also *Feng Shui* schools and a large range of *Feng Shui* books available in the bookstores. Moreover, many buildings and sites in Hong Kong were built according to *Feng Shui* theories. A recent and famous example is Hong Kong Disneyland.

* See First-hand account 14.1 for a fuller discussion of her national identity.

Redfield and Oscar Lewis, provide a classic example. The first study described a positive, cheerful people, with many mechanisms of cooperation; the second concentrated on negative aspects of the same society, illustrating the poverty of the people and a grasping, competitive character.

Various theories were put forward to explain these divergent results, and one put the difference down to changed demographic and economic conditions. Others saw the discrepancy in the character of the ethnographers. A third explanation might be related to the prior interests of each (Martin 2005 examines the issues). A more general literary examination of the work of anthropologists suggests that those who made most impact in the subject were simply good writers. The social and cultural features of the people they chose to study have therefore taken on a disproportionate value in the subject because of the clear and arresting language in which they were described (see, for example, Clifford and Marcus 1986). This is not necessarily a disadvantage, however, if it helps other people become aware of the relative nature of their own social and cultural assumptions, and therefore to understand the depth of difference which may exist in the views of their neighbours.

In another collection, anthropologists were invited to use autobiography, of themselves and of their informants, as a means to tackle head-on this problem of personal involvement in the research they carry out (Okely and Callaway 1992), and the resulting book has become a valuable aid to field work. Most anthropological studies make serious attempts to counteract the inevitable bias of the human studying humans – a phenomenon not unlike that known in physics as the Heisenberg uncertainty principle, which recognises the need to introduce a change to particles of matter in order to observe them. In a similar way, students of anthropology can learn from and about their own experience in the process of understanding people elsewhere.

Changes in Systems of Classification: The Issue of Gender

It was, in my view, no coincidence that this last collection of papers, about the personal involvement of the ethnographer, was edited by two women, for one of the biases identified in the work of their earlier colleagues was towards allocating much more importance in any society to the activities of men than to those of women. Sometimes the equally important roles of women even passed completely unnoticed. Steps have been taken to rectify this practice in the last few decades – steps that reflect an area of quite noticeable change in the wider systems of gender classification in the so-called 'civilised' societies from which the observers hailed. Indeed, the recognition of gender as a culturally relative notion has added a new dimension to the ideas of 'sex' as a biological feature. Here we can see the role of anthropology as a discipline that has forced its practitioners to challenge and reconsider their own assumptions about everyday life.

gender – a term of classification used to refer to conceptions of male and female, or masculinity and femininity in any society, and 'gender studies' refers to research and teaching that makes this distinction its primary focus.

This example also illustrates the way in which changes can be brought about in systems of classification over time within a particular society, or indeed through the influence of one people on another. One of the major distinctions learned is that between men and women, or, more importantly in this context, between the roles assigned to each of the categories. Within only one or two generations, there have been great changes in these roles in Western societies. Women have secured for themselves a much greater part in public life than their mothers and grandmothers played, and men are now much more likely than their fathers were to be found contributing in a significant way in the home.

This has been no mean feat, since the pioneers of women's 'liberation' found themselves fighting against the constraints of all sorts of 'social facts', in Durkheim's terms: legal and moral regulations, customs, and other collective representations about appropriate attitudes and behaviour. My own maiden aunt lamented the three years she spent waiting to marry and take care of a fiancé (who died while they were saving money) because, as a teacher in Scotland in the 1930s, she would have to give up work on marriage. My mother gave up her job as a nurse to

collective representations – symbols understood and used for communication between members of a particular social group (after Durkheim).

marry, and, throughout her life, saw her role in the 'work' of 'running the home'. The men of their class and generation were expected to provide for the whole family, and for long after women did begin to go out to work, it was still the men who were obliged, by law, to take care of the tax return in the United Kingdom.

In my own generation, expectations changed markedly, and some women experienced disapproval if they did not keep up their economic activities after marriage and even childbirth. We had been trained in the 'female' roles of housework, caring and comfort, but once we won our places in the wider world we were expected to maintain them, as well as attend to our homes and children. Some men were overtly supportive, but many found it difficult to do more than 'help' with the household tasks. Outside, men still tended to see other men as appropriate people to promote. Nowadays, men and women do, at least in some families, play an equal part in the rearing of their offspring, who will be unlikely to carry the same clear ideas in their heads as their grandparents did about 'men's and women's work'.

Anthropologists who noticed the male bias in their colleagues' work, perhaps projecting Western ideas onto the people of their studies, have over the years published a great deal of interesting material about women from different parts of the world, as well as attending to their own roles in society. In the wake of the early feminist works of influential writers such as Simone de Beauvoir, Kate Millet and Germaine Greer, two ground-breaking collections of anthropological articles appeared, first in America in *Women, Culture and Society* (Rosaldo and Lamphere 1974), and then, shortly afterwards, in the UK, in *Perceiving Women* (Ardener 1975). The latter was the first of a series of publications to come from a group of colleagues who eventually founded a Centre for Cross-Cultural Research on Women, later to become The International Gender Studies Centre.

Another of the early ones in this series, *Defining Females: The Nature of Women in Society*, originally published in 1978, examined the way in which even the so-called biological characteristics of women are culturally constructed:

> perceptions of the *nature* of women affect the shape of the *categories* assigned to them, which in turn reflect back upon and reinforce or remould perceptions of the *nature* of women, in a continuing process. (Ardener 1993:1; cf. Caplan 1987)

Hirschon's paper about a Greek community, for example, explains ideas about the appropriate behaviour for women in terms of beliefs about their sexuality. Only women are thought to be able to control their sexual urges, so both men and women should be married at an early age, and respectable women must be kept out of the way of other men, who might lead them into temptation. If a husband strays from the straight and narrow – in other words, from fidelity to his wife – it is the other woman who is blamed. Keeping their houses immaculate, cooking complicated dishes, preserving fruit in sweetmeats and cakes, and sewing and embroidery, are all time-consuming ways of keeping women occupied, and off the street (Hirschon 1993: 51–72; see also Photograph 1.2).

Documenting the roles of women, their variety, and their changes has meant there is now a veritable plethora of books and articles. These publications were for some time distinguished from regular anthropology by being called 'women's studies', but gender now forms just one type of social differentiation, alongside others based on age, generation, kinship, race, ethnicity, religion, region and social class. Women concerned with their own liberation from the constraints of Western society sometimes tended to focus overly on their counterparts in other

Photograph 1.2 Bereaved women in Greece express their loss by wearing black for at least three years as widows, sometimes for the rest of their own lives for other family members (photograph: Karpathos Island, Greece by Renee Hirschon).

societies, ignoring areas shared by men and women. They have also been accused of imposing, as universal, models subordinating women to men, whereas the situation in any one society might be much more subtle, even lacking hierarchical organisation at all.

Gullestad also advocates looking at gender 'in such a way that it is possible to study changes of cultural categories', pointing out that changes sought by women in their roles and definitions of themselves 'will have profound implications for the definitions of masculinity as well' (1993: 129). The Oscar-winning film *The Full Monty*, about a group of redundant steel workers seeking to reinstate their self-respect, is a poignant popular representation of this situation in the English city of Sheffield in the late 1990s. Anthropologists have now turned their attention to the new roles of men, and one interesting book, *Dislocating Masculinity: Comparative Ethnographies* (Cornwall and Lindisfarne 1994), is a re-examination of the notions of masculinity which have been displaced and replaced as women have moved into many of the spheres which were previously closed and almost sacrosanct to men.

Conclusion

In this chapter we have discussed systems of classification which affect and constrain the way in which people 'see' and understand 'the world'. We have considered various examples of difference in modes of classification: of objects, of life and death, of people, of space and time, and we have looked at how these may change. We have identified classificatory constraints (or bias) in the anthropologists as well as in the people they study, and pointed out the inevitability of this when human beings set out to study other human beings. In the next chapter, we begin to look at ways in which systems of classification are expressed, and in this and the following two chapters, the various ways in which anthropologists gather information about them.

Discussion Questions

1 Have you got a souvenir of somewhere you have visited that you feel is particularly representative of that place? Try to write down some of the reasons why you chose that object, and why it is special and different for you.

2 Make a list of words for colours which are also used as descriptions of sentiments, or have other meanings. Can you suggest reasons for the association? Do you know anyone who has different associations? You might want to compare your ideas.

3 Think of ways in which you have felt constrained to behave in a particular way because of your gender, age or religious background. Did the same constraints apply to your parents? Will you (or do you) impose them on your children?

4 In what way does *Feng Shui* offer an illustration of ideas about classification? Take a look at the First-Hand Account 1 on p. 28 for some more information. Can you imagine any instances where *Feng Shui* might influence an anthropologist's investigation? Should they try to avoid this and if so, how? Now look again at your answers to question 3, above, and consider how the constraints you have identified might influence your own thinking about anthropology.

References and Further Research

Books

Ardener, Edwin (ed.) (1971) *Social Anthropology and Language* (London: Tavistock).
Ardener, Shirley (ed.) (1975) *Perceiving Women* (London: Malaby Press).
Ardener, Shirley (ed.) (1993 [1978]) *Defining Females: The Nature of Women in Society* (Oxford: Berg).
Barley, Nigel (1997) *Dancing on the Grave* (London: Abacus).
Caplan, Pat (ed.) (1987) *The Cultural Construction of Sexuality* (London and New York: Tavistock Publications).
Clifford, James and Marcus George. E. (1986) *Writing Culture: The Poetics and Politics of Ethnography* (Berkeley, Los Angeles and London: University of California Press).
Cornwall, Andrea and Lindisfarne, Nancy (1994). *Dislocating Masculinity* (London: Routledge).
Durkheim, Emile and Mauss Marcel (1963) *Primitive Classification*, translated, with an introduction, by Rodney Needham (London: Cohen & West).
Gell, Alfred (1992) *The Anthropology of Time: Cultural Constructions of Temporal Maps and Images* (Oxford: Berg).
Hertz, R. (1960) *Death and the Right Hand*, translated by R. and C. Needham (London: Cohen & West).

Lévy-Bruhl, Lucien (1926 [1910]) *How Natives Think* (New York: A. A. Knopf; original text published in 1910 as *Les fonctions mentales dans les sociétés Inférieures*).

Lienhardt, Godfrey (1961) *Divinity and Experience: The Religion of the Dinka* (Oxford: Clarendon Press).

Martin, JoAnn (2005) *Tepoztlán and the Transformation of the Mexican State: The Politics of Loose Connections* (Tucson: University of Arizona Press).

Moore, Henrietta L. (1988) *Feminism and Anthropology* (Cambridge: Polity Press).

Needham, Rodney (1973) *Right and Left: Essays on Dual Symbolic Classification* (Chicago: Chicago University Press).

Okely, Judith and Callaway, Helen (eds) (1992) *Anthropology and Autobiography* (London: Routledge).

Rosaldo, Michelle Zimbalist and Lamphere, Louise (eds) (1974) *Woman, Culture and Society* (Stanford, Calif.: Stanford University Press).

Articles

Fukuda Kaoru (1997) 'Different Views of Animals and Cruelty to Animals: Cases in Fox-Hunting and Pet-Keeping in Britain' *Anthropology Today*, 13(5): 2–6.

Gullestad, Marianne (1993) 'Home Decoration as Popular Culture. Constructing Homes, Genders and Classes in Norway', in Teresa del Valle (ed.), *Gendered Anthropology* (London: Routledge), pp. 128–61.

Hirschon, Renee (1993) 'Open Body/Closed Space: The Transformation of Female Sexuality' in Shirley Ardener (ed.), *Defining Females: The Nature of Women in Society* (Oxford: Berg), pp. 51–72.

Rivers, W. H. R. (1926) 'The Primitive Conception of Death', in *Psychology and Ethnology* (London and New York: Kegan Paul and Trench Trubner).

Sherif, Bahira (1999) 'Gender Contradictions in Families: Official v. Practical Representations among Upper Middle-Class Muslim Egyptians', *Anthropology Today*, 15(4): 9–13.

Novels

Barker, Pat (1992) *Regeneration* (Harmondsworth: Penguin), is a trilogy of novels about the First World War, which feature W. H. R. Rivers, although not much direct mention is made of his anthropological work until the third book, the *Ghost Road*, where the effects of a British ban on head-hunting in the Solomon Islands are juxtaposed with reports of the atrocities taking place in war-torn Europe.

Bowen, E. Smith (1954) *Return to Laughter* (London: Victor Gollancz) is a fictionalised account of fieldwork amongst the Tiv of Nigeria by Laura Bohannan.

Durrell, Lawrence (1968 [1962]) *The Alexandria Quartet* (London: Faber and Faber) explores the encounter between 'Western' and 'Eastern' outlooks, through portraying events from a variety of different perspectives.

Mahfouz, Naguib (1994) *Palace Walk* (London: Black Swan), the first of the Cairo Trilogy, illustrates particularly well the contrasting life of men and women in a traditional Egyptian Muslim family.

Pamuk, Orhan (2001) *My Name is Red* (London: Powell's), a murder mystery that examines Islamic values in sixteenth-century Turkey as the Ottoman Empire declines.

Films

Doctors of Two Worlds (Natasha Solomons, 55 minutes, 1989) is about an English doctor administering health care in mountain villages of the Bolivian highlands who shares ideas and methods of healing with the local healer (*curandero*).

The BBC TV series *Life on Mars* (2006–7) was a popular series about a detective who was thrown back to the past, to 1973, where 'things were done differently' and many interesting culture clashes ensue.

Websites

http://www.relst.uiuc.edu/durkheim – The Durkheim Pages has extensive bibliographies and access to original texts.

http://durkheim.itgo.com/ – the Durkheim Archive, specifically for undergraduates.

http://www2.pfeiffer.edu/~lridener/DSS/INDEX.HTML – this link is for the Dead Sociologists Index – Durkheim pages written by L. A. Coser.

http://www.hewett.norfolk.sch.uk/curric/soc/durkheim/durk.htm – good introductory pages to Durkheim's ideas.

2

Disgusting, Forbidden and Unthinkable

Challenging Some Ingrained Ideas

One of the ways in which anthropologists find out about a system of classification is by looking at ideas which are strongly held by the people concerned. These are likely to be learnt early in life and are difficult to dislodge even when one becomes aware of the fact that they are culturally relative. They include ideas that would provoke expressions of shock and disgust should they be contravened – ideas which are at the root of prejudice and discrimination – for people who engage in practices contradictory to one's own may well seem barbaric and uncivilised.

In practice, these cherished ideas are usually challenged whenever we travel abroad. A resident of Southern England, for example, may need only to cross the Channel to France to find toilets which seem not only dirty, but constructed in a fashion unpleasant to use, to discover people relishing the consumption of creatures they cringe at the thought of eating, and to encounter customs that appear strange, perhaps even obsessive. They might be surprised, at least at first, to discover that their friends in France find a number of English habits disgusting too. Further afield, in India, for example, some of the activities taken for granted in

Europe are regarded as seriously polluting. A separation of the uses of the right and left hands, for eating and cleaning the body respectively, make passing food with the left hand seem quite disgusting.

Certain practices are also quite simply forbidden in the law and custom of each society. In many countries, it is against the law to appear in public in the nude, and 'streakers', who gain a few seconds of attention by running naked across a cricket pitch or other public place, would be promptly arrested. Those who wear very few clothes are accepted to different degrees in different places, and company on a beach will be much more tolerant than in a kindergarten, for example. Some exclusive clubs and restaurants have rules about dress, where men may be turned away if they have no jacket and tie; in Oxford, undergraduates are refused entry to the examination hall if they are not wearing the appropriate gowns and black and white clothes; and in my own London college in the 1960s, women were forbidden from appearing in jeans, or indeed, any trousers – though I found no serious sanctions came into operation when I decided to put the rule to the test.

Some of these regulations may sound quaint and perhaps old-fashioned to foreign visitors to Britain, even former compatriots whose families settled in Australia or the Americas, but there are conventions of dress everywhere which are difficult for people to break, even if there is no hard and fast rule. It would be 'unthinkable' for a man in most societies to turn up to work in a skirt – even in Scotland, kilts are usually only worn at weddings and other special occasions – and mothers who dress their daughters in dungarees, so as not to distinguish them overly from their brothers, would probably baulk at the idea of dressing their sons in little frocks. In some Islamic communities, women cover themselves from head to foot, a custom causing concern in Europe as this book was being written. In other parts of the world – the rain forest in South America is one example – it is acceptable for them to be quite bare down to the waist (see First-hand Account 10 on p. 194).

Men kissing in public is pretty unusual in Western countries (though this is another area which has been changing, along with new ideas about gender roles), but it is positively expected in greetings in other parts of the world. In much of the Middle East, men are freer about their bodily interaction than they are in northern Europe, but in the Far East kissing was not really a custom at all until recently, although men and women might think nothing of falling asleep on the shoulders of strangers in an underground train. In Japan, men and women used to bathe together in public until they saw how shocked Western visitors were in the nineteenth century. Now they bathe on different sides of a partition, but courting couples feel free to cuddle in public places, which they did not previously do, even until the early 1970s.

It is ideas such as these, which may form the basis of prejudice and suspicion when people from one culture visit, or move to live amongst members of another, that provide good starting places for anthropological investigation. Notions of pollution and taboo, which are essentially institutionalised versions of an antipathy towards 'dirt' and the 'unthinkable', are particularly useful in this respect because not only are they firmly held, they are also greatly concerned with classification. Things which are taboo and things which are regarded as polluted or polluting are very often things which fall between important categories. Thus, by studying the notions a people have about pollution (or dirt), and the things which they regard as taboo (or forbidden), we can learn more about the system of classification of that particular society.

Taboo

'Taboo' is a word which was brought back by Captain Cook from his voyages in the South Seas. His sailors noticed that in Polynesia the use of this word designated a prohibition and they found it useful themselves when they wanted to keep visitors off the ship, or reserve a particular girl for themselves. It was also a word for which they had an existing category, though they may have found this new word more instantly expressive and appealing than previous ones like 'prohibited' or 'forbidden', just as their countrymen did when they returned to introduce it to the English language. In any society certain things may be regarded as taboo.

In fact there are several possible translations of the word, as was discussed in some detail by Franz Steiner in another classic little book, named simply *Taboo* (1956). Its use in Fiji, for example, had been translated as 'unlawful', 'sacred' and 'superlatively good'; in Malagasy (Madagascar), a closely related word is translated as more like 'profaned' or 'polluted'. In either case, some special category is indicated, though the translations may seem opposed to English speakers. Steiner suggested that the best etymology is one which divides the word into two parts, where *ta* means 'to mark off', and *bu* is simply an emphatic suffix, so that the whole word means 'to mark off thoroughly' or 'to set apart'.

Steiner went on to show that there was a great range of types of taboo. In Polynesia, for example, a close association with political authority meant that the taboos a person could impose provided a measure of their power (or *mana* – see Shore 1989 and Chapter 3 in this book). To quote:

> The power to restrict was the yardstick by which power was measured; here was the social manifestation of power. Second, the exercise of this veto was in terms of taboo, that is, the actual sphere of any person's office or office's power was delimited by the kinds of taboos he could impose.

pollution/ purity – a pair of terms used by anthropologists to describe institutionalised ideas about dirt and cleanliness in any particular society, especially where these have connotations with notions of spiritual power.

taboo – something prohibited, usually for reasons associated with a wider system of classification, perhaps related to ideas of pollution, or with notions of the **sacred** in any society.

sacred/ profane – this dichotomy is used by anthropologists to describe a variety of distinctions made between things, people and events that are set apart (sacred) from everyday life (profane), though the deeper meanings vary between societies, some of which have no such distinction, and they always require further study.

Taboo thus provided the means of relating a person to his superiors and inferiors. One can imagine a Chancellor of the Exchequer declaring eight or nine shillings in every twenty taboo as a measure of the power conferred on him. It takes a stretch of the imagination to realize that in the Polynesian system this power could have been conferred on him only by somebody exercising an even more awful taboo, and that the Polynesian chancellor would use the same term for his share in your pound as for the rights of his superiors, because these rights would concern him only as infringements of his own rights, just as taking away eight shillings is a restriction on your use of your twenty shillings.   (1956: 39)

For a chief or king, this power could be so great and terrible that anything he touched immediately became polluting and dangerous for ordinary people. This explained why people of extremely high rank – including visiting members of the royal family in former British colonies – had to be carried by slaves. As these were owned by the king, polluting them did not cause too much inconvenience, otherwise the visiting dignitaries would pollute for everyone else the ground on which they had walked. Clearly these taboos are helping to delineate categories of social ranking in that particular society. In today's world, when widely shared ideas such as these can be less well relied upon, persons of high status and power are very often separated from their people by a ring of armed body guards, not only to protect them, but literally to 'set them apart'.

Further powerful examples of distinctions of classification based on taboos of one sort or another are to be found in rules about food. Hindus, for example, are

Photograph 2.1 The Yakha of East Nepal sacrifice pigs as well as other animals such as buffalo for the Hindu festival of Dasain, though the subsequent feast would be taboo to their Hindu neighbours (photograph: Tamara Kohn).

brought up always to use separate pots to cook meat and vegetables, a practice which expresses an idea so strong that many feel they cannot eat at all in non-Hindu restaurants which serve meat in case this rule may have been ignored. Amongst themselves, Hindus have a variety of food taboos, depending on their caste associations, which affect who cooks the food and who may eat with whom, as well as a series of complicated rules about what may or may not be eaten at any one time. The cow is sacred, so beef is taboo, but a dairy product like butter protects food fried in it, which can then be shared across caste lines. Food distinctions therefore express social divisions within Hindu society (see Photograph 2.1).

Muslims, on the other hand, who may live in close proximity to Hindus, have a taboo against eating pork, but this time it is because the pig is regarded as unclean. Although these animals appear to have been forbidden for different reasons from the Hindus' sacred cow, they are both 'set apart' and therefore 'taboo'. In both cases, too, the prohibition makes an important distinction between the categories of people involved. Other peoples have different food taboos. Orthodox Jewish rules prohibit eating meat and dairy products at the same meal, for example, and they also proscribe eating meat which has not been drained of blood, or made kosher. Jeremy MacClancy, in a book entitled *Consuming Culture*, describes these arrangements very colourfully:

> The Jewish dietary laws do not stop at the curly tail-end of a pig. They are made up of a whole set of kosher dos and dont's, of which the ban on pork and the separation of meat and milk are merely the most well known. Though these dietary rules are still central in the lives of many Jews, they were even more important in Jesus's time, when each Jewish sect interpreted God's gastronomic intentions in its own way. What foods you ate and with whom you ate them were a key means of saying what particular group you belonged to. The Essenes would only have a meal among themselves, and neither they nor members of the Pharisees, the Maccabees, the Sadducees, the Hasidim, the Sicraii, the Herodians, the Hellenists, or the Therapeutae, would even think of sitting down at the same table with a gentile. For Jews, their food rules came to stand for the whole of their law, and violating any of them was seen as equivalent to leaving the faith. God had founded his Covenant with His chosen people through the medium of food, and His followers were not going to break this holy agreement by nibbling the wrong edible in the wrong company. When forced to eat swine by the Romans, some chose to die rather than pollute themselves and profane their sacred pact with the Almighty. (1992: 33-4)

In many parts of the world there are taboos associated with the body and bodily functions, typically with pregnancy, childbirth and menstruation for women, and illness and death for anyone, regardless of gender. A study of pregnancy and childbirth amongst the Chinese in Hong Kong, by Diana Martin (1994), describes an abundance of food prohibitions during pregnancy, even amongst the most highly educated women. Martin discovered that her informants were expected to hand over the care of their babies and tiny infants to others almost as soon as they were born, and noted that the food and other taboos were observed openly in public situations. She suggests, therefore, that the prohibitions are an open expression of the fact that a woman is about to become a mother during the only time she has total responsibility for her offspring.

As for menstruation taboos, women in many societies are excluded from certain activities during their monthly periods. They may be required to live in a separate house for the duration, perhaps with other women in the same situation, or they may simply be banned from the fishing boats or not allowed to enter the temple. *The Red Tent*, a novel by Anita Diamant (2001) set in the biblical time of Dinah, sister of Joseph of the coat-of-many-colours fame, is much concerned with the lives of women in such a society, and vividly depicts the periods they spent in the separate quarters described in the title. Here, too, they gave birth, and attended to each other's feminine needs.

In rural Japan, where I did fieldwork in the 1970s, women observed taboos on certain foods, on bathing, and even on watching television for a period of 31–33 days after childbirth. After a death in the family, the bereaved relatives would avoid certain foods for up to 49 days. These customs were explained in terms of the relationship between the soul and the body. The soul of a person who has recently died is said to be prone to stay around the house for a while, and the taboos are concerned with avoiding trouble and seeing that a complete separation occurs. In the case of a baby, the soul is in danger of escaping in the early stages, and the prohibitions are to help avoid this kind of disaster. An examination of these ideas is thus revealing of Japanese notions about the constitution of the person, the relationship of humans with the spiritual world, and, by further examination of the range of people affected by the taboos, of the make-up of the Japanese family.

Pollution

Anthropologists use the word 'pollution' to describe ideas found to be held strongly in various parts of the world about the destruction of a parallel notion of purity. In most cases, purity denotes cleanliness, but in many societies there are religious associations with this concept so that it would perhaps be more accurately translated into English as 'sanctity'. It may be the case that rituals of purification precede any communication with the spiritual or supernatural world, for example, but in some societies there are strongly held views about the avoidance of pollution and polluting behaviour for reasons connected with ideas about social relations. In either case these are inevitably concerned with local systems of classification.

In the Japanese case above, taboos related to birth and death may also be explained in terms of the protection they will provide for others, since those observing the taboos may also be regarded as polluting at these times. Women after childbirth are thus prohibited from preparing food, entering a public bath, or participating in ritual activities, which they may spoil due to their polluted state. Similarly, a girl whose father had recently died had to instruct a group of friends in the plaiting of a straw rope for the shrine festival from a position just over the wall and therefore out of the sacred area that she would defile if she entered. After a death in Japan, a notice is posted on the front door of the house of the deceased to warn visitors of the polluting situation.

In the Indian subcontinent, on the other hand, the food taboos we discussed above express more permanent notions of pollution associated with a caste system which divides all human beings into classes of people conceptually distinguished from one another in such a way that the word 'class' seems inadequate (see Dumont 1980 and Quigley 1993 for two interpretations). The strength of the danger of pollution is evident in the existence of a caste of 'untouchable' people who are employed specifically to protect others (Deliege 1997). They sweep, clear sewage, deal with dead animals, and make leather goods, all tasks which are thought to be polluting for those of other castes. Brahmins, for example, must have nothing to do with excrement, an idea so firmly ingrained that a Brahmin girl working in a nursery in England preferred to alienate all her workmates rather than break the taboo and agree to change the nappies of her charges.

Such ideas of pollution demonstrate very clearly ways in which people divide themselves up, in this case initially into castes, an ancient system understood and observed in its own local context, but in practice in another society creating new reasons for emphasising old divisions. Actually, it is precisely for deeply ingrained ideas such as these that foreigners are regarded with suspicion, and often with distaste, wherever they are found. The system of classification, particularly when it is reinforced with taboos associated with ideas of pollution, is very hard to dislodge. It expresses the way the world is perceived, and changes in it can lead to a good deal of confusion, even to shock – that American phrase, 'culture shock', is no trite description.

The novels of Paul Scott's *Raj Quartet*, which were televised under the title of the first in the series, *The Jewel in the Crown*, opened with a forcible illustration of ideas such as these. Hari Kumar, a British public schoolboy of Indian parents, is returned to his relatives in India when his father dies suddenly, leaving no provision for the rest of his education. He finds himself in a society which includes people brought up like himself, but the colour of his skin excludes him from their company. His kinsfolk find his lifestyle entirely alien and indeed polluting to them, and they force him to drink the urine of the sacred cow, an abhorrence to him, but for them the only way to purge Hari of the pollution he has picked up by living overseas.

Purity and Classification

Various theories have been advanced to explain particular notions of pollution and taboo, but Mary Douglas has pointed out in her book *Purity and Danger*

(1966) that they all form part of a wider system of classification. The taboos, and the ideas about purity and pollution, are thus themselves fertile areas of investigation for anthropologists, who try to set them in the context of other knowledge about the peoples in question, and about the historical influences they have experienced. The analysis of the 'Abominations of Leviticus' in the same book is one of the best-known attempts to interpret an extremely complex and otherwise seemingly random system of rules and restrictions of this sort.

The lists of animals which were prohibited in the biblical book of Leviticus are many and varied, and previous attempts to make sense of them had been rather unsuccessful, according to Douglas. She argues, however, that they must not be considered piecemeal. Within the context of God's order for the world, laid out in the book of Genesis, important distinctions are to be made between the components of the threefold classification of the world into the earth, the waters and the firmament. Living beings which reside in each medium are described according to their type: flesh, fish and fowl, respectively, and each has an appropriate means of locomotion. In the firmament, for example, two-legged fowl fly with wings, in the water scaly fish swim with fins, and on the earth four-legged animals hop, jump or walk.

Those creatures which are forbidden turn out to be anomalous according to this system, Douglas argues. This includes four-footed creatures which fly, and creatures with two hands and two feet who move about on all fours. It particularly forbids creatures which swarm because these are neither fish, flesh nor fowl. They are matter out of place, and therefore forbidden.

> If the proposed interpretation of the forbidden animals is correct, the dietary laws would have been like signs which at every turn inspired meditation on the oneness, purity and completeness of God. By rules of avoidance holiness was given a physical expression in every encounter with the animal kingdom and at every meal. Observance of the dietary rules would thus have been a meaningful part of the great liturgical act of recognition and worship which culminated in the sacrifice in the Temple. (Douglas 1966: 72)

Mary Douglas's book has become a classic, and it was one of the first works to argue that rituals of purity and impurity create unity of experience in any society, not just those formerly regarded as 'primitive'. It brings the ideas discussed in this chapter right into the most domestic sphere, because in it she writes about *dirt* in a European household, or, to be more precise, in *her* type of household, since the ideas may not be shared by Europeans of all classes and ethnic origins; however, this anthropologist provides an excellent example of how the principles learned in exotic places may be most aptly applied in any society, including one's own.

She points out that cleaning is as much concerned with *order* as with hygiene. There is no such thing as absolute dirt, she tells us, 'it exists in the eye of the beholder', and if we abstract pathogenicity and hygiene from our notion of dirt we find it is simply 'matter out of place'. Cleaning expresses our own system of classification, so that an object likely to confuse it is regarded as *polluting*, that is, *dirty*.

> Shoes are not dirty in themselves, but it is dirty to place them on the dining-table; food is not dirty in itself, but it is dirty to leave cooking utensils in the bedroom, or food bespattered on clothing; similarly, bathroom equipment in the drawing room; clothing lying on chairs; outdoor-things in-doors; upstairs things downstairs; under-clothing appearing where over-clothing should be, and so on. In short, our pollution behaviour is the reaction which condemns any object or idea likely to confuse or contradict cherished classifications. (1966: 48)

In Japan, as elsewhere, shoes should not be brought into the house at all, and this is a rule enforced so strictly that even tiny children must obey it as soon as they are able to walk. A foreigner who stepped across a Japanese threshold with shoes on would soon be hustled back out again, for this error would contravene deeply ingrained ideas about dirt and cleanliness which further reflect a pervasive Japanese distinction between *inside* and *outside*. Shoes are to be left in the doorway to the outside world, where they should be donned before stepping out again. Within the house itself, there are further distinctions to be made between areas where slippers may be worn, and the fine floor matting which should only be crossed in stockinged feet.

The force of this distinction was illustrated clearly in the writings of Fukuzawa Yukichi, one of the first Japanese to visit America in the nineteenth century when the country was opened to the outside world after two hundred years of virtual isolation. He was shocked to see people going inside the houses in their shoes, which had come directly in from the outside world, but he was particularly affected to notice them walking on great areas of soft material (i.e. carpets) that looked to him identical to a substance highly valued in Japan for making small purses.

These foreigners seemed dirty to the Japanese just as people in Britain classify 'gypsies' as dirty because they throw rubbish out of their caravan windows and leave it behind when they move on. Judith Okely, who made a study of Traveller Gypsies in Britain in the 1970s, has nevertheless demonstrated forcibly how clean these people are within their own system of classification. Again, they make a clear distinction between the inside and the outside, this time of their caravans. Beyond the window is not their world, but within it they have such strict rules about cleanliness that if a dog were to lick a human plate, the owner would feel obliged to break the whole set.

This is part of a strict code of purity and pollution shared by the Traveller Gypsies, who keep their homes immaculate. They separate bowls for washing clothes (outside) from bowls for washing up pots (which hold food which goes inside), and they separate male and female washing as well. For them, cats are regarded as dirty because they lick their own fur and confound the distinction between inside and outside, whereas other members of the surrounding society admire cats for keeping themselves clean. Dogs are dirty, too, and should live outside; members of the wider society who allow cats and dogs to live in the house and eat off human plates fill the Travellers with disgust (see First-hand Account 2 on p. 46 and Photograph 2.2).

Photograph 2.2 Dogs are classified in very different ways by different peoples. To some, they are pets, though not always treated in the same way (see Fukuda 1997 in Chapter 1), to many they are work animals, including the hunt scenario pictured above, where they are referred to as hounds, and for others they are simply food (photograph: Robert Davis and Garry Marvin).

Animal Categories and Verbal Abuse

Edmund Leach wrote an interesting article about the role played by tabooed words in language. He was concerned with obscenities – dirty words, blasphemy and words of abuse – words that are unmentionable in some company, and therefore used to shock or impress in other circumstances. He argued that language in general is like a grid, in which words provide labels for important categories and break up the social and physical environment, which would otherwise be a continuum, into discrete, recognisable things. Words that are regarded as taboo help to reinforce this system and prevent confusion by inhibiting the recognition of the parts of the continuum that separate the things.

His first illustration of the argument concerns the boundary of the human being within its environment, particularly important, again, as a baby is learning

In a world where a cup of tea requires no more than the turn of a tap and the flick of a switch, it is easy for old ways to die, and equally easy to regard as quirky the way of life that went with them. For me, it is unthinkable to eat from a plate or cup or any other utensil that has been touched by a dog or cat; indeed, if I were aware of any such contact, I would break and discard the utensil so defiled. Horses and cattle would not cause such a reaction because they are clean or 'sweet' animals, but cats, dogs, pigs and many other animals are regarded as unclean or 'mockerdy', and by

First-hand account 2:

Mick Ganly, English Traveller – on Cleanliness among Travellers

definition, anything they touch becomes 'mockerdy covel', or a dirty thing. Likewise, when I eat I need to know that my eating utensils have been cleaned or, if you like, purified, in running water. I am aware in my rational mind that my prejudice no longer has a valid foundation in hygiene but something very deep rooted keeps it alive.

England

Equally difficult to overcome (actually, more so) was the matter of menstruating women, who were not welcome in the wagons when I was a boy, and who could not eat with us until they became 'clean' again, nor, might I add, were they encouraged to buy or handle food. Another section of society, subject to a variety of beliefs, placed somewhere between dogs and menstruating women, were those with mental impairments, i.e. Down's syndrome, madness in its various forms, or the downright simpleton. These were (and are) known as *raji*, or *radgy* people, and it would be a grave misfortune to have them handle one's food. The same sort of beliefs, I am told, are common in India, but that may be wholly untrue. In the matter of personal hygiene, things were equally clear cut. One's feet, mouth and private parts were cleaned scrupulously both morning and evening, but it is true to say that other parts of the body were not quite so important. This, I suspect, had as much to do with every drop of water having to be found and carried, and the same for firewood. There were no taboos, as far as I know, with regard to food itself.

> If it ran, swam, flew or grew, we killed it and ate it – in fact, I still do – but it is interesting that one could and would happily eat a hare or rabbit killed by a dog, or a bird killed by a cat, yet not eat the same hare or rabbit from a plate touched by its executioner.
>
> *Photograph taken by Władislaw Szulc*

to see and label the surrounding world. Here taboos are clearly associated with what Leach refers to as exudations of the body – 'feces, urine, semen, menstrual blood, hair clippings, nail parings, body dirt, spittle, mother's milk' is Leach's list (1966: 38), although in the case of the baby, vomit and nasal mucus could well be added. In an essay which was initially read to an audience, Leach notes that

> so strong is the resulting taboo that, even as an adult addressing an adult audience, I cannot refer to these substances by the monosyllabic words which I used as a child but must mention them only in Latin.   (Ibid.)

The child is not born with these inhibitions, of course, and it is an important aspect of the training of small children to see that they don't pay inappropriate attention to these same exudations of the body, which are apparently part of them, but which must be carefully separated from them. Failure to learn these practices would be regarded as dirty, although the behaviour regarded as 'clean' and appropriate is of course variable from one society to another. The substances themselves may also be regarded as powerful in some societies, like the cow's urine above, and hair and nail clippings are sometimes the focus of mystical attack. In any case, words for the substances may be used to make a forceful exclamation, and they are also inclined to provoke expressions of disgust.

Leach's second set of tabooed words comprises those which in a religious context would be described as blasphemous. He points out that although life and death are in fact inseparable, religion always tries to separate them, and the gap between this world of 'mortal men' and the next, inhabited by 'immortal nonmen (gods)' is bridged by beings who are ambiguous in terms of such regular systems of classification. Thus we find incarnate deities, virgin mothers and supernatural monsters which may be half-human/half-beast. These ambiguous creatures mediate between the two worlds, but they are also the object of the most intense taboos, and to speak in an inappropriate fashion about them may be regarded as a particularly dangerous endeavour.

The bulk of Leach's essay is about animal categories, and how these relate to categories of human being. Any number of animals are called into play – cow, pig, bitch, cat, rat, filly – but it is worth drawing attention to the fact that all the animal terms which are used to address or describe human beings, either in a derogatory or a familiar fashion, are those for beasts to be found in the households or countryside of Britain. An immediate concern is to distinguish between the human and animal worlds, then, and since it would be impossible to confuse animals from further afield with ourselves, it would therefore be less than forceful, as he points out, to address someone in Britain as a polar bear.

Leach chose to focus on the language of British English to illustrate his argument, but he suggests that similar mechanisms operate everywhere, and provides a further example in a consideration of the Kachin language of the people he worked with in Southern Burma. Leach's argument was later heavily criticised in an article in the anthropological journal *Man* (Halverson 1976), but the ideas do provide a forceful (if inaccurate) linguistic example of the general way in which taboos and ideas of pollution and purity help to delineate systems of classification.

Conclusion

It is clear that a look at ideas of dirt, cleanliness and prohibitions opens up avenues to the understanding of different systems of classification, which can evidently exist side by side, even within the same society. It is also clear how strong and powerful these ideas may be. Within one society, where such notions are shared, rules seem natural and normal. To members of other societies, however, the same rules may well appear unnecessarily strict, burdensome barriers to friendship and integration. In Chapter 4 we will return to these ideas when we look at ritual activities, but in the meantime, we turn to further aspects of social relations, this time expressed through material objects.

Discussion Questions

1   Think of a culturally variable situation you have found repulsive, perhaps in a foreign country. Think about why. Now try and imagine something a person from that country might find repulsive in your lifestyle.

2   Do you alter your greeting behaviour depending on who you are meeting and how well you know them? How would you greet the Queen of England, for example, or the Emperor of Japan? What about your own president or prime minister? Or a friend's spouse? Would you greet a strange child in the same way you would greet the child of a friend? Think about what a greeting can tell us about relationships.

3   Try out Leach's idea by making a list of words you might avoid in front of your mother. Consider when and whether you might use them and what force they might have. Do they illustrate Leach's categories of distinction?

References and Further Research

Books

Deliege, R. (1997) *The World of the 'Untouchables': Paraiyars of Tamil Nadu* (Delhi: Oxford: Oxford University Press).

Douglas, Mary (1966) *Purity and Danger* (Harmondsworth: Penguin).

Dumont, Louis (1980) *Homo Hierarchicus: The Caste System and Its Implications* (Chicago and London: University of Chicago Press).

MacClancy, Jeremy (1992) *Consuming Culture: Why You Eat What You Eat* (New York: Henry Holt & Company).

Martin, Diana (1994) 'Pregnancy and Childbirth among the Chinese of Hong Kong', DPhil thesis, University of Oxford.

Masquelier, Adeline (ed.), (2005) *Dress, Undress, and Difference: Critical Perspectives on the Body's Surface* (Bloomington: Indiana University Press).

Okely, Judith (1983) *The Traveller Gypsies* (Cambridge: Cambridge University Press).

Quigley, Declan (1993) *The Interpretation of Caste* (Oxford: Clarendon Press).

Steiner, Franz (1956) *Taboo* (Harmondsworth: Penguin).

Articles

Fassin, Didier (2001) 'The Biopolitics of Otherness: Undocumented Foreigners and Racial Discrimination in French Public Debate', *Anthropology Today*, 17(1): 3–7.

Gaborieau, Marc (1985) 'From Al-Beruni to Jinnah: Idiom, Ritual and Ideology of the Hindu–Muslim Confrontation in South Asia', *Anthropology Today*, 1(3): 7–14.

Halverson, J. (1976) 'Animal Categories and Terms of Abuse', *Man*, 11: 505–16.

Hendry, Joy (2007 [1984]) 'Shoes, the Early Learning of an Important Distinction in Japanese Society', in G. Daniels (ed.), *Europe Interprets Japan* (Tenterden: Paul Norbury Publications), reprinted in D. P. Martinez (ed.), *Japanese Culture and Society* (London, Routledge, 2007).

Leach, Edmund (1966) 'Animal Categories and Verbal Abuse', in Eric H. Lenneberg (ed.), *New Directions for the Study of Language* (Cambridge, Mass.: MIT Press).

Radcliffe-Brown, A. R. (1952) 'Taboo' chapter in *Structure and Function in Primitive Society* (London: Cohen & West).

Shore, Bradd (1989) '*Mana* and *Tapu*', in Alan Howard and Robert Borofsy (eds), *Developments of Polynesian Ethnology* (Honolulu: University of Hawaii Press).

Novels

Diamant, Anita (2001) *The Red Tent* (Pan). A novel built around the story of Dinah, who makes a brief appearance in the Bible; at the same time a well-researched account of the life of women at the time.

Fatima Altaf, (1993) *The One Who Did Not Ask* (translated from Urdu by Rukhsana Ahmad) (London: Heinemann), tells poignantly of the problems experienced by the daughter of a well-to-do Indian family when she breaks some of the taboos of her high class upbringing.

Hugo, Victor (1831) *The Hunchback of Notre-Dame*, is the story of Quasimodo, a man whose deformity causes others to reject him and to assume he is monstrous.

Scott, Paul (1996) *The Jewel in the Crown* (London: Mandarin) is the first of a series of four novels entitled *The Raj Quartet*, which depict, amongst other things, reactions to the breaking of unwritten taboos in the life of British India.

Films

Caste at Birth (Mira Hamermesh, 1990) explores the complexities of the caste system in the Indian subcontinent. It illustrates in particular taboos surrounding 'untouchables'.

The Lau of Malaita (Leslie Woodhead and Pierre Maranda, 1987), a film in the Granada

'Disappearing World' series, provides information about taboos amongst a group of Solomon Islanders and tells of how their long-standing 'Custom' is being defended (or otherwise) against Christian missionaries in the area.

Some Women of Marrakesh (Melissa Llewelyn-Davies, 1977), another 'Disappearing World' film, penetrates the enclosed world of female society in the male-orientated Muslim state of Morocco.

Websites

www.guardian.co.uk/obituaries/story/0,,2082621,00.html# – obituary for Mary Douglas, *Guardian*, May 2007.

www.samvak.tripod.com/taboo.html – taboos around the world and their history.

www.philosophersnet.com/games/taboo.htm – exercise to get one thinking about taboos.

www.catohoeben.com/lafti_film and www.lifeonlens.org/index.php?option=com_content&task=view&id=35&Itemid=37 – two films about the movement to raise the living standards of 'untouchable' people.

Gifts, Exchange and Reciprocity

The Anthropologist's Arrival

With all the complexity of possibility discussed in the last chapter, an anthropologist arriving in a society to make a study might well feel daunted by the task ahead. Where to start? This is a pertinent question and many students worry a great deal about it before they leave for fieldwork. In practice, once they arrive and settle in, there are so many details of daily life to be seen to that the work just seems to take on a pace of its own. In a strange situation, one must first of all learn to cope with very basic needs – eating, of course, but also cooking, bathing, laundry, disposing of refuse – all these things are highly relevant to an ethnographer, as we have seen, and for the participant observer, the work is begun.

While coping with the mundane, the fieldworker is also bound to enter into communication with other members of the society concerned and this forces an immediate consideration of the nature of social relations. My first days of fieldwork in Japan were greatly eased by the good nature and friendship of my next-door neighbour, whom I visited to inquire about refuse collection. To my good fortune, he not only explained carefully about dividing waste into the burnable and the unburnable (which began to indicate information about local systems of classification), but he also instructed me about the more orthodox way of introducing oneself to new neighbours – namely, by calling round with a small gift, such as a towel.

This turned out to be an important custom in a Japanese context, for it allows a relationship to be opened. Some foreigners return from working or studying in Japan complaining sadly that they never made any progress with their neighbours – they had lived there for a year, maybe more, but they had neglected to take that first important step of self-introduction. For an ethnographer, who can only begin to learn properly about the people under study through social interaction with them, the principle of opening relations is a vital one, and if the neighbours are part of the study, as they were in this first fieldwork of mine, it is an advantage to start out in a way that they can comprehend and appreciate.

Social relationships are themselves an important part of the study of social anthropologists, of course, but they are not actually visible without being signified in some way. The presentation of gifts or, indeed, any movement of material objects from one person to another can provide an observer with information which they can record, if only later to analyse and understand. It gives access to a visible medium of communication, and in the early days of study in a community, when only a limited amount of the spoken language may be understood, details about the movement of objects can help an ethnographer to build up a map of social ties between the people who live there.

Gifts

Gifts are also given at rather specific times, and an examination of the occasions involved may also help lead to an understanding of important events and stages in the lives of the people concerned. Gifts to individuals may be marking changes of status; exchanges within wider groups may be celebrating occasions important in their society. In many places, presents are given as one grows up and grows old, year by year; they are given as one attains important goals, like entry to a school or university, or achieving a new position at work; many are given if one decides to move from being single to being married, although rather fewer are given if the marriage breaks down; many are also given to mark a new life, and to mark the end of a life.

Gifts are also presented when one couple, or family, visits another, especially if they are to eat together, or to spend a weekend or holiday in the other's home. House-warming presents are made to families who have recently moved in most English-speaking countries, just as such families are expected to visit their neighbours in Japan. At certain festivals, everywhere, friends and relations express their relationships by making gifts to each other, or to each other's children, and Christmas has become such a global example of this custom that non-Christians may join in simply for the purpose of reinforcing their own social relations.

This has been described by Baumann in his study of Southall, mentioned in the Introduction (see Chapter 4, Baumann in de Coppet 1992).

All this gift exchange must be examined very carefully, however, for things that look familiar may be misleading. In theory, at least in some places, gifts are given voluntarily, but there are always rules and conventions involved. As well as knowing when it is appropriate to give gifts, and to whom, it is important to know how valuable they should be, how they should be received, and how and when they should be repaid. In some societies gifts are ignored by the recipient in front of the donor, in others they must be opened and admired, whether they actually bring pleasure or not. These rules vary from one society to another, and there are also sets of conventions about how the gift should be presented, and what form of words should accompany the presentation.

Another study which has become a classic in the field of social anthropology, and continues to invite comment, addresses precisely this subject. This book, *The Gift*, by Marcel Mauss, was written in 1925, at a time when Europeans still sought to learn about their own past by looking at so-called primitive or 'archaic' people. Mauss was interested in examining 'the realm of contract' and systems of 'economic presentation' by isolating

> one important set of phenomena: namely, prestations which are in theory voluntary, disinterested and spontaneous, but are in fact obligatory and interested. The form usually taken is that of the gift generously offered; but the accompanying behaviour is formal pretence and social deception, while the transaction itself is based on obligation and self-interest. (Mauss 1970: 1)

Through an examination of the practices found in various parts of the world, Mauss suggests that in small-scale 'early' societies, gift exchange is particularly important because it is a total phenomenon which may involve simultaneous expressions of a religious, legal, moral and economic nature. He argues further that exchange may often be between whole groups, through their chiefs, and may involve not only goods, wealth and property, but also courtesies, entertainment, ritual, military assistance, women, children, dances and feasts. These 'total prestations' are again in theory voluntary, but here, more than ever, strictly obligatory, with possible sanctions of private and open warfare.

total phenomenon – a social phenomenon that is found to involve all areas of life in a particular society. The term was chosen by Marcel Mauss in the case of *le don* – translated as gift or 'prestation' – which he saw involving simultaneous expressions of a 'religious, legal, moral and economic' nature.

He proposed that there are three clear obligations involved:

1 the obligation to give
2 the obligation to receive and
3 the obligation to repay

and examples of the mechanisms of gift exchange in several different societies illustrate the significance it may hold in the wider arenas of social life. In all cases, ethnographers have returned again and again to the societies he chose, and knowledge about the people concerned has been greatly deepened, but three examples from Mauss's material lay out an agenda for further discussion. They also illustrate principles which arise in all societies in one way or another – quite an achievement.

The first of these is the case of the *kula*, a system of gift-giving found in the Trobriand Islands and described and analysed in detail by Malinowski (1922), of whom we heard in the Introduction. He entitled his first book *Argonauts of the Western Pacific* after people who build elaborate boats and make long journeys to visit other islands in the area. The ostensible purpose of their voyages is to make gifts, gifts which are passed on to further islanders in time by the recipients, and which continue around in a wide circular progression. The gifts are made of local shells, and in one direction travel necklaces, called *soulava*, and in the other, expressed as a return for the first, according to Malinowski, armbands called *mwali*.

Despite a show of disinterest in the gifts when they arrive, often to be thrown down disdainfully, the *mwali* and *soulava* are greatly prized by the local people. The community as a whole is said to gloat over them while they are in their possession, handing them round with affection, wearing them as adornment, and even placing them over the sick to help them recover. Some of these objects have legends attached to them, and are particularly prized, but it is important not to keep the gifts too long before passing them on. The objects move around a much wider area of the ocean than any of their 'owners', but people gain status by being involved in the *kula*, and they take a lot of trouble to set up the voyages.

In practice, each visit involves considerable preparation, for the elaborate canoes must be built and maintained, and the presentation of gifts is accompanied by the regular exchange and barter of a multitude of other objects, or 'utilities', as Malinowski terms them, which are 'often unprocurable in the district to which they are imported, and indispensable there'.

> The Kula is thus an extremely big and complex institution, both in its
> geographical extent, and in the manifoldness of its component pursuits.
> It welds together a considerable number of tribes, and it embraces
> a vast complex of activities, interconnected, and playing into one
> another... (Malinowski 1922: 83)

Mauss's first example thus demonstrates that this system of ceremonial gift exchange is ensuring *communication* amongst island people who would otherwise be widely separated. The gifts are surely expressing social relationships.

The second example from Mauss proposes to help understand the force of obligation associated with gift-giving, which he finds lacking in Malinowski's account of the *kula*. He turns to Polynesia to consider practices and ideas of the Māori people, and those of Samoa, where spiritual forces are held to attack a person who fails to repay a gift received. Within the local system of thinking a person builds up a kind of honour or prestige, known as *mana*, which is conferred by wealth but lost if suitable gifts are not returned. This is said to be because *mana* includes a magical or spiritual element transmitted through the vehicle of *taonga*, which may be property, labour or merchandise, that has the power to turn and destroy the recipient if appropriate repayment is not made.

A part of the giver is thought to be sent with the gift, which gives him or her a kind of hold over the person who receives it, and also over anyone who may steal it! This view thus represents an explicit expression in spiritual terms of the obligation to repay goods or services received, which Mauss argues exists to some extent everywhere. It also demonstrates very clearly the way those who are unable to repay gifts received, for whatever reason, lose face and prestige within their own society. Indeed, the term *mana*, which is related to ideas of *tabu*, as we discussed in the last chapter, is sometimes translated as 'face' (see First-hand Account 3. 1 overleaf for the interesting 2007 interpretation of a Māori scholar).

This principle is illustrated forcibly in the third example we take from Mauss, namely the case of *potlatch*, which he explains was originally a Chinook word meaning to 'nourish' or 'consume', but that had come to describe competitive feasts held amongst peoples of northwest America like the Tlingit, Haida and Kwakiutl of Alaska and British Columbia. As elsewhere, the political hierarchy was based on wealth, which was said to indicate proof of favour with the spirits, and people would demonstrate their status in this respect by inviting each other to feasts during the cold winter months. Gifts would be handed out, and those who couldn't afford to repay would lose face, and could even be enslaved for debt.

The chiefs of each group invited would sometimes sit in hierarchical order at these gatherings so that everyone could see their ranking, and trade and marriage arrangements would depend upon an internally recognised relative standing of the groups involved. These people collectively became so rich during the late nineteenth and early twentieth centuries due to their skills at trapping animals whose furs were highly prized in the wider world, that their winter celebrations became extremely lavish, and they even began to destroy valuable goods to demonstrate their immense wealth. Beautiful blankets would be burned, and huge copper plates hurled over the cliffs, in their agonised efforts to humiliate one other.

This is evidently an exaggerated case, but the principles are quite recognisable. Where wealth is a mark of status, it is not enough to have the resources; others must be made aware of the fact. The notion of conspicuous consumption was discussed some time ago by Veblen (1899) for Western societies, and the wanton destruction of valuable goods is an extension of spending wildly to impress. In British society, there are subtle ways to gain status through diverting wealth into children's education, club membership, or perhaps land, sometimes even leaving a shortage of ready cash, a state which may be contrasted snobbishly with an excessively obvious display of wealth.

conspicuous consumption – the ostentatious consuming of food, drink or other goods interpreted (initially by Veblen) as a way of demonstrating wealth, or laying claim to a wealthy group or society.

Tikanga hau, the 'spirit of gift exchange' or the ethic of generosity, and its associated values are identified in my current research as a principal motivation of Māori business and cultural leaders. This is evident in economics, and significantly also in the politics of social relations. In anthropology, especially in the work of Marcel Mauss, who was informed on Māori thinking by Tamati Ranapiri of the Ngāti Raukawa tribe, exchange theory

and gift exchange are often presented in the form of the following propositions: that exchange is a fundamental social system; that gift exchange is a prior economic system; that a gift economy is animated by the spirit of the gift (*hau*); that the spirit of the gift creates an indissoluble bond between persons engaged in the exchange, and that it was Western societies which were responsible for the separation of persons and things.[1]

However, a focus solely on material and cognitive anthropology of gift exchange and generosity without recourse to its metaphysics and spirituality, or *wairuatanga*, is not adequate in the mind of Māori of Aotearoa New Zealand. While Mauss has, in my analysis of the Ranapiri letters of 1907, remained close to Ranapiri's metaphysics and indeed was informed by it, other commentators have concentrated on the material and social aspects of gift exchange, disputing a metaphysical explanation at all. Severe critiques were made by Raymond Firth, Claude Lévi-Strauss and Marshall Sahlins on Mauss's hermeneutics and treatment of *hau*, which reflect utilitarian, materialist, secularist, and psychological and Western rationalist critiques of Māori metaphysics as understood by a French scholar. The only ethnographer to have worked from the original Tamati Ranapiri letters was Elsdon Best, as they were in correspondence with each other. As far as I know, none of the commentators read or accessed the original letters in Māori of Tamati Ranapiri. They all therefore depended upon the accuracy of Elsdon Best and his transcribing and translating the letters correctly.

I found that Best had, when transcribing the letters and preparing extracts ready for publication in *Māori Forest Lore* (1909), made significant changes to key phrases. The effect of Best's changes turned Ranapiri's hermeneutics about Māori metaphysics into a secular materialist's explanation, thus reflecting Best's views more so than those of Ranapiri. The error was partly corrected by Mauss, albeit somewhat intuitively, but Firth, Lévi-Strauss and Sahlins followed Best's edited translation of the Ranapiri letters and the former's phenomenological approach. Many others have followed suit, including Weiner (1992) and Parry (1986). Following Best, Firth, Lévi-Strauss and Sahlins challenged Mauss's interpretation and his idea of the spirit of the gift itself. According to Firth: 'When Mauss sees in gift exchange an interchange of personalities, a "bond of soul", he is following not a native belief, but his own intellectual interpretation of it' (1972: 418).

Claude Lévi-Strauss wrote:

> Hau is not the ultimate explanation for gift exchange; it is the conscious form whereby men of a given society, in which the problem had particular importance, apprehended an unconscious necessity whose explanation lies elsewhere. (Cited in Schrift 1997: 55–6)

Finally, Marshall Sahlins presents a rationalist utilitarian criticism:

> Since Mauss ... anthropology has become more consistently rational in its treatment of exchange. Reciprocity is contract pure and mainly secular, sanctioned perhaps by a mixture of considerations of which a carefully calculated self-interest is not the least. (Cited in Schrift 1997: 93)

Ranapiri wrote of two distinct *hau* associated with a *taonga*, or the gift. The first is the *hau* intrinsic to the *taonga* itself, which is the *hau* infused at the creation of the *taonga*. The second *hau*, advises Ranapiri, is the original donor's *hau* that is associated with his or her possession or ownership of the taonga. Thus in Māori belief exchange and its spiritual–moral bases are therefore a central theme in contemporary social relations and economics. It is a Māori view of the exchange and its moral bases of the human action that matters. *Tikanga hau*, exchange or generosity, spirituality and morality, is part of a matrix of some thirteen associated ethics, which constitutes a moral system, based on a plurality of ethics.

Despite Elsdon Best's mistake in the translation of Ranapiri's explanation of *hau*, Marcel Mauss' intuitive explication of the meaning and significance of *hau* was correct all along and captured the spirit of Ranapiri's 'text capitale.'

Note
1. My thanks to Dr Amiria Salmond, Anthropology Department, Cambridge University, England for discussions on these points in 1999 and in New Zealand in 2000.

Dr Manuka Henare is associate dean of Māori and Pacific Development at the University of Auckland Business School. See the Henare entry under the 'References and Further Research' section at the end of this chapter to read about his research.

In 1928, the practice of potlatch was banned in British Columbia, by a Canadian government taking measures to try and assimilate their Native populations, and responding to complaints from local churchmen about the extreme measures being taken to acquire the necessary goods. The anthropologist Franz Boas wrote in defence of the system as an important part of the socioeconomic organisation of those peoples, but the ban was not lifted until the 1950s and masks confiscated at the time of the ban not returned until later (the film *Box of Treasures*, listed below, is the story told from the perspective of the Kwakwaka'wakw people, described by Mauss as Kwakiutl). The practice was in many cases continued in secret, for potlatch feasts also mark important occasions in people's lives.

Today, the gifts given include modern consumer goods such as coffee pots and tea towels, and the occasions include university and school graduation, marking the agreement of a land claim treaty, and memorials for people who have passed away. Jonaitis (1991) is a good source of information about the continuing feasts and their associated material culture.

The Indian Gift

Since Mauss's time there have been many refinements to the ethnography he used, but his ideas are still discussed, sometimes critically. One important contribution was made by anthropologists who have worked in India, where the obligation to repay gifts received is shown to be not as universal as Mauss seemed to be suggesting. Here a form of gift known as *dân* or *dana*, made to a priest or members of a different caste who can deal with residual pollution, is positively not to be repaid, because it is thought to carry away inauspiciousness and sin, which one would not want back. An interpretation of the Indian situation depends on an understanding of notions of purity and pollution, which are inextricably linked with the caste system, as introduced in the previous chapter.

This subject was the focus of a book called *The Poison in the Gift*, by Gloria Goodwin Raheja, who argued that the close examination of gift-giving in the North Indian village where she worked revealed a new theoretical interpretation of caste, based on the centrality of the landowners called Gujars:

> The structural position of Gujars in the caste configuration of the village and the region is dependent not only on their possession of the land, but also on the pattern of their relationships with the other castes in terms of the giving and receiving of specific named prestations, as the 'protectors' ... of the village.
>
> .... Gujars have a 'right' to give *dân* ... and it is always given in the context of ritual actions that are said to promote the 'well-being [achieved through] gift-giving' (*khairkhairât*) and 'auspiciousness'(*śubh*) of the Gujar donors through the transferral of inauspiciousness (*nâsubh*) to the recipients. (Raheja 1988: 18–20)

Raheja argues that her observations and analysis of the movement of objects, including gifts, reveals a new understanding of the relations between caste groups. She thereby challenges the previous work of both Mauss and Dumont (see Chapter 2), and her work is an excellent example of the value of the analysis of material culture for understanding social relations.

Jonathan Parry (1986) also discusses the *dana* gifts which positively reject a return. He proposes a rereading of Mauss's ideas to remind the reader that the ideological distinction between 'free gift' and 'economic self-interest' was part of Mauss's own society, distinguished from the practices of his ethnographic subjects by his choice of the word *prestation* to describe them. In the case of gifts unreciprocated materially, Parry points out that the act of giving builds up not only auspiciousness or status for the donor, but also allows them to accrue credit in their *karmic* destiny:

> I am suggesting, then, that an elaborated ideology of the 'pure' gift is most likely to develop in state societies with an advanced division of labour and a significant commercial sector. But what is also in my view essential to its articulation is a specific type of belief system, as is suggested by the fact that in all of the major world religions great stress is laid on the merit of gifts and alms, ideally given in secrecy and without expectation of any worldly return. (Parry 1986: 467)

In the world religions mentioned by Parry, teachings suggest that the donors might reasonably expect to build up credit for the afterlife for their generosity, and although the giver may never express things in this way, indeed it may be regarded as counterproductive to do so, the objective possibility of an eventual return of a non-material nature does conserve the principle of reciprocity. First-hand Account 3.2 overleaf provides an excellent Mexican example of the care and attention people may put into giving gifts that have no tangible return in view.

Another example of imbalance of this sort is where a person aspiring to leadership may give gifts in order to build up a following and, in this case, loyalty is the return that is expected. Indeed, in this last case, the return must necessarily

In Mexico, on 12th December we have one of our biggest celebrations: it's the day of our Lady of Guadalupe. We honour her as our mother, in a similar way as mother's day is celebrated basically around the world. People prepare gifts for her months in advance and they can take diverse forms.

Knitted tablecloths (similar to lace made in Bruges-Brussels) are one of the most popular gifts that our Lady of Guadalupe receives. They cover the permanent (or temporary) altar that some families have at their homes, where a picture or statue of the Virgin is placed and surrounded by fresh flowers – roses most of the time – and candles. Depending on the altar's size, women (mainly) start knitting the new gift several weeks or even months in advance, and every year they made a new one. The type of work can vary, but many of the pieces made are delicate, beautiful and perfect, and they should be white, meaning the purity of the Virgin. I had the opportunity to see an example of this work in progress. It was planned to be as grand as 4 x 3 metres approximately, requiring around 2 months of work, and consisted of small squares of 10 x 10 centimetres in a beautiful pattern. I was impressed both by the process and the final work.

First-hand account 3.2:

Maria Guadalupe Hernandez White, Mexican – on Gifts that need no Return

Another special gift for her is live music called a *serenata*. On the first minute of 12th December *mariachis* (a folkloric music band), soap opera stars, musicians, pop singers, composers and members of the general public go to *La Basilica de Guadalupe* (the Church dedicated to the Virgin) to sing *las mañanitas* – the Mexican happy birthday song – to the *Virgen* and thousands of people around the country follow the event by TV broadcast and sing along. Afterwards, a celebration with more songs and dances lasting more than one hour is performed in *La Basilica*.

Serenatas can also be offered to people on special occasions – always in the evening or at midnight. Mothers can receive *serenatas* on mother's day as a gift from their children; a woman (mainly) on her birthday or saint's day, when the first song is

USA

Mexico

©MAPS IN MINUTES™ 2008

always *las mañanitas* followed by other favourite tunes of the one who is receiving the *serenata*. A long time ago someone offered me a *serenata*, and that has been one of the most beautiful gifts that I received in my life: I love music and it was a very nice surprise.

Another reason for offering a *serenata* is when a man is wooing a woman, but contrary to the other events, the first song is not *las mañanitas*; it is different and it used to be one that the woman likes very much.

We also offer gifts on *el Dia de los Muertos* (The Day of the Dead). It is a complex celebration, very deep with meaning, that happens from the evening of 31st October until the evening of 2nd November. People elaborate an *ofrenda* (an offering in the form of an altar) dedicated to relatives and also loved friends who have died. An *ofrenda* consists of cooked food like *mole*, *tequila* and *pulque* (drinks), soft drinks, tea, coffee, *atole* (a corn-based drink), cigarettes, candies, fruits, and special bread baked for the dead. *Ofrendas* are made at home and also placed on graves in the cemeteries (see photograph 8.1 on p. 161).

At home, *ofrendas* are decorated with photographs of the people honoured and, as in graves, with objects they liked and used when they were alive, for instance toys for dead children. Other common gifts are candles, pottery, clothes, punched tissue paper with special designs related to death in a comic way; burning incense and myrrh; special flowers that are used only on this occasion: *cempansuchiles* – very similar to marigolds, skulls made from sugar and from *papier mâché*. Sometimes, both at home and at mausoleums, music bands offer live music also.

be blurred to avoid accusations of corruption, although views on what constitutes bribery are culturally variable, as can often be seen in reports of international politics. We will return to consider the question of power in Chapter 10, but the principles raised here are of course directly relevant, whether it be at an individual level, or in relations between nations. Those who can accumulate a surplus of wealth in any society are in a position to use that wealth to secure power in all kinds of ways, but it is sometimes necessary to be quite careful that the transactions not be too overt. The immense wealth that has been accumulated by the United States makes possible a political edge in all kinds of international negotiations, but, as the second edition of this book goes to press, many of the activities of that nation, under the presidency of George W. Bush, have gone way beyond the bounds of acceptable interaction for many onlookers, inside and out.

Exchange

In a wider interpretation of social life, gifts may be seen to form just one material part of a complex system of exchange, which is found in all societies in one form or another. Whether made in material form or not, exchange is an important means of *communication* which expresses social relationships at various levels. Within Western society, some of the ways in which social relationships are fostered are through dropping in to drink cups of tea or coffee together, inviting people to dinner (and other) parties, writing letters, sending Christmas cards, making telephone calls, buying drinks and doing favours.

In each of these cases, a degree of exchange is usually expected, and people would soon become tired of someone who was only on the receiving side or, indeed, only on the offering side. There are exceptions, but generally for a friendship or other relationship to develop, there needs to be a two-way flow. It need not be identical. One person may be better at writing, another at 'phoning; one may enjoy preparing dinners for their friends, another prefer spending time in the pub; but unless an individual has an extraordinarily magnetic personality, or a very depleted bank account, they would usually expect to engage in some level of give and take.

Even at the level of conversation, a social relationship does not usually thrive on one-way flow, and a person who failed to reply to an opening gambit could well be expressing a rejection of the relationship offered. This is of course always a possibility, and unwelcome overtures from strangers may be snuffed out by silence. Greetings are forms of exchange of a very basic kind, and it is not necessary to know someone well to say hello to them on a corridor. Refusal to reply, on the other hand, can be offensive. To try it out with people you see often is an excellent (if unpleasant) way to test the force of exchange in maintaining relationships!

In Japanese, even the smallest 'favours' are expressed in a giving or receiving verb which qualifies the main action verb and makes clear who is obligated to whom. Thus 'I'll carry your bag for you' is literally 'I'll carry-give your bag'; and 'Will you hold my books' is difficult to write literally because it asks the other person to hold the books but expresses the obligation using a word more akin to 'receive' in expressing the obligation incurred. Of course, it is not necessary to repay exactly every tiny favour in Japan, but the explicit language used is undoubtedly related to the very careful accounting found amongst Japanese people about the exchange of one sort or another in which they are involved.

Such precise accounting may seem more appropriate for economic transactions, but there is an overlap between the social and the economic in more societies than the so-called primitive ones that Mauss identified. In Mexico and Guatemala, for example, an interesting system developed in some regions which ties a number of villages into a single socioeconomic community. This is achieved by the fact that villages specialise in making only one particular product – bread,

pots, woollen goods, flowers, even fireworks. In order to provide for the necessities of life, then, the people of these villages must communicate with each other and this usually takes place at markets. Sometimes these circulate, visiting one village after another, nowadays usually arriving at the same place on a particular day of the week, although the system pre-dates the European calendar. In larger centres, a regular market attracts villagers from the whole area (see Photograph 3.1). In pre-Columbian times, the market day was also a day for sports and festivals, adding to its social function.

In areas where such a circulating marketing system operates, people tend to marry within the community so that they can use the skills of their own speciality and pass them on to their children. In other parts of the world, a preference for marriage outside the community may provide the means of communication across a wider area, and here *marriage* is sometimes interpreted as a form of exchange. This is usually described as an exchange of women, perhaps largely because the anthropologists were men and saw the world through the eyes of the men, as we discussed in Chapter I, but it may also be that this is the way the people (men?) themselves described the situation.

The influential French anthropologist Claude Lévi-Strauss identified two main types of exchange of this sort. One he called restricted (or direct) exchange, which may be a straight swap between brothers of their sisters, or anyway between women of one community for those of another. The other he called generalised (or indirect) exchange, where women move in one direction only, but several communities are eventually linked into a circle or more complicated arrangement. These different arrangements will be discussed in more detail in Chapter 11. Once marriages have been set up, further communication is effectively maintained through visiting, exchange of gifts, and probably further marriages in future generations. Again, this is a way in which smaller communities are drawn into larger systems with those around.

exchange, direct/ indirect, restricted/ generalised – words used to describe types of social interaction between individuals or groups, ranging from gift giving to marriage.

Reciprocity

In all the cases of exchange described above, some degree of reciprocity is necessary for the communication to continue in an amicable way, and the ultimate sanction for failing to maintain reciprocity may be, as Mauss predicted, private or open warfare. Warfare is itself a form of exchange, although in this case the reciprocity could be described as negative. Some villages of the Yanomamö Indians (in Brazil and Venezuela) go through cycles where they trade with one another for a while, even arrange marriages, but then relations break down and they go to war. Eventually they may patch up their quarrels and go through the cycle again, and there is even evidence that villages develop specialities and shortages which they didn't previously have so that they are forced to look for, or manage without, trading partners (Chagnon 1983: 149–50).

reciprocity – a return for something given, often part of a continuing arrangement expressing social relations, and analysed by Marshall Sahlins into three types: generalised, balanced and negative.

Reciprocity may be of various kinds, then, with more or less of a time factor involved and greater or fewer social or moral implications attached. An immediate exchange is less likely to represent a social relationship than a delayed one, since the transaction will be completed on the spot and there is no need for further communication. A small shopkeeper who gives credit is likely to be one with whom customers also have a social relationship of some sort, whereas it is possible to make purchases in a supermarket – an immediately agreed form of reciprocity – without even exchanging greetings with the cashier. Unbalanced reciprocity, on the other hand, is more likely the greater the strength of the relationship.

In another classic piece of work, entitled 'On the Sociology of Primitive Exchange' (1974), Marshall Sahlins drew up a typology of reciprocity, according to the social distance represented. Again, he is talking of so-called 'primitive people', but there are clear parallels with wider situations, and the article raises a number of examples which are quite transferable to any society. He identifies three main types of reciprocity, but he emphasises that these are the extremes and the mid-point of a spectrum of possible types to be encountered in practice.

The first type, which he calls generalised reciprocity, not to be confused with generalised exchange, as discussed above, is that found at the 'solidary extreme', that is amongst those with, or wishing to express, the closest social relations. In this case, there is no return stipulated and no definite obligation; indeed the return may never actually be fulfilled. Sharing of goods within a family is the example Sahlins gives as the extreme, where 'the expectation of a direct material return is unseemly. At best ... implicit' (1974: 147). In practice, the return is related to the circumstances of the recipient rather than to the value of that received, and failure to reciprocate does not necessarily stop the giving.

The mid-point of the continuum Sahlins calls balanced reciprocity and this is where goods of equal worth pass immediately between two parties, with no time lag and no moral implications. Here, we are more in the realm of economic than social transactions 'from our own vantage point', as Sahlins puts it, and while generalised reciprocities are characterised by a material flow sustained by social relations, balanced exchange is where social relations hinge on the material flow. The type of exchange involved will be akin to trade, but may also include peace treaties or alliances, some marital transactions, and compensation payments.

Sahlins's third type, at the 'unsociable extreme' of the spectrum, is negative reciprocity:

> the attempt to get something for nothing with impunity, the several forms of appropriation, transactions opened and conducted toward net utilitarian advantage. Indicative ethnographic terms include 'haggling' or 'barter', 'gambling', 'chicanery', 'theft', and other varieties of seizure. Negative reciprocity is the most impersonal sort of exchange. In guises such as 'barter' it is from our own point of view the 'most economic'. The participants confront each other as opposed interests, each looking to maximise utility at the other's expense. Approaching the transaction with an eye singular to the main chance, the aim of the opening party or of both parties is the unearned increment. . . . negative reciprocity ranges through various degrees of cunning, guile, stealth, and violence to the finesse of a well-conducted horse-raid . . . the flow may be one-way once more, reciprocation contingent upon mustering countervailing pressure or guile. (1974: 148–9)

Sahlins goes on to argue that the spectrum of reciprocity he has outlined may be related to degrees of social distance within any particular social world. In a well-known diagram, which applies to a tribal model of social relations (Figure 3.1), he maps the spectrum of types of reciprocity onto a series of concentric spheres moving out from the home, through to unrelated people from other tribes. Within the home, village, or even lineage, generalised reciprocity is expected, while for the rest if the tribe, a balanced arrangement is sufficient. Outside the tribe, with 'other' tribes or peoples, anything goes, and the moral system is, in effect, suspended. Sahlins's scheme also considers social ranking, relative wealth and the nature of the goods exchanged.

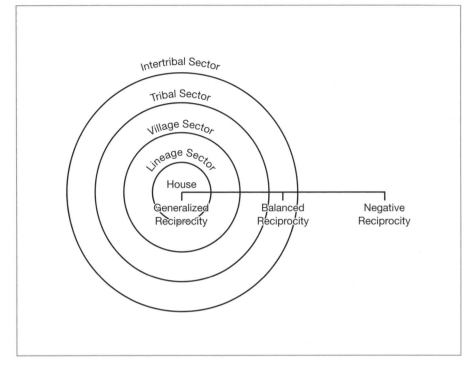

Intertribal Sector

Tribal Sector

Village Sector

Lineage Sector

House

Generalized Reciprocity

Balanced Reciprocity

Negative Reciprocity

Source: This has been adapted from Marshall Sahlins, 'On the Sociology of Primitive Exchange', in Michael Banton (ed.), *The Relevance of Models in Social Anthropology* (1974), p. 152, by permission of Tavistock Publications.

Figure 3.1 Reciprocity and kinship residential sectors

The basic principles outlined here are rather crude, and in any specific situation the details would need to be modified, but they give a feel for the contribution an anthropological approach can make to areas which have become associated with economists. Sahlins suggests that 'trade' should be classified as balanced exchange, but in an actual trading situation social factors are hard to eliminate, and in the global community, rules will vary depending on the nature of the market concerned. The capitalist world is full of people trying to make something out of other people, and social distance is invariably a factor, which may have little to do with geographical distance. It will also be related to perceived relative wealth and status. Former schoolmates, now trading between London and Auckland, New Zealand, for example, may well be kinder to one another than either will be to their Japanese business partners, but both could probably be persuaded to make concessions to a 'Third World' economy.

Neither should 'barter' always be classified as 'negative reciprocity', just because it does not involve a third medium of exchange, such as money. It may be part of a highly moral system in various parts of the world, including domestic babysitting circles in the English-speaking world, and exchanges of labour in Asia and South America. Furthermore, money may itself be valued in different ways in different parts of the world, and in the same parts of the world in different contexts (see Parry and Bloch 1989). Wrapping a bank note up in a special envelope, or placing a larger sum in a 'trust', may convert it into a gift, for example, and we are back to the various social and moral implications we considered above.

Objects Inalienable, Entangled and Wrapped

It is many years since the classic works referred to here were written, and their messages are clearly powerful, for they have probably inspired more reactions in the work of later scholars than any other related collection of ideas to be found in the subject. Some seek to refine the theoretical ideas put forward; others insist on a more thorough understanding of the ethnography, and, in between all this, the commentators comment on each other's reactions. It is particularly interesting to see whether the original peoples cited are still engaged in the forms of exchange described above, how they have been affected by outside influences, and whether subsequent studies have cast new interpretations on the material they collect.

One interesting study, which challenges the theories of both Mauss and Malinowski, was that carried out by Annette Weiner, who also travelled to the Trobriand Islands for her fieldwork, but who chose to spend more time with women than Malinowski did. She published several books, examining various aspects of the lives of Trobriand women, but most relevant to this discussion is a book entitled *Inalienable Possessions: The Paradox of Keeping-While-Giving* (1992), which puts forward theory based on practices observed throughout Oceania. The Māori and Samoan ideas of *taonga* and *mana*, examined by Mauss, are considerably refined in this book, as are the notions of reciprocity advocated by both writers.

The basic principle she advocates is a distinction between objects which can be given away, or perhaps consumed, and those that remain what she calls 'inalienable', even though they may be passed to another person. In other words, the first person retains ownership of the object, and therefore a kind of domination over the person to whom it is passed. Inalienable objects include mats, cloths and other materials made by women, each of which retains a special quality of its own, and the continued possession while passing around of these goods gives women a powerful political role previously ignored by ethnographers. Thus, not only were women ignored by a male bias in the early work of anthropologists, but, according to Weiner,

> the tenacious anthropological belief in the inherent nature of the norm of reciprocity ... impedes the examination of the particular cultural conditions that empower the owners of inalienable possessions with hegemonic dominance over others. (1992: 149–50)

Another study which attacks the notion of reciprocity is again located in the Pacific, but Nick Thomas (1991) focuses on the different uses Pacific Islanders and Europeans have made of each other's material artefacts. Entitled *Entangled*

Objects: Exchange, Material Culture and Colonialism in the Pacific, this book examines the way material objects are allocated significance in social life, but appropriated in different, but nevertheless entangled ways by the various parties caught up in the colonial endeavour. Thus objects may become something quite else from what they were made to be, depending on the context in which they are found, and they may be interpreted in different ways, depending on political factors inseparable from their acquisition or appropriation.

To make clearer some of the ideas behind both of these studies, consider the hypothetical case of a beautiful cloth, which forms part of a museum collection in a country that had colonised the island where it was made. The object, transformed into a work of art, adds kudos to the museum, and possibly also enhanced the reputation of the traveller who donated it. The traveller may have perceived the acquisition of the cloth as a purchase, or a straight exchange, whilst the producer expected continuing influence with the apparently powerful outsider. In the long run, the producer, or her descendants, may be right, as museums now find themselves negotiating terms with indigenous people seeking to repatriate objects they describe as their stolen heritage.

Situations of intercultural encounter are fertile areas for contemporary anthropologists to examine, and they may provide an interesting zone of contested

Photograph 3.2 A Japanese gift very often transmits more information in the wrapping than in its content. These envelopes simply enclose cash, but their size and shape is formal, probably the outer of three layers, and the decoration - of a turtle and a crane created out of special celebratory cord - symbolise a long and happy life for a couple getting married.

understanding in the global marketplace. In Japan, all sorts of social encounters are marked with gifts, and they are often presented in quite beautiful and elaborate wrapping (see Photograph 3.2). This *wrapping* conveys meaning way beyond the mere role of hiding the object inside, indicating the degree of formality, and whether the occasion is a happy one of celebration, or a sad one of condolence. This attention to presentation in Japan often delights the unsuspecting foreigner, but if they are serious about future relations with their Japanese partners, they should be aware of possible further meaning in the gift.

In Japan, the receipt of a gift is less likely to bring pleasure than a feeling of obligation, and this is the kind of information anthropologists could bring to people engaged in intercultural communication, who would be wise to be aware of such nuances. The Japanese donor is very likely to be aware that a gift will bring pleasure to a Westerner, so it is vital for the recipient to understand the reasons behind the overtures. The value of the gift will indicate the importance of the link, and although the price tag may not be there, the wrapping paper will probably display the name of the store where it was purchased, a clear indication to those who take the trouble to appreciate the significance of gifts.

It is also usual in Japan for the donor to belittle their own gift, as do the Trobriand Islanders, protesting in response to thanks that the object is nothing of value, even though it may actually be quite the opposite. This may be interpreted as another form of wrapping, namely the *social wrapping* of politeness formulae, and I have discussed the importance for anthropologists of looking beyond this social deception in a book entitled *Wrapping Culture: Politeness, Presentation and Power in Japan and Other Societies* (1993). Another example from the Japanese case is when you are invited to a meal, only to be greeted with the apology, 'There is nothing for you', whereas in fact the table is groaning with an abundant feast.

In Mexico, on the other hand, you are invited to make a house you are visiting your own: 'You are in your house', they assure you, although they would almost certainly be alarmed if you began to unpack your bags. 'It is at your service', they reply if you admire something, even a garment, though you would not usually expect to take up the offer. Little conventions like this are only gradually acquired during the course of field research, and investigators may make many social gaffes in the early stages, but they are usually indulged, as outsiders, for at least an initial period. Eventually, the social deceptions may turn out to have rather deep and vital significance, as I discovered to be the case in Japan, where non-verbal communication can be as important, if not more so, than verbal exchanges.

As the world is increasingly open to intercultural encounters of a social, economic and political kind, it provides a tremendous advantage to be aware of differences in the expectations of the people with whom one is dealing. This is a subject to which we will return in more detail in Chapter 14. As an anthropologist who has worked in Japan, my hunch is that many Japanese travelling abroad are more aware of local expectations than foreigners visiting Japan tend to be. This is because they are aware of some of their own idiosyncrasies – indeed they have been accused of being obsessed by their 'uniqueness' – so they take the trouble to find out how things are done elsewhere.

Some of my own compatriots have been known to be less humble. British business people travelling abroad sometimes don't even recognise a need to know much beyond the polite form of greeting in the countries they visit. As for bothering to understand local systems of distribution, or notions of value that might influence their marketing strategies, they are liable to dismiss 'all that' as meaningless cultural relativism. This is an area where anthropological knowledge can have very practical advantages, however, and the HSBC advertising campaign that sets out to demonstrate their care in such matters was actually informed by the advice of one of my students. Those who take the trouble to consult someone with such a speciality in their area of interest would be quite likely to reap benefits.

Conclusion

At the start of this chapter, I mentioned a small gift I was advised to take to my new neighbours in Japan – 'a towel or something'. The gift in this case could be quite small; indeed it *should* be quite small, for a larger one would incur unnecessary and possibly unwanted feelings of obligation, an issue I have discussed further in a whole paper about towels (Hendry 1995). The purpose is to open relations, but to do it too forcibly could be counterproductive, as we have also seen where wealth is used in the exercise of power. Just as presents may have many layers of wrapping, each with a meaning, exchange can be a complicated issue, with much subtle variation. A polite form of greeting may have different manifestations, too, with a multitude of further implications. The next chapter addresses these and many other such issues from the perspective of ritual activity.

Discussion Questions

1   Consider your own gift-giving behaviour. When do you give gifts? To whom? How do you know how much to spend? What do your answers tell you about your own social circle? And how do they fit into Mauss's theories?

2   How about receipt of gifts, or other goods and favours? Are there people to whom you feel no obligation to return? And when would you invite back someone who had you to their home for a meal? How does the gift-giving described in Maria Guadalupe Hernandez White's first-hand account (p. 60) relate to other theories discussed in this chapter, and your own? Try to draw a Sahlins-type map of your own social world in terms of reciprocity and social distance.

3   Now consider the power related to giving. To whom are you in debt? Have you considered the power they have over you? Do you ever give strategically? Why, and with what aims in mind? How do these obligations affect social life?

References and Further Research

Books

Chagnon, Napoleon (1983) *Yanomamö: The Fierce People* (New York: Holt, Rinehart & Winston).

Firth, R. (1972 [1929]) *Economics of the New Zealand Māori,* 2nd edn (Wellington: A. R. Shearer, Government Printer).

Hendry, Joy (1993) *Wrapping Culture: Politeness, Presentation and Power in Japan and Other Societies* (Oxford: Clarendon Press).

Jonaitis, Aldona (1991) *Chiefly Feasts: The Enduring Kwakiutl Potlatch* (Seattle: University of Washington Press).

Lévi-Strauss, Claude (1969) *The Elementary Structures of Kinship* (London: Eyre & Spottiswoode).

Malinowski, Bronislaw (1922) *Argonauts of the Western Pacific* (London: Routledge & Kegan Paul).

Mauss, Marcel (1970) *The Gift,* translated by I. Cunnison (London: Cohen & West).

Parry, J. and Bloch, M. (1989) *Money and the Morality of Exchange* (Cambridge: Cambridge University Press).

Raheja, Gloria G. (1988) *The Poison in the Gift* (Chicago: University of Chicago Press).

Schrift, Alan D. (ed.) (1997) *The Logic of the Gift: Toward an Ethic of Generosity* (New York: Routledge).

Thomas, Nicholas (1991) *Entangled Objects: Exchange, Material Culture, and Colonialism in the Pacific* (Cambridge, Mass.: Harvard University Press).

Veblen, Thorstein (1899) *The Theory of the Leisure Class* (New York: Macmillan).

Weiner, Annette B. (1992) *Inalienable Possessions: The Paradox of Keeping-While-Giving* (Berkeley, Calif.: University of Callifornia Press).

Articles

Benthall, Jonathan (2001) 'Time to Look "The Gift" in the Mouth', *Anthropology Today,* 17(4): 1–2.

Foster, Robert J. (2005) 'Commodity Futures: Labour, Love and Value', *Anthropology Today,* 21(4): 8–12.

Henare, Manuka (2001) '*Tapu, Mana, Mauri, Hau, Wairua*: A Maori Philosophy of Vitalism and Cosmos', in John A. Grimm (ed.), *Indigenous Traditions and Ecology: The Interbeing of Cosmology and Community* (Cambridge, Mass.: Harvard University Press for the Center for the Study of World Religions), pp. 197–221.

Hendry, Joy (1995) 'The Ritual of the Revolving Towel', in Jan van Bremen and D. P. Martinez (eds), *Ceremony and Ritual in Japan* (London: Routledge), pp. 210–26.

Lévi-Strauss, Claude (1997) 'Selections from *Introduction to the Work of Marcel Mauss*', in Alan D. Schrift (ed.), *The Logic of the Gift* (New York: Routledge) pp. 45–69.

Liep, John (2001) 'Airborne Kula: The Appropriation of Birds by Danish Ornithologists', *Anthropology Today,* 17 (5): pp. 10–15.

Parry, Jonathan (1986) 'The Gift, the Indian Gift and "the Indian Gift"', *Man,* 21: 453–73.

Riches, D. (1975) 'Cash, Credit and Gambling in a Modern Eskimo Economy: Speculations on Origins of Spheres of Economic Exchange', *Man,* 10: 21–33.

Sahlins, Marshall (1974) 'On the Sociology of Primitive Exchange', in Michael Banton (ed.), *The Relevance of Models in Social Anthropology* (London: Tavistock).

Schrift, Alan D. (1997) 'Introduction: Why Gift?', in A. D. Schrift (ed.), *The Logic of the Gift* (New York: Routledge).

Novels

McCullers, Carsten (2000 [1940]) *The Heart is a Lonely Hunter* (London: Penguin) is a novel about people giving companionship to one another.

Steinbeck, John (2000 [1945]) *Cannery Row* (London: Penguin Modern Classics) is a story about the attempts of a group of unemployed men to organise a party for their friend, the Doctor.

Wendt, Albert, (1994) *Leaves of the Banyan Tree* (Honolulu: University of Hawaii Press) is a poignant novel about a Samoan family struggling to balance the influence of outside ideas, notably Christianity, and their indigenous values.

Films

Box of Treasures (U'Mista Cultural Centre, Alert Bay, Vancouver Island) is a film about the return of the potlatch masks confiscated when the practice was banned by the Canadian government in 1928, but later returned when a culture centre was built to house them.

The Feast (Timothy Asch and Napoleon Chagnon, 1970) is a classic 28-minute film, a combination of stills with explanation, and moving pictures without, about exchange of goods, feasts and warfare amongst the Yanomamö people of the Venezuelan-Brazilian borderlands.

In Search of the Hamat'sa: A Tale of Headhunting (Aaron Glass, 33 minutes, 2004) traces the history of anthropological depictions of the Hamat'sa (or 'Cannibal Dance') – the most important and highly represented ceremony of the Kwakwaka'wakw (Kwakiutl) people of British Columbia – and how, through the return of archival materials to the community, diverse attitudes towards this history inform current performances.

The Kawelka: Ongka's Big Moka (Charlie Nairn and Andrew Strathern, 1974) is a Granada 'Disappearing World' documentary about assembling pigs and other goods for a feast which forms part of a long-term exchange system amongst the Kawelka of New Guinea.

See *Off the Verandah* (Chapter 1) for more detail about the *kula*.

Trobriand Cricket (Gary Kildea and Jerry Leach, 1975) is an amusing film about the introduction and adaptation of cricket to these same people.

The Trobriand Islanders (David Wasan, 1990), a 'Disappearing World' film, made with the help of anthropologist Annette Weiner, focuses on the female exchanges which complement the more famous *kula* practices.

Websites

http://www.peabody.harvard.edu/potlatch/default.html – gifting and feasting in the Northwest Coast Potlatch.

http://www.altruists.org/ – Altruists' International website!

http://rsnz.natlib.govt.nz/volume/rsnz_41/rsnz_41_00_003410.html – gives access to the article on Māori Forest Lore, by Elsdon Best, referred to in First-hand Account 3.1 on pp. 56–8.

The Ritual Round

Shoes and the Empty Ritual

Ritual is sometimes described as 'empty', or meaningless, and there are people who make conscious efforts to pare it away. They may decide to have a simple wedding 'without any fuss', or a small family funeral, with 'no flowers please'. Some Christian churches make a virtue out of simplicity of design, cast away the ecclesiastical robes, and even abandon their notion of an order of service on some especially open occasions. In each case, there is an expression of rejection of the more complicated forms which may be regarded as wasteful of time and resources, or unnecessary adornment of the event. In a way, it's like leaving the wrapping off a gift in the interest of saving trees ... but let us look at ritual a little more closely.

We talked in Chapter 1 about the importance of understanding systems of classification in order to understand the way in which people in different societies divide up the world into categories, and, in Chapter 2, about notions of pollution and taboo which may be associated with the places which fall between those categories. The places and situations which fall between categories, the interstitial places as they may be called, are also often associated with danger in any society, and a common response to this kind of danger is to institute some sort of ritual. By looking at ritual, then, we can again learn a lot about the system of classification held by a particular people.

To illustrate this idea, we can return briefly to the example of Japanese shoes. It is an inviolable custom in Japan to remove your shoes before entering someone's house, as was discussed earlier. The place in which you remove your shoes is usually a porch, which separates the inside of the house from the outside world, and this space may be described as an interstitial place between those two worlds (see Photograph 4.1). The act of removing shoes thus emphasises the importance of the distinction between them, and it is an act so firmly prescribed by society that in the Japanese case it may be regarded as having the force of a ritual act. In fact we find that further rituals very often accompany the removal or donning of shoes in that space.

Photograph 4.1 Shoes must be removed before entering a Japanese home so there is always a 'liminal' space between the outside world and the inside of the home where these may be removed and put back on.

These include greetings, with fixed words, depending on whether one is coming in or going out, and there is a response, again fixed, from anyone who is inside the house. The announcement of an arrival literally means 'now', and the response is something like 'welcome'. The call on departure means 'I go and come back'. A visitor to the house calls out 'I make disturbance' as they enter, and 'I make rudeness' as they leave. Mothers with small children will call out these greetings as they go in and come out whether there is anyone inside or not, because the rituals of crossing the threshold of the household are part of the training they feel they need to give to their child.

Further elements may be added to the ritual, such as the changing of clothes on returning home, and many mothers insist that their children also wash their hands and gargle. Husbands returning home from work may well head straight for the bath as a regular feature of their arrival, and some will change from their city suits into Japanese garments. The ritual for greeting guests includes bowing, and in the rural area of Japan where I did my first fieldwork, this was an elaborate performance involving kneeling on the ground and bringing one's head almost into contact with the floor. The guests would return the compliment, so this exchange would take place after the person had climbed up onto the matted floor.

Definitions of Ritual

It may be objected at this point that some form of greeting is carried out anywhere on entering or leaving a house, and people may also adjust their bodily attire. Why then should this be regarded as ritual? Let us turn first, then, to examine what exactly is meant by the term ritual in anthropology. In fact, there are several definitions of 'ritual', some of which restrict its use to describing behaviour of a religious nature (see, for example, Lewis 1980: 6–38 de Coppet 1992) but most anthropologists these days prefer to adopt a broader one which can include secular activities like greetings. For example,

> ritual - behaviour prescribed by society in which individuals have little choice about their actions; sometimes having reference to beliefs in mystical beings or powers.

> Ritual is behaviour prescribed by society in which individuals have little choice about their actions.

To test a form of behaviour to see whether it might qualify to be called ritual or not, one could try to change it, or omit it, and see how others would react. As mentioned in the previous chapter, refusing to reply to a greeting could be seen as most offensive. Omitting to greet someone on entering their house would seem churlish at the very least. In Japan, a visitor is expected to utter the appropriate phrases, and a child who failed to wash would soon be hustled into the bathroom, though the husband might get away with the odd lapse so that perhaps his practice would better be termed a routine, or custom, though a wife might read meaning into a lack of greeting anywhere! With this definition, rules about gift exchange can also be included, as can secular special occasions such as birthday parties.

After all, a birthday party, especially for a child, would hardly qualify to be such if it lacked certain elements: balloons, cards, presents, the cake, candles, the singing of a special song, and possibly the playing of games as well. In some areas, there are further expectations, perhaps about the provision of increasingly large gifts to take home, the wrapping up and distribution of pieces of cake, and a ceremony when the birthday presents are opened, one by one, to a series of 'oohs' and 'ahs' from the assembled company. A parent who put on a party without the appropriate paraphernalia would run the severe risk of disapproval on the part of their own offspring, and possibly voluble complaints from the young guests.

A more restricted definition of ritual, which several anthropologists have used and which may therefore be referred to, is:

> prescribed formal behaviour for occasions not given over to technological routine, having reference to beliefs in mystical beings or powers. (Turner 1967: 19)

Even in the case of religious ritual, the rites themselves must be examined separately from belief that may be associated with them, since people may participate for entirely social reasons. A funeral, for example, is attended by those who were close to, or who wish to express their respect for the deceased. Such participants will mourn, wear black or some other sombre colour and, if appropriate, they will attend a religious service. This says nothing about the individual beliefs of the participants with respect to God or gods and the service they are attending. It may not even say very much about their feelings for the dead. Perhaps they are attending to express sympathy for the bereaved.

Similarly, in the case of a marriage, or a christening, the participants may have very different views amongst themselves about the religious nature of the event. As the social anthropologist Edmund Leach (1969) pointed out, a Church of England wedding tells us nothing of the bride or her beliefs, only about the social relations being established (Photograph 4.2). In other words, we must separate personal beliefs from the social aspects of ritual behaviour. The latter is the domain of interest of the social anthropologist.

Photograph 4.2 According to Edmund Leach, a Church of England wedding tells us nothing of the bride and her beliefs, but only of the social relations being established.

Rites of Passage

Much has been written on the subject of ritual, and there have been many theories about its interpretation, but there is one classic work that has stood the tests both of time and of further research. This is the study by Arnold van Gennep, first published in 1909, in French, and translated into English in a book called *Rites of Passage* (1960). Again, this writer refers to the people under discussion as 'primitive', and he talks mostly of people in small-scale society, but his theories have been shown to have applicability in any society in any part of the world. Van Gennep's notion of ritual is also closer to the second definition about religious behaviour, but it applies to ritual which fits the first in many cases as well.

These rites of passage are those which accompany the movement from what van Gennep describes as 'one cosmic or social world to another'. In the terms we have been using in this book, it involves a move from one social category to another, the passage of a person or persons in a society from one *class* to another. There are four main types of move:

> **rites of passage** – rites that celebrate and protect the move of an individual or a social group from one 'class' or social category to another.

1. The passage of people from one *status* to another (for example, marriage or initiation to a new social or religious group).
2. The passage from one *place* to another (for example, a change of address or territory).
3. The passage from one *situation* to another (for example, taking up a new job or starting at a new school).
4. The passage of *time* (when the whole social group might move from one period to another, for example at New Year, or into the reign of a new king/queen or emperor).

If we think of occasions in our lives, and in those of people around us, when we might engage in some form of ritual, they are very often precisely the sort of passages which fit these descriptions. For example:

- birth, marriage, death
- christening, initiation, bar mitzvah
- changes of school, job or house
- going away, coming back
- birthdays, anniversaries, graduation
- changes of the seasons, New Year.

We ritualise these occasions in various ways, but some elements on which we draw are:

- dressing up
- sending cards
- giving presents
- holding parties

- making and consuming special food
- making resolutions
- ordeals.

By examining reports of rites of passage from various parts of the world, van Gennep noticed that certain characteristic patterns recurred in the order of the ceremonies even from places much too far apart to have influenced one another. First of all, there would be rites of separation from the old class or category, and these, he argued, are very often characterised by a symbolic death. There would also be rites of incorporation into the new class or category, and these would be characterised by a symbolic rebirth. Most striking, however, was the fact that these sets of rites would almost always be separated by a transition period when the participants would belong to neither one nor the other.

These rites he named as follows:

- Rites of Separation *or* Preliminal Rites
- Rites of Transition *or* Liminal Rites
- Rites of Incorporation *or* Postliminal Rites

Not all of these rites would be equally developed in each ceremony, since they would be of differing importance depending on the nature of the ceremony – for example, one might expect funerals to have more developed rites of separation – but van Gennep argued that this general structure is characteristic of rites of passage everywhere. Moreover, if the liminal or transition period is a particularly long one, for example during betrothal or pregnancy, there might be a set of each of the three types of rite at each end of it. He also noted that other kinds of rites – perhaps for fertility at marriage, or protection at birth – may be superimposed on the rites of passage. Let us examine some examples of the types of rite of passage he proposes.

Territorial Rites of Passage

Van Gennep's book is full of examples of rites of passage of different types, but most of these are set in small-scale societies which, he argues, imbue all such movements with ideas of a magico-religious variety. Since his book is still available and in print, let us turn here to examining some examples of secular rites of passage which may be familiar to a wider range of readers. The prototype for rites of passage is, according to van Gennep, a territorial passage from one social space such as a village to another, a passage which he argues often involves passing through a transitional area which belongs to neither side, a kind of no-man's-land in the middle.

Van Gennep discussed passages from one tribal area to another, or between different inhabited regions, but his ideas also work in a consideration of the bureaucratic rituals associated with making a passage from one nation to another. First of all, it is necessary to acquire a passport, sometimes quite a complicated and time-consuming process. In the case of many countries, it is also necessary to acquire a visa for entry. If the journey is to be of a considerable duration, friends and relatives may hold a farewell party and offer gifts and cards of good wishes. The moment of parting, at the airport, dock or station, will be marked with kisses, embraces and/or handshakes, and the passenger will be exhorted to telephone, text or e-mail on arrival.

In an airport, one is then forced to pass through a series of physical barriers involving the showing of passports and visas, the checking of luggage (and the body) through security screens, and, until arrival at the point of destination, one is quite literally in a zone of transition. Airlines use a technical explanation to account for their requests for mobile phones and other electronic equipment to be turned off during a flight, but the fact of doing it adds to the sense of liminality.

The rituals of departure are repeated in reverse on arrival, and if friends or relatives are waiting, despite a high probability of fatigue and overindulgence in food and drink, it would be regarded as most unfriendly to refuse the welcoming rituals of hospitality. The phone call of arrival is a reassurance for those left behind that the zone of transition is safely crossed, that the traveller has entered another social world. It may be a world relatively dangerous and unknown, but at least it is a world!

liminality – a term used by anthropologists to describe something separate from, or on the periphery of the wider society; thus used to describe those set apart during the period of transition in a rite of passage, or a people marginalised in a particular social situation.

Van Gennep also discusses rites for crossing thresholds, and the Japanese example given above would fit his theories perfectly. The zone of transition is most clear at the entrance to a Japanese house, and it is often filled with shoes, but there are parallel rites for entering a Jewish house, where the Mezuzah must be touched, and churches, mosques and temples have some form of ritual act as one moves from a profane space to a sacred one. This may involve the removal of pollution, with a touch of holy water; it may involve a bow, a sign of the cross, the removal or donning of shoes or headgear, or simply a lowering of the voice. Again, the crossing of the threshold involves a passage from one cosmic world to another, and visitors might be expected to observe the conventions regardless of their own religious allegiances. In Chapter 13, we will discuss a couple of examples of rites imposed on tourists visiting a specific cultural area that they should respect the rules and customs of that world.

These rites also represent a form of security for the world which is being entered. In the case of countries, the checking of the passport is a way of controlling immigration; in the case of a sacred building, there is an opportunity to remove the pollution of the mundane outside world. In any house or community a stranger may represent a threat, and ritual is a way of neutralising the potential danger. Van Gennep describes society as 'similar to a house divided into rooms and corridors' (1960: 26) and territorial rites of passage associated with entering and moving about in a house may thus be seen as a model in spatial form of the rites which accompany moves from one section of society to another.

Pregnancy and childbirth

The arrival of a completely new member of society is an occasion for ritual observance anywhere, and it also provides a threat to the mother who will give birth. In some societies women are regarded as polluting throughout their pregnancy and they must live in a special hut removed from the public arena. They are thus removed physically from their normal lives to live in a 'liminal' part of their social world. They participate in rites of separation before they go, rites of transition while they are there, and only become incorporated back into society after the baby has been born. The baby, too, must be welcomed into society through rites of separation from the mother and rites of incorporation into the new social world it has joined.

Although there are few formal periods of separation for pregnant mothers in the cosmopolitan world, the English language does still contain the telltale word 'confinement' which refers back to a period when it was considered inappropriate for heavily pregnant women to be out in the world at large. Moreover, pregnant women in almost all societies do observe various restrictions on their usual behaviour, perhaps in variations to their culinary practices, as we saw in Chapter 2, or the avoidance of alcohol and smoking, as well as the careful control of drugs and other remedies. Others who are aware of their condition will carry heavy objects for them, seek out titbits for them to consume, and generally offer special care during this transitory period. Women who suffer high blood pressure and other serious complications may be literally removed from society to hospital for the waiting period.

In Japan, many women bind themselves up in a special corset during pregnancy, and the first donning of this garment may be accompanied by a party which makes official the announcement of the impending arrival. The celebration is held on a day of the dog, according to the Chinese calendar, because dogs are said to give birth relatively easily and it is hoped that this birth will be likewise (see First-hand Account 4 overleaf). Women also often return to the homes of their own parents in order to give birth and they may stay away from their marital home for up to a month afterwards. Their return is celebrated with a visit to the local shrine to present the baby to the local protective deity, and a party will also be held to incorporate mother and child back into the community.

In most societies there is some form of celebration following a birth. Amongst Christians, the christening is a formal naming ceremony in the church as well as a presentation of the child to God, and the Church of England used to have a ceremony for mothers known as 'churching', which incorporated them back into normal life. During the christening service the baby is taken from its mother by the minister, who holds it throughout the most crucial part of the ceremony, and it may be handed to a godparent as well. Elsewhere, there is a rite of separation of the baby from its mother associated with the cutting of the cord, and the cord itself may be buried in a special place with some significance for the future. The

Jewish practice of circumcising a baby boy is also an important early rite of passage.

In some societies in South America, the father of a baby goes through a series of rites parallel to those undergone by the mother, partly as a way of expressing and confirming his paternity. This practice, known as couvade, implies the idea that the father shares substance with the mother and the unborn child, and they restrict their behaviour to avoid illnesses, particularly to avoid the child taking on the characteristics of animals eaten by humans. Although for very different reasons, this practice could be compared to the way fathers in the UK, USA and elsewhere attend and participate in antenatal classes with their pregnant partners so that they may assist at the birth of their children. These classes sometimes demand quite serious commitment on the part of the fathers, who must carry out breathing and relaxation exercises along with the mothers.

couvade – a practice in some societies in South America where the father of a baby goes through a series of rites parallel to those undergone by the mother as a way of expressing and confirming his paternity.

A role has been created here which has little to do with the 'safe' delivery of the baby in a purely medical sense. Rather it was created to provide psychological support for the mother in a highly intimate situation, which had become almost entirely impersonal. Before hospitals were deemed the appropriate place for childbirth, other women would usually surround and help a woman giving birth, and although a specialist may have been called in, it was for close kin to provide more familiar backup. The newly created role for the father reflects the increasing importance and isolation of the nuclear family unit, as well as a breakdown in the sexual division of labour which used to separate men from the care of their young in many societies.

Initiation Rites

During childhood, rites are held in different societies to mark various stages of development that are regarded as important. These may include regular events such as birthdays, or accomplishments such as a first outing, first food, first haircut, first teeth (or loss of same), first day at school, and so forth. In some societies physical changes are made, such as circumcision or ear piercing. The periods which are marked reflect the local system of classification of life into stages and some societies are divided into age sets where groups of children born within a particular period move through the stages together. Others move through on an individual basis. In either case, there will be rituals to mark the passages from one stage to another.

age set – a term used to describe a group of people who share a social position that cuts across kin ties. It is based on their birth within a particular period and they are therefore approximately the same age. Members of such a group share certain obligations to one another, and usually pass through age grades together.

Social recognition of the physical changes of puberty provide widespread

In Japan, it is common for an expectant mother to wear an *obi* (sash) or *haraobi* both to protect the baby and keep the mother's tummy warm. The ceremony associated with this is called *obiiwai* and is held on the day of the dog in the fifth month of pregnancy, according to the Shinto religious calendar. It is said that dogs give birth easily and women hope that their experience will be the same.

Obiiwai marks the official announcement of pregnancy in Japan not only to the family and friends, but also to neighbours. In general, women keep it secret until this time, from when a miscarriage is less likely. In some parts of Japan, the expectant mother and the baby's maternal grandmother distribute rice cakes (*mochi*) or red rice (*sekihan*) to neighbours as they announce the pregnancy.

First-hand account 4:

Hiroko Ford, Japanese – on Rituals associated with Pregnancy

Traditionally, the baby's maternal grandmother presents the *obi*. She and her daughter go to a Shinto temple together to get the obi from the priest and have it blessed, so that it has a sacred quality. Also, they bless pregnancy and pray for a good birth together. In general, it costs 5000 yen (£25) to be blessed. The *obi* is about 2 metres long and often has written on it 安産 'easy birth' or 寿 'celebration'. A formal *obi* consists of three sashes, two in red and white silk and one in white cotton. The imperial family celebrate the *obiiwai* in the ninth month of pregnancy as well, and when Princess Kiko reached that stage, the Emperor and Empress presented her an *obi* that was 4.5 metres long and had one side of white silk and the other red silk.

Japan

In modern Japan, more pregnant women wear a so-called pregnancy girdle instead of an *obi*, not only because it is fashionable to do so, but also because it takes less time to put it on. This is a significant factor for the increasing number of pregnant women who continue working during pregnancy. These days, there is a wide range of fashionable girdles in various styles – corset type, colours (pink, yellow, green), materials (cotton, lace, mesh) costing between 4000 yen (£20) and 12,000 yen (£60).

Most of my friends used the girdle type one instead of a traditional *obi* and I myself started to wear a maternity girdle on the day of the dog in my fifth month of pregnancy. My mother bought me three different maternity girdles at a department store where I saw some other pregnant women, accompanied by their mothers (or mothers-in-law), choosing maternity girdles. From my experience, wearing a maternity girdle was very comfortable and I felt very stable especially during later pregnancy when my tummy got bigger.

examples of clearly defined rites of passage which ritually turn children into adults, and these may again involve a substantial period of separation and/ or special treatment. Amongst African tribes such as the Maasai of the Kenya/ Tanzania borders, and the Ndembu of Zambia, for example, young men are turned out to fend for themselves in 'the bush', and they may be regarded as dead for the duration. Special rites precede and follow their absence, and their physical appearance will reflect their stage in the process (see First-hand Account 5, on p. 100). The Maasai allow their hair to grow long and unkempt in the bush, but shave completely on their return, painting their bare heads with shining ochre to mark their rebirth into society. The Ndembu have female puberty rituals which take place when a girl's breasts begin to form. They are confined to the village, but the girl is wrapped up in a blanket and lain under a tree where she must remain motionless for the whole of a very often hot and clammy day while others perform ritual activities around her (see Chapter 5 for further detail).

This kind of ordeal is characteristic of many initiation rituals, which may again involve mutilations of the body of one sort or another. The proximity of these events to the flowering of sexual maturity may focus attention on the genitals in the practice of circumcision again, or even clitoridectomy. This last practice has incurred something of a backlash from women around the world, although there have been fewer protests about the former, male practice. In some societies, incisions in the face will leave permanent scarring, indicating membership of a particular tribe or lineage. Undergoing the ordeal associated with these practices is supposed to demonstrate the readiness of the child for adulthood, and the permanent markings left behind will illustrate their new status once and for all.

Education of some sort is also often involved, and youths may be taken for the first time into the men's hut to be shown ritual objects, or taught tribal lore to be kept secret from the women and children. Likewise, girls may be taught certain esoteric elements of female life. In many societies, these young initiates are regarded as immune to social sanctions for the period of transition, and they may engage in all sorts of outrageous antisocial behaviour. Even if they are not in the bush, they may live for a period in a special house where they can experiment with adult activities and practise various social aberrations while they are in the intermediate stage between two categories.

Something of the same tolerance is accorded to youths for certain periods in many societies. For example, in universities in Britain, Holland and Ireland, an annual institution known as 'rag week' is the occasion for the tolerance of all kinds of scrapes and usually illegal activities in the interest of raising money for charity. For a few years in Britain, there was also an extraordinary amount of tolerance for a practice known as 'joy-riding', during which youths sometimes as young as 12 years of age would steal expensive cars and drive them wildly around the countryside before abandoning them. The vehicle would usually be returned to the owner within a few days, somewhat worse for wear, and even if the culprits were caught they were often let off with little more than a warning. They were too young to charge, and had few resources to pay for the damage they caused, so society seemed for a while to tolerate the practice.

Whether this represented a stage of transition between childhood and adulthood is a matter open to debate, but if the youths were not seen as responsible for their own behaviour, and their parents were not held responsible for them, it seems that they must have fallen between the categories of childhood and adulthood, at least in the legal system. In the more acceptable version of education, these youths may or may not have been doing well, and they may still have been living at home, but they were gaining the skills of theft and manipulation of powerful motor cars at an extremely early age, and they were exposing themselves to the risks and ordeals that other societies institutionalise for their youngsters.

The recent popularity of voluntarily piercing various parts of the body in countries such as North America, Britain and Australia is interesting in that these societies now have few clear ritual occasions to mark the transition from childhood to adulthood. The bar and bat mitzvah celebrations for the Jewish attainment of adulthood is an exception to this general rule, and some Native Americans and First Nations in Canada also practise their own versions of marking the occasion, but a 'Coming of Age' seems to be practised only rather sporadically now. In Britain, at least, it is not clear whether this should be at the eighteenth or the twenty-first birthday, since legal changes have scattered the rights, and neither has clear rules of procedure (and see Photograph 4.3). There is a sense of special occasion, and woe betide a parent who fails to do anything unusual on both occasions, but they are difficult ages at which to please. It may be that the people engaging in 'piercing' or possibly tattooing are actually trying to express independence from the parental fold by inventing an ordeal for themselves. In Chapter 13 we will return to this subject to consider another recently popular form of youthful activity as a rite of initiation into adulthood.

Other forms of initiation to secret societies or esoteric bodies such as priesthood, as well as the enthronement ceremonies for a king or emperor, follow the same principles as initiation to adulthood. There are rites of separation of the principals from their previous lives, periods of transition involving education and

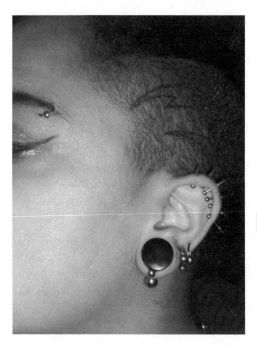

training, and rites of incorporation representing a rebirth into their new roles. In some societies the period of interregnum between one ruler and his successor allows antisocial behaviour for the whole people, and steps are sometimes taken to keep the death of a king secret until the arrangements are in place for a quick succession, in order to cut down on the disorder.

Marriage Rites

Marriage is a most important transition in most societies and it may coincide with the attainment of adulthood so that the rites associated with the wedding come at the end of the period of separation associated with the initiation into adulthood. In other societies there will be a long period of betrothal, which may be regarded as a period of transition with rites at the beginning and end. In any case, this is a passage well marked with rites of separation, transition and incorporation in most societies, although the details may differ.

In Mexico, for example, a party held for girls who have become engaged is called the *despedida de soltera*, or seeing off of the state of being single. Friends of approximately the same age gather to drink and eat together, and they dress up and act out some of the events which will follow for the bride, an occasion usually of considerable laughter and frivolity. The 'shower' for girls in the USA serves a similar role, and in the UK there is a 'hen party'. These rites separate the bride from her previous life in preparation for the new state to come. The version for the bridegroom is also commonly an all-male occasion known as a 'stag party' where serious drinking seems to be the order of the day.

In the country in Japan, where I did my own fieldwork, there were several rites of separation before the bride left her village to marry into a house elsewhere. A party would be held for her age-mates, both boys and girls this time, and there would be a display of the betrothal gifts she had received and the clothes and furniture she would take with her. Friends and neighbours would call round to see them, bringing gifts of money to send her on her way. On the morning of the wedding, there would be a farewell breakfast with the closest relatives, who would then travel together to the ceremony, and the bride would say a formal prayer of departure to the ancestors in the household Buddhist altar. After she had left, her rice bowl would be broken, just as if she had died to the house.

The bride in Japan wears a white garment under her colourful wedding kimono and this is said to represent a clean slate for her new life. In this way she resembles a corpse, as she dies to her old house, and a baby, to be born again into the new one. After the ceremony itself, the bride goes through a series of rites of incorporation into the new house and community, greeting her new ancestors, visiting the new local shrine, and being introduced to the new neighbours. According to Walter Edwards, in a book about modern Japanese weddings, the bride and groom are ritually separated from the rest of the party for the sharing of cups of *sake*, the crux of the marriage itself:

> In ethnographic accounts of pre-war and early post-war home weddings, ... the exchange is described variously as taking place in a separate room; as occurring behind a screen; and as being attended only by the nakōdo [go-between] or someone to pour the sake. In the contemporary Shinto ceremony the physical isolation is less extreme, but it is there nonetheless. Together with the nakōdo, the bride and groom sit in the center of the shrine room, apart from the rest of the group. (Edwards 1989: 107-8)

In many parts of the world it is customary for the bride and groom to go away for a honeymoon after their wedding and this practice can be seen as a rite of transition for the couple as a new unit. This time they will be formally separated from the crowd of family and friends who have come to wish them well, and various rites may be practised as they leave. Throwing of confetti is one example, tying boots to their car another. Some people go much further, and in Scotland my brother was kidnapped by his old friends, who tied his hands and feet together and hailed a passing van to drive him away around the streets of Glasgow. Again, this is a period of liminality when few rules apply. Later the couple will be regarded as properly married and treated as such. In the meantime, there would seem to be no end of fun to be had.

In recent years, there has been a noticeable breakdown in the institution of marriage in several countries. Many couples live together now without undergoing any formalities at all, and may split up just as easily if things don't work out. Even those who do marry seem to find themselves as likely to be divorced after a few years as to be still married, so the whole exercise seems rather hollow. Marriage is by no means disappearing, however, and people seem still to be happy to spend vast sums of money on their weddings. According to one of my students, a 'hand-binding ceremony' has also recently been instituted for a short-term union, and various rites of divorce are discussed from time to time in the media.

Funerals

Rites of separation are highly developed at a funeral, but there is again a period of transition, both for the deceased on his or her way to the afterlife, and for those who remain behind to come to terms with their loss. At Christian funerals, the custom of throwing a little earth into the grave is a way of saying farewell, as is the practice in Japan of adding a pinch of incense to the burning pile. In Roman Catholic and Afro-Caribbean communities, the custom of holding a wake allows a more elaborate venue for the final farewells, and elsewhere there is open house for the bereaved to receive the condolences of their friends and relatives.

During the period of mourning, people may alter their lifestyles, refraining from celebrations and jollification perhaps, and making regular visits to the grave of the loved one. In Japan, a notice is pasted to the door which not only identifies the house as one in mourning but also makes explicit the idea of pollution associated with the period in question. During this time, no meat is to be eaten, and there is a special diet for the bereaved. Various rites are held to mark stages in the progress of the soul, and these coincide with gatherings to thank those who helped at the funeral, and generally to redefine the social relations of the members of the family left behind. In some countries in southern Europe, a widow continues to wear black for the rest of her life, but in most cases there is a means of incorporating the living back into normal life.

Festivals and the Passage of Time

Finally, most societies have regular rituals to mark the passage of time. These reflect the classification of time in the way that the rituals associated with territorial passage reflect the classification of space into homes, villages, countries and so forth. As with the rites of passage through life, these events regularise in a social form natural cycles, though this time of the earth and moon, rather than the human body. Thus, the year is divided in various ways depending on the local climate, though provision is usually made for a festival to mark the harvest, at least in agricultural communities, and in countries with a severe winter there is usually a rite to herald the arrival of spring.

In the summer, in Europe, the year is clearly broken with holidays, and this ritual break in the normal routines of life is especially marked in countries such as France and Italy where there is a long and serious period of play which is virtually compulsory in its effective interruption of the ordinary. In France, the motorways are cleared of large trucks and roadworks, and it seems as though the entire population heads south to the sea and the sunshine. Certainly it is difficult to get anything done in government buildings, or, indeed, any number of other city offices. In Chapter 13 we consider further the way that tourism may be interpreted as a rite of passage.

The pattern of breaking work with play is of course repeated weekly in many parts of the world, but this is a system of classification originally based on the biblical story of the creation of the world. Elsewhere the breaks will come at different times. The lunar month is a more universal segment, and, especially before the advent of electricity, many people would organise events to coincide with the light of the full moon. Approaching the equator there is little difference in the climate between winter and summer, and seasons and their markings may be organised instead around wet and dry periods, or some other local climatic variable.

In many parts of the world, the year is broken clearly during the season of Christmas and New Year, when schools close and many government activities are suspended for a period of about two weeks, all preceded by preparations which may last for a couple of months. This 'festival' is, strictly speaking, a celebration of the birth of Jesus Christ, but it takes place at a time chosen by early Christians to coincide with winter solstice celebrations in northern Europe, and for many of its participants it is characterised as much by feasting and resting from usual routines as for any religious rites. Moreover, followers of other faiths observe their own rituals, such as the Jewish Hanukah and Hindu Diwali, close to the winter break, and a popular greeting card message, especially in the United States, has become 'Happy Holidays'.

These local differences are not actually as new as they may seem, for the Scots have long distinguished their winter celebrations from those of the English by placing greater emphasis on Hogmanay, celebrated on New Year's Eve, than on Christmas, whether they are Christians or not. Brought up as an ex-pat Scot in England, myself, I was made aware of this distinction from an early age, and our annual Hogmanay party encapsulated very clearly the elements of van Gennep's scheme: the old year seen off with a rendering of 'Auld Lang Syne', a liminal period passed listening to the chiming of Big Ben, and then greetings, accompanied by handshakes, hugs and kisses signalling a communal incorporation into the New Year which had opened.

At our parties, we would follow all this with a wild Eightsome Reel, as fellow Scots kicked their heels in an expression of togetherness as Scots, as well as to their specific friends and relatives. Although some English people I know have chosen to celebrate the New Year in this Scottish celebration, and they dress themselves in kilts and other 'Scottish' garments, they draw the line at a dance so common and apparently unrefined. These groups practise weekly all manner of complicated Scottish dancing, and although they incorporate a rite of 'first-footing' into their Hogmanay celebrations (another Scottish practice which echoes the theories of van Gennep), their togetherness is actually based on excluding dances that any outsider can do, just because they happen to be Scottish.

The element of abandonment which the Eightsome Reel signified for me, growing up, and which is expressed by the only element of Hogmanay that all Scots agree about – namely, that one must get very drunk – is a characteristic of the liminal period of many festivals for the people concerned, as were initiation rites for youths passing into a transition state before becoming adults. This is well illustrated by carnivals such as Mardi Gras, another Christian feast that has taken on wider appeal, but which is actually the beginning the period of fasting called Lent, and another example of a rite of passage marking a longer period of transition, culminating in Easter in the Christian calendar.

Edmund Leach (1961) wrote an interesting little article entitled 'Time and False Noses', where he examines the way people dress up, sometimes smartly and sometimes in quite bizarre ways, during ceremonies and festivals which mark the passage of time. He notes also that people sometimes even perform roles quite the opposite of their usual ones on these occasions – men dressing as women, kings as beggars, and vice versa. His thesis is that where rites of passage are marked by these examples of *formality* and *masquerade*, they form a pair of contrasted opposites to stand at either end of ritualised breaks in the passage of time. *Role reversal*, on the other hand, marks the middle period when normal time has stopped – another example of the period of liminality.

The British custom of performing plays known as pantomimes during the Christmas period is a good illustration of this phenomenon, for there is always a 'Dame', a buxom female role played by a man, and the main male role – who may be a prince in disguise as a pauper, for example – is very often played by a young woman. There is usually a 'princess', or some other female role played by a girl, too, so that the love scenes between her and the lead 'male' may seem physically homosexual, though the symbolism is clearly heterosexual. The general entertainment value of pantomime, carnival, holidays and the original holy days is commented upon in studies made around the world, and ritual, however solemn, usually has its fun side too, as Leach suggests.

Not surprisingly, then, an interest amongst anthropologists in the study of theatre, media and other types of performance is related to ritual (see, for example, Hughes-Freeland 1998). This, too, marks – for the audience, if not for the players – a break from the routines of working life. Like ritual, performances of one sort or another provide a place and period of separation from 'real life', a break in the relentless passage of time. For the players, theatre and media allows a period of (artistic) licence to behave quite outside the regular norms of social life, and in both ritual and theatre, people take on the task of performance of one sort or another.

My own research on theme parks was precisely about places which allow everyone to participate in a world of fantasy whenever they feel inclined – or, at least, when they have the funds available to take a holiday. Here, too, individuals may choose their own breaks in routine, but still with the possibility of reversing usual roles, and removing themselves from the exigencies of 'real life'. Some of the parks in Japan that I studied recreate the experience of visiting a foreign country, inviting their customers to spend a day or more imagining themselves to be in Canada or Spain, Germany or Holland, even dressing up to play the part of a native.

The apparent allure of cultural themes is found in many other countries, local culture being displayed for visitors in Taman Mini Indonesia Indah, just outside Jakarta, and parks in Taiwan, Singapore and China, although Shenzhen has a funfair of global culture in a park called Windows of the World. In Hawaii, there is a popular Polynesian Cultural Centre, and theme parks in other places offer a trip back in history, sometimes preserving buildings in the process. Colonial Williamsburg and Upper Canada Village in North America, Sovereign Hill in Australia, and Skansen in Sweden are all early examples of places which encourage visitors to remove themselves, temporarily, to a former period in time.

Conclusion

Rituals, wherever they are found, mark out the social categories for the people in question. They may be more or less related to the natural cycles of the seasons, the moon and the human body, but they will always order them in a cultural way related to ideas about the social world in which they are found. The range of possibilities offers an element of choice which might seem to contradict our initial definition of ritual, but the appearance of fixed elements of culture in a slippery flexible world may be the attraction to people seeking an identity to espouse – especially if they feel that more traditional rituals have become empty. In Chapter 13, we will look at some of the ways in which tourism has become a ritualised activity associated with the confirmation of identity, but meanwhile, in the next chapter, we look at some of the detail of ritual by turning to the subject of symbolism.

Discussion Questions

1   On what occasions do you dress up and/or cook special kinds of food? Make a list, and consider the extent to which they mark a point in the passage of life, yours or that of someone else. Are there elements of separation? transition? incorporation? See if van Gennep's scheme works in your life!

2   Have you been invited to a wedding or a funeral by friends in another social or religious setting to your own? How did you behave? Consider the constraints you felt, and compare them with an experience within your own family.

3   How is the year marked out where you live? What are the ritual events, and how do they make distinctions between participants? Do you know of any new events? Consider ways in which these reflect changes in the surrounding societies.

References and Further Research

Books

Bloch, Maurice (1989) *Ritual, History and Power* (London: Athlone Press).

Bloch, Maurice (1991) *Prey into Hunter: The Politics of Religious Experience* (Cambridge: Cambridge University Press).

Cannadine, David and Price Simon, (1987) *Rituals of Royalty: Power and Ceremonial in Traditional Societies* (Cambridge: Cambridge University Press).

de Coppet, D. (1992) *Understanding Rituals* (London: Routledge).

Edwards, Walter (1989) *Modern Japan through Its Weddings* (Stanford, Calif: Stanford University Press).

Fienup-Riordan, Ann (1994) *Boundaries and Passages: Rule and Ritual in Yup'ik Eskimo Oral Tradition* (Oklahoma: University of Oklahoma Press).

Van Gennep, Arnold (1960) *Rites of Passage* (London: Routledge & Kegan Paul).

Hendry, Joy (1986) *Marriage in Changing Japan* (Tokyo: Tuttle).

Hughes-Freeland, Felicia (1998) *Ritual, Performance and Media* (London: Routledge).

Huntington, Richard and Metcalf, Peter (1979) *Celebrations of Death* (Cambridge: Cambridge University Press).

La Fontaine, Jean, (1985) *Initiation* (Harmondsworth: Penguin).

Lewis, Gilbert (1980) *Day of Shining Red: An Essay on Understanding Ritual* (Cambridge: Cambridge University Press).

Ortner, Sherry (1977) *Sherpas through Their Rituals* (Cambridge: Cambridge University Press).

Turner, Victor (1969) *The Ritual Process* (London: Routledge & Kegan Paul).

Turner, Victor (1967) *The Forest of Symbols: Aspects of Ndembu Ritual* (Cornell, NY: Cornell University Press).

Articles

D'Alisera, JoAnn (1998) n in the USA: Naming Ceremonies of Infants among Sierra Leoneans Living in the American Capital', *Anthropology Today*, 14 (1): pp.16–18.

La Fontaine, Jean (1986), 'Invisible Custom: Public Lectures as Ceremonials', *Anthropology Today*, 2(5): pp. 3–9.

Leach, E. R. (1961) 'Two Essays Concerning the Symbolic Representation of Time: (ii) Time and False Noses', in *Rethinking Anthropology* (London: Athlone Press).

Leach, Edmund (1969) 'Virgin Birth', in *Genesis as Myth and other Essays* (London: Cape Editions).

Sprenger, Guido (2006) 'Out of the Ashes: Swidden Cultivation in Highland Laos', *Anthropology Today*, 22(4): pp 9–13.

Novels

Tartt, Donna *The Secret History* (London: Penguin, 1992) is a novel about a small group of college students who try to enact a Dionysian ritual, with some disastrous consequences.

Films

Adhiambo – Born in the Evening (Ruth Prince, Wenzel Geissler and Ruth Tuchtenhagen, 66 minutes, 2001) is a personal account of a woman's life, motherhood, children and the maintenance of bodily health in rural western Kenya. Set among the Luo, it follows NyaSeme, a married mother and grandmother in her late thirties, during the last month of her pregnancy and through the first weeks of her newborn daughter's life.

The Day I Will Never Forget (Kim Longinotto; Consultants: Fardhose Ali Mohamed and Eunice Munanie N'Daisi Kwinga, 92 minutes, 2002) is a documentary that explores the local dimensions of the female circumcision debate in Kenyan societies.

Imbalu: Ritual of Manhood of the Gisu of Uganda (Richard Hawkins and Suzette Heald, 69 minutes, 1988) is an insightful documentary about the male circumcision ritual among the Gisu of Uganda. The narrative follows one male participant through the ritual and contrasts his hopes and anxieties on this important day of his life with the expectations of the rest of the village.

Osōshiki ('Funeral, Japanese-style'), a 1987 Itami Juzo feature film, is an irreverent but interesting depiction of events surrounding death in modern Japan.

Masai Manhood (Chris Curling and Melissa Llewelyn-Davies, 1975), another classic 'Disappearing World' – film about initiation amongst these pastoral people of East Africa, also demonstrates cattle values, male–female relations and the power and influence of the elders. There is a companion film called *Masai Women*, made by the same team.

Good-bye Old Man (David MacDougall, 70 minutes, 1977). A last request of a Tiwi man on Melville Island was that a film be made of the *pukumani* (bereavement) ceremony to follow his death. The film follows his family, from the days of preparation to their final leave-taking of the old man.

The House-opening (Judith MacDougall, 45 minutes, 1980). When Geraldine Kawanka's husband died, she and her children left their house at Aurukun on Cape York Peninsula. In earlier times a bark house would have been burnt, but today a 'house-opening' ceremony – creatively mingling Aboriginal, Torres Strait and European elements – has evolved to deal with death in the midst of new living patterns.

Waiting for Harry (Kim McKenzie, and Les Hiatt, 1980, 57 minutes (AIATSIS-RAI). Set in Arnhem Land, east of Maningrida, we witness Frank Gurrnanamana as he prepares the final mortuary ceremonies for his dead brother, assisted by anthropologist Les Hiatt. The coffin is to be a hollow log covered with meticulous paintings. At the climax of the ceremony, all his close kin will be expected to be present, including Harry Daima, nephew of the dead man. As the relatives gather from outlying regions, Harry's unexpected absence provides a test of Frank's organisational ability. This film gives a view of the social context of Arnhem Land art, music, dance and song.

The Wicker Man, a feature film, directed by Robin Hardy (1973), in which an unsuspecting policeman falls prey to a ritual sect on an isolated Scottish island.

Websites:

http://www.msu.edu/~jdowell/miner.html – Horace Miner's brilliant 1956 paper in the *American Anthropologist* entitled 'Body Ritual among the Nacirema' (read the title backwards for a clue to who features here).

http://www.swcp.com/~ldraper/slim/biblios/morris.html – bibliography of social anthropological theories of ritual meaning and function.

5

Society: A Set of Symbols

What is a Symbol?

In the last chapter we talked of examining ritual to help our understanding of systems of classification. We referred to the scheme identified by Arnold van Gennep which seems to recur throughout the world in rites of passage, and we discussed various examples which would appear to illustrate it. This scheme makes sense of a wide variety of behaviour in an overall way, but let us turn now to see how we interpret these rituals in practice. What we can most easily look at when examining ritual behaviour are the material objects involved, the fixed elements of human behaviour, and the way the humans dress themselves. We divide the whole performance into small units – the clothes, the cards, the gifts, the food – all of which may be seen and interpreted as symbols. Symbols may be regarded as the smallest units of ritual and we can learn a lot by examining them in their own right.

symbol – a thing regarded as typifying, representing or recalling something else by possession of analogous qualities or by association in fact or in thought (*Concise Oxford Dictionary*). Symbols are particularly significant in the interpretation of rituals, but also as the visible features of invisible aspects of social organisation.

Symbolism is of course a huge subject which crops up in almost every sphere – in literature, art, religion and psychology, as well as in anthropology. There are certain differences in the way we interpret symbols in these different subjects, and there are various sorts of symbols to be interpreted. For example, there are private symbols which refer to emotional aspects of human behaviour and fall more into the domain of psychology or psychiatry. The symbols which interest social anthropologists are public symbols, shared by members of particular social groups. They express aspects of the ideology of the group, understood and interpreted within a specific social and moral system, and the same symbols may mean something quite different to members of another social group, or even different social groups within a single broad social system, such as a nation.

public symbols – are those shared by members of a particular social group, usually meaningful to all members of that group, though possibly in different ways.

Symbolism pervades human behaviour, at even the most mundane levels, and the ability to use symbols, including speech, is one of the ways in which the behaviour of humans is said to be distinguished from the behaviour of other animals. We have already seen examples of symbolism in the use of greetings and gift exchange, where we noted that social relationships would be invisible without some clearly defined way of expressing them. In anthropology we are particularly concerned with the variety of ways in which symbols may be interpreted in different societies, and between different groups in the same wider society. A large part of our work is to make sense of these units of communication in social life.

The definition of a symbol given in the *Concise Oxford English Dictionary* (1951) is:

> a thing regarded by general consent as naturally typifying or representing or recalling something by possession of analogous qualities or by association in fact or in thought.

These associations are specific to a particular society, though the analogous qualities could be clear to an outsider, and the 'general consent' is of course only general within a particular social or linguistic group. It is interesting that the definition uses the word 'naturally' because it is often the case that people within one society remain blissfully unaware of the relativity of their symbols. A connection which seems natural to one people may be quite contrived to another.

A sign is rather similar to a symbol, but it is a much more straightforward representation of something which is easy to describe in other ways. A symbol, on the other hand, is more open to different interpretations. It generally has more semantic content, more meaning, than a sign. As Jung put it (although he was referring to the analysis of dreams):

> The sign is always less than the concept it represents, while a symbol always stands for something more than its obvious and immediate meaning. (1964: 55)

A traffic light is a sign – red means 'stop', green means 'go' – now quite universally, though it is hardly natural. The wearing of red and green may be open to much more complicated interpretation – it may be nothing more than a fashion statement, or it may be associated with Christmas, or with the colours of a European flag. It could also be criticised, for there is a saying in the English language which goes: 'Red and green should never be seen except on an Irish Queen' – an Irish Queen?

Because public symbols are shared by members of a particular society, it is essential that an anthropologist studying that society learn to use them too. They are the visible features of invisible aspects of social organisation, as was demonstrated in the case of gifts. They provide objects of study, and of discussion, which lead to an understanding of that society. Symbols in any society must be used in a systematic way, or the members would be lost, just as the outsider feels lost on first exposure to the society. Within larger groupings, such as cities, nations, and now even cyberspace and the 'global village', people will also use symbols to express distinctions between differing social units. As in the case of language, an anthropologist must be careful not to make early assumptions about them. Let us examine some examples.

Bodily Symbols

Individuals in Western societies like to think of themselves as unique. They choose clothes and accessories to express their personalities, and they wear their hair in a style which they feel suits them personally. They are expressing themselves through the symbols of the society in which they live, however, and their range of choice for dress and adornment is limited to what is acceptable in that society. Even the most outrageous outfits must cover certain areas of the body, and a person who painted themselves and appeared on the streets with no further apparel would, at least in cities, be arrested unless the painting looked like very convincing clothes. Elsewhere, paint may be the appropriate attire for the most formal occasion.

Bodily attire provides a huge range of possibilities for symbolic communication, some relatively permanent, some entirely temporary, and the messages which are expressed may be interpreted at different levels by different groups of people within the same wider society. In societies less concerned with individualism as an ideology people are happy to dress much as their neighbours do, and they will express allegiances to certain groups in their appearance, or perhaps be more concerned to demonstrate the nature of an occasion in the way they present themselves. They may also indicate their level of status within their own society in the way they appear.

In markets in rural Mexico, for example, groups of Indigenous people may easily be identified because of the clothes they wear. Those groups who still live in relatively isolated communities continue to wear colours and styles that identify their groups rather than their personalities, and they may be picked out easily in a mixed crowd. Mexicans who have become part of the wider community have adopted more universal clothing, which may be judged according to taste and quality, but they would not necessarily be picked out in a cosmopolitan city as Mexicans – unless, of course, they chose to wear the sombrero, which has become a symbol of the Mexican people!

In some cities, people from different religious groups are easily identifiable by the clothes and hairstyles they choose to wear. In Jerusalem, for example, orthodox Jews may be picked out by the hats and black garments which symbolise their allegiance to the faith, and priests of the Armenian Church wear tall hats which distinguish them from other Christian groups who reside there. Visitors from religious orders, men and women, may also choose to wear the habits which express their particular allegiance in this holy city. In each case, the individuals express their membership of a religious order over any other allegiance. Here, too, however, the street vendors become adept at assessing the nationality of the tourists from their apparel so that they can guess what language to use in their sales patter.

These distinctions are more subtle, because the individuals concerned probably didn't get up in the morning intending to dress in their national costume. They may be wearing clothes to express their individuality, but their choices will reflect to an outsider something about their social group, national and regional. Many of them will be wearing jeans, a kind of universal unisex garment, it could be thought, but sometimes worn with sandals, sometimes with high-heeled shoes, sometimes with boots, and sometimes with trainers. Some jeans are shrunk, some are purposely faded, some are chosen for their designer label, and some are worn with colourful patches or indecently open holes in them. They may be worn with smart shirts and jewellery, or with a nondescript baggy T-shirt.

Some of these differences indicate information about the wearers which they may not consciously have thought about, although people are usually influenced by the way they think others will perceive them. Another almost universal garment is the two-piece (or three-piece) suit, yet almost no one would be willing to go to work in any garment just because it fell into that category. The tie is a particularly useful piece of apparel to be used symbolically, especially in Britain, where men express their allegiances to clubs, schools and colleges in the more traditional examples of the genre, assess one another's taste and judgement in the more decorative versions, and reject the whole system by leaving them off altogether. On special occasions the long variety is replaced by a bow, of course, and in some parts of North America the usual version is an object which would be used to lace shoes in the British Isles.

Within particular groups, different messages are communicated from those picked up by outsiders. Consider the case of headgear: although both may be Scottish, and sold to tourists for that reason, a deer-stalker – the mark of a country gentleman – tells quite a different story internally to a tartan cap with a peak at the front; in the England of Charles Dickens, a top hat would have conveyed different information from a bowler, though both are now sold as souvenirs in London. A Jewish skull cap will tell a non-Jew only that the wearer is probably Jewish. Within a particular Jewish community, however, these small items, where possible carefully crocheted in the home, allow women great scope to transmit messages, both to their menfolk for whom they make them, and to the wider world about their men's caretakers and loved ones. As a corollary of this, women are also said to be quite prone to judge one another on the basis of the skill they witness in these rather neat exhibitions of their handiwork (Baizerman 1991).

Jewellery and other types of adornment are highly symbolic, too. There is a kind of thick, gold jewellery abundantly available in airport shops which is a clear, international expression of wealth, just as designer scarves and handbags are. Amongst the nomadic Fulani people of West Africa, women wear coins in their hair to express the same meaning, and the Bella, their former slaves, decorate their hair with buttons to follow the style but without the same resources. The Rendille women of Kenya wear arm bands to show that they are married,

Photograph 5.1

A Wahgi man from the Highlands of New Guinea, in full festive adornment (photograph courtesy of Michael O'Hanlon, Pitt Rivers Museum, Oxford)

just as men and women elsewhere wear rings on their fingers, but the Rendille add further bands to demonstrate the stage of life their sons have reached. They also wear their hair in an enormous coxcomb from the birth of their first son.

In the Highlands of New Guinea, amongst the Wahgi people, men wear beautiful headdresses made of the feathers of local birds, and adorn their skin with the shiny fat of the pigs they value so highly. These forms of display (see Photograph 5.1) worn on certain special occasions, symbolise political and military might as well as status in the community. Michael O'Hanlon devotes a whole book, *Reading the Skin: Adornment, Display and Society among the Wahgi*, to the subject, but a few of his words give a feeling for the communicative possibilities:

> in a turbulent social landscape of shifting alliances and insistent rivalries, impressive displays are felt to intimidate rival clans, and to deter enemies from attacking ... the appearance of those displaying is thought of as an external reflection of their inner moral condition ... evaluations of adornment and display emerge as a dynamic idiom in terms of which moral issues are discussed ... in the rivalrous Wahgi social environment, displays are credited with exerting a direct influence over the military policies of spectator clans. (1989: 124–5)

In Polynesia, people tattoo themselves to make a more permanent statement about their role and place in society (see, for example, Gell 1993). In Japan, too, some gangsters wear beautiful tattoos which cover a large part of their bodies and depict scenes from the country's abundant religious and mythological artistic repertoire, but they keep them hidden under their clothes most of the time because the wider society finds them offensive and disgusting. To have one done – a painful process of more than a year – therefore symbolises an irreversible commitment to the life of the underworld, and could be seen as part of a rite of passage of initiation into the group. Even just part of such a tattoo, revealed at a strategic moment, makes a powerful statement about the allegiance, a statement sometimes illustrated in films about the Japanese underworld. In contrast, those with less extensive tattoos in Japan may merely be expressing a liking for a Western fashion, although this has in itself been much influenced by Japan over the years.

Hair on the head is an excellent medium for making symbolic statements of a striking if only semi-permanent nature. Shaving the head is a custom associated with initiation in several parts of the world, for example, as was seen with the Maasai in the last chapter, where leaving the hair to grow in an unruly fashion was also part of the process (see First-hand Account 5 overleaf for more detail about this symbolism). Where there is a prevailing custom about hairstyle, such as the short-back-and-sides arrangement for men, some people can express a rejection of the mainstream by allowing their hair to grow long. When this practice was first coming into its own in Britain, Raymond Firth (1973: 272), who had been working in Tikopia, an island in Polynesia, noticed that there had been a curious reversal of custom between the two places. When he left for fieldwork, men in Britain had worn their hair short, and women very often long, whereas in Tikopia he found this convention reversed. During his stay, the Tikopians began to follow outside influence and cut their hair to coincide with the Western way of doing things. Firth was surprised on his return to Britain to find that the situation seemed to have reversed there, too, at least among some of his students.

Young people in Britain have been through various stages since that time, often choosing a style that contrasts sharply with the previous generation of youth. The long-haired beatniks whom Firth encountered were a complete change from the 'Teddy' boys and girls who preceded them, with their neat quiffs and hair grease. These in their turn were rejected and opposed by the short-haired 'mods' who came afterwards, themselves contrasted with the unkempt 'rockers' of the same generation. Skinheads and 'bovverboys' wear their hair short to look threatening, as do the more lavishly turned-out punks, clearly expressing something animal or 'primitive' in their elaborate coxcombs, rejecting the society of both their parents and other elders. Variants of these differences are found in other Western countries, and young people travelling abroad may well identify potential allies by the way they cut and wear their hair.

This is not always the case, however, and one of my students recounted during a lecture on this very subject how he had chosen a punk hairstyle in order to be 'different' from everyone else. He was disappointed, however, for when visiting a night club he found the whole floor to be seething with variants of himself. As

Photograph 5.2

Tattoos can have various meanings for various people. What do you think this one might mean? (photograph by Tim Bauer, courtesy of Kaley Davis and Tiger Lily, Oxford).

The day after my friends and I were circumcised, other *isipolio* (new initiates) came to fetch us, and showed us how to tie cloths around the wounds. They brought us ostrich feathers to wear in our hair. We also had to put on the *esurutiei* necklace worn by women and the leather belt worn by young girls, and to carry the sticks of adult men. We would keep these things for several months. For the Maasai, the new initiates symbolically bring together all the different sections of society – men and women, young and old, humans and the environment – so that we were dressed as 'four in one'. With the *esurutiei* necklaces, we became bound by the same taboos as women, in that we weren't allowed to see any meat that would be eaten by the fully fledged warriors.

First-hand account 5:
Lesikar Ole Ngila, Maasai – on Initiation

As the new generation of warriors, *isipolio* are the future guards of the community, so during the first few weeks after circumcision we were greatly respected. While dressed in the black clothes of *isipolio* we were free to go wherever we wanted, like tourists, and nobody could harass us. New initiates aren't allowed to go to bed hungry, but nor can they handle blood themselves, so the warriors and elders had to slaughter rams and goats for us. We painted our faces with elaborate patterns in white chalk (*enduroto*) mixed with water, to symbolise the different birds, and greased our bodies with a mixture of sheep fat and charcoal to make them even blacker than usual. On our feet, we wore traditional leather sandals, to remind us of the old days when the Maasai pastoral economy was strong and nobody had rubber-soled shoes.

Tanzania

Four months after my circumcision, I asked my father to shave off my hair. Newly initiated warriors usually let their hair grow for a whole year, so that it becomes matted into something called *almasi*, and they aren't supposed to wash it. He had already bent the rules by allowing me to wash mine, as I was beaten in school for looking dirty. Now I needed to be shaved at home, because the teacher believed that the traditional Maasai education was outdated and should be left behind. 'If you waste your time with those old customs', he was fond of saying, 'you won't be able to focus on your studies'. So he had been going around with his scissors, chopping off the long hair of *isipolio* while they stood in lines, taking away the black jewellery that had been given to them by their elders as a blessing, and throwing all of it down the latrine.

One day a group of our *isipolio* age-mates, who weren't students at the school, had gone there to sing to him, 'Mr George, the curse of the *almasi* of the *isipolio* will follow you for the rest of your life, because of your disrespect! How could you throw our friends' hair into the latrine, instead of putting it in a safe place that is cold like the sacred *oreteti* tree?'

Mr George may have been cursed, but my friends and I believed that it would be a disaster for us too, if we were to fall victim to those scissors instead of following the proper customs. Every time we saw the other students standing in line, we would run away. My father, along with many of the other elders, thoroughly disliked the teacher and didn't want that fate for me, so he agreed to shave me at home even though it wasn't really the right time.

Lesikar Ole Ngila is the Director of Aang Serian, which means House of Peace, an organisation that has set up a school to value indigenous knowledge in Tanzania, among other things. See http://www.aangserian.org.uk/ *for further details.*

he put it, 'it seemed I had joined a convention of parrots'. He then decided to try another tack in his quest for individuality, and attended the same venue wearing a short haircut and a three-piece suit. He certainly looked different then – so different that he was beaten up.

In nineteenth-century Japan, people wore particular hairstyles to show their social status, and children in that world celebrated stages of life by altering their hair, the first haircut being a sort of initiation into childhood. Members of the *samurai* class had a topknot which was not allowed to lesser mortals, and although unmarried women could wear their hair loose, once married they were obliged to keep it in a kind of bun. In the film *Shinjū*, a couple who run away to commit suicide together, because they have developed a socially impossible relationship, let their hair down and cut it off to symbolise their rejection of society before they carry out the desperate act.

This relationship between hair, power and sexuality has been reported widely. For example,

> In pre-Christian Polynesia, the head was *mana* ... The Samoan word for head (*ulu*) can mean 'head' or 'hair'. Not surprisingly, hair was treated as if it too were *mana*. The hair of Samoan chiefs, for example, was cut by special attendants ... *Mana* was associated with the vital energies of the natural world and was synonymous with fecundity ... In pre-contact Samoa, women grew their hair long only during pregnancy ... The implication is that long hair alluded to the pregnant or fecund state.   (Mageo 1994: 410)

Several anthropologists have put forward theories about the way hair is used symbolically, some suggesting universal ideas, and Mageo's (1994) article examines these in the light of Samoan material she gathered over a period of eight years' residence there. This is particularly interesting because, like the Tikopian case mentioned above, the way hair is worn in Samoa has changed greatly over the period of colonial influence. Christian morals have come to play an important part, so that the positive role of fecundity has become tarred with a negative attitude towards excessive sexuality. Mageo also addresses the question of overlap between public and private symbols.

Symbolising Relationships

We have pointed out already that relationships are expressed in various symbolic ways, notably in Chapter 3 where we discussed gift exchange. We examined how gifts are given on particular occasions, perhaps wrapped in a locally appropriate fashion, so that the object and its presentation make statements about the relationship between donor and recipient. We discussed the importance of reciprocity in the exchange of gifts, and other modes of communication, if a relationship is to proceed smoothly, and we considered the problems that may arise when people from different cultural backgrounds misinterpret the significance of presents they may receive.

Again, the symbols are part of shared meaning peculiar to a particular society, and it is another role of the anthropologist to examine the local significance of such exchanges. Japanese people are well known for their generous and beautiful gifts to foreigners who have even the most tenuous of social relationships with them, but, as we mentioned, few foreigners are aware of the importance attached to the practice of gift-giving in Japan. Those who simply try to keep up with or outdo the cost of gifts they have received, and neglect factors such as relative status and non-material favours when they make their returns, could find themselves in a rapidly escalating and quite inappropriate contest of affluence.

Relationships may also be modified in a subtle manipulation of the local practice of gift exchange. An unexpected gift could, of course, signal a desire to intensify a relationship, but it could also mark the end of a series of exchanges, or be a way of expressing empathy for a situation difficult to discuss. Gifts of perishable food received may provide a good excuse to express friendship by inviting round a neighbour or colleague on the pretext of avoiding waste, but also purposely to further the acquaintance. A usual gift withheld, or noticeably cheaper than expected, can create distance when a relationship is becoming too close, or symbolise a rejection of an unwanted approach. A gift returned may seem like a clear symbol, but it must be interpreted within the range of possibilities of a particular social system.

Greetings are another important way of expressing relationships, and again these can be manipulated for more subtle communication within a particular society. The handshake has become an international symbol of agreement and accord, so that important treaties may be sealed in such a way, and photographs of handshakes frequently embellish the world press. Within Europe, customs vary, but generally handshakes express goodwill. In some countries they are practised daily within the family, in others they are reserved for first meetings and special occasions such as the conferment of a degree or a prize. People use them to seal a new arrangement, or to express the resumption of good relations after a quarrel.

In some situations a handshake would be too cool a greeting, however, and while hugging seemed to be rather common among the First Nations and others with whom I worked in Canada in 2003, various forms of kisses are practised within the continent of Europe. The lips are usually involved, though they may merely be pursed in the air as cheeks brush gently together, especially when women kiss one another in public. In some social circles, it is imperative to kiss on either cheek, and in Poland, at least according to my Polish niece-in-law, it is usual to kiss three times. This practice varies between different classes within Europe, as well as between regions, and people can express various degrees of intimacy by the kind of kisses – or hugs – they exchange within one group. The significance of a kiss in sexual relationships is also culturally variable, which may come as a surprise to some readers. In pre-modern Japan it was not even thought to be particularly erotic.

Kissing and hugging are rather intimate symbols in Western society, and they still don't seem to be practised as often between men as between women, as was discussed in Chapter 2, but in parts of the Middle East they may be more usual than a handshake, even in public situations. Before the historic meeting in 1993 between the Israeli Prime Minister Yitzhak Rabin and the leader of the Palestinian Liberation Organisation Yasser Arafat, speculation was rife about how their greeting would be expressed. Many hoped for a hug, but this was not forthcoming. Their handshake was celebrated all over the world, but for local people it may have seemed rather cool. The continuing differences between these two peoples reinforce the disappointment ... oh, for that hug!

In Japan, the usual form of greeting is a bow, and this has many variations. From a standing position the depth of a bow indicates the degree of deference, and two people bowing to one another will indicate their relative status in the angle of their acknowledgement. It is also expected that the lower-ranking person will allow the superior to rise first, so the situation can become quite comical if both parties are trying to defer to the other. In a *tatami*-matted room, where people habitually sit on the floor, there are various types of formal bows which may be carried out, and these involve bringing the head almost in contact with the floor. It is said that men in *samurai* times were taught to keep their eyes on their greeting partners, however, in case they proved to be enemies who would take advantage of the defenceless position.

Symbols are, of course, also used to express enmity and ferocity, and the *samurai* man would wear a pair of swords to demonstrate his invulnerability in this respect. The sword would also demonstrate his status in society, but in premodern Japan it could be used with impunity to decapitate a disobedient subject. In the United States, it is more acceptable to carry a gun than in some other countries, although the gentlemen's duel at dawn was for long a highly ritualised and therefore symbolic way of resolving a dispute in European countries. Suits of armour, now thankfully usually only on display in museums and castles, are also a repository of symbolic power and helmets or breast pieces very often sport a mark of allegiance as well.

Group Symbols and Their Interpretation

In battles and warfare, symbols such as these abound, representing the whole social group involved. Flags and banners represent a nation, town or the particular people concerned, and the human beings are decked out in clothes which make their adversarial activity their prime purpose. Battledress comes in a variety of forms, and uniform – or, previously, armour – is a powerful symbolic tool in rallying people to a cause. It clearly subordinates the individual to a greater social entity, in which personal qualms must be set aside for the wider common good. In such a guise human beings can carry out acts of terrible violence which would abhor them in normal life and which could well bring about their arrest and imprisonment. Similarly, police in uniform are empowered to pick up people who are disobeying laws agreed within a country, and to lock up people if they think they have committed a crime.

National anthems and marching songs are designed to invoke a pride of participation in those who listen to them, as are words of rhetoric turned out to whip up enthusiasm for a cause, whether it be bellicose or peaceful. The ban-the-bomb symbol has been one of the best known and most powerful in the last couple of generations, though it has various origins and interpretations in different parts of the world, for those who take the trouble to inquire. Anthropologists analyse the language and paraphernalia of the social groups they study in order to identify symbols that are important to the people concerned. These can in turn lead to an understanding of the ideology or ideologies they live by, and may be related to other aspects of social life.

A useful book, set in Britain and compiled and edited by Anthony Cohen, is entitled *Symbolising Boundaries* (1986). It considers the symbolism used to express and identify differences within communities, between the worlds of men and women in Devon, between households in Yorkshire and Battersea, between neighbouring settlements in Lewis, in the Outer Hebrides, and between Catholics and Protestants in Northern Ireland. The articles examine and illustrate the complexities and ambiguities of these distinctions. The second part of the book moves into the mechanisms used by certain groups to express their distinctions within the wider society, for example by adolescents in an adult world, by suburban occupants of a northern city, and by Glaswegians in reference to the image they portray abroad.

Cohen introduces the interesting idea of the malleability of symbols in a complex community:

> The efficacy of symbols which we recognise here is their capacity to express in ways which allows (*sic*) their common forms to be retained among the members of a group, and among different groups, whilst not imposing upon these people the yoke of uniform meaning. Symbols, being malleable in this way, can be made to 'fit' circumstances. They thus provide media through which individuals and groups can experience and express their attachment to a society without compromising their individuality. (1986: 9)

Anthropological Interpretation of Symbolism

Much has been written on the subject of symbolism, and there has been some dispute amongst anthropologists about how far an outsider should go in the interpretation of the symbolism of another people. As Cohen puts it:

> The ethnographic difficulty for us, therefore, is that not only is symbolism a matter of interpretation (as it is everywhere); but the interpretation of behaviour as symbolic in character is itself a matter of conjecture and judgement which is only demonstrable through notions of plausibility or of theoretical 'fit' ... The danger is, of course, that rather than using my imagination as an interpretive *resource*, I risk allowing it to constitute the data themselves ... I have written about the croft, the spree, the burial as symbolically significant... But significant for whom? The people we are supposedly describing. Or ourselves?   (Cohen 1986: 7)

Victor Turner is one of the anthropologists who has made a great contribution in this field. In his book *The Forest of Symbols*, he suggested that the structure and properties of ritual symbols could be inferred from three classes of data:

1 external form and observable characteristics;
2 interpretations offered by specialists and by laymen;
3 significant contexts largely worked out by the anthropologist (1967: 20)

It is this last category which is most contentious, because it goes beyond the second, and sometimes even contradicts it. Different anthropologists also disagree at this level, although this is not unusual in this subject, as was pointed out at the beginning of the book. Turner stresses the importance of putting sets of symbols in the total context of the ritual in which they appear, other rituals and their performance, and the wider society of which they form a part, including notions of class, lineage, generations and so forth. This, he argues, is easier for an outsider than for a subjectively involved participant, as the latter regards as axiomatic the ideals, values and norms expressed or symbolised.

Turner gives as an example the case of the Ndembu girls' puberty ritual, which was mentioned in the previous chapter, where a girl lies under a tree for a whole day. The tree, which is called a *mudyi* tree, exudes milky beads when the bark is scratched, and this, for the Ndembu, is its most important 'observable characteristic'. Women explain that this liquid stands for breast milk, and indeed, for the breasts which supply it. They further explain that the tree represents the relationship between mother and child, and the continuing line from woman to woman which stands for the tribe itself, including the men. When observing the ritual, however, Turner noticed that it actually serves to symbolise the separation of mother and daughter as the latter reaches puberty, to separate women from men, and even to separate some groups of women from others.

This was clear to him in the following ways. First, the mother of the initiate is excluded from the group of women who dance around the motionless girl under the tree. She is not allowed to participate in this important part of her daughter's puberty rite. Secondly, men are excluded from the ritual altogether, and the matter is handled entirely by women. Thirdly, when the mother brings out food for the participants, there is a kind of competition to be the first to take some, for that person's origin is said to indicate where the girl will marry. The Ndembu informants were unable to recognise these apparent contradictions, and Turner argues that it is only possible to infer them with a wider knowledge of the society, which is also made as a relatively objective outsider.

In societies which have a large number of Christians, a parallel may be made when anthropologists take a look at Christianity. Edmund Leach (1969) upset a lot of people in England when he discussed Christian practices in anthropological terms, writing essays entitled 'Genesis as Myth' and 'Virgin Birth', which will be considered in Chapter 7 of this book. His intentions were seriously academic ones, but putting Christian rituals in the context of those held in societies regarded as 'pagan' by Christian believers undoubtedly offended against their systems of classification, and struck a chord of taboo. Those people who are committed to one form of religious worship may find it difficult to stand back and view their practices in the context of other forms.

Nor may they necessarily understand all the elements of their activities. As John Beattie pointed out long ago, in an excellent article about ritual, the fact that a Christian communicant may not understand the doctrine and full meaning of the Eucharist (or Holy Communion) doesn't mean that it does not have such a meaning (1966: 67). Even specialists may disagree in explaining ritual events, and the Eucharist is a good example again, for while a Protestant minister will explain that the bread and wine represent (or symbolise) the body and blood of Jesus Christ, a Roman Catholic priest will say that the bread and wine *become* the body and blood of Jesus Christ. There is a fundamental difference of views here, which makes it difficult for believers and participants alike to make an objective analysis.

In Japan a similar problem may be observed. After the Second World War, the indigenous religion, Shinto, was officially denigrated as being associated with the notion of a divine emperor and the whole disastrous war effort. Buddhism, on the other hand, was unaffected in this way, and for many years people would talk only of Buddhism as religion, tending to describe Shinto activities, which did continue, as 'superstition'. It was thus rather easier to investigate Shinto practices than Buddhist ones, for the former had been stripped to some extent of their mystical elements. The mysticism attaches an awe to elements of religious faith which may make it difficult for people to discuss them without offending their own system of classification. They have been affected by the kind of taboos we discussed in Chapter 2.

Not so sacrosanct are secular elements of rituals, and people are usually quite happy to speculate about things such as the cakes and special clothing that mark rites of passage. An anthropological study carried out by Simon Charsley in Glasgow examined the meaning and purpose of the wedding cake in Scottish weddings. In fact, he was disappointed by the lack of ready interpretation of this apparently essential feature of the great day, but some ideas of his own were quite fruitful, if only in a negative way. He was impressed by the idea that the white wedding cake might stand for the white-clad bride, and 'cutting the cake', actually 'plunging the knife' into the centre of the cake, would then clearly represent a breaking of the 'virginal white outer-shell' (1987: 106).

Much of Charsley's article is a discussion about the degree to which an anthropologist is legitimately entitled to interpret beyond the explanations of the participants, just as Turner suggested, and an interesting twist to his investigation occurred when a couple actually came up with this meaning for the cake. They had heard it from someone else, but they were so horrified by the inequality they felt it expressed between bride and groom that they decided to do away with a cake altogether. Charsley then examines the interesting question of whether a rite can only be practised if a possible meaning for its symbolism has not been noticed. He rejects this idea, however, pointing out that it was not the idea of virginity and its loss that upset this particular couple, but the idea of inequality which they themselves felt it represented.

Interestingly, many people are more concerned in the arrangements of their own weddings, and even more so with those of their children, that things should be done 'properly'. They seek the 'right' way to do things, rather than examining the meanings in order to impose their own interpretations. A veritable barrage of wedding magazines stand ready at bookshops and newsagents to provide instant advice, and most people are quite happy to be informed of the appropriate etiquette. Rather than do away with a wedding cake, then, people may use it to express something personal about their relationship, according to Charsley's research, and he reported one couple who chose the icing decoration of a sofa depicting themselves and their children by previous marriages. British friends of mine who had worked in Japan chose to cut their cake with a *samurai* sword.

Conclusion

Ideas for symbolism may be discussed, then, and alternatives considered, but in any society there will be a set of underlying notions which form the basis of these deliberations. It is fine to be outrageous, if that is understood, and some may express messages selectively to a close group of friends or relatives, but it would be pointless in terms of communication to do something so unusual and different that nobody could discern the meaning at all. These basic tools of communication are the **collective representations** we discussed in Chapter 1, following Durkheim's terminology. They include the 'set of symbols' after which we named the chapter, and they form some of the most basic subject matter of social anthropology.

Discussion Questions

1   Can you think of an occasion when you, or someone you know, has described some kind of behaviour as 'natural'? Think again! Is it really universal to human life?

2   Do you think there is a symbolic element to body modifications such as tattoos and piercing? Think about what they might be at (a) an individual level, (b) a group level, or c) a relational level.

3   Do you think it legitimate for an anthropologist to go beyond the explanation of a member of another society in interpreting symbolic behaviour? How far?

References and Further Research

Books
Basso, Keith (1996) *Wisdom sits in Places: Landscape and Language among the Western Apache* (Albuquerque: University of New Mexico Press).
Cohen, Anthony (1986) *Symbolising Boundaries: Identity and Diversity in British Cultures* (Manchester: Manchester University Press).
Douglas, Mary (1975) *Implicit Meanings* (London: Routledge & Kegan Paul).
Eicher, Joanne B. (ed.) (1995) *Dress and Ethnicity* (Oxford: Berg).
Firth, Raymond (1937) *We, the Tikopia* (London: Allen & Unwin).
Firth, Raymond (1973) *Symbols, Public and Private* (London: Allen & Unwin).
Gell, Alfred (1993) *Wrapping in Images* (Oxford: Clarendon Press).
Jung, Carl G. (ed.) (1964) *Man and His Symbols* (London: Aldus Books).
Leach, Edmund (1969) *Genesis as Myth and Other Essays* (London: Cape Editions).

Needham, Rodney ((1979) *Symbolic Classification* (Santa Monica, Calif: Goodyear).

O'Hanlon, Michael (1989) *Reading the Skin: Adornment, Display and Society among the Wahgi* (London: British Museum Publications).

Turner, Victor (1967) *The Forest of Symbols: Aspects of Ndembu Ritual* (Cornell, NY: Cornell University Press).

Articles

Baizerman, Suzanne (1991) 'The *Kippa Sruga* and the Social Construction of Gender', in Ruth Barnes and Joanne B Eicher, *Dress and Gender: Making and Meaning* (Oxford: Berg).

Beattie, John (1966) 'Ritual and Social Change', *Man*, 1:60–74.

Charsley, Simon (1987) 'Interpretation and Custom: the Case of the Wedding Cake', *Man*, 22:93–110.

Edwards, Jeanette and Simpson, Anthony (1998) 'Diana and the Popular Imagination: An ICCCR Workshop' *Anthropology Today*, 14(3): p. 15.

Mageo, Jeanette Marie (1994) 'Hairdos and Don'ts: Hair Symbolism and Sexual History in Samoa', *Man*, 29:407–32.

Moretti, Daniele (2006) 'Osama Bin Laden and the Man-eating Sorcerers: Encountering the "War on Terror" in Papua New Guinea', *Anthropology Today*, 2006, 22(3): 13–17.

Watson, C. W. (1997) '"Born a Lady, Became a Princess, Died a Saint": The Reaction to the Death of Diana, Princess of Wales' *Anthropology Today*, 13(6): 3–7.

Novels

Lethem, Jonathan (2005 [1997]) *As She Climbed Across the Table* (London: Faber & Faber) is a campus novel, which mocks postmodernism through a symbolism of emptiness.

Mann, Thomas (2001 [1912]) *Death in Venice* (London: Vintage) is a novella about beauty and mortality, with multi-layers of symbolism.

Films

Altar of Fire, directed by Robert Gardner (1976), is a film about the performance of a Vedic ritual of sacrifice by Mambudiri Brahmins in Kerala, southwest India, known as the Agnicayana.

A Celebration of Origins: Wai Brama, Flores, Indonesia (E. Douglas Lewis, Patsy Asch and Timothy Asch, 45 minutes) is a record of rituals that also examines ceremonial leadership and the role of evolving religious practice in a changing society.

The Seventh Seal is a 1958 existential film directed by Ingmar Bergman, depicting a medieval knight playing chess with Death.

Shinjū: Ten no Amajima is a 1969 film, directed by Masahiro Shinoda, about the circumstances leading up to a double suicide set in eighteenth century Japan.

Websites

www.aangserian.org.uk/ – the website for Aang Serian (House of Peace), a Tanzanian non-governmental organisation dedicated to 'preserving indigenous traditions and knowledge, developing culturally appropriate programmes of education and training, and promoting inter-cultural dialogue across the world.'

http://hirr.hartsem.edu/ency/geertz.htm – an entry about Clifford Geertz in the *Encyclopaedia of Religion and Society*.

www-personal.si.umich.edu/~rfrost/courses/MatCult/content/Geertz.pdf – a reproduced online version of a famous paper on the symbolism of the Balinese cockfight by the American anthropologist Clifford Geertz.

Beauty and Bounty: Treasure and Trophies

Seeing and Value

An interesting aspect of the interpretation of objects and symbols in a particular society is the aesthetic one, and the anthropology of art and aesthetics is a particularly lively branch of the subject. There are various reasons for this, but one of the most important is reflected in the title of this chapter. One person's art is for another a **commodity** to be exploited, and the world of 'art' has truly become a *global* concern. At the beginning of Chapter 1 we talked of souvenirs and different ways of 'seeing the world', and then we went on to examine various ways of understanding these different worlds. In this chapter we return to 'seeing', but add the subject of value, notably but not exclusively aesthetic value.

In the cosmopolitan world, there are people who make a very tidy living by being acquainted with the value of *objets d'art*, while others feel excluded and possibly diminished by being

commodity – this word is used to describe articles designated an economic value, usually for the purpose of trade, and it may be applied to people and inanimate objects as well, if such an economic value is assigned.

objets d'art – literally, an object with artistic value, but used here in French to suggest the way that people in the world of very expensive art create a language of their own to make decisions about what (and who) may and may not qualify for inclusion.

uninformed on this subject. The value of art objects is, however, entirely relative to the place they are assigned in this exclusive world, and some people are able to take advantage of others in manipulating this system of categorisation which has come into existence. Indigenous (or, earlier, 'primitive') art has been increasingly valued in this cosmopolitan world, but in recent years some Indigenous artists have begun to join the fray, with interesting effects.

The value of objects for gaining access to an understanding of people and their views is still of prime concern, but it is also important to realise that interpretations may be seen in a particular light. Some people may feel aggrieved or misrepresented by the way in which their objects are used, and they may disagree with the interpretations assigned to them, whether by anthropologist or art historian. When people become aware of the value assigned elsewhere to their work, they may be influenced to respond to an apparent need, especially if it is economically or politically beneficial to them to do so. The outsiders, in their turn, may feel aggrieved that the 'pure' art forms of the people concerned have been corrupted. A good example of this phenomenon forms the subject matter of an ethnography of Japanese potters whose work gradually changed when it was chosen as the epitome of Japan's 'folk art' (Moeran 1984).

The relationship between art and the spiritual or transcendental is another source of interest to anthropologists, and this chapter will try to show how difficult it may be to separate works of art from their cosmological context. In practice, some objects have acquired different levels of interpretation in different situations, and the art of the Australian Aboriginal people is a case in point. Spiritual meaning is preserved for the artist and those of his or her own society while explanations provided for the tourist are much more limited, which would seem to be quite appropriate in a society that attaches value to secrecy, as is the case in many Aboriginal communities.

It is possible that there is also a certain attraction for the consumer in knowing that their purchase may carry some esoteric value, and although the layers of meaning may not be appreciated by indigenous artists, it is likely that their advocates are aware that those who wish to acquire it may be seeking more than just an attractive souvenir. Early Western paintings of the native inhabitants of the various idyllic isles discovered by Captain Cook and his sailors depicted people in a situation resembling the Garden of Eden, a fictional paradise quite in keeping with the Rousseauan ideas of the noble savage current at the time. Indigenous art may still carry a tinge of spiritual healing, which appeals to those seeking solace from the fast city life of the high-tech world.

Aboriginal refers to the first status of **Indigenous** peoples around the world, used by explorers and travellers who arrived in their lands. Its negative connotations in the English language made it an unacceptable term in many countries for years, though it was still used in Australia. Now it has become a preferred term again by some of the people themselves (e.g. Aboriginal Peoples Television Network in Canada).

Living Art

The anthropology of art is not confined to the study of marketable objects, how-ever. In many societies people assign aesthetic qualities to the decoration of their own bodies, sometimes spending days in the preparation of a particular display. Some cases of bodily decoration, and its symbolic associations, were raised in the previous chapter, but a particularly striking example of the aesthetic appreciation of bodily decoration is to be found amongst the Nuba people of Southern Sudan. Here, young men and women spend time every day making themselves up and rubbing oil into their whole bodies to make them shine, some of the most attractive designs being found amongst pubescent boys between the ages of about 15 and 20.

According to the anthropologist J. C. Faris (1971), this activity is purely aes-thetic, to express the beauty of healthy nubile bodies, which are idealised in this society. The attachment of aesthetic value to an idealised form of the human body is of course found in many societies, possibly universally, and examples probably overlooked by art historians abound in television series such as *Bay Watch* or *Footballers' Wives*, where the story line would seem much less important than the health and youthful vigour of the characters on display. The technical term for displaying and admiring nubile bodies in their physical and sexual prime is ephebism, although how the ideal body is conceptualised will vary from culture to culture.

> **ephebism** – displaying and admiring nubile bodies in their physical and sexual prime, although how the ideal body is conceptualised will vary from culture to culture.

Tattoos are a permanent type of bodily adornment requiring considerable investment of time and resources which may also bestow a long-term political advantage, as we discussed in the previous chapter. In some societies they express a man's place in a hierarchical scheme, in others they are chosen to demonstrate a kind of *macho* ability to endure pain, but people also choose them for their aesthetic appeal. The 'dis-gusting' Japanese tattoos we mentioned draw on the same fund of mythological inspiration as do woodblock prints, exported as examples of Japanese cultural achievement, and tattoo artists around the world have chosen elements of them to offer their clients, along with a range of examples from other cultural sources.

Aesthetic appreciation can also be expressed towards aspects of everyday life which might, by others, be considered mundane or functional; for example, Jeremy Coote (in Coote and Shelton 1992) shows how Nilotic herding people such as the Nuer and the Dinka demonstrate an artistic focus of attention on colour, shading, shapes and patterns of the cattle which form the basis of their livelihood (see Photograph 6.1). The languages of these people have extensive vocabulary with which to discuss and express the finer variations of the animals' markings, and a conversation about them is said rather to resemble one of antique dealers or wine connoisseurs than what might be expected elsewhere from stockbreeders. In the Nuer and Dinka languages, words which might be translated as 'piebald' and 'guernsey' take on a whole new set of values.

Photograph 6.1 An example of Dinka cattle, whose aesthetic qualities are discussed in this chapter (photograph courtesy of Jeremy Coote)

Another interesting area of living art brings us back to a most conventional form for Europeans, namely the area of gardens and landscape. The story of decorative gardens is a history of cultural influence, appropriation and creativity, and signs of the Far Eastern influence in European countries provide a good example of the process. Indeed, many of the flowers which are highly valued by horticulturalists have their origins in China, as do features of the Japanese garden to which they attribute many favoured varieties of trees and shrubs. Several wealthy families in Europe and elsewhere in the nineteenth century created Japanese gardens, and finding and restoring these has become an aim of the Japanese Garden Society, created in Britain in 1993.

The appeal of these Japanese gardens does not often derive from a wider interest in Japanese culture, but their intrinsic aesthetic qualities seem to offer something intangible to their aficionados, sometimes described as 'haunting' or 'spiritual'. They provide a way of creating a 'scene' or a possibly miniature 'landscape' which has been a European endeavour for centuries. Whether in practice in a tiny space or a country estate, or in two-dimensional form in a painting, creating a landscape has been an important part of the artistic worlds in the East, too, and this has been an area of the deepest cultural reciprocity. It is not necessarily the way in which the world is depicted or perceived in all societies, however.

In several of the major galleries of Australia (and undoubtedly other countries with a similar history) it is possible to observe a selection of depictions of the local landscapes made through the period of colonisation and beyond by artists who variously came from Europe, were born in Australia, and those whose origins are largely Aboriginal. Since many of the galleries also boast a collection of European art, it is quite easy to discern the same periods and styles in the early European paintings of Australia, and distinguish these from the later Australian schools which developed as people born and brought up in the Australian landscape perceived their surroundings in a way less dominated by European traditions.

The stark contrast with Aboriginal depictions of some of the same scenery, which forms much of the subject matter of Howard Morphy's (1991) book *Ancestral Connections*, immediately opens up questions about the systems of classification which underlie the whole endeavour of two-dimensional representation of an environmental landscape (see First-hand Account on p. 124 for an Aboriginal account). Landscape paintings, like maps, illustrate a culturally specific form, dating back to classical antiquity in the West, where it was rediscovered in the Renaissance, but even the idea of a landscape is not as universal as might be imagined. The collection of papers in *The Anthropology of Landscape* (Hirsch and O'Hanlon 1995) provides some excellent examples of alternative ways in which this notion, which the editors see as a relationship between ideas of 'place' and the here-and-now of foreground actuality, and 'space' of background potentiality, may be understood.

> The model of landscape developed ... is one predicated on the idea of landscape as process ... this process is one which relates a 'foreground' everyday social life ('us the way we are') to a 'background' potential social existence ('us the way we might be'). It is a process that attains a form of timelessness and fixity in certain idealized and transcendent situations, such as painted landscape representation, but which can be achieved only momentarily, if ever, in the human world of social relationships.   (1995: 2)

One paper, which discusses the Piro people of Amazonian Peru, makes the point that in the rain forest the horizon does not recede away from the point of observation. The vegetation pattern that surrounds villages is 'seen' in terms of kinship and past activities associated with it:

> It is hard to see Amazonia as a landscape ... The land does not recede away from a point of observation to the distant horizon, for everywhere vegetation occludes the view.   (Gow 1995: 43)
>   For the native people of Bajo Urubamba, the local environment is a lived space. It is known by means of movement through it, seeing the traces of other people's movements and agency, and through the narratives of yet other people's agency.   (Ibid. 59)

In Australian examples, too, notions of kinship are intimately bound up with ideas of place and space, through the ancestral connections with which they are attributed, and these are also bound up with notions of time and the passage through life and death. In another paper about a people who inhabit dense forest, this time Papua New Guinea, we are told about the importance of sounds to an understanding of the landscape. Here 'hiddenness' is perceived as inaudibility, rather than invisibility, and the landscape is one of 'articulation' (Gell 1995: 238). Clearly, the way that our senses are trained locally to perceive aesthetic value can be quite variable.

Art for Gaining Access to 'Seeing the World'

As an anthropologist embarks upon a study, however, material objects in any society provide a useful focus for attention, a concrete set of phenomena for investigation and discussion with informants, and a fertile source of information about the people who make and use them. Local interpretations and evaluations of objects offer an excellent way to gain access to indigenous systems of classification, which underpin the modes of thought and expression of the people under study. As Coote and Shelton point out in the introduction to their book on the anthropology of art and aesthetics, 'the art of a society can provide a fruitful starting-point for the analyst's explication of its world-view' (1992: 5).

A good explicit example of this is to be found in the paper by Ross Bowden in the same book, on the art and architecture of the Kwoma people of the Sepik River region of Papua New Guinea. Bowden (1983) has also written a fascinating book about the sculpture found amongst these same people. In all cases – art, architecture and sculpture – intricately carved and painted material objects strike the visitor as the epitome of what we have come to call primitive or tribal art, and examples are to be found on display in the most famous museums of the Western world. For the Kwoma themselves, these objects are assigned quite different value – political, spiritual and symbolic – and they thus offer a particularly enlightening window to understanding the way they 'see the world', or their **collective representations**.

Bowden argues, for example, that the lavishly decorated ceremonial houses form visual counterparts for the roles men, in contrast to women, play in the structure of Kwoma social groups. These houses, where male members of a community meet for informal social interaction and to perform ceremonies, are located in the centre of villages, a geographical location which corresponds to the structurally central position men have in clan organisation. Villages are made up of a group of related men, who remain together throughout their lives, and women move in and out of the village on marriage, which, in a society where divorce is common, may be quite a frequent occurrence.

Reflecting this, domestic homes, where individual men live with their wives and children, are scattered adjacent to the forest on the margins of the village. Unlike men, women do not form groups except in relation to those of their husbands, and they are excluded from the ceremonial house. Bowden argues that women's peripheral geographical position within a village expresses their 'peripheral' position structurally: that is the way they, as wives, form the links between groups rather than constituting their residential and social cores. Interestingly, Kwoma women display the art with which they are associated in the form of elaborate decorative scars on their own bodies (Williamson 1979), art works which are of course carried with them when they move.

The construction of the ceremonial house, on the other hand, expresses male attributes sought and admired in Kwoma society. Men aspire to be killers in warfare, and to produce many children and great gardens, and these same qualities of homicidal aggression and human and horticultural fertility are attributed to ceremonial houses as well. This is explicitly expressed in the choice of timbers used to construct the elaborately carved and painted ridge pole and the longitudinal side beams, customarily made from the wood of a tree which in myth is ascribed superabundant masculine sexual potency. In the story this tree stands

Photograph 6.2

Detail of the sculptures and bark paintings that decorate the ceiling of the Kwoma ceremonial men's house named Wayipanalin Bangwiss village, 1973. The sculpture depicts a clan spirit and the paintings are clan totems (photograph courtesy of Ross Bowden).

beside a forest track and whenever a woman, or girl, steps over one of its roots she immediately becomes pregnant, but girls who are not yet sexually mature are condemned to die in childbirth.

The splendid figures found in the carvings on the posts and beams in these buildings (see Photograph 6.2) also depict culture heroes which feature in Kwoma myths about the creation of fundamental features of Kwoma culture, such as the types of plants on which Kwoma rely for food, sago plants, which yield the highest quantities of edible starch, and the central role played by exchange in the structure of Kwoma society. The literally hundreds of bark paintings on the ceilings illustrate the species of plants and animals that belong to the different clans, and Kwoma people say that any knowledgeable person who walks into these buildings can immediately determine the clan composition of the community from the paintings on display.

Art and Status: The Status of Art

An important aspect of the way in which objects may be interpreted in an ethnographic context is to see how they express and relate to systems of hierarchy and power. Amongst the Kwoma, described above, the Yena sculptures represent the spirit world which guarantees the continued fertility of the gardens and people, and underpins their system of morality and law. In the men's house they look down on discussions of social concern, and protect the human protagonists who may not strike one another in the presence of the spirits. They stand for the authority and continuity of the wider community, and the skills men display when carving and painting these objects are thought to come directly from the supernatural world.

Elsewhere, notably in Africa, masks are used to disguise individuals handing down the judgements of the ancestors or spirits, and to separate the authoritative role being played from the person who is called upon to play it. The voice used during judgement will also very often be changed. Some art objects are shown only to people in certain positions in society. In several parts of the world it is an important feature of adult initiation rites to reveal ritual objects, which are often so beautifully carved that they are also easily classified in the West as works of art. Antony Forge wrote of the Abelam people, again in Papua New Guinea, that showing the ritual objects for the first time towards the end of a traumatic initiation procedure heightens their apparent power, as well as increasing the significance of the whole ritual. Knowledge of how to perform such rituals, and even more of the creation of the art objects, demonstrates a special relationship with the supernatural world and a sure way to success in the local system of politics.

We will return in the next section to examine further the meaning of art objects in a particular context, but it is interesting that an association with secular art is also capable of bestowing status. It was mentioned in the introduction that in cosmopolitan societies people accrue considerable status, and potentially wealth, through knowledge of the value and authenticity of *objets d'art*. Furthermore, those in the most powerful positions influence the extent to which a work will be assigned a high value in artistic terms, or even whether it will be classified as art at all. In an exhibition I once saw at the Victoria and Albert Museum in London, one of the most appealing exhibits was an arrangement of garden gloves. For a collection of garden gloves to be deemed a work of art requires not only the declaration of the artist, but the agreement of a number of other agents along the way. In this case, members of the viewing public seemed to acquiesce with the decision, but they are sometimes left bewildered as to why mundane objects are attributed such status.

In practice, it is not even necessary for people to understand why art is assigned a high value in order to acquire status through its ownership or display. Collections of art are commonplace in the homes of the wealthy, and in the public rooms of royal palaces and other aristocratic houses, where they may also express a family heritage, but it has become fashionable for companies to buy and display paintings in their foyers and executive rooms as an expression of sophistication and economic power. The ownership of these paintings says little about the understanding of the company employees of the aesthetics and meaning of the object, rather the aim is to demonstrate corporate access to the elite and expensive world of high art with which it gains kudos by association.

We should perhaps, therefore, not be surprised to discover that some Indigenous people also display apparently meaningful objects largely for the kudos they acquire, rather than for any deep significance they display in the designs. According to Anderson (1989), an example of this is to be found in the elaborate totem poles owned by Northwest American Indian peoples such as the Kwakiutl (now corrected locally as Kwakwaka'wakw), Tlingit and Haida (whom we met in Chapter 3). They depict animals and, possibly, characters from their folk tales (see Photograph 6.3). These features are sometimes quite stylised, and they are open to symbolic interpretation, but their chiefly owners are said to be much more concerned with the status they represent than with any stories they might depict:

totem – thought by some early anthropologists to be a sacred symbol, which represented a specific part of society known as a clan, but eventually discovered to have more complex meanings, which were different in Australia and in North America.

> A piece carries with it a message that bears no palpable resemblance to the image itself: It is a 'status symbol'. The totem poles, houseposts, and most of the masks were signs of the high social standing of their owners. Even if a native viewer did not accurately decipher the iconic message of a given art work, he or she undoubtedly appreciated the social significance of the piece. The quantity and elaborateness of the works of art possessed by a person were public statements of the individual's relative position in the social hierarchy. As we know, members of Northwest Coast

societies were vitally concerned with their relative social standing, so to them the symbolic messages transmitted via their art were far from trivial. (Anderson 1989)

In both cases, corporate art and totem poles, the iconography is supposed to be less significant than the possession of the objects, but another factor has become important since Anderson published his book. Many of the totem poles that once stood proudly on the Northwest Coast are now to be found in museums (as in Photograph 6.3) around the world and, in some cases, members of the groups that once made those poles are seeking to have them returned. A major reason for this is that the displays are of old, sometimes rotting poles, and give the impression (as does Anderson's use of the past tense) that the practice has died out. In fact, in one case in Sweden, a new pole was carved to replace the old one. Poles are carved and raised to this day to mark important occasions, and they can be seen in many locations in Northwest Coast Canada and in Haida Gwaii (formerly the Queen Charlotte Islands).

In an international context, people allocate one another status in a preconceived view of aesthetic value, and evidence of a highly developed aesthetic sense may be cited as an index of civilisation. The reciprocal influences which have run between East and West for millennia are an illustration of this process, and in Europe the value placed on the acquisition of Chinese ceramics and Turkish carpets are just two examples where status has been assigned in one society to an art form developed in another. This is an area open to considerable negotiation, of course, and Japan now sports many art forms originally developed in China as characteristically Japanese.

Indeed, some Japanese writers claim that their country is superior to all others because their artistic accomplishments are developed in such subtle and deceptively simple ways. A single leaf, or a simple twist of paper, may be regarded as aesthetic achievements of the highest quality, and attention accorded to the wrapping and presentation of objects and ideas, as already discussed, is said to be greater than in any other civilisation. Even objects wrapped for the most mundane reasons will receive a meticulous care – demonstrating the same kind of attention to detail which has brought Japan into the forefront of microchip technology – but it is the appreciation of aesthetic qualities which raises the level of civilisation in a Japanese view.

One Japanese author who has written on this subject is Iwao Nukada (1977) who proposes an evolutionary theory that wrapping was first used everywhere for practical reasons: to carry food safely from the fields to the home, to keep the body warm in winter, and to protect from the elements. With the development of spiritual and religious ideas, this material form acquired all kinds of new significance in the realm of the sacred, he argues, and he cites examples from different parts of the world. The third and fourth stages of development, in his view, are those of art and courtesy. The wrapping forms took on an aesthetic quality, and provided a medium for the elaboration of beauty, but they also enabled their creators to communicate deeper expressions of concern and appreciation. They offered a way to communicate the status which an appreciation of beauty implied, both on the part of the donor and in recognition that the efforts would be appreciated by the recipient.

This kind of subtlety of communication is highly regarded in a Japanese view, and it is by no means limited to material culture. The choice of words and language is also tinged with an aesthetic quality, even in everyday discourse, as is the choice of clothes and interior design. These concerns are not, of course, unique to Japan, but the areas of artistic achievement recognisable in a Western context bring Japan into a universe of discourse more readily shared in the cosmopolitan world than are some of those found in societies technologically less developed. The Dinka appreciation of the beauty of their cattle might be one example. This apparent Western understanding of Japan is deceptive, however, because it may well mask some of the deeply ingrained differences, which could thus be overlooked.

Art and Meaning

In Chapter 3 I gave some examples of the kinds of meaning that may be transmitted in the wrapping of a gift, but it is important to remember that the whole notion of gift wrapping may carry different messages in a Japanese view from that expected in many Western countries. In formal presentations, the wrapping may even be more important than the gift inside, and I know several Japanese people who put away the gifts they receive without even opening them, perhaps to use again when they need to make a presentation. The wrapping is not 'mere decoration' to be ripped off and thrown away. It is itself, in all its glory, the medium of the message of the gift.

This quality of what outsiders may see as 'mere decoration' to carry deep and meaningful messages was raised in the last chapter when we considered the work of Michael O'Hanlon (1989) in his book about the Wahgi people of the Highlands of Papua New Guinea. Like Japanese wrapping, the adornment provides the medium which carries the message, the beautiful headdresses exhibiting directly the political clout of their wearers, and the use of the special shining qualities of pig's fat to embellish the skin is a direct demonstration of the health and fertility of the most important medium of wealth and exchange in this society. O'Hanlon elsewhere examines the implications of this lack of exegesis about artistic accomplishments among the peoples of Papua New Guinea (O'Hanlon 1992).

Also talking of Papua New Guinea, other writers have emphasised the competitive element of the ritual bodily attire. Just as gifts from one group to another are lined up in an ostentatious display of wealth, one of the aims of the headdress is to impress and overawe the spectators who attend. The body is decorated to an enhanced, idealised form, which in this case is a general representation of the collective health and prosperity of the wider group. In the Trobriand Islands, it is the canoe boards which play this role:

> The function of the Trobriand canoe-boards is to dazzle their owners' Kula trade partners, making them take leave of their senses and trade more of their valuables than they otherwise would have done. The designs on the canoe-boards identify the boat with the original flying canoe of Trobriand mythology, and symbolise slipperiness, flowing water, and wisdom, all of which help to attract the luxury goods the expedition hopes for. In this example, the form and content of the art work together to produce magical, aesthetic effects. (Coote and Shelton 1992:9)

This is essentially the same competitive element mentioned above in reference to corporate art, and bodily and other art is also found in complex societies as an index or reflection of structural divisions within that society. The hairstyles discussed in the previous chapter provide an excellent example, as do other forms of bodily attire. People in complex societies do not necessarily share taste and the fact that punk bodily art differs from more acceptable tastes expresses their rejection of wider society. Similarly, if one section of society expresses a preference for art forms of a certain kind, another section may well define their own boundaries with that section by belittling it. Popular music is a particularly apt example.

The notion of 'taste' underlies this phenomenon, as social groups express their shared ideas in terms of what they admire and seek to acquire. 'Taste' becomes a way of expressing values which are clearly 'contested' by different social groups, and this notion of contested value is an area of recent interest for anthropologists. The French anthropologist Pierre Bourdieu wrote a classic text entitled *Distinction: A Social Critique of the Judgement of Taste* in which he relates the idea of taste to the way people classify one another in a particular society, and hence to the classes into which society divides, or 'distinguishes' itself.

> Taste classifies, and it classifies the classifier. Social subjects, classified by their classifications, distinguish themselves by the distinctions they make, between the beautiful and the ugly, the distinguished and the vulgar, in which their position in the objective classifications is expressed or betrayed. (Bourdieu 1992 [1984])

Lines along which divisions of opinion occur indicate lines of education and social class. Interestingly, however, artistic taste would seem to be one area where there is little difference based on gender.

Aesthetics

These aspects of the communicative properties of art and decoration are again difficult to describe in detail. Why one object should be regarded as tasteful by one social group and distasteful by another is beyond easy explanation. Indeed, the explanation may be couched in terms of upbringing and education. One learns how to recognise a valuable object by being around objects assigned value in a similar value system. One acquires a gut reaction which will coincide with those whom one respects and admires, or, in the case of punk and other revolutionary art, one specifically sets out to flout those accepted values and produce something that will shock. In all these cases, there is meaning which lies embedded in the art itself, and one area of meaning is concerned with the quality we call aesthetic. This is an area about which anthropologists themselves disagree.

aesthetics - strictly speaking, a branch of philosophy concerned with beauty and the physical ability to recognise it.

On the one hand, there is the view that the whole idea of aesthetics is culture bound, like the notion of taste, so that an aesthetic appreciation is itself a product of a particular society which can only be properly applied within that social context. Those who hold that view see others applying this culture-bound aesthetic sense in other societies, but feel that their judgements are misplaced. They may even feel that the idea of universality of aesthetic sense is a kind of faith, held in the context of art as theology is with religion. Alfred Gell, who expressed this view in his paper in the Coote and Shelton book, goes on to suggest that art has become a sort of religion, whose shrines are theatres, libraries and art galleries, and whose priests and bishops are the painters and poets.

The other view is that there exists a universal aesthetic sense possessed by human beings, whatever their society, although it will of course be interpreted and evaluated in socially appropriate ways. This view argues for a human capacity to appreciate beauty and experience a sensory reaction to the physical qualities of an object, such as form and texture, which will be related to non-material aspects of that object within its cultural system of knowledge. In his introduction to *Anthropology of Art*, Howard Morphy (1994) gives an example of the way a particular aesthetic effect, namely that of shimmering or shining brilliance, may be highly valued, but with different interpretations, in three different societies.

Amongst the people with whom he himself worked, the Yolngu of Northern Australia, the shimmering effect applied to paintings with a cross-hatching technique is interpreted as the power of the ancestral beings shining out of a creation which is anyway seen as a manifestation of their existence. The value of brilliance is reiterated in myth and song in Yolngu social life. The Wahgi, too, value a shining effect, this time created on their bodies, as described above, but here the association is with health and fertility, with the power and strength of the group as a whole. Morphy's third example is of the shining effect of a black mask valued by the Mende people of Sierra Leone, particularly during a ritual dance display as an expression of female health.

In all these cases, shining is itself a quality selected for particular note. Elsewhere, efforts may be made to reduce shine, such as when a woman powders her nose, or a set of photographs is ordered with a matt finish. The value of shine has undergone a major change in Western society, perhaps reflecting an underlying economic and political shift of values. Hard polished wood is still highly prized in antique furniture, but there has been a shift of appreciation towards the originally cheaper pine, which is not only easier to care for, but also more politically correct. In the days of shiny polished hardwood, and bronze and silver ornaments, their ownership and display was a way of demonstrating the economic resources to engage staff to maintain their quality. Interestingly, the lower-quality wood, which has been stripped of its glossy paint, is now quite expensive to acquire!

Definitions of Art

The problem with defining the notion of aesthetics is only part of the wider problem of defining the notion of 'art'. We have been applying both terms throughout this chapter, without pausing to define them, partly because an understanding of some of the issues we have raised is vital to an appreciation of this problem.

In the Yolngu worldview there are two moieties, one is Yirritja and the other is Dhuwa. They are two halves of one whole. Our view of the world is holistic. All knowledge is interconnected. Art is connected to songs and songs are connected to people. People are also connected through song lines and stories. Stories are connected to art and art is connected to country and land through clans and totems. Everything in our world is linked to all these things. Our Yolngu world view consists of all these things.

First-hand account 6:

Raymattja Marika, Yolngu – on Art through Indigenous Science

Everything in the Yolngu world view is made up of two moieties. One is Yirritja and the other one is Dhuwa. Dhuwa and Yirritja make up our worldview. They are two halves of our holistic world view.

Yirritja and Dhuwa are a bit like ying and yang. They fit together perfectly. Everything in Yirritja and Dhuwa is connected. For example, Yirritja and Dhuwa intermarry into each other and vice-versa.

Everything in the land is Yirritja and Dhuwa.

Yothu-yindi and mari-gutharra are the two main relationships for Yirritja and Dhuwa. Mari and gutharra means grandmother and grandchild relationship. Yothu and yindi means mother and child relationship.

Everything in our world view is interrelated. For example, Yirritja land and Dhuwa land can come together at a certain point and that land becomes Dhuwa and Yirritja. Also, Yirritja country being looked after by a Yirritja clan, that has a mari-gutharra connection (grandmother and grandchild). Yes, Yirritja and Dhuwa have these relationship terms, through yothu-yindi and mari-gutharra.

This world view is expressed through songs, through stories, through art, through rituals, and through paintings. Paintings consist of maps, abstract maps of the land, trees, the animals, the plants, the rocks and so on. All have meaning, they're either Yirritja or Dhuwa. So everything is integrated – science, language, culture, law, they're all integrated – whereas in the non-Aboriginal world view all these things are taught separately.

Northern Territory
AUSTRALIA

Science is taught differently, language is taught differently, art is too, they are all taught in their own components. For Yolngu, in the Yolngu world view everything is interconnected and interrelated in a holistic way.

This piece was videotaped in May 2002 at Yirrkala, Community Education Centre, by Katie Hayne.

Many of the books cited below tackle the issue of definition, and you may pursue the ideas presented for yourself, but in the end the whole endeavour of definition is also so culturally bound that it seemed better not to engage in it at the outset. The next chapter is almost entirely devoted to the problems of defining the term 'religion' which runs into parallel problems, and the reader will probably find that exercise taxing enough.

A few words are in order, however, by way of summary, for the main problem centres around the varying and disputed attitudes to the concept of art in European languages. Morphy (1994) points out that in the nineteenth century a Western definition of art involved such a strong notion of civilisation that the idea of 'primitive art' was almost a contradiction in terms. Even now, the three aspects of a European definition of art that he identifies are very revealing of European ideas: first, the institutional one, whereby objects are deemed art or otherwise depending on whether they are chosen to be displayed in galleries as opposed to museums, and therefore classified as 'fine art' as opposed to 'folk art' or 'craft'; secondly, a definition in terms of attributes makes reference to aesthetics again, but also skills and semantic properties; and finally, Morphy sees the *intent* of the artist as important:

> art objects are ones that are *intended* to be works of art by their makers. With most types of object, intention is subordinate to functional or institutional specification – the intention to make a boat is insufficient if the object is incapable of floating. In the case of art objects the individual has a little more freedom, since the category is always open to persuasion (1994: 652)

This leads to the extraordinary situation we find in art galleries where almost anything, or indeed, nothing, can be designated as 'art'.

The boundaries that exist between fine arts, crafts and artefacts are now beginning to break down, however, since no clear distinction, anyway often a product of Western hegemony, is made in all social settings. The garden gloves referred to earlier were part of an interesting exhibition of Japanese 'Studio Crafts', which combined a wonderfully irreverent mix of functional artefacts, sometimes called 'traditional', with a dramatic display of abstract 'modern' artistic constructions, one of which, a steep upward slope, is entitled *The M25*, presumably after the usually clogged London ring-road. As mentioned above, Japan is a country where the beauty of an apparent simplicity of form has for long been recognised amongst the most mundane objects, as well as in the creations of the aristocracy, a point illustrated in a book now well known in many countries, entitled *How to Wrap Five Eggs* (Oka 1967).

Intent is therefore also a problem, although this is also cited in Layton's (1991) introduction to the anthropology of art, where he gives a possible definition as concerned with objects made primarily to be aesthetically pleasing rather than for a pragmatic functional purpose. He considers discussions of ancient Greek philosophy about the formal properties of beauty, but also the capacity of art to represent the world around us in a way which enhances our perceptions of it and, indeed, which induces emotional response. Art historians in the Western world look for innovation in artistic accomplishments, and associate these advances with particular periods in the past. Their approach is premised in an idea of the creativity of the artist.

This premise is not necessarily shared by people in other societies whose work has been deemed 'art' by the outside world. In some societies, including those of Australian Aborigines and the Sepik people discussed above, any one of them is thought capable of creating their painting and sculpture. Indeed, the skills are not thought to be talents given only to certain individuals, but to be revelations of the spiritual world through the human beings involved. Neither is there an indigenous concept of originality in art, for since the source of the works is to be found in the spirit world, it is regarded as vital to replicate them to keep them in good order. Thus, the older Kwoma houses are burned down to be rebuilt; and ancient sculptures sold to early travellers, and now maybe carefully guarded in Western museums, are apparently less valuable to the people whose ancestors made them than some purists might think. Indeed, letting them rot away back into the earth that provided the source material might well be thought the most appropriate treatment for them once they have lost their lustre.

Conclusion

In the Western world, replication of a work of art is considered acceptable as part of the learning process, but passing it off as one's own would be a forgery. Of course, in the past, schools of a single artist produced work now attributed only to that one name, and during certain periods art was also much more closely associated with religion than it is now. Some Western people might still argue that they receive their artistic talent from God, but those whose 'art' is a revelation of the spiritual world would possibly not classify their work as art in a Western sense at all! In the next chapter we turn our attention to what it is we mean by the term 'religion'.

Discussion Questions

1 Consider the meaning of the word 'art' in your social world. Does it apply only to things that are beautiful? Who has authority in that art world and how much status do they have?

2 What is a craft? If a craftsperson is good at their job, would their production need to be beautiful? How beautiful would it need to be before it became classified as 'art'? What are the cultural implications of this classificatory device?

3 Do you agree that aesthetics has a universal value? Is a cow aesthetically pleasing to you? How would you make a judgement about that?

References and Further Research

Books
Anderson, R. L. (1989) *Art in Small-Scale Societies* (Englewood Cliffs, NJ: Prentice Hall).
Banks, Marcus and Morphy, Howard (1997) *Rethinking Visual Anthropology* (New Haven and London: Yale University Press).
Bourdieu, Pierre (1992 [1984]) *Distinction: A Social Critique of the Judgement of Taste* (Cambridge, Mass.: Harvard University Press).
Bowden, Ross (1983) *Yena: Art and Ceremony in a Sepik Society* (Oxford: Pitt Rivers Museum).
Coote, Jeremy and Shelton, Anthony (1992) *Anthropology, Art, and Aesthetics* (Oxford: Clarendon Press).
Faris, J. C. (1971) *Nuba Personal Art* (London: Duckworth).
Hirsch, Eric and O'Hanlon, Michael (1995) *The Anthropology of Landscape: Perspectives in Place and Space* (Oxford: Clarendon Press).
Layton, Robert (1991) *The Anthropology of Art* (Cambridge: Cambridge University Press).
Moeran, Brian (1984) *Lost Innocence* (Berkeley, Los Angeles and London: University of California Press).
Moeran, Brian (1997) *Folk Art Potters of Japan: Beyond an Anthropology of Aesthetics* (Richmond, Va.: Curzon).
Morphy, Howard (1991) *Ancestral Connections: Art and an Aboriginal System of Knowledge* (Chicago and London: University of Chicago Press).
Nukada Iwao (1977) *Tsutsumi* (Wrapping) (Tokyo: Hosei Daigaku Shuppansha) – in Japanese.
Oka, Hideyuki (1967) *How to Wrap Five Eggs: Japanese Design in Traditional Packaging* (New York: Weatherhill; Tokyo: Bijutsu Shuppansha).

Articles
Bowden, Ross (1992) 'Art, Architecture, and Collective Representations in a New Guinea Society', in Jeremy Coote and Anthony Shelton, *Anthropology, Art and Aesthetics* (Oxford: Clarendon Press), pp. 67–93.
Gell, Alfred (1992) 'The Technology of Enchantment and the Enchantment of Technology', in Jeremy Coote and Shelton, Anthony, *Anthropology, Art and Aesthetics* (Oxford: Clarendon Press) pp. 40–63.

Gell, Alfred (1995) 'The Language of the Forest: Landscape and Phonological Iconism in Umeda', in Eric Hirsch and Michael O'Hanlon, *The Anthropology of Landscape* (Oxford: Clarendon Press), pp. 232–52.

Gow, Peter, (1995) 'Land, People and Paper in Western Amazonia', in Eric Hirsch and Michael O'Hanlon, *The Anthropology of Landscape* (Oxford: Clarendon Press), pp. 43–62.

Forge, Anthony (1970) 'Learning to see in New Guinea', in Philip Mayer (ed.), *Socialisation: The Approach from Social Anthropology* (London: Tavistock).

Morphy, Howard (1994) 'The Anthropology of Art', in Tim Ingold (ed.), *Companion Encyclopedia of Anthropology* (London: Routledge).

O'Hanlon, Michael (1992) 'Unstable Images and Second Skins: Artefacts, Exegesis and Assessments in the New Guinea Highlands', *Man* (n.s.), 27: 587–608.

Scheper-Hughes, Nancy (2003) 'Anatomy of a Quilt: Civil Rights, Art and Anthropology', *Anthropology Today*, 19(4): 15–21.

Schneider, Arnd (1993) 'The Art Diviners', *Anthropology Today*, 9(2): pp. 3–9.

Strathern, Marilyn (1979) 'The Self in Self Decoration' *Oceania*, 49: 240–56.

Williamson, Margaret Holmes (1979) 'Cicatrisation of Women among the Kwoma', *Mankind*, 12: 35–41.

Novels

Carey, Peter (2007) *Theft: A Love Story* (Canada: Vintage) is a novel centred around the themes of art and fraud.

Chevalier, Tracy (2006) *Girl with a Pearl Earring* (London: HarperCollins) is a novel that speculates about the relationship of a servant and muse to the artist Vermeer.

Ishiguro, Kazuo (1986) *Artist in a Floating World* (Harlow: Faber) is a novel that illustrates the relationships between Japanese artists in the turbulence of pre-Second World War Japan.

Films

The Wodaabe (Leslie Woodhead and Mette Bovin, 1988), a film in the Granada 'Disappearing World' series, is about the nomadic lives of a Fulani people of Nigeria who are described as 'obsessed with male beauty'. A part of the film is devoted to the extraordinary facial decorations they apply.

Parts of the *Strangers Abroad* film on Sir Walter Baldwin Spencer (see Chapter 2) is about Australian Aboriginal art and its meaning.

Deep Hearts is a (1981) film directed by Robert Gardner about a male 'beauty contest' among the Bororo Fulani of Niger.

In and out of Africa (Ilisa Barbash and Lucien Taylor, 59 minutes, 1993) – the negotiation of cultural values between European and American collectors and African artists and traders is revealed by following Nigerian Gabai Baare, from the Ivory Coast to Long Island, USA, as he conducts transnational trade of African art.

Singing Pictures – Woman Painters of Naya (Lina Fruzzetti and Ákos Östör, 45 minutes, 2005) illustrates the daily lives of Muslim Patua women from West Bengal, who have formed a scroll painters' cooperative, thus following the generations of the Patua (Chitrakara) communities of painters and singers of stories depicted in scrolls.

Websites

http://www.societyforvisualanthropology.org/ – Society for Visual Anthropology.

http://www.socialsciences.manchester.ac.uk/visualanthropology/ – Visual Anthropology Centre at Manchester (UK) University.

http://nymag.com/arts/art/features/16542/ – Article about the Western art world.

http://www.iep.utm.edu/a/aestheti.htm – history of Western aesthetics.

7

Cosmology I: Religion, Magic and Mythology

Religion, Science and Cosmology

Until the last chapter, we were looking rather broadly at the way in which anthropologists observe and make sense of particular societies, the way they try to understand systems of classification and value, and the social relationships into which they enter. In Chapter 6 we began to look at contested ideas about objects and their meaning. It was mentioned at the outset of this book that another important task for anthropologists is the translation back of their findings into their own language and their own system of categories. This is what makes it possible to compare their findings with those of people working elsewhere, or, at least, to present a description capable of comparison with those produced elsewhere.

Important categories of analysis have therefore been those which represented divisions made in the societies of the academics doing the analysis – religion, politics, economics – and broad headings for the chapters which follow include these very three. However, as we have begun to see, problems arise when anthropologists try to fit the indigenous categories of other parts of the world into their own clearly defined notions, and all kinds of other descriptions are needed to describe local ideas. In the pages that follow we will examine some of these problems as well as some of the descriptions, and we will introduce some analytical notions which have fewer restricting connotations to detract from our understanding of people with very different ideas.

This and the next chapter are concerned with what anthropologists have come to call cosmology, or, in other words, broad ideas and explanations which people have about the world in which they live and their place in that world. These include ideas about the creation of the world, or the arrival of the people in question into that world. They include notions of other worlds, worlds from which they may believe they have come, and to which they go after death in this world, or indeed during transcendental experiences in this world. Until now we have concentrated on social relations between living beings, but in all cultures there are notions about beings beyond that living world, about places and events beyond those of the strictly tangible, and these are usually related to explanations about life itself.

cosmology – broad ideas and explanations that people have about the world in which they live and their place in that world

We are in the area of *religion*, but, as we shall see, some of the theories and practices found around the world make the drawing up of a valid universal definition a virtually impossible task. In this chapter we will consider some of the problems of definition of the categories used in the European world of the first anthropologists, in the English language in this text, sometimes translated from French, but also undoubtedly influenced by Scandinavian ideas as well as those of Latin and Greek. In the next chapter we will turn to examine examples of non-European indigenous ideas and some actual situations. We are also in the area of *science*, and some readers may feel that this is where we should now turn for answers to all the above questions. A minimal definition of science is 'a body of knowledge', with further qualifications about observation, experiment and induction, but let us examine that concept too.

Definitions and Distinctions

Various attempts have been made to define the word '*religion*'. Edward Burnett Tylor tried to be very broad when he suggested religion be defined as 'the belief in spiritual beings' (1913: 8). A problem arises immediately, however, for there are plenty of people whose devout religious activities involve no spiritual beings. Buddhists, for example, are concerned with achieving a state beyond the spiritual, a state which does not require the intervention of a god or gods. Indeed, a Buddhist specialist working in Sri Lanka enjoys telling people about how two different monks there told him quite clearly that the word usually translated as 'religion' has nothing to do with gods (Gombrich 1971: 46).

This statement may sound crazy to a reader brought up in the Abrahamic religious traditions of Islam, Judaism and Christianity, but it makes perfect sense in the local language of Sinhala where 'religion', as far as Buddhism is concerned, refs to a path leading beyond this world. Other ideas about spirits and gods are part of worldly life and defined quite differently. The names of some of the gods come from Hinduism, but this set of beliefs is not classified as 'religion' as far as local Buddhists are concerned. As discussed in Chapter 5, a parallel situation was found in post-Second World War Japan, where Buddhism is again regarded as 'religion', but indigenous ideas about gods and spirits, which form part of a complex known as Shinto, were described by many as 'superstition'.

Tylor's definition above may also include notions such as *magic* and witchcraft, which many would object fall outside the area of' 'religion' as such, and a category was subsequently developed of *magico-religious beliefs* which was broad enough to include all the above phenomena as well as ideas of pollution and taboo. Perhaps because of their own prejudices, based on deeply felt distinctions, several scholars tried to find ways of distinguishing between magic and religion, however (see Tambiah 1990 for a detailed historical analysis of this propensity from a Sri Lankan anthropologist). Sir James Frazer, whose monumental 12-volume The Golden Bough, addresses just these issues, argued for the following distinction:

> *Magic* assumes that in nature one event follows another necessarily and invariably without the intervention of a spiritual or personal agency. Thus its fundamental conception is identical with that of modern science; underlying the whole system is a faith, implicit but real and firm, in the order and uniformity of nature.   (1922: 49)

In contrast,

> *Religion* is a propitiation or conciliation of powers superior to man which are believed to control and direct the course of nature and of human life. Thus defined, religion consists of two basic elements, a theoretical and a practical, namely a belief in powers higher than man and an attempt to propitiate or please them   (ibid. 50)

With an abundance of examples, Frazer demonstrates that there are but two basic principles underlying the practice of magic. The first is that like produces like, so that a magician trying to bring about an effect may imitate the effect he wants to produce, for example by sticking pins into a model of the victim. This is what he calls *homeopathic* or *imitative magic*. The second, *contagious* magic, assumes that 'things which have once been in contact with each other continue to act on each other at a distance'. Thus, acting on something which was once part of a person will still affect that person even when no longer attached to them, leading to spells involving the hair, finger nails and so forth.

Frazer was writing in the evolutionary mode characteristic of his time when he suggested that there had been, everywhere, an Age of Magic, which was followed by an Age of Religion, when at least the more intelligent people realised the falsity of some of these theories and turned instead to superior beings. This move involved an assumption that nature is to some extent elastic or variable and subject to deflection by a mightier power, the opposite of the assumption which underpins both magic and science. Close observation proved this to be untrue, he argues, so thinking people moved into a third Age of Science, which rejects both the previous modes of thought. He then makes a wonderfully futuristic statement:

> Yet the history of thought should warn us against concluding that because scientific theory of the world is the best that has yet been formulated, it is necessarily complete and final. We must remember that ... the generalisations of *science*, or, in common parlance, the laws of nature are merely hypotheses devised to explain that ever-shifting phantasmagoria of thought which we dignify with the high-sounding names of the world and the universe. In the last analysis magic, religion, and science are nothing but theories of thought; and as science has supplanted its predecessors, so it may hereafter be superseded by some more perfect hypothesis ... (Ibid. 712)

In practice, it seems that magic and religion persist, even in a world dominated by scientific thought, and the 'more intelligent', or 'thinking people', as Frazer would have them, are by no means excluded. Malinowski took up this subject, and argued moreover that scientific thought exists everywhere, alongside ideas about magical powers. Based on his own experience with the 'savage' people of the Trobriand Islands, he argued in his essay *Magic, Science and Religion* (1974) that they were aware of and distinguished all three modes of thought, as defined above, demonstrating the existence of 'rational' explanations for technological routines, which form a body of knowledge easily comparable with what we call *science*.

He argued for a clear distinction between these and ideas of *magic* and *religion* to which people turned in times of uncertainty, and explains that Trobriand Islanders fishing in a lagoon, where conditions are known and quite safe, practise no magic, but when they venture out into the ocean, where there may be sudden changes in the weather, they take ritual precautions to seek to avert the possible danger. Furthermore, on the subject of the failure of magic always to succeed, he wrote:

> we should vastly underrate the savage's intelligence, logic and grasp of experience if we assumed that he is not aware of it and that he fails to account for it. (1974: 85)

Malinowski's distinction between magic and religion refines Frazer's on two levels. He proposes:

> *magic* as a practical art consisting of acts which are only means to a definite end expected to follow later on; *religion* as a body of self-contained acts being themselves the fulfilment of their purpose ...
> *Magic* ... had to be handed over in direct filiation from generation to generation ... it remains ... in the hands of specialists ... *Religion*, on the other hand, ... is an affair of all, in which everyone takes an active and equivalent part. (Ibid. 88–9)

One of the problems here is that, according to Malinowski's distinction, some of the practical aspects of religious worship in Roman Catholic countries look pretty much like magic: for example the conversion of bread and wine into the body and blood of Jesus Christ is an act with a very specific end, as are rites of exorcism, and so forth, and they are both carried out by priests who have been given much training, in other words experts whose role is hardly 'equal' to that of their parishioners.

Durkheim had proposed a similar distinction to the second half of Malinowski's one, however, when he insisted that religion needs a moral community, whereas in magic, laymen are merely clients. He formulated a definition of *religion* as:

> A unified system of beliefs and practices relative to sacred things, that is to say, things set apart and forbidden – beliefs and practices which unite into one single moral community called a Church, all those who adhere to them. (1915: 47)

This definition, while useful, presupposes the acceptance of a universal division of the universe into the two categories, sacred and profane, as well as a very corporate concept of the community, neither of which always hold up in practice. Indeed, in several societies the sacred, as we might understand the term in English, is found to pervade all spheres of life, and religious practice, where there are ascetics and other individuals who seek personal salvation, may also be found to be a very lonely and isolated pursuit. The case of Buddhism is a very pertinent one again, for the search for *nirvana* is precisely concerned with removing oneself from the social, though those who achieve it may be expected to return to help others along.

It has, over the years, proved very difficult to find an acceptable universal definition of religion, though there are clearly resemblances between the ideas of these different thinkers. Before continuing with the examination of indigenous ideas, let us turn to examine some of the ways in which those who drew up the definitions have investigated ideas about 'religion'.

Origins of Religion

In the nineteenth century people were greatly concerned with the origins of religion and they looked to the so-called primitive societies for ideas about how religion might have developed. This approach reflected contemporary scientific advances which were apparently disproving religious beliefs. By their very nature, these theories were speculative, but some of them had a great impact on the thinking of the time, and a few influenced social anthropology in quite a profound way. The various theories are discussed in a very readable manner in the book by Evans-Pritchard entitled *Theories of Primitive Religion* (1965) where they are divided into the psychological and the sociological.

Notable amongst the psychological were the rather similar, though independently developed theories of Herbert Spencer and Edward Tylor, which argued that notions of the spiritual were derived from the apparent existence of a dual self. There was the self of the waking world and the self of dreams, trances and death, as Spencer imagined the primitive person reasoning. He argued that as dead people could appear in dreams, the earliest idea of the supernatural must be associated with ghosts, so that ancestor worship must have been the first form of religion. It was inevitable, he argued, that ghosts would develop into gods, so that the offerings to the dead to please them would gradually become libations and sacrifices to the gods to propitiate them.

Tylor's theory was also rooted in the idea of a self of dreams, but he focused on the notion of a soul which could act separately from the body. He saw primitive people attributing souls also to animals and even to inanimate objects. These ideas constituted a primitive religion known as animism, according to Tylor, and these souls became the spirits of his minimal definition, which eventually developed into the gods and God of more highly developed religions, in which they took control of the destiny of man. Although anthropologists have come up with detailed descriptions of religions of this sort, which show great differences between them, common parlance still seems to describe animism as a kind of universal earlier form of religion.

animism – the attribution of souls or a spiritual existence to animals, plants and other natural objects, such as mountains and rocks, thought by early anthropologists to be an early stage of religion, a theory now shown to have no supporting evidence.

Evans-Pritchard points out that in both cases the arguments were mere speculation. Each of the writers simply imagines himself in the shoes of some so-called primitive man, but neither has any evidence at all that things did indeed develop in this way. Dreams may have led to speculations about souls and ghosts, but there is no real way of knowing, and there is no particular reason why these should have developed into gods. There were many other attempts to explain religion in this 'psychological' way, but Evans-Pritchard dismisses them all, pointing out that psychological states vary from one individual to another, and in one individual from time to time; therefore these states could not serve to explain social behaviour which exists independently of the psychological states it might or might not induce:

> in an individual's experience the acquisition of rites and beliefs precedes the emotions which are said to accompany them later in adult life. He learns to participate in them before he experiences any emotion at all, so the emotional state, whatever it may be, and if there is one, can hardly be the genesis and explanation of them. A rite is part of the culture the individual is born into, and it imposes itself on him from the outside, like the rest of his culture. It is a creation of society, not of individual reasoning or emotion, though it may satisfy both; and it is for this reason that Durkheim tells us that a psychological interpretation of a social fact is invariably a wrong interpretation. (1965: 6)

Evans-Pritchard goes on to discuss sociological theories, and the most ingenious is that of Durkheim himself explained in his book *Elementary Forms*

of the Religious Life (1915), where he also proposed the working definition quoted above. Durkheim was convinced that the simplest form of religion was a system known as a *totemic clan cult*, found amongst Australian Aborigines called the Arunta, and also in North America. This religion brought together the worship of ancestors with the notion of a totem to represent them. The totem was a sacred symbol which stood for the clan that it represented, and rites of worship served to recharge the sense of belonging and solidarity of the clan itself. God, for these people, was simply the clan itself divinised.

Durkheim argued that all the elements of more advanced religions were to be found in this system, which had elsewhere gradually developed over time, so that other religions were simply more complicated versions of the same idea. He marshalled evidence to demonstrate that rites in any religious system served to draw people together and to renew in them a sense of solidarity and communality as they worshipped their gods, which stood for the society, and eventually God, when **polytheism** gave way to **monotheism**. These actions were carried out by individuals, but they existed in collective form which transcended individual participation. The driving force was society itself, also the object of worship, so that God was simply society divinised.

Durkheim argued that in secular times the same function could be performed by patriotism. In the French Revolution a cult had arisen around the notions of the Fatherland, Liberty and Equality, and he hoped that humanitarian values would replace the spiritual ones. Evans-Pritchard admires Durkheim's 'brilliant and imaginative' theory, but he calls it yet another 'just-so story', based on insufficient and atypical ethnographic evidence (1965: 64). He chose totemism to discuss, assuming people with simple technology would have a similar simple religion, but this is only one kind of totemism, and even in other Australian groups it was quite different, nor was it particularly characteristic of all people with simple technology.

totemism – a term used by Émile Durkheim to describe what he thought was the earliest form of religion, which brought together the worship of ancestors with the notion of a **totem** to represent the clan to which they belonged.

Indeed, as we saw in the previous chapter, the 'totem' poles of Northwest America, where the word originated, have no such function. Again, the seeking of origins must be little more than conjecture, Evans-Pritchard argues. The theories may be true, but equally they may be false. As for totemism, the whole subject became something of an anthropological red herring, eventually dispensed very firmly by Lévi-Strauss in the early 1960s, when he applied his (then) new form of **structural analysis** to the subject to argue that theories about it said more about the theorists than the people under consideration, illustrating views prevalent at the time. In Europe, anyway, the word seems less used now than animism, and totem poles are, in popular thought, probably firmly back in place in Canada.

In the period since the first edition of this book was published and the second edition goes to press, there has again been some serious research on the evolution of religion, this time drawing on advances in cognitive science and cultural transmission. It is still an area of much discussion and debate, but one of its chief protagonists, Harvey Whitehouse, has set up two research centres on the subject called the Institute of Cognition and Culture and the Centre for Anthropology and Mind (websites listed below). More recently still, he has set up a new Institute for Cognitive and Evolutionary Anthropology to be headed up by the distinguished evolutionary anthropologist Robin Dunbar. Whitehouse's own theories focus on two divergent 'modes of religiosity', which he calls the imagistic and the doctrinal, around which different kinds of activity cluster depending on how behaviours are remembered. In the first case, highly arousing ritual plays a stronger part, leaving a lasting visual impression on the mind; the second is more concerned with the teaching, learning and interpretation of doctrine and narrative. Both draw on the findings of evolutionary psychology, and, as these theories develop, we may well have a new approach to this theme (see First-hand Account 14.2 on pp. 292–4 for further detail).

Explanations of Religious Phenomena

Eventually, anthropologists turned from trying to establish the origins of religious phenomena to seeking explanations of them within their social context. Durkheim's grand evolutionary religious theory may have foundered, but his insistence on the identification of **social facts** in any study continued to be much more influential. Instead of working out explanations of behaviour by trying to enter the mind of those participating, he urged researchers to seek social constraints which exist outside the individuals. Religious faiths and moral systems provide a rich source of such constraints into which any one individual is gradually socialised, and these also provide the social facts an anthropologist should seek.

The interpretation of these facts within the wider social context falls into various types, two of which have subsequently been described as '**functional**' and '**structural**', though they are not completely separate and the latter has at least two distinct forms. Examples of these will be given below, along with an attempt to explain this classification. We will also examine briefly the association of religious phenomena with moral systems, a subject which will recur in Chapter 9, and we will look at explanations of some new manifestations of religious phenomena which have arisen in times of great social change. Other examples of reactions to social change will emerge in the next chapter.

Functional Explanations

One set of sociological explanations of religion seeks to analyse religious rites for their capacity to promote social cohesion, to encourage a spirit of cooperation, and to support the social structure of a particular society, just as Durkheim proposed. These explanations also sought to relate religious systems to the social and political system in which they were found, and, as detailed ethnography became available, religious behaviour could be analysed as part of the total set of **social facts** to form a coherent system. Radcliffe-Brown's work was of this type, and his analysis of the religious life of the Andaman Islanders was a specific example of his more general theory on the subject, later to be dubbed **structural functionalism**.

Malinowski's approach, on the other hand, related religion, magic and the related subject of mythology to very specific human needs, providing what became known as essentially functional explanations. For example, he explained the magical practices associated with fishing at sea, where sudden storms might bring danger, as efforts to control adverse, unknown factors as opposed to the predictable ones associated with fishing in the safer lagoon. *Mourning rites* he explained as serving to reintegrate the group's shaken solidarity on losing a member, and to re-establish the morale of the community. There were personal benefits in comforting the bereaved, Malinowski argued, but he also saw the anthropologist's job as showing the value of phenomena for social integrity and the continuity of culture.

mythology – a term used by anthropologists to describe the study of myths, bodies of stories held by a people about themselves and their origins, described by Malinowski as a codification of belief, which acted as a charter for ritual, justifying rites, ceremonies and social and moral rules.

Mythology he saw as a 'codification of belief', which acted as a 'charter for ritual', justifying rites, ceremonies and social and moral rules. Thus, for example, myths about the points of origin of local groups he explained as justification for the clan hierarchy, and myths concerned with death as a kind of screen between man and 'the vast emotional void' which would otherwise gape beyond death (1974: 38). It may sound sacrilegious and somewhat trite to say so, but this line of argument brings the great books of world faiths, such as the Bible and the Qur'an, into the category of mythology, because they serve much the same purpose. We need to recognise that the English-language use of the word 'mythology' implies a disbelief which is disrespectful of people who may hold their own myths as truth.

Following the line of argument which sees *science* as another type of faith, we can better understand the conflicts and rows which arose in the nineteenth century when Darwin proposed a theory of evolution which appeared directly to disagree with the explanation of the origins of the human race propounded in Genesis. Those who took both seriously felt they had to decide which one to 'believe', and this period could be seen as a turning point in the dislocation of security. In complex societies, people have come to live with apparently conflicting world views, and their cosmologies may include elements which could also be described as 'scientific', 'religious' and even 'magical'. Indeed, in Japan, a sick person may well consult a diviner as well as a doctor, as we will see in the next chapter, and he or she may also visit a shrine or temple to pray for recovery (Ohnuki-Tierney 1984).

Let me start from the perceived tension between objective analysis, on the one hand, and belief and participation in a religious 'world view', on the other (see p. 137) for this is matter on which I have had to reflect, being both an ordained Anglican priest and a trained academic anthropologist.

It is worth observing that different Churches and Denominations hold different and distinctive attitudes towards the world, towards the society they are part of and the political structures of that society. Different Denominations will find specific social scientific approaches attractive as being compatible with their particular approach; Anglicanism finds its broad world view readily supported and confirmed by the practices and concerns of (British) social anthropology.

First-hand account 7:

Timothy Jenkins, English – on Anglicanism and Anthropology

I have found the experience of fieldwork a good preparation for parish ministry, and there is compatibility between the tasks of the priest and those of the anthropologist. For example, the clergy live in their parishes, taking an interest in the well-being of the place and the people it contains over a long period of time, just like anthropologists. But more importantly, there is a congruency in the two disciplines of paying attention to a place and the forms of life that it contains, and to the resources for living well or badly that underwrite these forms. Clearly, the knowledge is not required for the same purposes, but it is the same kind of knowledge.

The task of the priest is to enter into the lives of the people who make up the parish, to understand their concerns, limits and opportunities, and to respond to some of these concerns on the basis of the Christian tradition they represent. For example, the occasional offices concerned with marriages, births and deaths cannot be conducted well without involvement in and knowledge of the lives of those who attend the services. A parish ministry from this perspective might be seen in terms of a double apprenticeship of the meanings both of those lives and of the ceremonies themselves.

England

From an anthropologist's point of view, it is a good thing to have a particular role to fulfil – in my case, that of a priest – which also gives a privileged access to all kinds of institutions, lives and activities. But the priestly task always takes precedence over anthropological interest, both at the time and in any writing up, and this imposes clear restrictions upon what can be said. However, these constraints operate in all kinds of knowledge; all human knowledge is ethical, and everyone has to judge what may be said under the particular circumstances they are in. In this sense, the good informant, the good priest and the good anthropologist are all in the same situation: the information they give will be on the basis of a series of judgements and responsible decisions. Anthropology as a human science is inescapably concerned with moral knowledge.

Doubts as to whether the anthropological conflicts with the priestly task may also be expressed from the Christian side, on the grounds that it is not a priest's task simply to understand, but also to make a difference and to cause an alteration in the circumstances being considered. There is a tension observed between the 'is' of description and the 'ought' contained in a particular Christian world view. This perspective, of course, mirrors the reservations implied in the sociological account; the fear that an objective account will be interfered with by the demands of faith matches the resistance to a properly objective account on the part of believers. And the same sort of answer can be given in either case: knowledge of any kind, including objective knowledge, is constructed through complex, collective moral practices, and sound or reliable knowledge is constructed carefully in each case, while unreliable knowledge is constructed hastily and without due procedure.

So the contrast is less between the motivated nature of faith engagements and the objective nature of sociological ones, than between good judgement and less well-founded judgement in either case. In short, truth – whether religious or sociological – is a difficult business; what matters is the calibre of the persons you deal with rather than their presuppositions about what counts and does not count as knowledge. Participation and belief are, indeed, an integral part of objective knowledge, and not to be contrasted with it.

See the Jenkins entries under the 'References and Further Reading' section at the end of this chapter to find out more about these views.

In some ways, Malinowski went too far in making such a clear distinction between magic, science and religion, because his definitions did not always apply elsewhere, as we noted above. However, it is useful, if sometimes a little alarming, to consider that even experimentally based 'science' is part of a wider cosmology, in the same way as magic and religion. They all aim to provide theories about the world, as Frazer suggested, and they all also offer practical, functional ways of dealing with problems. After all, for many readers, 'science' may also be rather mystical, even if you may have more faith in it to offer explanations of illness and disaster than you do in magic or religion – but it is *faith*, rather than knowledge, in many cases!

Even practising scientists are aware of the mysteries that remain to be explained, and the extent to which they make assumptions that may later prove to be unfounded. Much of their learning is of 'theories', which are based on the best available understanding of a phenomenon at the time they were made, but which may well be disproved as further knowledge comes to light. Medical doctors are aware too of the enormous psychological value of their prescriptions, and they are not averse to offering what is known as a *placebo*, which has no specific pharmaceutical value, if they feel their patients will benefit. Practitioners of East Asian medicine tend to allow more time and attention to their patients than Western doctors do, because they see this as an important part of the healing process. Indeed, indigenous knowledge from most societies offers a whole range of efficacious healing mechanisms which lack the kinds of explanations that Western experimental scientists would accept.

The most frightening diseases are those which appear to have no cure, or worse, no understanding, such as AIDS and certain forms of cancer. Once diagnosed by 'scientific' rationale as a hopeless case, sufferers and their families anywhere are often open to suggestions about alternative healers, and they may travel long distances if they feel there is a chance that they could be 'magically' cured. A friend of mine who was told she was suffering from terminal cancer travelled from Oxford to Mexico to learn about a special diet, which held her symptoms at bay for several years. The strength of public support for this kind of venture may be seen when communities raise the funds to send a local child halfway around the world to be treated at a clinic of special renown. Functional explanations work rather well with this kind of faith that somewhere there may be an effective way of dealing with a life-threatening problem.

A Structural Approach

Another influential approach, which differs quite fundamentally from the structural functional, as it was called (which examined the **functional** role of components of a particular society for maintaining the social **structure**), is the **structural analysis** of the French anthropologist Claude Lévi-Strauss, who was more interested in a universal organisational capacity of the human mind. We have mentioned that he applied this method to the subject of **totemism**, but he developed his ideas most successfully in the analysis of **mythology**, including nursery rhymes, just-so stories and other collectively owned materials, when he noticed amazing similarities in the structure of stories from widely separated parts of the world.

> Mythology confronts the student with a situation which at first sight appears contradictory. On the one hand it would seem that in the course of a myth anything is likely to happen. There is no logic, no continuity. Any characteristic can be attributed to any subject; every conceivable relation can be found. With myth, everything becomes possible. But on the other hand, this apparent arbitrariness is belied by the astounding similarity between myths collected in widely different regions. Therefore the problem: If the content of a myth is contingent, how are we going to explain the fact that myths throughout the world are so similar?   (Lévi-Strauss 1963: 08)

Lévi-Strauss collected huge volumes of stories, including several different versions of the same tale, divided them up into what he perceived as their smallest elements, and analysed the structure which he felt was common to all, by looking at the relations between these elements. He concluded that they act as devices for apparently mediating important and usually impossible oppositions such as those between life and death, man and god, nature and culture. The analyses are often long, complicated and not always immediately convincing, but to give a flavour of the idea let us examine part of his attempt to explain why the role of a *trickster* is so often played by a raven or a coyote in many native American myths.

> If we keep in mind that mythical thought always progresses from the awareness of oppositions towards their resolution, the reason ... becomes clearer. We need only assume that two opposite terms with no intermediary always tend to be replaced by two equivalent terms which admit of a third one as a mediator; then one of the polar terms and the mediator become replaced by a new triad, and so on.   (Ibid. 224)

Through this process, Lévi-Strauss identifies a mediating structure in the Native American myths in which the initial pair *life* and *death* is replaced by a triad of agriculture (on the life side), warfare on the death side, and hunting in the middle (as having qualities of each). This is in its turn replaced by a further triad, where herbivorous animals replace agriculture, beasts of prey replace warfare, and carrion-eating animals, such as the ubiquitous raven and coyote, appear in the mediating position, again as having some qualities of each of the others. A story centred around one of these ambiguous characters thus usually appears to mediate the actually irreconcilable opposition between life and death.

Further details of this analysis, and other aspects of Lévi-Strauss's work, may be pursued in his book *Structural Anthropology* (1963), which serves as a good preliminary to the more difficult tomes of mythological analysis which he has also published, with intriguing titles such as *The Raw and the Cooked* and *From*

Honey to Ashes. Another good and relatively accessible analysis of myth is to be found in his essay, the 'Myth of Asdiwal' (Lévi-Strauss 1967). Because the oppositions he considers are usually impossible actually to mediate, characters who appear in the myths tend to be the same anomalous or abnormal beings such as monsters, incarnate deities or virgin mothers, which, we noted in Chapter 2, provide the focus for taboos and ritual observance.

Edmund Leach, who introduced those ideas in a consideration of language, also put forward an interesting structural analysis in his *Genesis as Myth* (1969), mentioned in passing in Chapter 5, where he sets out to resolve the paradox that Christians, who forbid incest, are all descended from Adam and Eve. He argues that a series of stories which offer a number of examples of incest, some worse than others, place the tribal neighbours of the Israelites in varying degrees of inferior status. By comparison, the marriage of Abraham to his paternal half-sister seems almost virtuous, he argues. This, and indeed some of Lévi-Strauss's analysis, actually confirms a functional role, as Malinowski suggested, justifying the status quo in a particular social configuration.

The structural approach to religion may actually supplement the functional explanations discussed above, which have also been called *instrumental* explanations. As well as looking at the function of certain rites, the idea is to look for *meaning* which may be described as *expressive*, which may tell us something about the delineation of the important categories of society, or, as Radcliffe-Brown put it, 'express ... their fundamental notions of life and nature' (1964: 330). In a more formal structural mode, however, we are back to the identification of systems of classification, and the association of anomalous and abnormal beings with mediation of impossible oppositions is another way to identify the liminal middle ground between these categories.

In the case of **rites of passage** people are moved from one category to another – an *instrumental* aspect of the rite, creating new adults, or members of a particular group, or moving people safely from one area or time zone to another, but the rites themselves divide up life into meaningful chunks, just as they divide up space and time for that particular people. This is the *expressive* aspect. Looking at religious activities in a structural way therefore also means looking for what they can tell us about the dividing up of people and their world. In a very readable ethnography about how the Zapotec people of Oaxaca, Mexico, categorise and celebrate the dead members of their society (Haley and Fukuda 2004), we can also learn how the teachings of the Catholic Church have been adapted and accommodated to strong expressive and instrumental ideas that pre-dated their arrival.

Many other studies demonstrate the structural role of religious activities in any one case. My own work in Mexico revealed a neat parallel between the Holy Family emphasised by Mexican Catholics, which places the Virgin of Guadalupe (see First-hand Account 3.2 on pp. 60–1) in a position of greater importance than God, or even Jesus, and the actual Mexican family, where the mother very often plays the dominant role in holding things together. Mexican men sometimes have two or three different nuclear families they have fathered, and they are peripheral in the maintenance of even one. The real source of stability in any particular case is the mother who must find a way to provide for her children, so it is small wonder that Mexicans of both sexes prefer to bring their important prayers to a female source of divine power.

John Middleton's book *Lugbara Religion* (1960), based on fieldwork in the Uganda/Belgian Congo borders in the 1950s, is an excellent example of an ethnography organised to present the expressive role of religious activities, which centre around ancestor worship held at shrines associated with the lineage groups important in everyday life:

> The cult of the dead is intimately connected with the maintenance of lineage authority. The exercise and acknowledgement of this authority are bound up with the cycle of lineage development. Senior men attempt to sustain their authority against their juniors' claim to independence, and the consequent conflict is conceived largely in mystical and ritual terms ... I show how the men of a single lineage group manipulate the cult of the dead as a means to the acquisition and retention of authority. (Middleton 1960: v)

The chapters of the book are organised in such a way that the background information about Lugbara social and political life is presented first, then the details of the cults of the dead, both material and conceptual, after which the chief focus of the book – the ritual action – may be understood in its proper context. Finally, Middleton addresses the effect of the religious ideas on the moral community. The overall picture is one in which religious ideas reflect the social life of the Lugbara people, which is physically mapped out in the arrangement of shrines within the village compound.

Religion as a Moral System

Clearly, in considering large world religions such as Christianity, Islam, Judaism and the Indian religions, an important aspect of their role in society is to lay out the moral order by which people are expected to live. They are associated with books and teaching, much of which is concerned with spelling out these ethical codes. As mentioned briefly in Chapter 3, giving freely is usually a part of these codes, and it is their basis in soteriology or salvation of one sort or another which allows the principles of reciprocity to be applied to this apparent generosity, though it may not be seen in exactly that way. In these cases explanations of this world and the next will be inextricably linked to ideas of behaviour acceptable to the wider society.

soteriology – a term used to refer to ideas about salvation in any particular system of cosmology, notably in the religious traditions that are based on written scriptures, where they form part of a broad moral system.

In most Western countries, the legal system is influenced by Judaeo-Christian ideas, though now often tempered with a fair degree of 'humanism', and in the Islamic world much legislation is rooted in the Qur'an. Punishment meted out to criminals and others who break the law is often justified in moral terms, and those who escape the earthly justice system may fear retribution in heaven, or 'the other place'. The idea of 'burning in hell' is still part of common parlance, or at least it was until early 1996 when the Church of England declared hell a much less fiery place, perhaps in recognition of the fact that people are probably less worried that this will be their fate than they used to be.

Not all religious traditions include such a clear connection with laying out a moral code. Indeed, in small-scale societies, moral values and the ideas that may be termed religious pervade social life so completely that neither can be clearly separated from the rest of social interaction. Ancestors may be seen as the repositories of moral order, and illness and other misfortunes may be interpreted as an expression of their wrath, incurred almost immediately because of contraventions of moral or social rules. However, there may be no notion of sacredness associated with the activities of these former human beings. Explanations of misfortune may also manifest themselves in other ways, as we will see in Chapter 8. A more detailed consideration of social rules and the various mechanisms for their enforcement will be the subject matter of Chapter 9, on social control.

Cults: The Persistence of Religious Movements

Contrary to the evolutionary expectations mentioned at the beginning of this chapter, and despite the predictions of sociologists and others that modernisation would bring with it secularisation in the world at large, religion does not seem to be giving way to more 'rational' ways of explaining the world. Indeed, new religious sects are appearing abundantly around the world – and there is quite a variety to choose from. In Japan, some people turn from one to another, seeking solutions to problems they may be experiencing, and in several countries around the world Japanese new religious groups are quite active. The neighbour in Japan mentioned in Chapter 3, who introduced me to the niceties of meeting further neighbours, became a Christian shortly after I left, and I came back to find two or three Japanese Buddhists among my students.

New religious movements have often appeared in times of great social change and upheaval, according to another variety of anthropological explanation, and some special *cults* demonstrate an interesting expression of cultural confusion. Typically where the lives of one people have been profoundly affected by the invasion, however peaceful, of another, religious reactions can be shown to express efforts to adjust in one way or another to the new situation. In North America, for example, there was widespread practice of a 'ghost dance' amongst the Plains Indians whose land and livelihood had been devastated by the arrival of Europeans. The aim of the dance was to rid the ancestral land of these cruel and destructive invaders and bring about a return of the native bison they had hunted. The medium was prayer to the ancestors through dance.

Native Americans, called First Nations in Canada, have in fact made some considerable progress in renewing their association with their lands and their ancestors, though they may not have succeeded in expelling the 'invaders', and there are now even new herds of bison being bred. The Red Power movement of the 1960s was perhaps the turning point, with the occupation of the Island of Alcatraz and the site of their massacre at Wounded Knee. A first-hand description of this period, and its religious associations, is graphically portrayed in the book *Lakota Woman* by Mary Crow Dog (1991), who gave birth to her first son during their siege at Wounded Knee. Local activities of a spiritual or 'religious' nature are practised all over the Americas, but there is an interesting Pan-Indian movement that has emerged, and the annual Sundance gathering that takes place at Pipestone, Minnesota is one event that expresses this new form of identity.

Even more spectacular examples of religious reaction to the arrival of outsiders sometimes took place at considerable distance from the new settlement so that knowledge of the invaders was largely second-hand. Cults would grow up whose aim was to achieve the greater standard of living which had been observed, possibly only by one or a few prophet-like figures, and the aim was again a kind of moral regeneration of society. Usually, there would be a charismatic leader, and the results were sometimes devastating. In one part of South America, for example, a whole congregation of indigenous people jumped off a cliff, believing that they would subsequently be reborn white, with all the advantages they had heard that would bring.

In Melanesia, cults arose which have become known as 'cargo cults', for their practices were aimed at attracting the goods to which they saw white people had access. Some of these have been brought to the attention of the public in film and on stage. A Jacques Tati film showed a group of people building an airport in the hope that they could attract the enormous birds they saw delivering all manner of good things to the white people who had settled nearby. A stage play entitled *Sergeant Ola and His Followers* illustrated even in its title the role of the charismatic leader. In this production, local people dressed up as whites and spent their time trying to replicate their activities, reading newspapers and tapping away at a typewriter, although they were in fact still illiterate.

Peter Worsley's book *The Trumpet Shall Sound* (1970) includes a comprehensive survey of these cults, which were found in various parts of New Guinea as well as in Fiji, the Solomon Islands and the New Hebrides. He also calls them millenarian movements because of their similarity to movements found all over the world that are characterised by a belief in the imminence of the end of the world, some of which occurred in Europe in the run up to the year 1000. The expectation is that a cataclysm will destroy everything, but that the ancestors, or some prior god, will return and liberate the people from their new oppressors, incidentally making available all the goods these same oppressors seem to own. Hence the preparations.

These movements are, of course, not peculiar to Melanesia, as Worsley himself points out, nor are they only to be discovered in the anthropological fieldnotes of the past, especially as another new millennium has now been entered. The shocking release of poisonous gas in the Tokyo underground in 1995, and the mass suicide/murder of members of the Branch Dravidian cult in Waco, Texas, two years before that, may both be seen as examples of the continuing power of people preaching about the end of the world. The tale of the Japanese group Aum Shinrikyo, which has been blamed for the deaths and injuries in Tokyo, is a textbook example of a millennium cult. In a well-informed study of the group, Ian Reader writes of its leader, Asahara Shōko:

> He ... achieved prominence because of his frequent, drastic prophecies, which stated that an apocalypse would occur before the end of the century to engulf the vast majority of humanity and sweep away the corrupt material world and destroy Japanese society. He proclaimed that he was a messiah who had come to save his followers from the apocalypse and lead them forward to form a new, ideal spiritual universe that would emerge from the ruins of the old.   (1996: 2)

Worsley's survey concludes by putting the Melanesian material in a broader anthropological and historical context, where he identifies common features in a wide range of different movements. Resistance to oppression is a common theme, as is the drawing together of a new, and possibly powerful amalgamation of smaller groups. The promise of a better life is of course another powerful characteristic, and the charismatic leader is a virtual *sine qua non*. These cults allow a kind of generalisation, which is rare in anthropological literature, and Worsley's book is an accessible example of how this may be done.

Conclusion

This chapter has been concerned with several ways in which anthropologists have dealt with categories like religion, cults, magic and mythology, but largely in their own terms, or applying their own terms across the board to draw up theories that hold good in a comparative context. Many of these theories were short-lived and floundered on the ethnographic evidence, although one or two, like our last example, have stood better the test of time, and the arrival of new phenomena. In the next chapter we turn again to an examination of the more culturally specific, which allows a more informed interpretation of the 'magico-religious' phenomena found in any one place.

Discussion Questions

1 What does the word 'religion' mean to you? Compare your idea with those of some of your friends. Do you have a collective view?

2 Remember the functionalist questions at the end of the Introduction to this book? Consider the extent to which religions may respond to those basic needs? What are the limitations to this approach?

3   Consider the idea that 'science' is a world view, like a faith or a belief system. For example, how much 'science' do you take on trust? Can you think of occasions when 'scientists' have been discredited? Does this undermine your faith in 'science', and if not, why not?

References and Further Research

Books
Bowie, Fiona (2005) *The Anthropology of Religion*, 2nd edn (Oxford: Blackwell Publishing).

Boyer, Pascal (2001) *Religion Explained: The Human Instincts That Fashion Spirits and Ancestors* (London: Heinemann).

Burridge, Kenelm (1960) *Mambu: A Melanesian Millennium* (London: Methuen).

Durkheim, Emile (1915) *The Elementary Forms of the Religious Life*, translated J. W. Swain (London: George Allen & Unwin).

Evans-Pritchard, E. E. (1965) *Theories of Primitive Religion* (Oxford: Clarendon Press).

Frazer, Sir James George (1922) *The Golden Bough: A Study in Magic and Religion*, abridged edition (London: Macmillan).

Gombrich, Richard (1971) *Precept and Practice: Traditional Buddhism in the Rural Highlands of Ceylon* (Oxford: Clarendon Press).

Haley, Shawn D. and Fukuda, Curt (2004) *Day of the Dead: When Two Worlds Meet in Oaxaca* (Oxford: Berghahn).

Hendry, Joy (2005) *Reclaiming Culture: Indigenous People and Self-Representation* (Basingstoke: Palgrave Macmillan).

Jenkins, Timothy (1999) *Religion in English Everyday Life: An Ethnographic Approach* (Oxford: Berghahn).

Jenkins, Timothy (2006) *An Experiment in Providence: How Faith Engages with the World* (London: Society for Promoting Christian Knowledge).

Leach, Edmund (1969) *Genesis as Myth and Other Essays* (London: Cape Editions).

Lévi-Strauss, Claude (1963) *Structural Anthropology* (Harmondsworth: Penguin Books).

Lindstrom, Lamont (1993) *Cargo Cult: Strange Stories of Desire from Melanesia and Beyond* (Honolulu: University of Hawaii Press).

Malinowski, Bronislaw (1974) *Magic, Science and Religion* (London: The Free Press).

Middleton, John (1960) *Lugbara Religion: Ritual and Authority among an East African People* (London: Oxford University Press for the International African Institute).

Morris, Brian (1987) *Anthropological Studies of Religion: An Introductory Text* (Cambridge: Cambridge University Press).

Ohnuki-Tierney, Emiko (1984) *Illness and Culture in Contemporary Japan* (Cambridge: Cambridge University Press).

Radcliffe-Brown, A. R. (1984) *The Andaman Islanders* (New York: Free Press).

Reader, Ian (1996) *A Poisonous Cocktail: Aum Shinrikyo's Path to Violence* (Copenhagen: Nordic Institute for Asian Studies).

Tambiah, Stanley Jeyaraja (1990) *Magic, Science, Religion, and the Scope of Rationality* (Cambridge: Cambridge University Press).

Tylor, Edward B. (1913) *Primitive Culture*, vol. 2 (London: John Murray).

Whitehouse, H. (2004) *Modes of Religiosity: A Cognitive Theory of Religious Transmission* (Walnut Creek, Cal.: AltaMira Press).

Worsley, Peter (1970) *The Trumpet Shall Sound: A Study of 'Cargo' Cults in Melanesia* (London: Paladin).

Articles

Caplan, Lionel (1985) 'Fundamentalism Pursued', *Anthropology Today*, 1(4): 18–19.

Engelke, Matthew (2002) 'The Problem of Belief: Evans-Pritchard and Victor Turner on "the Inner Life"', *Anthropology Today*, 18(6): 3–6.

Leach, Edmund (1969) 'Genesis as Myth', in *Genesis as Myth and Other Essays* (London: Cape Editions).

Lévi-Strauss, Claude (1963) 'The Structural Study of Myth', in *Structural Anthropology* (Harmondsworth: Penguin Books, 1963).

Lévi-Strauss, Claude (1967) 'The Myth of Asdiwal' in Edmund Leach (ed.), *The Structural Study of Myth and Totemism* (London: Tavistock).

Webber, Jonathan (1985) 'Religions in the Holy Land: Conflicts of Interpretation', *Anthropology Today*, 1(2): pp. 3–10.

Novels and Other Works of Interest

Crow Dog, Mary (1991) *Lakota Woman* (New York: Harper Perennial) is the moving first-person account of the wife of a medicine man during the Native American revival movement.

Eco, Umberto (1983) *The Name of the Rose* (London: Vintage Classics) is a murder mystery set in an Italian monastery in 1327.

Endo, Shusaku (1976) *Silence* (London: Peter Owen) tells the story of two European missionaries whose less than successful work in Japan finds them seeking some sign from God that their work is not in vain.

Hillerman, Tony (1993) *Sacred Clowns* (Harmondsworth: Penguin) is a murder mystery involving two Native American detectives and a sacred festival.

Kneale, Matthew (2001) *English Passengers* (London: Penguin) is a novel set in the nineteenth century about a fanatically religious traveller and his encounters with people of different origins, notably Manx and Tasmanian.

Trollope, Joanna (1992) *The Choir* (London: Black Swan) takes the reader into a fictional world of politics, scandal and social relations in a Church of England community.

Films

The Dervishes of Kurdistan (Brian Moser, André Singer and Ali Bulookbashi, 1973) illustrates some of the extraordinary feats people with strong faith are able to perform.

The Kalasha: Rites of Spring (John Sheppard and Peter Parkes, 1990) is another very good 'Disappearing World' film about a minority people living in the mountains of Pakistan who resist the surrounding Islamic influence.

Koriam's Law, or the Death Who Governs (Gary Kildea and Andrea Simon, 110 minutes, 2005). Australian anthropologist Andrew Lattas and Peter Avarea of Pomio, New Britain, Papua New Guinea explore the Pomio Kivung movement and the phenomenon of the Melanesian cargo cult.

Native Spirit and the Sun Dance Way (World Wisdom, 2007). Thomas Yellowtail, a revered Crow Medicine Man and Sun Dance Chief for over 30 years, describes and explains the ancient ceremony that is sacred to the Crow tribe.

Tantra of Gyuto: Sacred Rituals of Tibet (1985), a documentary, introduced by the Dalai Lama and directed by S. Rochlin *et al.*, about the lives and spiritualism of Tibetan tantric monks, with coverage of various historical events.

Websites

http://www.isca.ox.ac.uk/research/cognitive_research.shtml – the site for the Centre for Anthropology and Mind.

http://www.qub.ac.uk/schools/InstituteofCognitionCulture/ – the site for the Institute of Cognition and Culture.

http://66.249.93.104/search?q=cache:Xm3xEWhGSDEJ:www.routledge-ny.com/ref/modfrenchthought/levistrauss.PDF+%27levi-strauss+anthropology%27&hl=en&client=firefox-a – a general overview and introduction to Lévi-Strauss and other anthropologists.

http://varenne.tc.columbia.edu/bib/info/taxoosol53appranth.html – a discussion between Lévi-Strauss and other anthropologists

http://varenne.tc.columbia.edu/bib/auth/levstcld0.html – a list of some of Lévi-Strauss' works and links to extracts from various texts

http://www.geocities.com/axeopoafonja/ – a site with information about Candomblé, an Afro-Brazilian spiritualist movement.

8

Cosmology II: Witchcraft, Shamanism and Syncretism

Indigenous Categories of Cosmology

In this chapter, we will turn to examine in detail some important categories which have interested anthropologists over the years, and in which they have sometimes engaged in interesting dialogue with historians. The first subjects are witchcraft and sorcery, which are not without intriguing meaning in the English language, but we will turn for our initial definitions to an African people studied by one of the better-known British anthropologists introduced in the last chapter, namely Edward Evans-Pritchard. The people are the Azande, a tribe of the Southern Sudan, for whom the word *mangu*, translated as 'witchcraft', was perhaps the most commonly used in their language when Evans-Pritchard lived among them. It was a matter of daily discussion, irritating rather than frightening, and, as an ethnographer, he could hardly ignore it.

Evans-Pritchard chose this subject for his study because it clearly pervaded the thinking of the Zande people and he real-ised that an understanding of their social life depended upon an understanding of their ideas about witchcraft. He became aware that their moral universe was not constructed around a Supreme Being, or the ghosts of ancestors, but around their ideas about witchcraft. The practice of witchcraft he found was almost synonymous with bad character, with greed and jealousy:

> witches tend to be those whose behaviour is least in accordance with social demands. Those whom we would call good citizens – and, of course, the richer and more powerful members of society are such – are seldom accused of witchcraft, while those who make themselves a nuisance to their neighbours and those who are weak are most likely to be accused. (1976: 52)

The study of witchcraft thus provided an essential key to understanding Zande systems of thought and paved the way to deciphering many related aspects of their social and political life.

Evans-Pritchard's work among the Azande also allowed him to devise theory about witchcraft which proved highly influential amongst ethnographers making observations in a wide range of other societies. His analysis has thus provided a basis for comparison with almost all the further studies which have been made. Some of these agree with his ideas, providing further examples of the general principles, others offer modifications or alternative types of analysis. None ignore his work, and even if only for this reason, it seems essential to start with his study and the theory it engendered. It is also a fascinating case, written in an extremely accessible style, so it is an excellent introduction for the student of witchcraft phenomena.

It is not everywhere that notions of witchcraft were found to be important, however, and other indigenous categories are thought better translated as spirit possession, shamanism, and so forth. These phenomena are discussed in the second part of the chapter, again with an emphasis on local understanding. In the last part of the chapter some attention is paid to places where ideas and beliefs from more than one religious tradition appear to coexist quite happily, a phenomenon again quite difficult to comprehend from the perspective of Europe and the Middle East, where history would be decimated if it ignored the many times people and places have been ravaged by religious wars. This is another area in which the knowledge acquired by anthropologists might be put to good use, were people convinced to listen.

Terminology

The terms witchcraft and sorcery were, until Evans-Pritchard's time, used rather unsystematically to describe a wide variety of ideas held in different parts of the world about mystical powers which people may possess. This power may have been thought to be a psychic one, with which a person is born, or a skill which can be learned, and perhaps passed on through an initiation ceremony. It may have been thought to emanate from the body, perhaps even unconsciously, or to be manipulated con-

witchcraft – ideas about psychic powers thought to be held by certain people, and the associated practices held to harness them, or sometimes to oppose them.

sorcery – ideas about the use of medicines and other occult powers, usually for evil ends, and the ways in which these are passed on from one practitioner to another.

sciously through the use of spells. Evans-Pritchard, in his classic book *Witchcraft, Oracles and Magic among the Azande* (1976), made clear a distinction between witchcraft and sorcery, which he saw as an evil form of magic, based on these sorts of characteristics. The distinction includes the following elements:

Witchcraft	*Sorcery*
• a psychic power	• use of medicines for evil ends
• often hereditary	• anyone can learn it
• may be unconscious	• conscious

This distinction was based initially on the Azande case, where witchcraft was said to be inherited in the male or female line, i.e. passed from father to son, or mother to daughter, although Evans-Pritchard did notice that this was not always the most important criterion when people were trying to identify a possible witch to accuse. The power was thought to reside in a substance in the belly, but this power could lie dormant or 'cool' indefinitely, and would only be activated if its owner became angry or jealous. People could also be entirely unaware of their power and it was held to be something of an individual quality for it to become active. If the witch died, an autopsy was said to confirm whether or not the substance had been present; however, the colonial government banned these operations, so Evans-Pritchard was not able to observe them.

Sorcery, on the other hand, was held to be a skill which could be learned, and passed on through conscious study. It was defined as the evil use of medicines, a practice also known as black magic, thereby seen as parallel to white magic used for positive purposes. Anyone with an interest could learn these skills and put them into practice, whereas the activation of witchcraft power was held often to be unconscious as well as limited to those with the substance in their bodies. The distinction is also held to distinguish kings and princes in Zande society from commoners, for the former are said to be both incapable of and immune to witchcraft, whereas they may be subject to the evil effects of sorcery.

wizardry – beliefs which people have about the capabilities and activities of others and the action which they take to avoid attacks or to counter them when they believe they have occurred (Middleton).

Evans-Pritchard's distinction holds up rather well cross-culturally, but it is not possible to make in every society, and other efforts have been made to delineate the same sort of subject matter. For example, in their book *Witchcraft and Sorcery in East Africa* (1963) the authors John Middleton and E. H. Winter suggest the term wizardry to cover all such mystical activities. Another suggestion, made by I. M. Lewis in an article he contributed to the collection edited by Mary Douglas, entitled *Witchcraft: Confessions and Accusations* (1970) was that spirit possession be included together with witchcraft and sorcery in a notion of *mystical attack*, which could

spirit possession – an engagement with the spirit world distinguished from others (by Raymond Firth) as largely involuntary, though some (like Lewis) interpret possession as invited – either way, a spirit is thought to express itself through a human being, causing the latter to engage in extraordinary behaviour.

be classified as *oblique* or *direct*, depending on the perceived motives of the accuser, rather than the accused. Lewis pointed out that it is after all the accuser who initiates the attack of public opinion against the witch, who in the end is the victim of social action, and this is parallel to some of his ideas about spirit possession. We will return to the subject of possession later in the chapter. In the meantime, however, let us turn to examine further the ideas of Evans-Pritchard, gleaned from the Azande.

Roles of Witchcraft and Sorcery Beliefs

The most influential aspects of the theory about witchcraft which Evans-Pritchard drew up were his considerations of the roles ideas about witchcraft played in relation to norms of good behaviour in Zande society. His discussion about these roles can be laid out under four headings, and in the pages that follow we can draw also on comparisons from other studies of witchcraft and sorcery. Perhaps most widespread of all is the way witchcraft could provide an explanation of misfortune.

(1) Witchcraft as an Explanation of Misfortune

Amongst the Azande people, witchcraft would be blamed for all kinds of unfortunate events which occurred in everyday life. Crop failure, illness, or simply a lack of fish could all be put down to witchcraft, although Evans-Pritchard emphasises that the Azande were not unaware of natural causes, such as adverse weather conditions, as well. Perhaps his most famous illustration of this principle is when he describes the Zande explanation of the collapse of a granary on a group of people eating their lunch. They know that the granary supports had been eaten by termites, he asserts, and they knew that the people sitting under the granary were doing it to take advantage of the shade it offered. It is witchcraft, however, which explains why the granary fell down at that particular time on those particular people.

In Evans-Pritchard's view, witchcraft carries an explanation to its logical conclusion. It explains why misfortune happens to certain people at a certain time, and in this way, explanations are carried one stage further than they may be elsewhere. A common view for someone involved in a car crash, for example, may be to ponder whether if they'd left home a few minutes later they would not have been hit by that person jumping a light. Someone missing a plane or bus that crashed might feel strangely lucky or protected. They may wonder about 'fate', 'destiny', 'luck' or 'acts of god', but with less immediate confidence than the Azande have, who are quite sure about why particular people are in the path of misfortune at a particular time – it's due to witchcraft.

Other belief systems have a similar confidence, however. For example, a Muslim's view of misfortune may see it immediately as an act of God. Indeed, an expression commonly used in Islamic circles allows for this intervention when a person modifies an arrangement by adding *insh'Allah*, meaning 'God-willing', to their proposed plans. In Western countries there seems to be a need to find a human cause for misfortune, so that a disaster will be followed by a court of inquiry to see where the blame lies. In an air crash, it is always important to seek the 'black box', for example, and ferry disasters have led to considerable modification to the design and execution of the journey. A disaster seems somehow less destructive in the long run if some action may be taken, and this is another role which notions of witchcraft allow.

(2) Witchcraft Provides Some Action which May Be Taken

The second role played by witchcraft is that ideas about it offer clear steps which may be taken to alleviate the misfortune. Just as one feels better about illness if someone knows what it is and how to treat it, the Azande can take action to find out who is bewitching them and why. They turn to oracles for this purpose. The most famous of these is known as the chicken oracle, when a series of chickens are fed doses of strychnine which are on the borderline of being lethal. Questions are presented as each chicken is given the dose, and the answer is provided by the death or otherwise of the chicken. Less expensive oracles involve putting sticks in a termite mound to see which is eaten faster, and the use of a 'rubbing board'. This last is described, by Evans-Pritchard, as:

> a miniature table-like construction ... carved out of the wood of various trees. They have two parts, the 'female', or the flat surface of the table supported by two legs and its tail, and the 'male', or the piece which fits the surface of the table like a lid.
>
> When the operator jerks the lid over the table it generally either moves smoothly backwards and forwards or it sticks to the board so firmly that no jerking will further move it, and it has to be pulled upwards with considerable force to detach it from the table. These two actions – smooth sliding and firm sticking – are the two ways in which the oracle answers questions. They correspond to the slaying or sparing of fowls by the poison, the eating or refusing of the branches by the termites.   (1976: 168–70)

(3) Witchcraft Brings Social Tensions out into the Open

Questions put to the oracles are usually in a form which requires a yes/no answer, and Evans-Pritchard noticed that those conducting the investigation consider not who is a known witch, but who might bear malice against the afflicted person. Witchcraft among the Azande is supposed to occur spontaneously if a person with the innate power is angry with or jealous of another, so that considering who might feel that way is thought likely to elicit a positive answer from the oracles. There is then a procedure to approach the person, most formally by presenting the wing of the dead chicken. The accused is likely to deny malice, but will probably go through a rite of blowing water on the wing to cool the witchcraft and exorcise any ill-feeling. This procedure serves a simultaneous purpose of bringing underlying tensions between people into the open, Evans-Pritchard argues, and deals with them in a way acceptable to both parties.

(4) Witchcraft has a Normative Effect on Society

These beliefs about witchcraft may serve as 'corrective to uncharitable impulses', argued Evans-Pritchard, 'because a show of spleen or meanness or hostility may bring serious consequences in its train' (1976: 54–5). In other words, people will try to curb their jealousy and other forms of unpleasantness for two important reasons:

- to avoid being accused of witchcraft, and
- to avoid incurring the wrath of a witch.

Accusations are usually made to those who are rude, dirty, and jealous, he notes, those with a generally bad character, so the whole system is a discouragement to people to behave in an unpleasant manner. 'Since Azande do not know who are and who are not witches, they assume that all their neighbours may be witches, and are therefore careful not to offend any of them without good cause' (ibid.).

Reactions and other Theories of Witchcraft

Most people who have discussed witchcraft since Evans-Pritchard wrote his classic book have reacted in one way or another to his work, many reinforcing his ideas about the roles played, particularly about the way it provides an explanation of misfortune. An interesting article by the historian Keith Thomas (1970), for example, describes the situation in sixteenth- and seventeenth-century England. He points out that misfortune could also be explained by the wrath of God, but witchcraft offered people more scope for action (see (2) above) than the new Protestant church did.

> A man who decided that God was responsible for his illness could do little about it. He could pray that he might be cured, but with no very certain prospect of success, for God's ways were mysterious, and, though he could be supplicated, he could not be coerced. Protestant theologians taught that Christians should suffer stoically like Job, but this doctrine was not a comfortable one. The attraction of witchcraft beliefs, by contrast, was that they held out precisely that certainty of redress which the theologians denied. A man who feared that a witch might attack him could invoke a number of magical preservatives in order to ensure his self-protection. If the witch had already struck, it was still open to him to practise counter magic ... Best of all, the victim could have the witch prosecuted and executed. For the point of such witch trials was not merely that they afforded the gratification of revenge, but that, according to contemporary belief, they positively relieved the victim. (Thomas 1970: 57)

The Roman Catholic Church had had clearer procedures to be followed, and this difference could account to some extent for the rise in witchcraft trials after the Reformation, Thomas argued. He also offers support for (3) above by suggesting that accusations of witchcraft may well have followed feelings of guilt at having offended a neighbour, or refusing a person asking for alms, and that these ideas might therefore have encouraged neighbourly behaviour and generally reinforced moral standards. As in (4) above, people would try to avoid behaviour which might lead to accusations of witchcraft or the curses of a witch.

Both Keith Thomas and Evans-Pritchard point out, however, that it can sometimes be advantageous to have a reputation for power. In England, old ladies begging for alms could benefit from the fear that their potential benefactors might have of their bewitching capabilities. Among the Azande, those with a reputation for witchcraft were often offered extra meat when the spoils of a hunt were being divided up. This was thought to protect against possible interference during a further hunt, indeed it would be an incentive for the witch to ensure good hunting fortune, they argued.

Writing of the Amba of Uganda (Middleton and Winter 1963), Winter argues that witchcraft is not always beneficial to society, however. Indeed, he shows how notions of witchcraft tend to disrupt the social cohesion of the village. Witches in an Amba view exhibit an inversion of physical and moral qualities of human beings. They hang upside down, eat human flesh, quench their thirst with salt, go about naked and, unlike the situation in the case of feuds, they take their victims from their own villages and share them with witches in other villages.

> Thus if witches in a particular village kill a person they invite the witches from another village to share the ensuing feast. At a later date, the witches of the second village must reciprocate by inviting their previous hosts to a feast at which they will serve the corpse of a victim from their own village. (1963: 292).

The behaviour of witches is thus precisely the opposite of that expected of ordinary people, who abhor the idea of eating human flesh, and always go about with clothes on their bodies. The notions of witchcraft should be examined in the context of the whole moral universe, Winter argues, when they can be seen as a *structural inversion* of the social order. This argument is thus an example of an *expressive* role of witchcraft, in the same sense as we used the idea in the previous chapter, in that it tells us something about important categories in society. It thereby goes beyond, and complements the *instrumental* or functional role presented by Evans-Pritchard and others, when they identify the normative effect witchcraft has on society.

Other structural interpretations are found in the analyses of sorcery accusations made in South America. Peter Rivière's chapter in *Witchcraft: Confessions and Accusations* (1970) describes the way lines of sorcery accusation reflect the sociopolitical structure of the Trio Indians of Surinam in helping to demarcate divisions between villages. In the case of the Akwe Shavante of southern Brazil, they reflect lines of division between political factions. In both cases, the groups are somewhat fluid. Allegiances can alter, and people move to rearrange their neighbourly links. Confirmation of a new division is clear when sorcery accusations are made, for these do not occur amongst people who share a village, or a faction.

In the introduction to the same book, Douglas describes witchcraft as 'essentially a means of clarifying and affirming social definitions' (1970: xxv). If the witch is an outsider, there is a reconfirmation of the inside, whatever that may be. If the witch is an insider, witchcraft may have the function of controlling deviants in the name of community values, it may promote factional rivalry, or it may redefine a hierarchy. In *Purity and Danger* (1966) she argued that uncontrolled witchcraft is attributed to people in dangerously ambiguous roles, people who may be potential sources of disorder. They may have their own niche in one group, but be an intruder from the point of view of another. 'Witches are the social equivalents of beetles and spiders who live in the cracks of the walls and the wainscoting' (1966: 24). An example she gives is Joan of Arc, 'a peasant at court, a woman in armour, an outsider in the councils of war' (ibid.) – small wonder she was accused of witchcraft.

Peter Brown, in another chapter in the Douglas collection (1970) points to so-called flashpoints of sorcery accusation at times of crisis and social change, suggesting an increase when areas of the social structure are ill-defined. Some of his examples are the fourth-century remains of the Roman Empire, sixteenth- and seventeenth-century England, which he relates to the undefined position of the poor until the passing of the Poor Law, and a rise of witchcraft in Africa with colonisation and missionary work.

It is difficult to say whether current witchcraft practices in England are related to any kind of crisis or social change, or, indeed, whether they have ever really abated over the intervening years. It is certainly true, however, that magic and witchcraft continue to intrigue members of the wider society, and practising witches are found amongst the most apparently staid and middle-class of professions. These subjects have occasionally attracted undergraduate students at Oxford Brookes, and those who have gained access to local covens have written very interesting dissertations. A Cambridge PhD thesis which became an excellent ethnography of British Witchcraft – *Persuasions of the Witch's Craft* (Luhrmann 1989) – is a good introduction to the subject, which also addresses the thorny question of rationality.

Another good book to follow up links the ideas about witchcraft that we have discussed in this chapter with the powers of rumour and gossip that we will discuss in the next. *Witchcraft, Sorcery, Rumors and Gossip* (2004), by Pamela Stewart and Andrew Strathern, ranges across Africa, India, New Guinea and Europe, and from the Middle Ages to the present day, in looking at the way that rumours and gossip lead to accusations of witchcraft and sorcery. They investigate the relationship of all these things with situations of conflict and violence, and examine how the latter is justified in the interests of some greater social good that also happens to bring benefits to powerful people in that society.

Possession and Shamanism

Explanations of misfortune form part of the **cosmology** of a society, and in industrialised societies, science is very often invoked for this purpose. Thus, people visit a doctor when they are ill, ask a forensic expert to help solve a murder, examine fingerprints in the case of theft, and seek the 'black box' to explain a plane crash. In many societies people also turn to spirits for explanations of all these kinds of eventualities, usually by asking a specialist such as a shaman, a diviner, or a witch-doctor to intervene in communicating with the spirit world. Communication with the spirits may take place on behalf of an individual or it may take place at a large gathering, often with much ribaldry and enjoyment, and ethnographers have commented on the entertainment value of these occasions.

shaman – a person thought to have the power to communicate with the spirit world, perhaps by travelling there or receiving a spirit into his or her body, and also sometimes to influence and control the activities of those spirits.

The different words used for these practitioners tend to be associated with particular regions. 'Shaman', for example, is a word taken from the Tungus tribe of Siberia, although it is used elsewhere, particularly to describe practitioners who claim to have a soul which can leave their body and travel to a heaven or an underworld. People of South America often have practitioners such as these, although of course with their own local names, who may train to go into trances, perhaps by drinking tobacco juice or taking hallucinogens, and then claim to go on trips to visit the spirit world. They may also learn a technique for receiving spirits into their

diviner – a person thought to have powers to explain the past, anticipate the future and to advise about related decisions, such as causes of illness, marriage partners and travel plans.

own bodies, which will then speak to the assembled company (in any number of different voices!) about their problems and requests.

Audrey Colson, who worked amongst the Akawaio people of British Guyana, describes such occasions in lively detail (Colson 1977). Indeed, one of my strongest memories as a student learning anthropology was listening to Audrey's tape of an Akawaio seance, because the audience is extremely participative and the whole thing sounds immensely exciting. The visiting spirits are asked to deal with misfortune, to help find lost articles, including determining who may have stolen them in case it was a matter of theft, and to identify the causes of sickness, and recommend ways to bring it to an end. People in the audience join in with their own suggestions throughout the procedure, and Colson argues that the shaman, or the spirits who are possessing the shaman, make decisions which reflect public opinion.

In this way, the Akawaio seance plays some of the same roles as described by Evans-Pritchard for witchcraft beliefs. It provides an opportunity for underlying tensions to be expressed in a legitimate fashion, for people in a contained situation to throw out accusations against others whose behaviour could have brought about the misfortunes – perhaps by upsetting the spirits who would bring about illness, for example. Because names of possible transgressors are brought to the visiting spirits, Colson argues that this is a strong disincentive to people to behave in an antisocial way, and the whole procedure again has a normative effect on Akawaio society.

'Diviner' refers to a broader category of people who may address themselves to similar problems. In Japan and other parts of the Far East their roles include divining the causes of illness (perhaps by claiming to enter the body of the afflicted), assessing the suitability of a marriage or a proposed alteration to a house, and determining auspicious days for a venture of any sort. A complicated calendar may be consulted for these purposes, and this is drawn up according to astrological ideas, in association with ideas about the division of the world into *yin* and *yang*. The classification of time, discussed in Chapter 1, is influential here too, so the work of a diviner is not only concerned with communication with spirits.

However, Japanese diviners may also be consulted to explain misfortune, and some of their explanations may involve dissatisfied ghosts and ancestral spirits. Memorials for the dead should be carried out on certain death days, for example, and forgetting these could cause trouble. A relatively recent reaction to misfortune has been to attribute it to the souls of aborted babies, and Buddhist temples have set aside areas for small memorial statues, as well as running monthly rituals to appease these lonely souls. New temples have even opened which cater exclusively to the souls of aborted babies (see Lafleur 1992 for more detail). Japanese people anyway think nothing of consulting a variety of diviners *and* doctors about the same ailment, as was mentioned in the last chapter.

Practitioners of this sort in Africa are more commonly described as spirit mediums or witch-doctors, though their roles may be very similar, that is divining the cause of illness, and finding out how to appease an offended spirit. In talking of communication with spirits in different societies, Raymond Firth suggested that a distinction be made between:

spirit mediumship
– an engagement with the spirit world where communication is thought to be voluntary so that the medium makes deliberate efforts to call spirits into the presence of gathered company, although he/she may have limited control.

- **spirit possession**, which is largely involuntary
- **spirit mediumship**, where communication is voluntary, and
- **shamanism**, which involves some control over spirits.

There have been many different approaches to this subject, and I. M. Lewis (1971) discussed some of them in *Ecstatic Religion*. As was mentioned in the last section, Lewis (1970) compares the interpretation of spirit possession with that of witchcraft. He considers possession as a strategy employed by a person seeking an outlet for distress. Amongst the BaVenda of Southern Africa, for example, the treatment for a woman's possession involves the husband and family according the afflicted person special respect and kindness, and, perhaps not unexpectedly, this kind of possession is said to recur rather frequently. A similar form of spirit possession occurs elsewhere amongst men of low status, who thereby have their position at least temporarily enhanced. Persistence of the 'affliction' may lead to suspicion of witchcraft and *direct* rather than *oblique* mystical attack, in Lewis's terms.

There are several ethnographies that give pride of place to the practice of spirit possession, and some of these are listed below. A useful article which examines Lewis's broader theories about spirit possession in the context of the particular case of the Newar people of the Kathmandu Valley is that by David Gellner (1994), entitled 'Priests, healers, mediums and witches'. A classic collection is that by Beattie and Middleton, which focuses on the role of spirit mediumship in Africa, and a nice introduction to interaction with spirits in Japan is the book by Carmen Blacker entitled *The Catalpa Bow* (1975).

Syncretism

In complex multicultural worlds, different cosmologies must needs coexist. Tolerance of different faiths is one way of seeking a peaceful life, and people of varying backgrounds do manage to live alongside one another in many cities of the world. In urban schools, these days, children may learn a veritable medley of ideas about the faiths which the teachers find amongst their charges. They may encourage children to share their notions of this world and any other they have been taught to believe in, and the school may play host to all manner of different festivals and rites. The aim is to teach tolerance, but it may also engender a degree of confusion, and some of my students who have been brought up in this climate of opinion are only devout when they talk of environmental issues.

Those who become most serious on this subject may turn to a form of nature worship known as Paganism, which has become quite influential in Northern European countries. Although there are many forms of this movement, which has adopted as a name the word used to describe pre-Christian religious ideas, there is in Britain an overarching organisation which aims to keep different groups in touch with one another (http://www.paganfed.org/). One of the common themes seems, appropriately, to be the revival of ideas which were prevalent in Europe before Christianity, but there is also a common concern with the conservation and protection of the environment. Anthropologist Charlotte Hardman, writes:

> the state of Paganism in the UK has been changing ... Ecologically, although Paganism has always had behind it a romantic view of the land and has always been 'green' philosophically, it has now also become more clearly an activist movement in this area .... Respect for Nature, being 'green', is no longer just part of the philosophy; the eco-magic of Pagan ritual can be activated towards environmental, social and spiritual change. (1996: xiv – xv)

There is some overlap here with Luhrman's witches, but she also had informants who did not classify themselves as Pagans, and some even practised Christianity (Luhrman 1989: 5).

People who turn to paganism and witchcraft in Europe are revitalising old categories into new systems of cosmology. They draw on an abundant fund of ancient ideas to create a new way to impose order on an increasingly confusing world. Sometimes in despair at the way scientific discovery appears to ignore the fragility of natural resources, people look back to times which seem idyllic from the perspective of nuclear power and mass destruction. Like the art collectors mentioned in Chapter 6, who seek solace in aboriginal paintings, these people look for wisdom in ancient or disappearing worlds. They reject the excesses of a scientific world view, and seek to find a spiritual life which reflects the concerns of the world in which they find themselves.

Drawing elements of different cosmological systems into a new world view is a practice as ancient as cultural exchange, and the results are sometimes called syncretism, literally the coexistence of beliefs, although in practice one set may virtually subsume another, when it may be called synthesis. As Christianity has spread around the world, it has often incorporated elements of previous belief systems into its range of varying ideas and practices. The timing of the celebration of the birth of Christ to coincide with mid-winter conveniently replaced previous northern

syncretism – the coexistence of cosmological systems which can still be identified as distinct, although in practice may become quite intermingled.

European festivals, for example, as mentioned in Chapter 4, and the celebration of Hallowe'en, now a 'religious' practice only in Pagan circles, is not by chance

Photograph **8.1** Offerings to departed relatives in Mexico, made on the days of All Saints and All Souls in the Christian calendar, also reflect pre-Christian customs for what is known as el Dia de los Muertos, or the Day of the Dead (photograph: Raquel Hernandez-White).

held on days known in the Christian calendar as celebrations of All Saints and All Souls.

In Mexico, these days are amongst the most important in the calendar, when people remember their departed loved ones and visit their graves. Principally known as the Day of the Dead (see also First-hand Account 3.2 on pp. 60–1 and Photograph 8.1), the period is marked by the construction and sale of an abundance of goods and sweets with ghoulish themes, such as rubber skeletons and chocolate skulls. In the book referred to in the last chapter by Haley and Fukuda (2004), it is clearly shown how the pre-Christian Zapotec ideas have been interwoven with the Roman Catholic ones in contemporary practice. It is several centuries since Christianity was introduced to the Mexican people, but there is evidence in the writings of the missionaries of the time that efforts were made to incorporate indigenous practices, and it is interesting that the Virgin of Guadalupe made her first appearance on a hill sacred to Tonantzin, an important Aztec Earth Mother.

The 'Disappearing World' film *Witchcraft among the Azande* noted below, also gives a demonstration of how the ideas described above have found ways to coexist with the more newly introduced Christianity.

Photograph 8.2 Three Buddhist *chityas* (cult objects) outside the Bhimsen Temple, Kathmandu. The *chitya* in the foreground is of the style popular in the 17th and 18th centuries, the other two are the syncretic form which became popular in Kathmandu in the later 19th and early 20th centuries, a time of intensive Hinduisation. They incorporate as part of the base a water course that is copied from the most common Hindu cult object, namely the *shivalinga* (photograph courtesy of David Gellner).

When I was about 10 years old, I was given a paper in school that asked what religion I was. As I didn't know, I went back home and asked my grandfather. He said, 'We are Udays. Our caste is Tuladhar and we are Buddhists'.

Almost all the Udays live in the densely populated ancient city of Kathmandu. I grew up living in two houses: one in the mountain town of Pharping and the other in Kathmandu. My grandparents taught me how to act like a Tuladhar and how to speak according to my audience. I learned that within the

First-hand account 8:

Bhawana Tuladhar-Douglas, Newar – on Syncretism in Nepal

Udays there are lots of castes, but Tuladhars are the highest. I was told that Bajracharyas and Shakyas come before the Udays, so the language I should use with them, especially with those Bajracharyas that are acting as our Buddhist priests, has to be very polite. It is almost a different language.

We do our morning worship, or *puja*, before breakfast. There are various special days when we do *puja* for specific deities: our lineage deity (each caste branch has their own), the stupa at Svayambhu, the Avalokiteshvara of Jana Bahal, Akash Bhairav, Kal Bhairav and other deities. There are festivals where every Buddhist can walk in a procession called a *jatra*, like Mataya, the procession of lamps that remembers the recently dead. When we are someplace other than the Kathmandu house – such as the Pharping house, where I lived – we remember exactly where our (lineage) god is located, visualise them, and do the *puja* from our roof. To worship the lineage deity you must come from a family which has been accepted as part of the caste association, called a *guthi*. Almost every Newar family is part of a *guthi*.

People say that there used to be 10 Buddhist monasteries in Pharping, but none of them are there anymore, nor are there any proper old Buddhist families. There are two Bajracharya families, but just as we were really from Kathmandu, those families were from Lalitpur. The only son in one family married a Jyapu, a Newar farmer, so that family collapsed and became

Jyapus. After that they could no longer work as priests. The other family still stays at the Vajrayogini temple and they work as priests there. There had been another Uday family, Sthapits, but the son married a Jyapu, and his son married a Balami so that family lost their membership in their *guthi*, and now have no communication with their relatives.

During the Buddhist festival month of Gumla in Pharping people do Vajrayogini *pujas* all month and at the end of the month there is a big procession. In Kathmandu, during Gumla every town square has its own devotional music (*bhajans*). Usually a few musicians come to play early in the morning to wake people up. Everybody follows the musical group and we visit lots of Buddhist deities in a long procession that finishes back at our square. For the Buddha's birthday we usually go to Svayambhunath in Kathmandu. In Pharping, on the same day, there is a Buddha image on a cart that goes around to each of the seven town squares of Pharping. All Newars do annual *pujas* as part of their *guthis*. For Udays, this is a big *puja* done together with a Bajracharya priest, and we have a special feast afterwards.

My parents had a love marriage. My mother was born in a Parbatiya Brahmin family. Because she was a very high caste Brahmin, my grandparents and our *guthi* were prepared to accept her. However, one of my father's mother's cousins fell in love with a Shrestha girl, and they married. She was neither allowed in the kitchen nor in *guthi*. It was real luck that my mother – and so also us, her children – were allowed in our society.

I didn't visit my mother's family house until I was 13 years old. There was a fight about our religion and caste system, poor and rich, between two families. For Parbatiyas all the Newars are Jyapus, a farmer caste. They do not have any knowledge of the Newar caste system. In school my Parbatiya friends called me 'Jyapu'. When I visited my mother's family, in Palanchok, my grandmother was very happy to see me but she was upset by the fact that my mother had married a Jyapu. In her house I saw only Hindu deities but not Buddhist ones. I found their way of worshipping gods and the way I was taught were very different indeed. I did see a picture of the Buddha in my mother's brother's new house at Kathmandu, but only in the sitting room as a part of room decoration.

Until 2006 Nepal was a Hindu monarchy with a Parbatiya king. I remember reading in my school book that 'Nepal is a multi-religious and multi-lingual country'. All our course books are either in Nepali or in English. There are pronunciation differences

– Newari does not distinguish a retroflex 't'- so Newars get teased by Parbatiyas. As a result our language is dying. So far as religion goes, in school I read one small chapter about Buddha, his birth place and his enlightenment. There were lots of chapters about Hindu deities.

Every week we had Hindi Dharawahik show on NTV, about the Hindu epic, Ramayana, Mahabharata and then the Vishnupuran. These shows are still a constant feature of the national broadcast programme. Nepalese people wonder if the gods only speak in Hindi. Yet they do like watching Hindi films. In films if anything goes wrong the hero or their relative goes to pray in a Hindu temple, and then everything turns out okay. We all talked about these films in school with friends – it was a kind of pressure on people to worship some Shiva or Vishnu, directly or indirectly.

My great-grandmother became a Buddhist nun for a few years. She does not really know the differences between Theravada and Mahayana Buddhism. What she does know is Sakyamuni Buddha and his life, and about the secret initiations that she has been given, and how she will be treated after her death by the funeral *guthi*. Because she had secret initiations from the Bajracharya priests, she believes her dead body will be carried to the cremation ground with special Newari music.

In a proper Buddhist Newar family we are given secret mantras by the Bajracharya priest. Once you have the mantra you are not allowed to tell anyone. If you did tell another person then, according to the priest, your head would explode. I don't think any one would want to die like that – so the pure Buddhist mantras die with people. Hindu mantras, however, you can learn in a book or from a television programme where some Babaji says it clearly so you can pick it up. I know both Hindu and Buddhist mantras – though probably more Hindu mantras because they're so easy to find.

So far as I can tell, both for Newars and other groups, people don't make much of a distinction about going to Hindu or Buddhist shrines. Hinduism dominates Nepalese culture, though, for all the reasons I have given. I still believe of myself that I am Buddhist. My grandfather said that Buddha is the 'light of Asia'. I believe Buddha is the light of the world.

In Japan, the situation is rather different, and provides a better example of syncretism. The indigenous Shinto, which literally means 'path of the gods', was a set of rather miscellaneous ancient beliefs without a name, possibly related to Taoism, until they needed to be distinguished from other more established traditions which were introduced from the outside. These now coexist with ideas and practices from Buddhism, Confucianism and Christianity. These, of course, have their own dogma, teachings and ritual experts, but ordinary Japanese people seem to find little difficulty in drawing on anything available in turning to what might be called religion.

We have already noted that the Japanese language sometimes classed Shinto ideas 'superstition' in the postwar disapproval of its support for imperial expansion, but the word usually translated as religion (*shūkyō*) is also more appropriately used for the teachings introduced from outside than for these indigenous ideas. The word for 'believer' (*shinja*) is also applied rather to someone who chooses a special (often 'new') religious path than to the many Japanese people who incorporate various strands of religious influence into their life almost imperceptibly. Visits to Shinto shrines at birth, Buddhist funerals, Christian weddings, and the consultation of a (possibly Taoist) shaman may all be practised by the same person in Japan.

Analysis of the practices of the people who lived in the rural community where I carried out fieldwork (Hendry 1981) coincided with the findings of those who have specialised in looking at religious practises in Japan. On the whole, Shinto is found to be drawn upon in celebrations associated with life and health, Buddhism with death and memorials for the ancestors. The former are usually community celebrations, perhaps held at the community shrine, the latter are household ones which make use of the household altar. Clearly, these practices may again be seen as playing an *expressive* role, one which is reinforced when we notice that the consultation of the less well defined shaman takes place in times of illness, marriage and housebuilding, when the important categories are threatened or undergoing change.

Christianity in Japan has not made much progress, counting less than two per cent of Japanese as practitioners. Perhaps this is because the syncretic system, which now also includes a number of 'new' sects of Buddhism and Shinto, is not only at odds with the more exclusive nature of Christianity, but also still serves to accommodate the changing structures of Japanese society. Looking back over 1500 years of Japanese history, the two major strands of what are now called Shinto and Buddhism can be seen to have undergone much separation and assimilation, but certain elements have also continued to persist. Confucianism has been a long-term influence too, but largely in the underpinning of morals and ethics, a subject we will consider in more detail in the next chapter.

Some discussants (Stewart and Shaw 1995) of syncretism have argued that all religions have drawn on different traditions over the centuries, so little is to be gained by using the term, but the notion is useful for contrasting with the relatively ethnocentric nature of the idea that one religion should make an exclusive call on its adherents. David Gellner (1997), in a critique of the Stewart and Shaw book, considers different varieties of syncretism, and makes a comparison between the Buddhism found alongside Shinto and Confucianism in Japan and the case of the Newar people of the Kathmandu Valley, in Nepal, who continue to practise Tantric Buddhism in a predominantly Hindu state. His book *Monk, Householder and Tantric Priest* (1992) is a detailed ethnography of the Newar people who live in the Hindu Buddhist city of Lalitpur, and focuses on the religious activities which provide many good examples of syncretism in practice (see Photograph 8.2). First-hand Account 8 on pp. 163–5 includes an account of one person's life in this kind of syncretic situation.

Conclusion

This chapter has laid out a selection of the indigenous categories of cosmology that have been studied by anthropologists, and focused in on a few of the more influential, in order to give a feel for some of the different ideas held by people in what might be called their spiritual life. We have also considered some of the ways in which people communicate with worlds that are held to exist beyond the mundane. In the next chapter we draw again on ideas that may be termed religious or spiritual, but among many others that serve as constraints in everyday social life.

Discussion Questions

1   How do you explain misfortune in your own life? Do you call on a religious faith, or science, or the interference of spirits? Or do you use words like 'luck' or 'fate'? What do your explanations tell you about your own upbringing?

2   Do your explanations of misfortune relate to norms in your own society? Can you think of any 'structural' or 'expressive' roles they might play?

3   Consider the value of syncretic ideas in the contemporary world. How might they work to the long-term survival of our planet?

References and Further Research

Books

Beattie, John and Middleton, John (1969) *Spirit Mediumship and Society in Africa* (London: Routledge & Kegan Paul).

Blacker, Carmen (1975) *The Catalpa Bow: A Study of Shamanistic Practices in Japan* (London: Allen & Unwin).

Blain, Jenny, Ezzy, Douglas and Harvey, Graham (2004) *Researching Paganisms* (Oxford: Altamira Press).

Douglas, Mary (1966) *Purity and Danger* (Harmondsworth: Penguin).

Douglas, Mary (ed.) (1970) *Witchcraft: Confessions and Accusations* (London: Tavistock).

Eliade, Mircea (1964) *Shamanism: Archaic Techniques of Ecstacy* (Princeton: Princeton University Press).

Evans-Pritchard, E. E. (1976) *Witchcraft, Oracles and Magic among the Azande* (Oxford: Clarendon Press).

Gellner, David (1992) *Monk, Householder and Tantric Priest* (Cambridge: Cambridge University Press).

Haley, Sharon D. and Fukuda, Curt (2004) *Day of the Dead: When Two Worlds Meet in Oaxaca* (Oxford: Berghahn).

Hardman, Charlotte (1996) 'Introduction' in Graham Harvey, and Charlotte Hardman (eds), *Paganism Today: Wiccans, Druids, the Goddess and Ancient Earth Traditions for the Twenty-First Century* (London: Thorsons).

Hendry, J. (1981) *Marriage in Changing Japan: Community and Society*, (London: Croom Helm).

LaFleur, William R. (1992) *Liquid Life: Abortion and Buddhism in Japan* (Princeton, NJ: Princeton University Press).

Lewis, I. M. (1971) *Ecstatic Religion: An Anthropological Study of Spirit Possession and Shamanism* (Harmondsworth: Penguin).

Luhrmann, Tanya (1989) *Persuasions of the Witch's Craft* (Blackwell: Oxford).

Marwick, Max (ed.) (1982) *Penguin Readings on Witchcraft*, 2nd edn. (Harmondsworth: Penguin).

Middleton, John and Winter, E. H. (eds) (1963) *Witchcraft and Sorcery in East Africa* (London: Routledge & Kegan Paul, 1963).

Stewart, Charles and Shaw, Rosalind (eds) (1995) *Syncretism/Anti-Syncretism: The Politics of Religious Synthesis* (London: Routledge, 1995).

Stewart, Pamela J. and Strathern, Andrew (2004) *Witchcraft, Sorcery, Rumors and Gossip* (Cambridge: Cambridge University Press).

Articles

Boddy, Janice (1988) 'Spirits and Selves in Northern Sudan: The Cultural Therapeutics of Possession and Trance', *American Ethnologist*, 15(1): 4 – 27

Brown, Peter (1970) 'Sorcery, Demons and the Rise of Christianity from Late Antiquity into the Middle Ages', in Mary Douglas (ed.) *Witchcraft: Confessions and Accusations* (London: Tavistock), pp. 17–45.

Colson, Audrey (1977) 'The Akawaio Shaman', in ed. E. B. Basso (ed.) *Carib- Speaking Indians: Culture, Society and Language* (Tucson: University of Arizona Press).

Gellner, David (1994) 'Priests, Healers, Mediums and Witches: The Context of Possession in the Kathmandu Valley, Nepal', *Man,* 29: 27–48.

Gellner, David (1997) 'For Syncretism. The Position of Buddhism in Nepal and Japan Compared', *Social Anthropology,* 5(3): 277–91.

Humphrey, Caroline (1999) 'Shamans in the City', *Anthropology Today*, 15(3): 3–10.

Jencson, L. (1989) 'Neo-paganism and the Great Mother-Goddess: Anthropology as the Midwife to a New Religion', *Anthropology Today*, 5(2): 2–4.

Lewis, I. M. (1970) 'A Structural Approach to Witchcraft and Spirit Possession', in Mary Douglas (ed.), *Witchcraft: Confessions and Accusations* (London: Tavistock), pp.293–309.

Riches, David (1994) 'Shamanism: The Key to Religion', *Man,* 29: 381–405.

Rivière, Peter (1970) 'Factions and Exclusions in Two South American Village Systems', in Mary Douglas (ed.), pp. 245–55.

Thomas, Keith (1970) 'The Relevance of Social Anthropology to the Historical Study of English Witchcraft', in Mary Douglas (ed.), *Witchcraft: Confessions and Accusations* (London: Tavistock), pp. 47–79.

Willis, Roy (1994) 'New Shamanism', *Anthropology Today*, 10:(6): 16–18.

Novels

Lowry, Malcolm (1962) *Under the Volcano* (Harmondsworth: Penguin Books) is a novel about a disillusioned and alcoholic British consul living in Mexico, but it is of interest here because much of the action takes place on the Day of the Dead.

Mantel, Hilary (2005) *Beyond Black* (London: Fourth Estate) is a novel about the life of a spirit medium in suburban London.

Miller, Arthur (1996) *The Crucible* (London: Methuen) is a play about the Salem witch trials in seventeenth-century United States.

Okri, Ben (1991) *The Famished Road* (London: Cape) is a novel full of African spirits and mysticism.

Warner, Sylvia Townsend (1978 [1926]) *Lolly Willowes* (London: The Women's Press) is a comic novel about a spinster who joins a coven – an allegory for feminist subversiveness.

Films

Bridewealth of a Goddess (Chris Owen, 72 minutes, 2000) is a unique insight into a secret spirit cult among the Kawelka people in the western Highlands of Papua New Guinea.

Witchcraft among the Azande (André Singer and John Ryle, 1982), a 'Disappearing World' film that depicts the world of Azande witchcraft within the new context of widespread conversion to Christianity.

The Guardian of the Forces (Anne Laure Folly, 52 minutes, 1991) explores the significance of sacrifice and possession in communicating with spirits of ancestors and voodoo deities.

Kataragama, A God for All Seasons (Charlie Nairn and Gananath Obeyesekere, 1973) is another 'Disappearing World' film set in Sri Lanka (then, Ceylon) which, at least at first, illustrates the variety of ways a people may seek to understand the misfortune of losing an 11-year-old son.

Shamans of the Amazon, a documentary by Dean Jeffreys about a visit, with his family, to shamans on the Amazon in Equador.

The 'Strangers Abroad' film about Evans-Pritchard, entitled *Strange Beliefs* (see Chapter 1) includes an examination of Zande material too.

The Crucible, Nicholas Hytner's 1997 feature film of Arthur Miller's play.

Websites

http://personalwebs.oakland.edu/~dow/courses/an271/bswmr.html – James Dow's bibliography for witchcraft studies.

http://www.bbc.co.uk/religion/religions/paganism/ataglance/glance.shtml and http://www.paganfed.org/ – two websites about Paganism.

http://www.shamanism.org/ – homepage for The Foundation for Shamanic Studies.

http://www.drugnerd.com/archives/435/shamans-of-the-amazon-great-documentary/ – weblink to a film about Amazonian shamanism.

Law, Order and Social Control

Rules and Norms

In this chapter and the next we are again taking as a focus categories from the English language, and we will examine manifestations of behaviour observed in different parts of the world which conform approximately to the specifications these terms encompass. The terms in question – 'law' and 'politics' – overlap in any society. When a formal political system is distinguished from a legal system, it is still the politicians who design and discuss the laws, while a different set of professionals – lawyers and judges – put them into practice. In both cases we deal, on the one hand, with persons in positions of power – the subject matter of Chapter 10 – and, on the other, with the constraints imposed on members of the society at large by the mechanisms of control. In most societies, too, the people themselves constrain the acts of others amongst them in a variety of less formal ways.

In this chapter we will focus on the constraints. Any society needs mechanisms which ensure that its members behave for the most part in a reasonably ordered fashion. In countries at national level, there are laws, together with systems of policing and courts which execute the enforcement of these laws. There are also prisons and other institutions to exact punishment or rehabilitate offenders. And there are norms of behaviour, which may or may not coincide with these laws, that people learn as they grow up within social groups, and everywhere there is some kind of reaction on the part of most other people if these norms are transgressed. Details vary from one group to another – indeed, within one group – but some form of social control is found everywhere.

norms - aspects of expected behaviour that people learn as they grow up within social groups, and which provoke some kind of reaction from those groups if transgressed.

social control - mechanisms within a society that act to constrain members of that society to behave within a range of acceptable norms.

At a local level, and within specific communities, informal constraints on the behaviour of individuals are rather effective, sometimes more effective than the laws of the land, and in this chapter, we will concern ourselves particularly with these mechanisms for 'keeping order' in society. The experience of anthropologists, working for long periods amongst smallish groups of people, sometimes very isolated from any wider legal system, has given them a special insight into the workings of these informal methods of social control. They are able to observe the kinds of pressures which induce people to conform to certain norms and standards, and they can identify incentives people cite for complying with the expectations of their friends and neighbours.

Actually, we have already considered several methods of social control in previous chapters. In the last one we looked at the shaman's seance, where we noticed that the likelihood of being picked out as a possible transgressor was thought to induce people to behave within accepted norms amongst the Akawaio of British Guyana. It was also suggested that ideas about witchcraft and spirit possession had a normative effect on the behaviour of the Azande of the Southern Sudan and the Bavanda of Uganda respectively. In Chapter 7, on religion, we talked of the prospect of salvation, or divine retribution, as well as the wrath of ancestors and fears of burning in hell, as incentives to conform to the behaviour expected by the moral system.

During my own first fieldwork in Japan, when I was focusing on patterns of marriage, I noticed an interesting mechanism of social control in the way people would check up on the families of prospective spouses. Meetings are often arranged by relatives so that young people can meet likely candidates for marriage, and if there is serious interest between them, each family will take steps to find out about the other. In the countryside this may involve a visit to the village where they live, and simple enquiries amongst neighbours and in the local shops. The owner of the general store in my village told me that she was regularly approached in this way. She also explained that she felt a moral obligation to tell the truth as she saw it. If a family were to set up a marriage with a family she knew to be difficult or unpleasant, she would forever feel responsible.

There was also an economic element at play here, since the shopkeeper would clearly lose custom if she protected people who turned out to make life miserable for a new housewife and potential customer. For the existing village families, well aware of the system, it was a powerful incentive to keep on good terms with the shopkeeper, again bringing her custom, especially as one's children approached marriageable age. Amongst neighbours too it could be very difficult if one were to acquire a bad reputation, and two families in the village had had to set up a marriage between themselves, although marrying out of the village was usually preferred, because of their reputation for rudeness and bad temper. There is clearly an element of social control at play here.

There have been several attempts to make general statements about social control, and in this chapter we will examine two of these in some detail and make reference to a third. In all three cases, the anthropologists have drawn heavily on material from small-scale societies, but their findings may also be usefully applied to segments of more complex societies. First, we will look at the approach of Radcliffe-Brown, who sought an understanding of this subject by looking at *social sanctions,* which he defines as follows:

> A sanction is a reaction on the part of a society or of a considerable number of its members to a mode of behaviour which is thereby approved (positive sanctions) or disapproved (negative sanctions).   (1952: 205)

The standards of behaviour by which people judge one another are based on the norms of that society, ideas of right and wrong, which are learned early, as we discussed in Chapter 2. These may be highly complicated, however, and quite situationally specific. Indeed in some societies the situation may be a more important consideration than any absolute rules, as is sometimes argued for Japan. To take an example which will be recognisable in most societies, there is usually a rule or law against killing another human being. However, under certain circumstances this rule may be broken. In most societies, war is a sufficient excuse, though its definition may vary; in some societies, vengeance, 'honour killings' or the legal retribution of capital punishment is accepted; and in Japan – as well as certain fundamentalist religious groups – people are sometimes admired … for, and helped in … taking their own lives.

In any society it is possible to learn about the norms which people share by observing the sanctions which come into play to encourage some kinds of behaviour and discourage others, and Radcliffe-Brown drew up a system for classifying these, which we will shortly consider. It must also be remembered, however, that different members of any one society will have somewhat differing views, and the degree to which variation is tolerated is another aspect of this subject of social control. In some societies, it is possible to live quite an idiosyncratic life; in others the leeway is far less broad. The examination of sanctions is not so good at identifying this kind of range of acceptance, or, indeed, the possibility of contested norms within one society.

The second approach we will consider can be more effective in this respect. Laid out in detail by Simon Roberts in his book *Order and Dispute* (1979), there are some areas of overlap with looking at sanctions, as we will see, but Roberts decided to focus on the resolution of disputes. He starts with the assumption we made above, that there must be order in any society, and he also takes as given that disputes are inevitable. His interest is in the variety of methods which come into play to resolve them, and we will examine these in some detail. In our third example, we will turn to a collection of papers which considers actual disputes from a detailed ethnographic perspective (Caplan 1995), and here we will encounter the ability to detect contested norms in a specific case.

Sanctions

Radcliffe-Brown drew up a very useful list of different types of sanctions which come into play as part of the regulation of social behaviour. He first made an important distinction between *positive* and *negative* sanctions, helping us to identify some of the positive forces for action which are present in any society, but particularly in places like Japan and Melanesia where a strong emphasis on harmony discourages open disputes. These positive sanctions include

sanction - a reaction on the part of a society or of a considerable number of its members to a mode of behaviour which is thereby approved (positive sanctions) or disapproved (negative sanctions).

material rewards such as prizes, titles and decorations, but they also include things less easy to define such as the good opinion of neighbours and workmates, prestige and status within the community, and general support and success in social activities.

Negative sanctions are those which form some kind of penalty for stepping out of line, for behaving in a way which is unacceptable to members of the wider society. These include definite, regulated punishments such as the fines and prison sentences meted out by courts of law, and those of other constituted organisations such as the Church, which may defrock a priest, or excommunicate a parishioner, and professional bodies which may strike off a medical or legal practitioner. They also include more spontaneous expressions of disapproval through gossip, avoidance and ridicule within the local community. Radcliffe-Brown's second distinction, between *organised* and *diffuse* sanctions, corresponds to these two extreme sets of examples, as well as to the different types of positive sanctions mentioned above.

Organised sanctions are characteristic of large-scale, anonymous societies, but diffuse ones are found amongst any group of people who live in face-to-face contact. They are particularly effective in small-scale societies where it is difficult for people to move away if they fall out with their neighbours, for these are people whom one must meet constantly. In an agricultural or horticultural society, where a good deal of time and effort has been invested in the cultivation of land, they are strong, but they work effectively amongst the employees of large companies in industrial society too, if people want to keep their positions. In practice, sanctions may fall on a continuum between the highly organised at one end and the totally spontaneous at the other in almost any situation. Let us look at a few examples.

Japanese people discussing their own society often turn to the cultivation of rice as an explanation for the strong emphasis on harmony and cooperation, for much mutual support is necessary for a successful crop. The fields must be flooded when the rice seedlings are planted out, and complicated irrigation networks have been built up over the years to ensure this process. However, the water supply must be shared out, so villages work to a rota, and families used to help one another to do the planting, and later the harvesting, to gain maximum advantage from the period when they are allocated sufficient water, on the one hand, and when the ears ripen, on the other. Now that there are machines to do many of the tasks, it is not so vital to share out these roles, but people still turn to this process to explain the cooperative nature of Japanese society.

The most severe sanction which could be brought into play in a Japanese village, especially during the premodern period when it was forbidden to move from one part of the country to another, was called *mura-hachibu*. This means 'village eighth-part' and it restricts neighbourly cooperation to the bare minimum required for the family to survive, which is seen as one-eighth of the usual level. Otherwise, members of the whole household could be totally ostracised. No one was to speak to anyone concerned, not even the children, and no one was to invite members of the family to participate in village meetings, celebrations or festivals. Personal events such as birth, marriage and death would receive none of the usual support; indeed arranging a marriage with such a family would be well-nigh impossible. This was a highly organised sanction, arranged by the village assembly and limited to a specific period, after which the offending behaviour would supposedly be curtailed, although the only case I know personally involved the expression of disapproval about the building of a factory, which is in fact still in place.

Ostracism may also be a much more diffuse sanction, of course, and the avoidance of a person who has offended in some way is a common occurrence in many societies. In English, there is an expression, 'sending to Coventry', which is a relatively organised arrangement made by some people to cut off communication with another. The expression probably dates back to the historical decision of the people of Coventry (in Warwickshire) to pull their curtains and look away when the unpopular King of Mercia's wife, Lady Godiva, was forced to ride around the streets naked to achieve the pardon she had sought for some local prisoners. In the Irish film *Ryan's Daughter*, there are impressive scenes where a family was ostracised because of the association of their daughter with a British soldier.

House-burning is another sanction which may be more or less organised. In the Highlands and Islands of Scotland, where it was for long the custom to close down all forms of business on Sundays, including cafés, restaurants and even bed-and-breakfast establishments, to all those who were not booked in on the Saturday, a few places were mysteriously burnt to the ground when they began to try and alter the custom. No one was arrested, and the police could find no witnesses. Word had it that the fires were clearly 'an act of God'. Opposition to the opening of businesses on a Sunday is still strong in the Island of Lewis, and an article that appeared in the *Stornaway Gazette* in August 2006 reported that a man who had planned to open a convenience store on Sunday in the community of Bragar on the west coast of the island changed his mind on receiving a message direct from the Almighty (see website below).

In the almost abandoned village of Hampton Gay, just outside Oxford, a ruined house is said to stand witness to a similar occurrence (see Photograph 9.1). Local people say that the nineteenth-century occupants were extremely angry when their peace was shattered by the coming of the railway, which ran very close to the house. When an accident took place nearby, and nine railway carriages fell into the river, it is said that they refused to open their doors to help the injured, and they would lend no blankets to keep them warm. The house burnt down some time later. Historical records show that the fire actually happened several years after the accident, so the stories relating the events may be apocryphal, but their existence can in itself be seen as a potential form of social control, expressing shock at such selfish and unsympathetic behaviour.

A third kind of more-or-less diffuse sanction is of a type described by Radcliffe-Brown as *satirical*, usually involving some kind of public mockery. In the same film, *Ryan's Daughter*, the British soldier's woman has her beautiful hair cut off in a manner reminiscent of the 'tarring and feathering' practised in earlier times. A custom known in part of Spain as the *vito* brings neighbours round to sing abuse outside the house of a person of whom they disapprove, typically for a transgression of a sexual nature, such as adultery (see Pitt-Rivers 1971: 169–77). A similar custom in rural England is known as 'loud-shouting' or 'rough music'

Photograph 9.1 The ruined house at Hampton Gay, near Oxford (photograph: Joy Hendry).

(Thompson 1991: 467–533) – and some evening-class students I taught in rural Oxfordshire described singing repeatedly: 'We know you're in there' outside the house of an adulterous couple of whom they all roundly disapproved. Under these circumstances, in an English village, the recalcitrant(s) may see such a display as unreasonable, but if they want to stay together, their only option would probably be to move out of the community.

Fear of such unpleasant sanctions is an even more powerful force for social control in countries where the avoidance of ridicule and laughter is tied up with strong values of honour and shame. An excellent ethnographic example of this situation is to be found in an article by Juliet du Boulay (1976), about rural Greece, where she analysed in some detail the relationship between mockery as a force for social control and the use of lies to conceal misdemeanour in the maintenance of family honour in the community where she worked.

Social relations in the community were characterised by competition between different families over wealth and reputation, and people constantly sought faults in others apparently in order to maintain their own relative superiority:

> On discovery of some offence, the discoverer immediately relates it to his or her friends and relations, and in no time at all the story is all round the village and everyone is, as they say, 'laughing' (velame). The more serious or ludicrous the offence is, the more people mock the principals of it. The more they laugh, the more the victims of the laughter are humiliated, because the chief ingredient of laughter is lack of respect, and it is this above all that is the enemy of reputation and self-esteem ... Mockery, therefore, may be said to work through shame to preserve honour. (1976: 394–5)

Clearly nobody can be perfect at all times, however, and as a form of defence in this hostile environment, the local people used lies in a systematic way to protect their reputations. Du Boulay identified no fewer than eight different kinds of lies, and she makes very clear that some forms of lying are not only tacitly accepted, but almost expected, especially when they become opposed to betraying another family member. Others are quite taboo, however, and understanding the system is evidently an important aspect of the maintenance of honour. As du Boulay puts it:

> Because the reputation for which everyone strives is something which is given by the community, this reputation, and, in the last extreme, honour itself, in a very literal sense only has reality if the rest of the community grants it that reality ... it is [thus] more important to be thought to be in the right than it is actually to be in the right, and ... deceit comes to be regarded as an indispensable element in social relations ... Deceit, therefore, and the avoidance of public mockery, appear as phenomena ultimately connected with the structure of the value system and as part of the legitimate means by which the honour of a family is preserved and the prosperity of a house maintained. (Ibid. 405–6)

This value system may be quite difficult to understand for those brought up in a society where frankness and honesty are granted high value, though they may think nothing of telling a 'white lie' in a social situation where 'politeness' is called for. 'Lies' are assigned negative value in many societies which have a high regard for diplomacy, but most peoples have acceptable forms of indirect communication which could also be described as a type of deceit. We will return to this subject in the next chapter, but du Boulay's paper is an interesting examination of these issues as well as providing a good example of mockery as a form of social control. Some other ethnography from Mediterranean societies illustrates more broadly how these kinds of values play out in everyday life (see, for example, Pitt Rivers 1971; Herzfeld 1985; Cowan 1990; Sutton, 1998; Just 2000).

Radcliffe-Brown also talked of *religious and ritual sanctions* which depend on a system of belief. Some people avoid certain types of behaviour because of the fear that ancestral ghosts will take retribution, others may regulate their lives in a way conducive to a favourable position in a life after death. The terrible threats of hell preached in Christian, Muslim and Buddhist faiths alike are certainly strong forces for social control, as are the positive images of heaven and 'nirvana', and here a further distinction is made between 'immediate' and 'delayed' sanctions. In many societies, illness and other misfortunes are put down to the wrath of god(s), spirits or ancestors, as we saw in the last chapter, and it is the role of priests, shamans and other mediums to intercede and find ways to make retribution.

The reciprocal principle which may underpin such recourse is also to be found in economic sanctions, which were picked out by Malinowski as particularly important because they were often related to survival. In the Trobriand Islands, people are careful to get on with their neighbours because they are involved in the exchange of goods essential to their diet, he argued, and this must be the most important sanction of all. The 'do as you would be done by' principle is part of many forms of religious and moral dogma, although it may not always be practised. Nor are economic sanctions always effective, as we see from time to time when countries express disapproval of one another by cutting off certain supplies, or by boycotting goods. A worldwide avoidance of French wine and other goods had no effect whatsoever on nuclear testing in the Pacific, but its avoidance again in the USA when France refused to support the invasion of Iraq apparently caused some hardship (McCartney 2003).

Reciprocal principles may be useful in bringing about a neutralisation of the infringement of rules and norms of society. The payment of compensation may go some way towards appeasing an angry customer, or a person hurt by another, although in litigious cultures monetary demands for every small misfortune has also been described as more of an act of opportunism on the part of eager lawyers. In some societies a recognised form of 'blood-money' is paid in the case of murder, and there are also all sorts of ritual ways of cleansing people and bringing them back into the fold, as it were. Many peoples have some way or other of giving their recalcitrants a second chance, as long as they appear to be sorry for what they have done, and in Japan, judges try to bring about reconciliation between parties to a dispute, rather than deciding clearly who is right and wrong. This undoubtedly again reflects the emphasis on maintaining, where possible, a harmonious front for social relations.

Order and Dispute

Simon Robert (1979) takes a slightly different approach to the subject of social control, as we outlined above, and his focus is on possible reactions to *dispute*. He assumes it to be inevitable that disputes will arise in any society, and he identifies different types of reaction which come into play. Of course, the expression of dispute will vary from one society to another too, but this is something we will leave until the last section of the chapter. Here, Roberts is concerned with 'legal anthropology', or the reactions he sees as in some way equivalent to or comparable with the exercise of law. However, he is at pains to point out that there may be quite different ways of keeping order, which involve nothing like the application of law, and his aim is to seek these mechanisms.

The first he discusses is the permitted exercise of *interpersonal violence*. Here, the principle is very often the reciprocal one, discussed above, where a limited amount of interpersonal violence is seen as an appropriate response to the suffering of the same. Thus, vengeance is approved in some societies, although usually only up to the limit of the hurt received, as in an 'eye for an eye, a tooth for a tooth'. Of course, in practice, the side suffering the vengeance may perceive things quite differently from the side meting it out, and the continuation of such disputes into a long-term feud between groups is not at all uncommon. Indeed it forms the stuff of well-known dramas such as *Romeo and Juliet* and *West Side Story*, and it may underpin a wider political system, as we will see in the next chapter when we consider the Nuer people of the Southern Sudan.

In some cases, an organised arrangement of interpersonal violence may divert attention from the original object of the dispute and bring about a resolution. In New Guinea, among the Minj-Wahgi people, for example, Roberts describes an institution known as the *tagba boz*, which involves men from two opposing sides lining up, clasping their hands behind their backs, and kicking at each other's shins until one side withdraws. Another example was reported to be found among several Inuit groups (still called Eskimo in the Roberts text, but see the website listed below for a more recent Inuit comment, and Photograph 9.2), who would either sit opposite one another and engage in head-butting, or stand up and deliver straight-arm blows to each other's heads. In either case, the battle continues until one side falls over.

In case this sounds uncivilised behaviour, the reader might like to consider the dawn duel between gentlemen, or the trenches of The First World War, as ways of resolving quarrels in Europe. In the cases cited by Roberts, on the other hand:

An essential feature of controlled conflict of this kind is that there are recognised conventions which delimit the struggle, and ideally have the effect of preventing death or serious injury on either side ... thus making continuous and escalating violence unlikely.   (1979: 59)

There is an element of ritualisation of the dispute in these cases, but a complete representation of the violence forms a second type of reaction which Roberts calls *channelling conflict into ritual*. Another good example he gives is also taken from Inuit societies, where a song contest allows both sides to enunciate their grievances at a public gathering, but only through the medium of song and dance. After each side has exhausted itself in hurling as much melodious abuse as it can at the other, one party apparently usually emerges in receipt of greater public acclaim, but in any case each has had plenty of opportunity to get the problem off their chests. A similar practice is reportedly found amongst the Tiv people of Nigeria.

The practice of sport may be seen to some extent as a ritual form of channelling conflict, for it allows in the same way representatives of two opposing groups to exercise skills in the enactment of a battle. People living in neighbouring towns and villages very often build up resentment against each other, and a weekly sporting event allows the expression of competition between them usually

Photograph 9.2 The new Canadian province of Nunavut has a large majority of Inuit population, and the Legislative Assembly likewise was 85% Inuit control in 2005, and rising. Decisions about dispute resolution are therefore now in a state of flux again. The objects in this photograph – all essential to Inuit life in the past – have pride of place in the centre of the Assembly hall.

to be carried out in a controlled fashion. Of course, *interpersonal violence* may still break out, and it could be argued that the sporting event incites this violence, but such a breakdown of control is then subject to considerable censure on the part of the wider society. When the popular footballer Eric Cantona crossed 'the magic line' dividing the field and the fans to kick a member of the audience who shouted abuse at him in 1995, he was punished severely and roundly condemned, even by his own supporters (see website).

A side-effect of the Inuit-type song contest is that it makes public all the aspects of a misdemeanour, which may well shame the guilty party into future compliance, and it is this *shaming* which forms Roberts's third type of reaction to dispute. He cites various examples, but one of them, the public harangue, will illustrate the point. In parts of New Guinea, a person who feels he has been mistreated will stand at his door, usually in the middle of the night or very early in the morning, and simply deliver a harangue against the person or persons he believes responsible. The villages are compact enough, and the night sufficiently silent, for all to hear clearly what is said. The response is typically absolute silence, the guilty party to be found 'with his head bowed under the imagined stare of the whole community' (Roberts 1979: 62, quoting from Young 1971: 125).

The next two types of response discussed by Roberts are very similar to examples of sanctions cited by Radcliffe-Brown, namely the appeal to *supernatural agencies*, and *ostracism*. The latter we have already discussed in some detail, and Roberts gives further examples of the principles involved. The former includes consideration of societies which hold ideas about **witchcraft** and **sorcery**, which were the subject matter of our last chapter. Where misfortune of one sort or another is put down to witchcraft or sorcery, the response either involves identifying the witch or practising retaliatory sorcery. Various ordeals may be administered to suspected witches, as they were in Europe, and very often the ordeal itself becomes a punishment if the person accused is proved guilty. In West Africa, for example, an accused person is made to drink a concoction prepared with the poisonous bark of the Sasswood tree. If they vomit and survive, they are pronounced innocent. If they die, they were clearly guilty.

The last type of dispute resolution discussed by Roberts is *talking*, and this common form of response he considers under three further headings, namely *bilateral negotiation*, *mediation*, and *umpires*. In the first case, the two parties concerned address one another directly, to air and try to iron out their differences; in the second case a third party becomes involved, perhaps to carry the grievances to and fro between them, or to set up a meeting. The role of the mediator is to ease communication and to advise, but if a third party is engaged to make a decision about the dispute, this Roberts classifies as being an *umpire*. He also distinguishes two types of umpire, the first an *arbitrator*, who is someone the disputants ask to make a decision on their behalf; the second an *adjudicator*, a person who already holds authority in the society concerned.

The last case will, of course, cover most systems of courts, where the judge and jury play the roles of umpire, but we should remember that the punishment they mete out for a misdemeanour may represent forms of the other types of response discussed above. Imprisonment is an example of formal ostracism, for example, and capital and corporal punishment are clearly examples of interpersonal violence, though this time removed from the disputants themselves and carried out by the wider, impersonal state. Nor are courts confined to industrial societies. In small-scale communities, there may be formal trials for those accused of misdemeanour, and the classic work of Max Gluckman (1955) is an excellent illustration of such a case.

In a monograph entitled *The Judicial Process among the Barotse of Northern Rhodesia* (now Zimbabwe), Gluckman analysed the processes used by this Indigenous people, identifying and illustrating concepts parallel to English notions invoked in legal situations, and describing methods used in the examination of crimes, the interviewing of witnesses, and the application of the notion of 'a reasonable man'. Another classic work is that of Paul Bohannan (1957), in his book *Justice and Judgement among the Tiv*, about a Nigerian people, which emphasises the motives and rationale of the individuals involved rather than the overall structure of the system which comes into play. A recent issue among Indigenous peoples in different parts of the world is that they resent having their own legal systems, which they regard as perfectly fair, sidelined by a national system which they feel (probably with some justice) treats them unfairly.

Contested Norms and Social Control in a Context

A collection of papers, entitled *Understanding Disputes: The Politics of Argument* (ed. Caplan 1995), examines in various contexts the work of a man, Philip Gulliver, who spent much of his life observing *disputes*. The papers move from national disputes over access to water sources, through 'gentlemanly values' in two sets of political circles, to family wrangles over failed marriages, intra-family strife about death and funerals, and concepts of passion and compassion. The contexts considered are also extremely various, and the reader is introduced to discrepant values in locations as far apart as nineteenth- and twentieth-century Ireland, rural Nepal, London, Lagos, and more specific African locations in Kenya, Tanzania and Uganda.

Some of the broader themes covered include discussion of a move from judicial institutions to negotiation as the more 'civilised' means of dispute resolution, including a realisation that both these systems still favour the more powerful partner, despite ostensible efforts to incorporate approaches previously more characteristic of weaker peoples. There are also examples of resistance, and some of these illustrate the ways different parties draw on different values and methods of approach, just like the situation of colonised Indigenous peoples mentioned above.

An excellent example is a paper by Stephen Gaetz about disputes between the leaders and members of an Irish youth club, where the latter resort to violence because they feel excluded from decision making. The leaders respond to this plea by setting up committee meetings, and then can't understand why the youths don't turn up, or fail to air their views. From the point of view of the youths, who have no experience of committees and little confidence that they would make a difference, these are just another way for the leaders to exert their authority. Here the important point is illustrated that the disputing *process* may be more significant than any resolution.

Most of the papers follow Gulliver's emphasis on understanding the political and historical context of any dispute and 'categories of meaning by which the participants themselves comprehend their experience'. Sometimes the parties to a dispute do not even share these categories of meaning, and each seeks to manipulate the situation to suit their own understanding. In another case, the same people under different circumstances may invoke different sets of norms. Pat Caplan shows how the three sets of Islamic law, Tanzanian law and local custom available in Mafia Island, Tanzania, where she did her fieldwork, make possible a continual negotiation of rules and behaviour, allowing a situation of contested norms to be counterpoised to relations of unequal power. Those who are at ease with the three possibilities have a distinct advantage over those who know only one.

In this detailed discussion of a specific long-term dispute, Pat Caplan, who is also the editor of the papers, illustrates her contention at the start of the book that the study of disputes leads us:

> straight to the key issues in anthropology – norms and ideology, power, rhetoric and oratory, personhood and agency, morality, meaning and interpretation – and enables us not only to see social relations in action but also to understand cultural systems. (1995:1)

What her paper also illustrates very nicely is the fluidity of norms, and their manipulative possibilities, an issue we raised in the introduction to this chapter.

Attempts to classify responses to dispute, and sanctions which come into play, are extremely useful in the understanding of methods of social control which people exercise upon one another in different parts of the world. The work of anthropologists is particularly valuable for a deep understanding of the constraints which inform the organisation of undisputed life, for it is only with long-term observations that strongly held, underlying forces of influence may be identified and evaluated. It is a pity that the governments of politically powerful countries do not take into account the work of their own anthropological experts in particular parts of the world, alongside that of their economists, before they make decisions about dealing with, and especially invading, other countries. As I wrote the second edition of this book, the situation in Iraq and other war-torn countries of the Middle East was clear testament to decades of misunderstanding of local issues on the part of the leaders of the big economies who think they should make decisions on behalf of the world.

In my own study of Japan, a focus on child-rearing methods revealed some of the complicated mechanisms of peer pressure which profoundly affect the lives of Japanese adults and the decisions they make about how to behave. One of the overt aims of kindergarten education, for example, is to inculcate an understanding of the way that subordinating self-interest to the needs of a wider group will have long-term benefits for all involved. Teachers use various means to encourage children to discipline one another in this endeavour, thus imparting a principle which underpins the success of the whole education system and later working life. Two books by the Japanese anthropologist Emiko Ohnuki-Tierney (2002, 2006) reveal a lot about the way this kind of upbringing filtered through into the behaviour of the so-called *kamikaze* pilots of the Second World War, revealed by their diaries to be frightened but compliant young lads, intelligent but obedient – in fact, the cream of a generation.

The present good relations between Japan and the powerful countries of the West are of course related to the country's postwar economic success, but I would like to think that the work Ruth Benedict carried out in the internment camps where Japanese citizens of the Allied countries were held during the Second World War – mentioned in the Introduction to this volume – might have influenced the Occupation policies and hence laid the foundations for them. Likewise, I suggest that the work of some of the anthropologists who have studied in Japan, both insiders and outsiders, contributes to continuing cooperation. Certainly, one of my former students has established an organisation with the specific aim of helping to 'defuse and prevent ethnic and religious conflict' (see www.oicd.net for further details).

We end this chapter by looking at a book that focuses on social control in a particular society, and which approaches it from an angle which might not at first have been anticipated. In *Power and Persuasion*, subtitled *Fiestas and Social Control in Rural Mexico*, Stanley Brandes (1988) examines in minute detail the events and processes leading up to annual festivals which find the villagers relaxing in a frenzy of fun and fireworks. The villagers almost certainly enjoy themselves, for each fiesta is a culmination of months of arrangements and planning, financing, purchasing and allocation of tasks, and the successful accomplishment of the various elements of the event demonstrate that things in the village are operating in an orderly fashion.

Various aspects of the moral universe are played out during the course of a festival, and power relationships are expressed in the relative financial contributions made by each household in the village to the huge pyrotechnic displays of material wealth and influence. Masked figures in a dance performance known as 'La Danza' portray in symbolic form the system of religious and moral values which underpin social life. They break normal social rules in the way they dance, but the figures they portray, like Death and the Devil, are so abhorrent that Brandes argues that they actually exert and demonstrate a strong force for social control.

Fiestas in general are expected to find people reversing the expectations of normal everyday life, and turning upside down the moral system. This they do, but their production offers an excellent window on the workings of social and political relations within the village. In Brandes' words:

> To be successful, fiestas of all types depend on two predictable circumstances: cooperation among leaders and order among the participants. When a fiesta is over, and both order and cooperation have prevailed, villagers know that their society is intact. Perhaps the constant threat of disorder and uncooperativeness ... actually keeps the whole fiesta cycle in motion, as people demand periodic affirmation of cooperation and social control. (1988:165)

Conclusion

In another location, the details might be different. We have now seen several examples of approaches identified by anthropologists as important for understanding systems of social control. We have looked at witchcraft among the Azande, shamanism among the Akawaio, marriage in Japan and fiestas in Mexico. The anthropologists concerned could possibly have chosen a different focus and come up with something equally interesting, but they could not easily have anticipated all that they would find before they got to the field. Unearthing a system of social control is a long-term endeavour, but it is a satisfying one, and it is one which demonstrates the value of the kind of qualitative research anthropologists engage in.

Discussion Questions

1   Think about constraints again. What or who makes you adjust your behaviour, or avoid certain activities? What are the positive influences in your life? Can you relate these to general norms and values in your society?

2   Under what circumstances would you consider it acceptable to tell a lie? What would be your motivation? Would your peers approve of your actions? What about other members of your society?

3   Think about Roberts's various methods of solving disputes. What would work best in situations in your own life? Have you any others to add to his list?

Reference and Further Research

Books:
Alia, Valerie (2007) *Naming and Nunavut: Culture and Identity in Arctic Canada* (Oxford: Berghahn).
Bohannan, Paul (1989[1957]) *Justice and Judgement among the Tiv* (Prospect Heights: Waveland Press.

Brandes, Stanley (1988) *Power and Persuasion: Fiestas and Social Control in Rural Mexico* (Philadelphia: University of Pennsylvania Press).
Caplan, Pat (ed.) (1995) *Understanding Disputes: The Politics of Argument* (Oxford: Berg).
Cowan, Jane K. (1990) *Dance and the Body Politic in Northern Greece* (Princeton, NJ: Princeton University Press).
Desjarlais, R. (1997) *Shelter Blues* (Pittsburgh: University of Pennsylvania Press).
Gluckman, Max (1955) *The Judicial Process among the Barotse of Northern Rhodesia* (Manchester: Manchester University Press).
Herzfeld, Michael (1985) *The Poetics of Manhood: Contest and Identity in a Cretan Mountain Village* (Princeton, NJ: Princeton University Press).
Just, Roger (2000) *A Greek Island Cosmos: Kinship Community on Meganisi* (Oxford: James Currey Publishers).
Moore, Sally Falk (1978) *Law as Process: An Anthropological Approach* (London: Routledge & Kegan Paul).
Nader, Laura and Todd, Harry F. (1978) *The Disputing Process: Law in Ten Societies* (New York: Columbia University Press).
Ohnuki-Tierney, Emiko (2002) *Kamikaze, Cherry Blossoms and Nationalisms: The Militarization of Aesthetics in Japanese History* (Chicago: University of Chicago Press).
Ohnuki-Tierney, Emiko (2006) *Kamikaze Diaries: Reflections of Japanese Student Soldiers* (Chicago: University of Chicago Press).
Pitt-Rivers, Julian A. (1971) *The People of the Sierra* (Chicago: University of Chicago Press).
Roberts, Simon (1979) *Order and Dispute* (Harmondsworth: Pelican Books).
Sutton, David (1998) *Memories Cast in Stone* (Oxford and New York: Berg).
Thompson, E. P. (1991) *Customs in Common* (London: Penguin Books).
Young, Michael (1971) *Fighting with Food* (Cambridge: Cambridge University Press).

Articles

Bazin, Laurent, Gibb, Robert, Neveu, Catherine and Selim, Monique (2006) 'The Broken Myth: Popular Unrest and the "Republican Model of Integration" in France', *Anthropology Today*, 22(2).
Bergsma, Harold M. (1970) 'Tiv Proverbs as a Means of Social Control', *Africa: Journal of the International African Institute*, 40(2) 151–63.
du Boulay, Juliet (1976) 'Lies, Mockery and Family Integrity', in J. G. Peristiany (ed.), *Mediterranean Family Structures* (Cambridge: Cambridge University Press).
Cohen, Abner (1980) 'Drama and Politics in the Development of the London Carnival', *Man* 15: 65–87.
Gaetz, Stephen (1995) '"Youth Development": Conflict and Negotiation in an Urban Irish Youth Club', in Pat Caplan (ed.), *Understanding Disputes* (Oxford: Berg), pp. 181–201.
Goldschmidt, Walter, Foster, Mary Lecron, Rubenstein, Robert A. and Silverberg, James (1986) 'Anthropology and Conflict', *Anthropology Today* (special issue on Anthropology and Conflict), 2(1).
Gulliver, P. (1969) 'Dispute Settlement without Court: The Ndendeuli of Southern Tanzania' in L. Nader (ed.), *Law in Culture and Society* (Chicago: Aldine).
McCartney, Robert J. (2003) 'US Boycott being felt, French say', *Washington Post*, 16 April, p. A32.
McNamara, Sean Cush (1986) 'Learning How to Bribe a Policeman', *Anthropology Today*, 2(2): 2–3.
Radcliffe-Brown, A. R. (1952) 'Social Sanctions', in *Structure and Function* (London: Cohen & West).
Roberts, Simon (1994) 'Law and Dispute Processes', in T. Ingold (ed.), *Humanity, Culture and Social Life* (London: Routledge & Kegan Paul).

Novels

Blythe, Ronald (1972) *Akenfield* (Harmondsworth: Penguin Books) is a detailed historical account of life in a medieval English village.

Gulik, Robert van (1989) *The Chinese Maze Murders* (London: Sphere Books) is a series of detective stories which demonstrate the value of an understanding of indirect and non-verbal cues, rather in the manner of Sherlock Holmes, but in a more openly culturally specific mode.

Kafka, Frank (2004[1925]) *The Trial* (London: Vintage Classics) is a story about a man who is arrested and tried, although he is not told what his crime is. It is about the power of bureaucracy.

Mo, Timothy (1990) *Sour Sweet* (London: Hodder & Stoughton) is a novel about a Chinese family that settles in Britain, and the social constraints they experience, more from the Chinese community than the wider British one.

Nafisi, Azar (2004) *Reading Lolita in Tehran* (London: Fourth Estate).

Orwell, George (2000[1949]) *1984* (London: Penguin Classics) is a novel about a totalitarian state, seen as the future when it was written in 1949.

Ouzo, Mario (1969) *The Godfather* (Greenwich, Conn.: Fawcett Publications) is a classic novel about the social control exercised among members of Sicilian/American mafia groups.

Films

Atanarjuat: The Fast Runner is a 2002 Inuit-produced film, directed by Zacharias Kanuk, which depicts a legend that at the same time illustrates Inuit mechanisms of social control.

Divorce Iranian Style (Kim Longinotto and Ziba Mir-Hosseini, 80 minutes, 1998). This documentary film, set in the Family Law Courts in central Tehran, concentrates on ordinary women who come to this court to try and transform their lives.

The Lives of Others (*Das Leben der Anderen*) is an originally German feature film (by Henckel von Donnersmarck, Florian), which illustrates state control of East Germany through secret service observation of the detail of its citizens' lives.

The two 'Disappearing World' films, *The Mehinacu* (Carlos Pasini and Thomas Gregor, 1974), about a people of the Brazilian rain forest, and *The Kirghiz of Afghanistan* (Charlie Nairn and Nazif Shahrani, 1976), about a people virtually imprisoned on a mountain top between Russia and China, which they may not legally enter, both illustrate aspects of social control discussed in this chapter.

Romeo and Juliet and *West Side Story*.

Ryan's Daughter is David Lean's 1970 film which tells the story of an Irish girl who has an affair with a British soldier during the First World War.

Sisters in Law is a 2005 Cameroonian documentary film, directed by Kim Longinotto and Florence Ayisi, about the everyday work of a female judge dispensing justice in her own way in a small town in Cameroon.

Websites

http://www.stornowaygazette.co.uk/ViewArticle.aspx?SectionID=2629&articleid=1668591 – an article in the local newspaper on the Island of Lewis about Sunday trading.

http://www.erudit.org/revue/etudinuit/2002/v26/n1/009271ar.pdf – a detailed discussion about a workshop held with Inuit Elders on the subject of social problems and social control.

http://news.bbc.co.uk/onthisday/hi/dates/stories/january/27/newsid_2506000/2506237. stm – reports on the severity of the reaction to Eric Cantona's crossing of the line.

10

The Art of Politics

Political Possibilities

It was pointed out in the introduction to the last chapter that it is not always possible to make a clear distinction between the concepts of 'law' and 'politics', but our discussions there fell more into the realms of 'law' than politics. However, we took pains to broaden our approach to include mechanisms of social control which could hardly be described as legal, even in the broadest sense of the word, although our approach was certainly not confined to societies which have no overarching legal system. In this chapter we will turn to areas more usually associated with what the English language might term 'politics', though again the reader must be prepared to have a broad and flexible mind. We will start with the internationally familiar, however, but we will move gradually into examples of societies whose political systems, if we may call them such, were at first quite impenetrable to observers from outside nations.

Much of the early work in the area of political anthropology was carried out by anthropologists in a colonial situation, itself a prime example of the ruthless exercise of power, which is still a topic of concern in the field, especially in former colonies where Indigenous people are now trying to reclaim their lands. Ethnographers were inevitably caught up with helping their own governments to maintain order in unfamiliar circumstances, although they may also have found themselves acting as advocates for the people they came to know better than any other outsider, and even taking a critical stance towards the colonial rule. At the time, they were dependent on the goodwill of the local administrators for their continued presence in a fieldwork location, however, and their positions were at best ambiguous.

The influential early British examples of local political systems were African, and they were classified under two main headings, namely *centralised* and *acephalus* (Fortes and Evans-Pritchard 1940). The first were known as *kingships*, with relatively stable hierarchical units, and the second were 'headless', the Greek meaning of the term. Two famous anthropological studies which are cited to illustrate these types are again by Evans-Pritchard, both of peoples of the Sudan. The first, the Shilluk, exemplify a kingship, and the Nuer people of Southern Sudan have been held up as a model for the second, acephalus type. We will discuss both cases so that the reader will become aware of the base line in this area of the field.

acephalus (literally, 'headless') **political system** – a system without any easily recognisable head or system of hierarchy.

kingship – a centralised system of hierarchy, not necessarily responsible for political activity, in which the holders of high rank have a status and authority that were compared by European anthropologists with their own systems of monarchy.

As ethnographic material became available from different parts of the world, however, it became clear that these two approaches were actually better described as opposing ends of a continuum of types of political system, with interesting and sometimes rather recognisable cases in the middle. We will consider some cases from the Latin American rain forest as an example of the middle ground, in a section entitled 'leadership', but we could have chosen to look at people from any number of other locations for all these sections. It is a good exercise to read a complete ethnography to get a feel for the intricacies of a particular political system, and the books at the end of the chapter by Ahmed, Barth, Maybury-Lewis, Leach and Strathern are a few excellent examples.

This chapter is named 'the art of politics' in deference to the stunning ingenuity of human beings in creating and manipulating relations of *power* and authority in a rich variety of ways in different parts of the world, so after the examination of classic political 'types' we turn to consider some of this variety and ingenuity at the level of human interaction. The importance is noted again of guarding against carrying assumptions about behaviour from one political system to another, particularly where the unspoken is almost as important as the spoken word. By its very nature politics often involves disputed ideas of the type we discussed towards the end of the last chapter, and anthropologists are well placed to contribute to this arena too (see, for example, Shore 1990).

In the end this chapter must be a cursory glance at a huge subject, for political science forms an academic discipline in its own right, and anthropologists themselves devote whole books to the political branch of their subject (for example, Balandier 1967; Bloch 1975; Godelier 1986; Gledhill 1994; Vincent 2004; Vincent and Nugent 2006), but it is useful to examine some of the findings of anthropologists in this sphere for three reasons. First, in the classic works we can identify an interesting range of ideas about the distribution of *power* in society, which may now be interpreted within the context of colonial endeavour (Gledhill is particularly good on this subject). Secondly, we can identify in all the variety some persistent themes which run through the gamut of political life, which can inform for anyone the familiar exercise of power, but with unusual twists. Thirdly, the chapter will demonstrate the importance of anthropology for seeing beyond the social science concepts of political science, which were developed along European lines and which cannot take account of the range of variety to be found in the world.

Types of Political System

Centralised systems

The political system which was most familiar to European nations setting up colonies was a centralised one with various forms of hierarchical arrangements. There are clearly a great number of possibilities for how such a system may work, but we can identify some characteristic features. First, in its most organised form, a centralised system will have a *head* at the top and layers of lesser positions with degrees of authority and dependence below that. The position of the head may be *hereditary*, and it may even have some divine qualities, or it may be filled by a person elected by the people at large. These two possibilities may seem quite different within conventional approaches to politics, but they are both part of centrally organised systems. Several countries, including Belgium, Britain, the Netherlands, Norway, Sweden and Thailand, manage to maintain both types of centralised system, as indeed does Japan, and the two types play different roles, but they are both *centralised*.

In both cases, the people indicate submission to the system, willingly or unwillingly, by paying tribute or tax, and this makes available public funds that allow for certain other possibilities, for example:

tribute – goods or other forms of wealth paid to a central person or body, which shows recognition of that body, and enables the central body to administer the public funds made available on their behalf.

- a *ruling class* with officials to carry out activities on behalf of the group;
- *protection* in times of dispute;
- *courts* for dealing with disputes;
- buildings and other *facilities* for public use;
- *feasts* and *aid* for the needy;
- *ritual* support, perhaps in dealing with spirits.

A classic example from the anthropological literature is provided by the case of the Shilluk people, who have a hereditary *kingship*, legitimated by the idea that the spirit of their god, Nyikang, passes from one king to another. The king symbolises the people and the changeless moral order, but his role is sacerdotal rather than governmental. He reigns, and others do the ruling. The Shilluk nation is divided into settlements, each with a chief and council, and further subdivided into hamlets, each with a head, usually of a lineage. Myths validate the overall hierarchy, as all can trace their descent from characters in a saga which tells of Nyikang dividing up the land on conquest. Lineage heads have ritual duties to the king, who is a mediator between man and god. He must keep ritually pure and healthy to avoid natural disaster. If he falls ill or senile, he should be killed for the sake of the people.

sacerdotal, a term meaning 'priestly', used by anthropologists to refer to the role of communicating with higher powers, such as gods and spirits, often played alongside the more mundane **governmental** role in a system of dual leadership or authority.

When colonists encountered a society such as this, they had relatively little difficulty in understanding the political arrangements, and they were able to incorporate the system under their own overarching umbrella. By respecting the king, and his entourage, for something akin to their own, they could communicate in a relatively trouble-free manner, from their point of view, though things did not always proceed smoothly, as history has taught us. The case of India is a particularly good example of where things at first fell neatly into place to provide 'the jewel in the crown' of the British Empire, but then became more complicated, as Paul Scott's 'Raj Quartet' novels made clear in an anthropologically interesting manner.

In some cases potential colonists were understandably opposed in their efforts to impose a new order, but a centralised system was relatively easy to defeat. If the head is deposed, and the new rulers observe most of the niceties of social life as far as keeping the underlying hierarchy in place, they can simply rely on existing mechanisms to impose their new regime, and this happened for centuries within Europe. This is also what happened in many cases of centralised systems elsewhere, and the pre-existing culture became gradually eroded. One well-known example is the case of the Aztec empire in precolonial Mexico, a highly organised centralised system, under the rule of the Emperor Montezuma. However, it espoused a set of beliefs which happened to see the arrival on their shores of the Spanish conquistadors as fulfilling a legend that one of their gods would return.

It was therefore relatively easy for Hernando Cortez to step into the position of supreme ruler in the Aztec court, and he and his party could set about colonising Mexico for Spain. It was not long before Aztec culture was destroyed, although many other Indigenous people remained, and there is now even a revival of Aztec customs such as dancing. This is the society we mentioned in Chapter 1 where the curtailment of the practice of human sacrifice, seen as a way to keep the gods content and the society prosperous, coincided as predicted with the end of the period of cultural supremacy. The other example of a centralised system in South America was the Inca empire and this suffered a similar fate in the country which became Peru; however, not all of South America was so easy to colonise, as we will see in the next section.

Meanwhile, the centralised case of Japan may be cited to illustrate some of the complications of the too-easy application of a 'political type' for understanding the locus of power in any situation. Although Japan has never been a colony to another power, it was occupied after defeat in the Second World War, when the Allied Forces insisted on 'democratising' the political system, already modelled on European prototypes when Japan set out to 'modernise' in the latter half of the nineteenth-century. Japan's system thus has recognisable elements such as a parliament, political parties and constituencies, as well as full adult franchise and free and fair elections. According to political observers from the outside world, this is a system they can analyse and understand.

In practice, however, in a large part Japan's system still works according to principles which pre-date even the first modernisation process. The confrontational nature of the chambers of the parliament is not a mode of communication in which decisions are easily reached in Japanese discourse; large political parties tend to operate at a factional level more reminiscent of social relations found elsewhere in Japan; and voting is not always an individual decision in a society where reciprocity and loyalty to local benefactors counts highly. This is a good example of why it is useful to examine politics in the context of a wider social system, rather than making assumptions about categories such as 'centralised', and we will return to consider some strategies for the exercise of power in the last part of this chapter.

Leadership

Amongst the peoples who inhabit the tropical rain forests of Latin America, politics is much less clear cut than the centralised systems we have sketched above. Nevertheless, their leaders have recognisable qualities and their arrangements are still open to comparison with the politics of the industrialised world. Some people become *leaders* and others are content to follow them. There are many societies we could consider here, but the work carried out by anthropologists on the Yanomamö people of Venezuela and Brazil, encountered in Chapter 3 (see also Ferguson 1995), and the Akwe Shavante, also of the Brazilian rain forest (Maybury-Lewis 1974, see website also), provide good cases for examination. The following characteristics are generally common to the area.

No Central Administration

Here is the first major difference to the societies we have been considering so far, because these peoples have no formal system of authority, and they have therefore posed many problems to the governments of the countries where they are found.

Typically, such governments will try to appoint a local chief amongst Indigenous people and work through that chief to maintain communication. They will offer remuneration to such a chief, and possibly a uniform or some other badge of office. Those who accepted such an incentive to represent their people to outside bodies very often found themselves the laughing stock of the community, however, and any pretensions to leadership they may have held before such an arrangement would soon disappear. In some areas only a person regarded locally as an idiot would contemplate such a role.

Village Autonomy

One of the reasons for this situation is the strong value placed on village autonomy in this part of the world. Leaders can come and go, and if there happened to be two in conflict within one community, the community itself might well split and redefine itself. We referred in Chapter 8 to Peter Rivière's argument about how, amongst the Trio of Surinam and the Akwe Shavante, these divisions may be initiated through sorcery accusations. Ultimately, the villagers follow a leader only as long as they see it to be in their interest, and they are not inclined at all to be dictated to by outsiders, even if the latter do try to work through their own people.

The Leaders Lead

As the word implies, leaders in this area have none of the coercive power or accepted authority of the 'chiefs' discussed in the previous section. They simply lead, and if others approve, they follow. Thus, if the leader thinks it time to clean up the central square he will start doing it, perhaps calling to his companions to join him. He has no power to instruct others to carry out such tasks for him, and if others fail to see the sense of his plan, he will be left unsupported. It is even said amongst the Akwe Shavante that they are likely to kill bossy leaders! Putting on airs would also clearly be unacceptable, and this would explain why the provision of a uniform and a salary might disrupt an otherwise effective relationship.

Environmental factors

These are undoubtedly important in the political life of these communities. This is an area where slash-and-burn cultivation is the norm among many peoples, requiring commitment to a particular patch of land for only a few years at a time. A smallish area of the forest is cleared for cultivation (see Photograph 10.1 and the First-hand Account 10 overleaf for an illustration from the Trio people of Surinam) but its nutritional value is limited so communities are small and where possible people move on regularly. The diet is supplemented with sporadic hunting and fishing, but none of these economic activities requires much managerial organisation, as was pointed out by Anthony Leeds in a consideration of the Yaruro people of south-central Venezuela:

> Given the techniques and tools of the Yaruro, all the subsistence activities
> ... can conveniently be done by one person. ... the logic of tools and

Trio Indians in Surinam clear the rainforest for planting in the slash-and-burn cultivation style (photograph taken from a print in the Rivière Collection, Pitt Rivers Museum, University of Oxford, PRM 2001.33.262.4).

> techniques concerned demands utilization by single persons. Activities of all sorts may be done by aggregates of persons, each utilizing his own tools and techniques individually but neither the activity, the tools nor the techniques entail the aggregation of individuals. Thus, from the point of view of human organization, the technology, by itself, entails no managerial functions, no coordination of tasks which must be overseen by someone occupying an appropriately defined status.   (1969: 383)

The major cooperative venture is choosing and clearing land and setting up a village to administer it. Decisions must be made about when and where to move, and a potential leader is able to judge his support by the response he gets to an initiative to seek a new site. The length of a longhouse, which is shared by the men in the group, is a spatial indication of a leader's support, for it will be tailored to suit the size of the community, although people can of course leave if they grow tired of a particular leader, and moving is a time for realignment, as we have seen.

The qualities required by an aspiring leader in these rain forest communities are interesting to observe, for they are mostly quite recognisable. First of all, a leader is usually an example of a successful person by local standards, so an *athletic, well-built* person who is good at hunting would be an appropriate type. A leader needs to display *generosity* with goods, and a good hunter is well placed to share his spoils as well as to attract several wives so that he can maintain a surplus of cooked food. *Oratorical skills* are admired here as elsewhere, and they are

We have a field, we have an older field and right now we are preparing a new one. We still have some cassava and cotton and sweet potatoes and bananas and sugar cane and pineapples on our oldest field. Right now we are making a new field, because it is sun time [1 November 2006] and we always plant before the rain begins to come back. We only plant once a year, then we have enough food. Pananakiri [strangers, white people] say one can plant more than once a year, but we have plenty when we do it when our field is ready.

Everybody grows cassava [i.e. bitter cassava] and corn and watermelons and bananas and different sorts of sweet potatoes and also cotton for hammocks. Close to our houses we have peppers and sometimes papayas and other fruit trees. No, we don't grow green vegetables, we are not like caterpillars [most Trio are scared to death of caterpillars]. Some people grow more watermelons or corn than others do. I always grow lots of sweet cassava, but hardly any corn.

Cutting a field is much easier for the Trio men than it used to be in the past, when the men had to cut a field in the forest with axes. Now they have chain saws and moreover they don't even need to cut the tall trees. Why? Well, since we have been living at Tepu for so many years now [since 1970], we are cutting our new fields in areas where the forest has not become real forest yet [i.e. in long-deserted fields].

This year the rainy season was very bad. Many fields were flooded for more than six days. When the flood was over, a great deal of our food was spoiled, in particular our bread [i.e. cassava]. It smelled very, very bad, because of all the dead worms that had come out of the earth and than drowned. At first the children had a lot of fun playing in the flooded village, but afterwards many of us had terrible stomach problems. Nobody died, but we were very sick indeed. There was no famine, because the higher fields came out all right and the soldiers [government, WHO] brought us lots of rice. We like rice, but we did not really need it. But when they ask: 'Are you hungry? Do you need rice?' our village leader says on our behalf: 'Yes, our cassava is spoiled and we don't have rice. So send us many bags of rice.' And that is what happened. We got many bags of rice. Rice is nice.

Some people lost all their cassava, others still had plenty. In those cases we always help others who are in need without asking for payment. And we always plant larger fields than we really need, because we know that floods may ruin part of the crops and it is not only heavy rains. Sometimes there may be enormous numbers of caterpillars that eat all the leaves of all our young cassava plants. However, the worst threats are the many, many ants that cut the cassava leaves and carry those leaves all underground.

Merinto Taje is living at Tepu, Upper-Tapanahoni (river), in the Sipaliwini District of Surinam. This text was translated and annotated [using square brackets] by Cees Koelewijn.

sometimes used in formal negotiations between villages known as ceremonial dialogue, for resolving potential disputes, as well as for trade, to arrange marriages, and so forth. These skills are also important to resolve disputes within the local group, and the skills of a *moderator, mediator* and *peace-maker* are highly regarded. Amongst the Nambikwara, for example, the word for leader is, literally, 'one who unites'.

ceremonial dialogue
– a way of transacting formal negotiations between villages for many peoples in the rain forests of Latin America, used for resolving disputes and potential disputes, as well as for trade and to arrange marriages.

Amongst the Akwe Shavante, who are a large enough group to be split into factions, their leaders are permanently in a state of competition over minor disputes, and their skills need to be flexible. The leader of the dominant faction at any one time may emphasise his skills of impartiality, tolerance and wisdom to maintain peace and harmony within the wider community. If threatened, he needs to be ready to become more assertive and aggressive. As Maybury-Lewis notes (using the term 'chief' for the most dominant Akwe Shavante leaders):

> A chief is therefore in a difficult position. The qualities ideally required of him and the behaviour expected of him while he is in office are diametrically opposed to those of which he had to make use when he aspired to the chieftancy. Indeed, in a community where the dominant faction is not firmly established, they are opposed to the talents he must display in order to maintain himself in office at all … chiefs [therefore] tend to veer from one type of behaviour to its opposite. Sometimes they handle seemingly intractable situations with great patience and forensic skill. At others they deal summarily and ruthlessly with only incipient opposition. (1974: 204)

Finally, some leaders may need to have **shamanistic** qualities, although this may be a separate but influential role. This split between the *sacerdotal* and the *governmental*, also noted above for the Shilluk, is actually found in many societies. A system found in ancient Japan, for example, held a brother and a sister at the top of the hierarchy. The sister was a religious figure in constant touch with the deities, while the brother took care of everyday political matters. The twin imperial/ governmental system still in practice in Japan evidently has ancient roots. Other contemporary monarchies become quite commonplace too in view of these examples, although the role of the monarch is usually more symbolic than religious for most people.

Other examples of leadership and how it may be acquired abound in the ethnography, but the Latin American case gives a good example of the importance of placing a particular political system in its local environmental, ecological and demographic context. This is also an area where anthropologists can hardly fail to get involved in helping the people with whom they work to represent themselves to the outside world. The rain forest habitat is constantly threatened by developers, now seeking oil as well as timber and pharmaceutical products, and anthropologists need to address questions of compatibility between the different political strategies involved in the negotiations. According to Laura Rival, an anthropologist specialising in this area:

> We need to study ethnographically how, when communities encounter the oil transnationals, they come to think in a new way and to take decisions about their futures; and how they come to abandon their self-reliant marginality as they envisage their sustainable integration into wider spheres ... We need to understand how, in the course of unequal negotiations, emerging forms of political agency are built up through the strategic use of particular rhetorical styles. Under what conditions can the abstract notion of 'equal partnership' become a reality?   (1997: 3)

The film cited below about the Kayapo people of the Altamira region of the Xingu valley, is an excellent illustration of such negotiations. Thanks to the help of an anthropologist who had worked in the area, and the film crew who helped the Kayapo to record their deals with the Brazilian authorities, the outcome was relatively positive. Others have not been so fortunate, and there is still much work to be done, according to Rival. However, there has been a successful resurgence of indigenous political power in several South American nations, most notably Bolivia, where the president Evo Morales is a member of the Aymara, a local indigenous people, so it will be interesting to see how this works out in the future.

Acephalus societies

Segmentary systems
Anthropologists from states with highly centralised political systems for a while found it difficult to understand how some African societies were organised at all.

They seemed to have very little in the way of political organisation, and yet retained order in everyday life. Detailed field research eventually revealed some of the principles underlying this order, and Evans-Pritchard made a breakthrough in describing the segmentary system of the Nuer of Southern Sudan, a people who 'hate authority', and who 'strut about like lords of the earth .... equals who regard themselves as God's noblest creation' (1940: 182). It is important in reading the description that follows to distinguish between the *ideal* system and that which operated in practice. Bear in mind also that the lives of the Nuer have been badly affected since the time of Evans-Pritchard by the continuing war in Sudan (see website below).

> **segmentary system** – An abstraction of a social and political system, first described by Evans-Pritchard for the Nuer people of the Southern Sudan, as a 'set of structural relations between territorial segments'.

The Nuer are a cattle-keeping people who live a transhumant life, spending the dry season in camps by the rivers, when they also fish, and moving away to villages on high land, where they also grow millet, during the wet season when the river floods. They thus spend part of the year in territorially defined communities separated from each other by flooded land, and part in larger, more fluid

> **transhumant** – a type of lifestyle spent between two distinct locations, usually related to annual changes in the climate, such as dry and wet, or hot and cold seasons.

settlements when people can move amongst each other. The basic economic unit is conceptually, or *ideally*, a group of relations who move to and fro together, but each move is also an opportunity for *political* realignment, and some members of a village may thus be together for political reasons and not in fact be related. This *territorial* unit is therefore described by Evans-Pritchard as the smallest *political segment*, which in turn belongs to larger *segments* occupying a particular region.

The whole tribe or clan is made up of people related in this way. However, Nuer men *think of themselves* very much in terms of belonging to a group which shares descent from a common ancestor. They *ideally* share living arrangements with close relatives, described by Evans-Pritchard as a minimal lineage, and carry out economic and ritual activities of various sorts with larger groups of relatives, which he describes as minor, major or maximal lineages. The largest group defined in this way is a *clan* of people ultimately descended from one founding ancestor, who is described as related to the founding ancestors of the other clans in a way that binds the whole Nuer people.

> **descent** – **unilineal descent groups** – groups of people related on the basis of lineal descent from a common ancestor.

This *ideal* model is distinguished in Evans-Pritchard's description from groups which align themselves in practice into what he calls *political segments*. The smallest, the villages, belong to *tribes*, which correspond approximately to

> **lineage** – a group of relatives based on **lineal** connections.

the *clans*, but they may also align themselves for particular political issues with *segments* of varying sizes, which Evans-Pritchard calls primary, secondary and

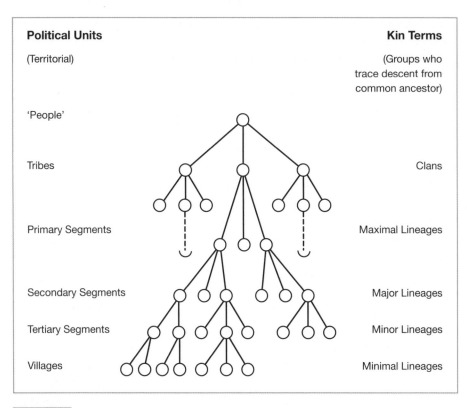

Political Units (Territorial)

Kin Terms (Groups who trace descent from common ancestor)

'People'

Tribes — Clans

Primary Segments — Maximal Lineages

Secondary Segments — Major Lineages

Tertiary Segments — Minor Lineages

Villages — Minimal Lineages

Figure 10.1 A representation of the social and political organisation of the Nuer

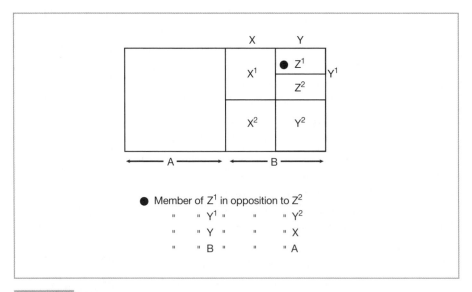

● Member of Z^1 in opposition to Z^2
" " Y^1 " " " Y^2
" " Y " " " X
" " B " " " A

Figure 10.2 The segmentary system

Source: E. E. Evans-Pritchard, *The Nuer* (1940), p. 144, by permission of Oxford University Press.

tertiary (see Figure 10.1). The moral universe varies depending on a specific issue which may arise, and people may only conceive of themselves as members of a particular segment in opposition to others in a different one.

To give an example, if a dispute arises between members of two different villages, their relatives will support them according to principles of common ancestry, which in practice is translated into common territorial segments. Thus, in reference to Figure 10.2, if a member of Z^1 fights with a member of Z^2, the quarrel is between the two Z groups. If a member of Z^1 fights with a member of Y^1, then the differences between the two Z groups will be put aside as the two align in opposition to Y^1 as Y^2. Similarly if a member of Y^1 quarrels with a member of X^1, the whole of Y will align in opposition to X, overriding their previous differences. A common political phenomenon in Nuerland is the feud, and it is more difficult to resolve the larger the groups involved. A feud may be between camps, or villages, or any larger group up to the whole tribe, versus neighbouring people like the Dinka.

This description forms the basis of what has been described as a segmentary system. Evans-Pritchard described such a political system as a 'set of structural relations between territorial segments'. A man is a member of a group by virtue of opposition to another group, and thus group membership is relative to the situation:

> political values are relative and … the political system is an equilibrium between opposed tendencies towards fission and fusion, between the tendency of all groups to segment, and the tendency of all groups to combine with segments of the same order. The tendency towards fusion is inherent in the segmentary character of Nuer political structure, for although any group tends to split into opposed parts these parts must tend to fuse in relation to other groups, since they form part of a segmentary system. Hence fission and fusion in political groups are two aspects of the same segmentary principle, and the Nuer tribe and its divisions are to be understood as an equilibrium between these two contradictory, yet complementary tendencies … the tendency towards segmentation must be defined as a fundamental principle of their social structure   (1940: 48)

Similar principles were found amongst other African peoples, after Evans-Pritchard had published his study, but these principles can be used in other parts of the world too. Consider the case of sporting activities, where people alter their allegiances depending on the magnitude of the occasion. Thus supporters of a local town team in any country would oppose another town in a match between the two, but would join forces to support a larger team drawn from both towns to represent a wider area. In an international event, supporters of all these teams would become supporters of their national team against another country. A very readable ethnography that draws heavily on the ideas of the segmentary system is *The Social Order of the Slum*, a fascinating account of 1960s life in the poorer areas of Chicago (Suttles 1968). Herzfeld's *Poetics of Manhood* (1985), to which we referred in the last chapter, demonstrates its value in a Greek society as well.

Age sets and age grades

The Nuer also divide themselves up into **age sets** and **age grades**, but Evans-Pritchard didn't think that these had much political importance. In other African societies, it is the system of age grades which is seen as the basis of the political system. Examples are to be found in the books cited below by Paul Spencer (1973) and Monica Wilson (1963). Typically, all men in the society participate in such a system, women less often. All those born during a particular period of time are automatically members of a particular *age set*, and they share this membership with their *age mates* throughout life, moving gradually through *age grades* as they get older. Typically, these will include:

age grade – divisions of society through which people pass, and which may determine various roles, particularly ritual and perhaps political, during the course of a lifetime. They are found quite commonly in Africa, but also to a lesser extent in Japan and other Asian countries.

- *youths* – who will be learning the ways of their people;
- *warriors* – who will be responsible for defence and protection; and
- *elders* who – will be responsible for political decisions and dispute resolution.

In some larger tribes, the members of age sets will co-operate with their contemporaries in other groups to form *age regiments*. The Southern African Zulu people had such a system.

Examples of people with an age grade political system are the Nandi and the Maasai people of East Africa. The Nandi, for example, have no fewer than seven age grades, and each age set recruits for about 15 years, so there is some overlap in practice with the functional roles they are able to play. The youngest group is *small children*; the next one is *initiates* who have some free sexual access between the girls' and boys' groups; the next are *warriors*, who are expected to get married; and there are four groups of elders, each of whom is expected to defer to and obey those above them. Members of the same age set are seen as equals and should help one another, even to the extent of sharing spouses. The names of the age sets circulate so that each new group takes the name of the last oldest group, who would by then usually have died out. Important political roles may thus be allocated throughout the society on the basis of age.

Again, this system uses a principle of social order which is found in any society, whether or not it is part of the political system. A cohort of young men may be called upon anywhere to take part in the defence of a nation, or smaller group, although the extent to which age brings greater respect is more variable, especially in the industrialised areas, where people are expected to retire from active work at a certain age. In some parts of Japan there are *age grades*, just as in Africa, with functions that operate in a rather similar way at a local level, and this provides an opportunity to keep even the oldest members of the community valued. These comprise:

- *children's groups* – which meet for sports activities, entertainment, and to play a ritual role in festivals;

- *youth groups* – which also have ritual roles at festivals, meet each other for sports tournaments, and go on trips together, sometimes as a kind of *ordeal;*
- *fire brigades* – which are groups of young married men who are responsible for *protection* in times of danger or local disaster;
- *adults in the prime of life* – who make *decisions* about community affairs, resolve *disputes* and plan *festivals;*
- *old peope* – who also meet for sports, travel together, and carry out tasks in the local community.

In some parts of Japan there are also age sets who meet regularly for social events. They may collect money regularly, help out in times of need, and make journeys together. These groups have little to do with the political system, but they are important for interpersonal relations in everyday life. In general, in Japan, people are expected to defer to their elders, using polite language to address them, and they can only be really relaxed with members of their own age group, hence the importance of age sets and other age-related groups such as old class mates. This is a factor which feeds indirectly into political life in Japan, as the implicit hierarchical difference in relations between those of different ages impinges on the way that they can treat one another, at least in public.

Acquiring and Achieving Political Power and Status

Age is in fact a universal way of measuring *status*, and determining people's *roles* in social life. This is an *ascribed* status, which we cannot choose, like gender and inherited qualities such as membership in a lineage or a royal family. *Achieved* status is that gained through one's occupation, skills and success in other fields. In democratic societies, this latter is generally regarded as the more important and acceptable type of status, although acquired characteristics may in practice be vital to achieving success in political circles. In age-set and lineage societies, formal status is *ascribed*, though informal status may be acquired through oratory and other interpersonal skills.

In any society people interested in the acquisition and manipulation of power will need to negotiate the system as they find it, and anthropologists have adopted different approaches in understanding the rich variety of material they encounter in the field. Evans-Pritchard's studies, cited above, set out an abstract 'structural' system only really accessible to someone who is not caught up within it. He is trying to make clear the way in which the world is classified by the people involved, and thus help a reader to understand the social background within which the behaviour of the individuals he observed may be interpreted.

Others have focused directly on the point of view of the individual members of a society in practice in everyday life, seeking through analysing their personal and interested behaviour to work out how social patterns emerge. The protagonist in this field was Fredrik Barth, a Norwegian anthropologist who worked in several locations, but who made his name writing about the political leaders of the Swat Pathan with an approach he termed transactionalism. This emphasises looking at the way individuals make choices, usually in their own self-interest, in order to *achieve* status and power (Barth 1965). This approach has been highly influential, but has also been criticised for failing to lay out the important categories within which the Pathans were working, and Ahmed's (1976) subsequent work sets out to rectify some of this by placing the Swat Pathan material within the context of the state.

transactionalism – a theory about political behaviour, developed by Frederick Barth, which focuses on the negotiations of individuals and the choices they make in order to achieve political power.

Another ground-breaking study that emphasised again the importance of looking at people in the wider context in which they found themselves was carried out by Edmund Leach (1970). His book *Political Systems of Highland Burma* involves members of several different language groups, and he lays out the formal possibilities for political action by presenting important categories of a system of classification shared across the area in all the languages. This is a structural overview again, and Leach has been criticised for presenting the situation as if it were static, but he argues that he is describing *ideal* systems. As we saw above, it is important to distinguish these from practice, and since this case involves marriage alliances as a vital part of the system, we shall discuss it further in the next chapter.

Opposing principles of equality and hierarchy underpin much of Leach's study, as we shall see, and these also form the focus of a collection of papers, edited by Brenneis and Myers (1984), which examines the situation in a variety of Pacific communities. Entitled *Dangerous Words*, this study approaches the subject of politics through the use of language (cf. Bloch 1975), and indeed, through the suppression of language, or the use of non-verbal and other indirect means of communication in the pursuit of political power. Many of the communities under consideration place a high value on harmonious interaction, as discussed in the previous chapter, and great pains are taken to avoid direct and open confrontation. Such an avenue to political power is quite unfamiliar to people who have been brought up in a society where government is carried out through debate between a party in power and others in open opposition, but it is precisely an anthropological approach which can reveal the mechanisms of political interaction in societies that do not prize the dialectical means of resolving issues.

In my book *Wrapping Culture*, referred to in Chapter 3, I set out to demonstrate some of the layers of indirect communication which could enter into a struggle for power, and although Japan was the main ethnographic focus, and gifts and their wrapping the prototype, there are many other examples. We considered cases of the power of 'wrapping the body' in Chapters 5 and 6, when we looked at the adornment of the Wahgi people of New Guinea and the political implications of the body tattoo. The use of castles and palaces to express authority as well as demonstrating physical power is an example of the 'wrapping of space', and I have also suggested a notion of 'wrapping time' in the subtle forms of organisation and presentation which may be used in meetings.

In all these cases there is political advantage to be gained by those who can exploit these indirect forms of communication. In a society such as Japan which apparently has a rather fixed set of principles ordering people into hierarchical frames, the skilful use of various forms of 'wrapping' allows considerable manipulation of the *status quo* by people who understand the system. In Japan, these different layers of operation are clearly recognised, and in any formal situation there is a 'front' and 'rear' or inside activities, going on. It was my view, in using the notion of 'wrapping', that an understanding of the Japanese case might help people to see parallel cases in other societies, especially those which value harmony and avoid direct confrontation.

In approaching the subject through a consideration of polite and formal language in order to address the question of hierarchy and how it is perceived in Japan, it might be thought beneficial to be from an eminently hierarchical society such as Britain, which also has a complicated set of rules about politeness and etiquette. There may be some truth in this, as there are historical and practical parallels between the two systems, but there is also a danger of expecting things to operate in a recognisable way, as we shall also see in the next chapter. Children in Japan learn about the responsibilities attached to being older, and the advantages of being younger, before they learn about the reverse, which I contend is commoner in many Western countries. This sets up values and expectations that colour future relationships in quite a different way, though direct translation may reveal little of this discrepancy. Much of my research was also carried out amongst women, who demonstrated clearly the power attached to skill in the manipulation of different forms of language, and it is here, too, that perceptions of outsiders about the 'meek and demure' Japanese housewife can be shown in practice to be quite false.

There are many societies in which women carry more power than was recognised by anthropologists who came from a male-dominated political background. Even if the researchers were women, they tended to look to the men they worked with to understand the political system, whereas more recent work–like that of Annette Weiner, which we discussed in Chapter 3, and Lynn Stephen's (2005) work with Zapotec women – has revealed different forms of power that reside with the female members of a society. The Six Nations of the Haudenosaunee people have a confederacy of chiefs, a system which is supposed to have influenced Benjamin Franklin and others when they drew up the American constitution (see website below), but less well known is their system of clan mothers, who choose those chiefs, and wield much power behind the scenes (see website).

Conclusion

We have identified several examples where looking at a political system in its wider social context is vital to a deep understanding of where power is located and how it is used. This theme will persist into the next chapter, where we consider the importance of seeing kinship and marriage in their social context, and again warn of the dangers of making assumptions too quickly when we find something similar to the system with which we have been brought up.

Discussion Questions

1 Do you think democracy is the only acceptable way to run a country? Why? Does it actually fulfil those reasons in practice?

2 What qualities would you admire in a leader in your society? How do they reflect the wider system of values? Are 'managers' leaders?

3 Do you consider economic power to be ultimately the most effective? What other forms of power do you use in your own life? How about others around you?

References and Further Research

Books

Ahmed, Akbar S. (1976) *Millennium and Charisma among the Pathans* (London: Routledge and Kegan Paul).

Balandier, Georges (1967) *Political Anthropology* (London: Allen Lane).

Barth, Fredrik (1965) *Political Leadership among the Swat Pathans* (London: Athlone Press).

Bloch, Maurice (ed.) (1975) *Political Language and Oratory in Traditional Societies* (London: Academic Press).

Brenneis, Donald Lawrence and Myers, Fred R. (1984) *Dangerous Words: Language and Politics in the Pacific* (New York: New York University Press).

Evans-Pritchard, E. E. (1940) *The Nuer* (Oxford: Oxford University Press).

Evans-Pritchard, E. E.(1948) *The Divine Kingship of the Shilluk of the Nilotic Sudan* (Cambridge: Cambridge University Press).

Ferguson, R. B. (1995) *Yanomami Warfare: A Political History* (Santa Fe, NM: School of American Research Press).

Fortes, M. and Evans-Pritchard, E. E. (1940) *African Political Systems* (Oxford: Oxford University Press).

Gledhill, John (1994) *Power and Its Disguises: Anthropological Perspectives on Politics* (London: Pluto Press).

Godelier, Maurice (1986) *The Making of Great Men* (Cambridge: Cambridge University Press).

Gupta, A. and Ferguson, J. (eds) (1997) *Culture, Power, Place: Explorations in Critical Anthropology* (Durham, NC: Duke University Press).

Hendry, Joy (1993) *Wrapping Culture* (Oxford: Clarendon Press).

Herzfeld, Michael (1985) *The Poetics of Manhood: Contest and Identity in a Cretan Mountain Village* (Princeton, NJ: Princeton University Press).

Leach, E. R. (1970) *Political Systems of Highland Burma* (London: Athlone Press).

Maybury-Lewis, David (1974) *The Akwe Shavante* (Oxford: Oxford University Press).
Shore, Cris (1990) *Italian Communism: The Escape from Leninism* (London: Pluto Press).
Spencer, Paul (1973) *Nomads in Alliance* (London: Oxford University Press).
Stephen, Lynn (2005) *Zapotec Women: Gender, Class and Ethnicity in Globalized Oaxaca* (Durham, NC: Duke University Press).
Strathern, Andrew (1971) *The Rope of Moka: Big Men and Ceremonial Exchange in Mount Hagen, New Guinea* (London: Cambridge University Press).
Suttles, Gerald D. (1968) *The Social Order of the Slum: Ethnicity and Territory in the Inner City* (Chicago and London: University of Chicago Press).
Vincent, Joan (2004) *The Anthropology of Politics: A Reader in Ethnography, Theory and Critique* (Oxford and Malden, Mass.: Blackwell Publishing).
Vincent, Joan, and Nugent David (2006) *A Companion to the Anthropology of Politics* (Oxford: Blackwell Publishing).
Weiner, Annette B. (1992) *Inalienable Possessions* (Berkeley: University of California Press).
Wilson, Monica (1963) *Good Company: A Study of Nyakyusa Age-Villages* (Boston, Mass.: Beacon Press).

Articles

Anthropology Today (2005) Special Issue on Policy and Islam, 21(1).
Jakubowska, Longina (1990) 'Political Drama in Poland: The Use of National Symbols', *Anthropology Today*, 6(4): 10–13.
Keenan, Jeremy (2006) 'Conspiracy Theories and "Terrorists": How the "War on Terror" is Placing New Responsibilities on Anthropology', *Anthropology Today*, 22(6): 4–9.
Khazanov, Anatoly M. (1996) 'Anthropologists in the Midst of Ethnic Conflicts', *Anthropology Today*, 12(2): 5–8.
Lecomte-Tilouine, Marie (2004) 'Regicide and Maoist Revolutionary Warfare in Nepal: Modern Intricacies of a Warrior Kingdom', *Anthropology Today*, 20(1): 13–19.
Leeds, Anthony (1969) 'Ecological Determinants of Chieftanship among the Yaruro Indians of Venezuela', in Andrew P. Vayda (ed.), *Environment and Cultural Behaviour* (Austin and London: University of Texas Press).
Rival, Laura (1997) 'Oil and Sustainable Development in the Latin American Humid Tropics', *Anthropology Today*, 13(6): 1–3.
Seneviratne, H. L. (2001) 'Buddhist Monks and Ethnic Politics: A War Zone in an Island Paradise', *Anthropology Today*, 17(2): 15–21.

Novels

Clavell, James (1975) *Shōgun* (London: Hodder & Stoughton) is a well known-novel, subsequently filmed for television in a less anthropologically interesting way, about the encounter between a British sailor–explorer and the Japanese power structure during a period in the sixteenth century when Japan was relatively open to outsiders.
Heller, Joseph (1994[1961]) *Catch-22* (London: Vintage). A general critique of bureaucratic operation and reasoning.
Mishima Yukio (1967) *After the Banquet* (Tokyo and Rutland, Vt.: Tuttle) is a novel which portrays life behind the scenes of early twentieth-century Japanese politicians, showing also the potential power of women close to the men with big names.
Primary Colors (London: Vintage, 1996) was first published anonymously, but was later revealed to be by the journalist Joe Klein and based on Clinton's first presidential campaign.
Rand, Ayn (2007[1959]) *Atlas Shrugged* (London: Penguin Modern Classics) sets out to portray any form of state intervention in society as systemically flawed. Rand claimed that the politics portrayed in the novel are a result of her attempt to display her image of the ideal person and the individual mind's position and value in society.

Scott, Paul (1996) *The Jewel in the Crown* (London: Mandarin) and the subsequent three novels in the *Raj Quartet* portray life in the closing years of British rule in India.

Films

Gandhi (Richard Attenborough, 1982) tells the story of Mahatma Gandhi's leadership through his philosophy of non-violent but direct-action protest.

The Kawelka: Ongka's Big Moka (see Chapter 3).

The Kayapo: Out of the Forest (Michael Beckham and Terence Turner, 1988), another excellent 'Disappearing World' film discussing the resistance and reunification of peoples of Altamira against a huge hydroelectric dam project on the Xingu River, a large tributary of the Amazon.

The Masai (see Chapter 4).

Metropolis (Fritz Lang, 1927) is a silent futuristic film depicting an urban dystopia of 2027 and is about a society brutally divided into 'thinkers' and 'workers'.

The Mursi: War with the Bodi: Decision-making and *Relations with the Kwegu* (Leslie Woodhead, 1985) are anthropological films about a cattle-keeping people of South-West Ethiopia who have no formal chiefs or leaders.

Nixon (Oliver Stone, 1995) tells the story of American president Richard Nixon's political and personal life.

The Shilluk of Southern Sudan (Chris Curling, Paul Howell, Walter Kunijwok and André Singer, 52 minutes, 'Disappearing World' series) is a compelling analysis of Shilluk kingship in 1975. See the website below for a more recent update on the situation.

Websites

http://www.centrelink.org/ANTH423/bibliography.htm – a bibliography of political anthropology.

http://www.sudan101.com/nur.htm – an evangelical website about the Nuer in war-torn Sudan.

http://www.paxchristi.nl/files/Documenten/afrika/soedan/040505_report_shilluk_kingdom.pdf – a report from Nairobi about the current situation of the Shilluk people.

http://www.ratical.org/many_worlds/6Nations/ – an account of the history and politics of the Iroquoian (Haudenosaunee) people.

http://www.peace4turtleisland.org/pages/womensbelt.htm – concerned with women of the Haudenosaunee.

http://www.mnsu.edu/emuseum/cultural/southamerica/shavante.html – a website about the Shavante people of Mato Grosso, Brazil.

11

Family, Kinship and Marriage

Varieties of Kinship

Within the subject of social anthropology, *kinship* and *marriage* are amongst the oldest and most debated topics. It is within a family group of some sort that most of us are reared, and therefore where most of us learn about social relationships. As we discussed briefly in Chapter 1, it is here that we learn to classify other human beings, and how we should behave towards them. Because these distinctions are learned so early, they are hard to dislodge, and, as we shall see, they tend to colour our views of other peoples, and their relations. We may or may not see much of our close relatives, but it is with these that we celebrate important life crises such as birth, marriage and death, and it is to these people that we may well turn in times of need.

In different societies, people have different ideas about how to classify their relatives, and how to calculate their degrees of relatedness. They even have different ideas about how people become related in the first place. Ideas of genealogy are found in all societies, but ideas about conception and the development of a new human being are rather varied, and with the advent of *new reproductive technologies*, virulent debates have emerged. Not everyone is exclusively concerned with 'blood ties', as the

English language would suggest: some attach as much importance to relatives according to the nurturing roles of parents who might be described as 'adopted' in English; others derive relationships through a common bond with the land.

The sharing of a household is often an important factor to consider, and in several systems of kinship, this will override relationships which may be described as 'natural' or 'biological'. The film *Secrets and Lies* illustrated in a bitter-sweet way the social and emotional problems that can arise when people reared in an adoptive family take steps to make contact with their parents of birth, compounded here when details of an interracial union had been concealed from even those closest to the parties involved.

The immediate family group varies from one society to another, too, and there are numerous possibilities for residential arrangements. In Western societies, the familiar nuclear family has undergone a great deal of change in recent years, and the 'single-parent family' has become a common phrase, though the actual form, where it comprises a mother and her children, is not unusual in the world at large although that of a father and children is rarer. The terminology implies the lack of another parent, however, and expresses

nuclear family – a basic unit of parents and children, as defined by English language usage.

an ideological preference for two parents to be involved with the rearing of children, even if they are not both related to the children, and the children may have 'parents' in more than one home. Another recent addition to Western societies can be found in same-sex marriages and parentage (see First-hand Account 11.1 overleaf), and we will see that this is not unheard of elsewhere as well. In any case, so-called 'natural' features have become complicated. When a child is conceived in a test-tube, now called *in vitro* fertilisation or IVF, and possibly carried to the point of birth by a *surrogate* mother (who has not donated the genetic material), the maternal biological link is confused, and if the paternity is assisted, too, the child's parenthood becomes very unclear. In an early anthropological comment on the Warnock Report, the first official British response to scientific developments which made possible 'human-assisted reproduction', Peter Rivière's article 'Unscrambling Parenthood' (1985) argued for the role social anthropology might play in helping to sort out some of the confusion.

Two of the important points he made were, first, that any construct of genealogy and parenthood is cultural, and secondly, that examples from societies anthropologists have studied may help to disentangle the issues involved. For one thing, in considering the problems of artificial insemination, we already have the vocabulary to distinguish between a child's genetic father and a man who has taken on a social role with regard to that child. Based on work with African people like the Nuer, for whom we saw in the last chapter that lineal relations are politically very important, anthropologists devised a distinction between a genitor, for the genetic father, and a pater for the social role.

genitor – a term devised by anthropologists to describe the genetic father of a child, when this might be distinguished from a social parent, who would be named **pater**.

In cases already considered by anthropologists, some of which we will encounter in this chapter, the genitor could be a person who made it possible for another man, known as the pater, to have a child to carry on his line, so there were in fact precedents for the issues which arose in considering the legal, ethical and social issues surrounding the donation of sperm for artificial insemination. The distinction has been useful in understanding arrangements in many socie-

pater - a term devised by anthropologists to describe a man who plays the social role of father to a child when this needs to be distinguished from a genetic parent, who would be named **genitor**.

ties, and, where genealogy is a vital element of social and political life, there are various forms of social construction to overcome problems such as infertility or premature death.

It is not conceptually difficult for this distinction to be modified to apply to the case of the donation of an egg for an infertile mother to carry, when she might be termed *mater* and the donor *genetrix* but, as Rivière pointed out, there was no precedent for the separation of roles of conception and gestation which technology has made possible. In some systems of thought, the period of gestation has been regarded as more important than the moment of conception for the development of the new human being, and the father may be expected to keep 'feeding' the foetus with further sexual encounters. This may sound a little bizarre, but one of the concerns of the British public, and therefore the Warnock Committee, was certainly about how a child should be treated once it is born if it is to develop into a well-balanced member of the society in which it lives, as mentioned above in the case of the 'single-parent family'.

Rivière discussed the further complications which arise if all three roles – provision of an egg (the role of the *genetrix*), the carrying of the child, and the subsequent rearing of that child – are separated. The need to use Latin words for these roles already indicates the linguistic problems which arise in English, but there are all sorts of other issues related to cultural constructions of the family, legal ideas about legitimacy and inheritance, religious, scientific and social ideas about the nature of a human being, and the rights of men and women to be in control of their bodies.

There has been much debate amongst anthropologists on this subject since that time (see, for example, Franklin 1997; Shore 1992; Strathern 1992; Carsten 2004) but Rivière wrote rather cautiously:

> I am not advocating ... that we should therefore adopt the ideas and practices of other people. I am merely suggesting that it might help if we removed our cultural blinkers and saw our problems in a wider perspective. If we did this, the surrogate mothers might not appear to be the threat to civilization that some people make them out to be.   (1985: 6)

In a sense, this is a plea which could apply to many social issues, and the article expresses a concern at the time of writing which has dissipated over the years, but as we have already seen in our examination of the work of anthropologists, we too find it hard to escape those 'cultural blinkers'.

Same-sex relationships are not new in the United States, as is evidenced in calling them 'Boston marriages' in Victorian days. This phrase was used to describe two women living together, while discreetly avoiding the true nature of the relationship. It has only been in modern times that same-sex relationships between women, and men for that matter, have been openly discussed and, to some degree, regarded as an acceptable coupling. When you throw children into the mix, it becomes more controversial. As a lesbian couple living in San Francisco, California (which is known for its liberal attitudes), we do not face the prejudice and misunderstanding that may exist in other parts of the United States.

First-hand account 11.1:

Mary Martha Beaton, American – on Same-Sex Parentage

Having two adopted girls (Jesse and Sara – five years' age difference – both two and a half years old at adoption), we felt it was important to give them the support they needed and an exposure to an accepting society. We did not want to subject them to name calling and other prejudicial labels that might have been applied, so we moved from Boston to the liberal West Coast. In reality, I think we could live anywhere, but I wanted it to be easier on the girls.

Not having been in a traditional marriage, I cannot draw direct comparisons, but I can say that I feel our family was (and still is) as normal and healthy and functional as any traditional parent–child relationship. We laughed together, cried together, grew together, had the usual mother–daughter conflicts and, while there were two mothers, the girls always seemed to know exactly who they could get what they wanted from, and how. They soon learned how to work each parent to their advantage, and learned to avoid asking 'that mother' when they knew the answer would be 'no'. To them, having two mothers was natural, and because they were brought up to be proud of their family, and knew they were loved, and in a supportive school system, for the most part, their having two mothers was not an issue. This is not to say there were not real struggles in raising Jesse and Sara.

There were the usual parent–child fights and arguments about curfews, boyfriends, slumber parties, party attendance, school grades, cleaning their rooms, choirs, and the usual conflicts parents all have. Speaking specifically about same-sex parents, I would say when adolescence hit, our younger daughter, Sara, was less secure about telling people she had two parents of the same sex than her older sister, Jesse. Sara struggled with that and we let her come to terms with it in her own time. Eventually, as she matured, she found that her friends thought it was 'fun' to have two mothers, and even labelled her as lucky, so she came to appreciate her family configuration.

Our girls are now 21 and 25 years old, with intact self-esteems, living on their own and both in healthy relationships with men. We raised them with the same values that any family would: respect for others, acceptance of others, tolerance for differences, and knowing the importance of spirituality, love of family, and tradition. I feel we made the same sacrifices, the same commitments, the same decisions, and had the same devotion to family as any parents would.

Some anthropologists have tried over the years to draw up typologies of 'kinship systems' which would eventually encompass all possible varieties; others have concentrated on developing often very complex theories about logical possibilities for kin relations. In the 1970s, as part of a 'rethinking' vogue within anthropology, a book entitled *Rethinking Kinship and Marriage* (Needham 1971) focused on basic difficulties, first about defining something universal which could be called kinship, and then about isolating such a thing from wider aspects of the social system in which it was found. The authors suggested that early anthropologists were somewhat blinded by their own expectations of kinship, based on deeply ingrained ideas about biological links, and later ones followed their lead without enough reflection about what they were doing and how they might be taking some aspects of social life out of their context.

kinship – a term used by anthropologists to describe sets of relationships considered primary in any society, also called *family* and *relations*, but demonstrating huge variety in different societies in practice.

The editor, Rodney Needham, wrote:

There has been a fair amount of discussion about what 'kinship' really is. My own view is that much of this debate is pretty scholastic and inconsequential ... Let me simply adopt the minimal premiss that kinship has to do with the allocation of rights and their transmission from one generation to the next. These rights are not of any specific kind but are exceedingly various: they include most prominently rights of group

membership, succession to office, inheritance of property, locality of
residence, type of occupation, and a great deal else. They are all, however,
transmissible by modes which have nothing to do with sex or genealogical
states of transmitter or recipient.   (1971: 3–4)

In Britain, kin relations are often relatively isolated from the rest of social life,
and an overlap of family loyalty into economic and political life may be perceived
negatively as *nepotism*, or regarded with suspicion. The rise to wealth of Mark
Thatcher, son of the former British Prime Minister, is a good case to illustrate this
point, especially in view of his later dubious African affairs. Becoming wealthy in
his own right by taking advantage of his mother's name is one less than admirable
thing, but a hint of overlap with political decision making was totally unacceptable to the British press. A similar reaction can be found among some Americans
about politicians and their families, and there is some resentment about access to
Hollywood (see website below). In fact, most people expect to help their kin to
get on in the world, but there is sometimes quite a sharp dividing line between
acceptable family support and confusing the needs and desires of one's relatives
with one's wider public duty.

In the previous chapter we began to discern an example of a situation where
kin relations were entirely bound up with political life – indeed it would have
been impossible to understand one without an idea of the other. Although actual
neighbourly relations amongst the Nuer may be more important than kin when
people work out who to support in a particular political situation, they use the
genealogical vocabulary to classify one another. **Lineage** membership is a most
important principle for calculating relationships, so if a man dies without issue, a
ghost marriage may be arranged between him and a woman
who takes a living man as genitor, providing children to   **ghost marriage** – a
continue the line through the dead man (known as the   marriage arranged
pater). In this case the child inherits group membership   posthumously to
without a 'biological' relationship.   ensure lineal continu-
                                                             ity and thus perhaps
In the world at large, there is a huge variety in the way   care of the soul of the
in which people classify others around them, and relations   dead in the afterlife.
whom we might at first think of as *kin* may actually have little to do with genealogical connections. They may also be inextricably tied up with economic transactions, the political system and the religious beliefs of the people concerned.
It is thus very important to understand how people's *relations* fit into the wider
society in which they are found before trying to isolate them. It is for this reason
that the whole subject of kinship has been left until we have covered other areas,
and in this chapter we will consider a specific case to illustrate this point, but first
we need introduce some of the terminology.

Within multicultural societies, people from specific ethnic backgrounds still
grow up within their own families, and it is here that they learn to look out at the
social life within which their family is lodged. The great variety mentioned above
is not confined to certain locations, then, it is scattered throughout the world. It

is thus not only possible for a wide range of people to broaden the assumptions and expectations associated with relatives by simply taking an interest in those around them; it can also be crucial to good neighbourly understanding. The material presented here is not only curious and interesting, then; it may be an important part of everyday life across the globe.

To introduce some of the conventions adopted by anthropologists for describing kin relations, we examine first what we will call a *standard English family*, a kind of model of how people using the English language classify one another as relatives, wherever the language is used. We will then place this system in a wider context by turning to look at unilineal descent groups, which offer a completely contrasting way of classifying relatives, found in various forms in different parts of the world. We will then give a concrete example of how relatives may be perceived in a multicultural situation by focusing on the Pakistani community in Oxford. This case study will lead us into the last part of the chapter, where the focus will be marriage.

Classifying Kin Relations

In order to discuss family relationships at all, various conventions have been adopted. Some of these are familiar to those who take an interest in family trees, others are understood readily only by the professional anthropologist. If we start with the so-called 'standard English family', we can draw a diagram which depicts people in terms of their nearest relations, namely parents and siblings, and, by extension, to their more distant aunts, uncles and cousins. We can place marriages on this diagram, and there is a convention for depicting serial marriage in the case of death or divorce and remarriage.

Figure 11.1 is a representation of this 'standard English family'. It uses a small circle (○) to represent a woman and a triangle (△) to represent a man. An equals sign (=) represents a marriage or an informal union which results in offspring, and a line joining a circle and a triangle from above stands for a brother–sister relationship. It is important to remember that this is not a representation of an actual situation, but a set of logical possibilities. Thus, there is only one brother and sister in each unit, because these stand for the two possible positions that children may occupy terminologically. This becomes significant in the next generation when the pair would take on new roles to each other's children.

By examining the diagram that results we can work out a number of implications which can be drawn from the English-language system of designating relatives. The terms used separate off units of parents and children from more distant relatives by having unique terms for each category of member–mother, father, son, daughter – as opposed to blanket terms like uncle, aunt and cousins which cover a wide range of people outside that unit. All of the latter may have special characteristics for their actual relations, and the terms may even be used for friends, but the terms themselves make no such distinctions. The marked

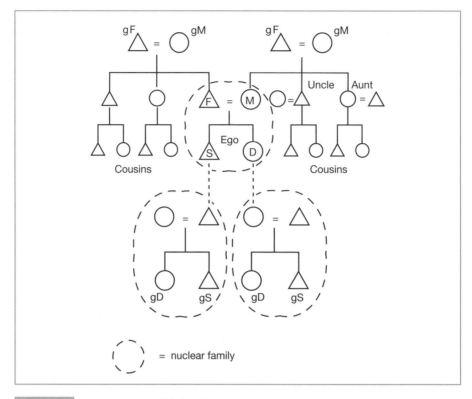

Figure 11.1 A standard English family

family units, comprising people who do have distinct terms, are technically called *nuclear families*, and in many English-speaking and other countries people live in units that express degrees of closeness in a similar way.

Up and down the diagram, the terms used in the nuclear unit are qualified for the people outside it by adding the prefix *grand* to the four distinct terms (as in grandmother, grandson, and so forth) or a number of *greats* to indicate further generational distance (as in great-grandmother, and so on). These terms distinguish the lineal relatives, named after the line which can be traced through the generations, from uncles, aunts and cousins, essentially related through siblings, which are termed lateral, after the Latin for 'out to the side'. This use of terminology suggests another marking which may have practical implications too.

Rights and obligations concerned with inheritance rules are one example, and these are usually determined by family relationships in any particular legal system, which

lineal relatives – individuals related along a line which can be traced through the generations; see also **patrilineal** and **matrilineal** relatives.

lateral relations – the term used to describe relatives who are connected through siblings, distinguished in many languages in the next generation (i.e. for the children of siblings) as **matrilateral** or **patrilateral** in order to mark important kin divisions in a society.

inheritance – rules for passing on status, roles, goods and membership in particular social groups from one generation to the next.

will distinguish different degrees of proximity, though the details vary from one country to another. In some cases, there is a system of primogeniture, for example, which indicates a special role for an eldest son. In Japanese, where terminology makes distinctions otherwise rather similar to the English case, there are terms to mark the birth order among the children, especially marking the eldest son, and in Nahuatl, an indigenous Mexican language, it is the youngest son who may be denoted in this way.

primogeniture – indicates a special role of inheritance for an eldest son.

Terminology does not always indicate practice, however, and an interesting aspect of our 'English' diagram is the lack of a distinction based on gender, let alone birth order. From the point of view of a child in the middle nuclear family, a reference point often termed *ego* by anthropologists, no terminological distinctions are made between relatives on the mother's or father's side. In practice, however, children's surnames are usually taken from the father in English-speaking societies, and women may well turn to their mothers for help with their own children, for example, and perhaps to pass on certain material objects, such as porcelain and jewellery.

Inheritance is of course important in all societies, and in many other languages distinctions of this sort are made. Anthropologists therefore decided to use Latin terms to devise a system of talking about inheritance in cases where the English language is lacking in appropriate distinctions. Thus, when something is passed through the male line, as is usually the case for English names, it is said to be passed patrilineally. When it is passed through the female line, the term used is matrilineal inheritance (see Figure 11.2 for a way of depicting these lines).

In some societies matrilineal inheritance may still be passed from man to man, that is, a man receives his share of his inheritance from his *mother's brother* (rather than from his father, as in a patriline), and, likewise, a man passes it on to his *sister's son* (in Figure 11.2, the share would then pass between the triangles

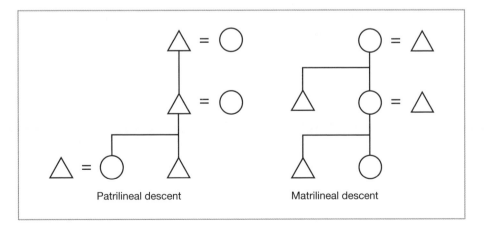

Patrilineal descent   Matrilineal descent

Figure 11.2 Patrilineal and matrilineal descent

on the left-hand side of the second diagram). Where this latter preference predominates, the whole society has sometimes been termed a **matrilineal** society. It is important to consider *property*, *status*, *titles* and *group membership* separately, however, as these may not be the same. In the following section the last will be the focus of attention.

Unilineal Descent Groups

Principles of **descent** are particularly important in societies where they lead to the formation of groups descended from one common ancestor. In Figure 11.3 the situation is depicted of a *patrilineal descent* group, where the shaded brother and sister pair at the bottom are again in the position of *ego*. This time their rela-

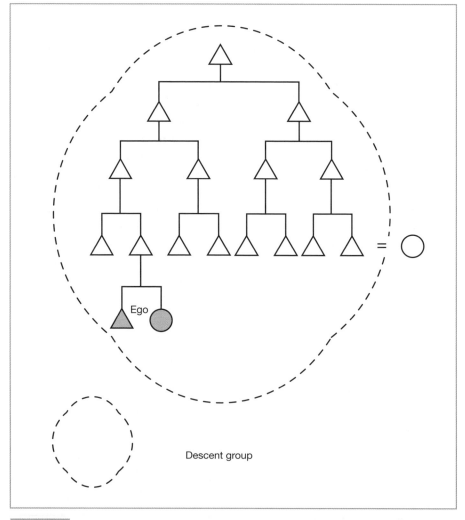

Figure **11.3**   A unilineal descent group

tives are worked out by virtue of membership in a group traced through men, as shown in the diagram. Women who are born into the group, like the female *ego*, usually marry out, so they are not shown. Wives of the males are members of other groups, as shown in the case of the example of a wife at the right hand side of the diagram.

Groups of this sort may be *clans* such as those of the Ancient Romans, Hebrews and Scots, or they may form a complicated lineage system like that seen amongst the Nuer and discussed in the previous chapter. Membership in such a group may determine residence possibilities, as well as economic partners such as companions for herding, hunting and agriculture, and it may define political allegiances and obligations in case of war, although the latter may also be affected by one's membership in an age grade. It is also very likely to affect possibilities for marriage, since people are usually expected to marry out of their own group.

Ancestors who preceded the present incumbents as members of unilineal descent groups may appear as important characters in local legend and mythology, and they may also play a part in religious and ritual life. These may be the beings to be blamed and consulted in the case of misfortune, as we have seen, and their help may also be sought in times of need. Association with particular ancestors may bring rights and/or obligations, and they will certainly play a part in the identity of a living being in their social world. In return, the living will perform rites for the care of their ancestors in the afterlife, and arrangements are very often made for a person with no issue to have descendants through some kind of social adoption, or ghost marriage, as described above for the Nuer.

In some relatively closed societies everybody may be classified as a member of a lineage, and the relationship with everyone else in the society determined by relationships between these groups. Naming terminology will reflect these allegiances, and appropriate behaviour follows depending on the type of relationship involved. Members of one's own lineage would be in a more intimate relationship than those of the lineage into which one had, or expected to be, married, and in-laws may be treated with special respect or even avoidance. Anthropologists approaching such people found it necessary to be adopted into a group of relatives in order to communicate in a meaningful fashion at all. Once they had found a niche, everyone was able to work out the appropriate behaviour.

Such arrangements make it quite difficult to translate kin terms into the English language. For example, the term which might be translated as *brother* refers in some societies to all male members of one generation in the same lineage, and *father* to all those of the senior generation. Earlier anthropologists called such usages *classificatory terminology*, to distinguish them from terms which applied more exclusively to categories they recognised, which they called *descriptive terminology*. However, if the range of people denoted by the term is understood, the terms are *descriptive* in each situation, and they may indicate some important social categories, so seeking to identify the *descriptive* significance of a term is a good way to proceed.

Terms of address may also carry further significance in making sense of the system of classification in a particular society. For example, in a society where group membership is inherited matrilineally, but passed from man to man, as discussed above, there may be a lineage term for *father's sister* which literally means *female father*, and similarly *mother's brother* may mean *male mother*. Here the terms for father and mother will be less concerned with gender than with group affiliation. The 'male mother' will simply be a male of the senior generation in one's own lineage, and the 'female father' a representative of the group to which a father owes his allegiance and inheritance. To the first a young person may owe obedience and respect, to the second, deference and distance.

Siblings usually form a unit related to others in the same way, and many people make terminological distinctions between matrilateral (related through one's mother) and patrilateral (related through one's father) relatives, sometimes because these are automatically members of different clans, and one might have to marry out of one's own clan. Cross-cousins (related through siblings of the opposite sex) are also very often distinguished from parallel-cousins (related through siblings of the same sex). These distinctions are illustrated in Figure 11.4, where the sibling pair in the centre of the diagram take the position of *ego*, and their matrilateral and patrilateral cousins, on the right and left of the diagram respectively, are marked as parallel or cross, depending of their parents' relationships.

matrilateral relatives – those in the same generation related through the mother's family.

patrilateral relatives – those in the same generation, but related through the father.

cross-cousins – are the offspring of siblings of opposite sex.

parallel-cousins – are the offspring of siblings of the same sex, male or female.

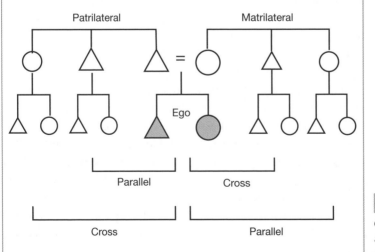

Figure 11.4

Cross-cousins and parallel-cousins

Kinship in a Multicultural Context: A Case Study

To pick up the point made earlier by Rodney Needham about the advisability of looking at 'kinship' in its social context, this section of the chapter will be devoted to a detailed examination of one particular case. The example has been chosen to illustrate another, earlier point about the multiplicity of systems now found in many parts of the world, and the need to understand our neighbours. The case is the Pakistani community in Oxford, and the section is largely based on the ethnography of Alison Shaw (1988, 2000), with some personal insights from second-generation members of the community. Photograph 11.1 illustrates the mosque built by members of this community to which neighbours and other faith groups were invited as it was being built.

Throughout her books, Shaw makes comparisons with the situation of continuing relations in Pakistan and elsewhere, and argues that the similarities between the old and new communities outweigh the differences brought about by coexistence of the new one with the wider community in England. She is also keen to break down prejudices and assumptions which are commonly made by the wider community about the Pakistanis in Britain, and sometimes vice versa, and her study takes pains to present the point of view of the people with whom she worked.

Most members of this community come from the Punjabi district of Pakistan, many from the Jhelum area, south-east of Islamabad, and they maintain contact with their forebears through visits, by sending money and other resources, and by arranging marriages and funerals back in Pakistan. Many families also feel it important to send their British-born children to spend time with their Pakistani

Photograph 11.1 The mosque in Oxford built by members of the Pakistani community described in this chapter (photograph: Bob Pomfret).

relatives. Within Britain, the group which would seem to be most significant for members of this community is known as the *birādarī*, commonly translated as 'relations'. This group is not clearly defined as a group of kin, although it may comprise a set of brothers or cousins and their offspring, but it is the most immediate circle of people on whom a member may depend, and to whom a person feels obliged.

The limits of the group are contextual, somewhat in the spirit of the segmentary system of the previous chapter, and the whole Pakistani community in Oxford could be described *birādarī* in contrast with the wider cosmopolitan citizenship. In other situations, the *birādarī* is conceived to include members of the family who have remained behind in Pakistan, on whom one can call to put up one's children, and to whom one may well be expected to send goods and money (a situation we will raise again in Chapter 14). In practice, in everyday life, this group will consist of a set of people who live together, or in close proximity, and it is the women of the group who seek to preserve the strength of the immediate set of close relations through the explicit exchange of gifts.

The composition of a Pakistani household in Oxford sometimes confuses their non-Pakistani neighbours, as may their arrangement of rooms, and Alison Shaw works from the plan of a typical house in Pakistan to explain the modifications of more traditional British use to the often Victorian houses. The most important distinction is between the male and female worlds, for these are Muslim families who seek to preserve Islamic ideals:

> A notable feature of all east Oxford Pakistani houses is that despite the different physical layout of the houses considerations of *purdah* are very important. This is best illustrated by the arrival of visitors. If male visitors arrive and a male family member is at home, the visitors may first be detained at the door while the women of the household, modestly adjusting their *dupattās* over their heads, leave the front room and retreat to the backroom or kitchen. For as long as unrelated men are present, the women of the household will not usually enter the front room; instead the men of the household will go or send children to the backroom with requests for food and tea for the guests. The men may themselves carry the food or drinks from the kitchen to the front room, though sometimes the women will do this, without speaking to the male visitors.   (Shaw 1988: 63)

The children of a house come under the guidance of the women, but young married couples very often live with the parents of the husband, and the grandmother is sometimes addressed with the same term as 'mother' in Urdu and Punjabi, namely '*ammi*', which can be confusing when the children begin to translate things into English. Similarly, they may use the same Urdu/Punjabi terms for brother and sister in reference to their cousins, especially if they are co-resident, because the strict terms are simply 'aunt/uncle-born brother/sister', with distinctions for matrilaterality and patrilaterality. On the male side, too, the term for father may also be used for grandfather, and the term for father's brother is appropriate for father's cousins and may also be used for friends' fathers and fathers' friends, as a sign of respect to the senior generation.

Clearly, the view of a child growing up in this community will be somewhat different from that of a child whose first language defines the 'standard English family' detailed above, although that was of course only a model. When a small child from the Pakistani community goes to school and is asked about his or her relatives, the response of an unsympathetic teacher could be withering, but it could also be creative and helpful – a good reason for welcoming students of education on anthropology courses. In practice, the Pakistani children living in Oxford have adapted some of their relationships to make more sense when they speak in English, and a local young informant gave me the terms which fitted a 'standard English' view as well as his own indigenous one.

Expectations of behaviour within the Pakistani family are sometimes quite shocking to outsiders in British communities, especially on the touchy subject of gender. Men are in a position to order their female relatives to attend to their needs, it seems, and the same informant reported gleefully that his sister is obliged to bring him things in the home. He also noted that this expectation only starts as the girls grow up, however, and if he tries to get his youngest sisters to wait on him he is given short shrift. This expectation is part of a wider view still maintained in the more conservative families that men are the ones to earn the money and women to take care of the home, but a stronger constraint on all family members is usually to play an appropriate part in contributing to the wider needs of the *birādarī*.

Alison Shaw started her first book with an example of her own initial misunderstanding of the decision of a promising member of the community she had studied to turn down a place at university. She goes on to present his rationale in terms of the expectations of the wider Pakistani community, and compares this with her own reasons for being disappointed on his behalf. She uses this example to illustrate the difficulties of undoing one's own preconceptions in looking at those of people brought up with a different set, but also to introduce the value of belonging to a wider group such as the Pakistani *birādarī*.

Later in the book, Shaw details several cases of real material help people have received from their relatives – for house purchase, building, education, marriage and so forth – and this is of course the positive side of the commitment which imposes the constraints that she had initially interpreted negatively. Being part of a large social group such as we have described here clearly involves fitting in at least to some extent with the wider expectations of the group. Those who wish to receive the benefits must also make a contribution. They will be continually involved in the exchange of gifts, and they will participate in the perpetuation of the society through marriage as well as in maintaining economic security.

Within the family, youngsters are expected to defer to the wishes of their elders, and it is the elders who make arrangements for the marriages of their children, both boys and girls. Some children have rebelled and made their own marriages outside the community, occasionally successful, but all can also site cases where a new, second marriage has had to be arranged for such tearaways when the first one broke down. Whether an outside spouse is accepted depends partly on the extent to which they are prepared to adopt and contribute to the social life of the community.

Marriages are usually arranged between members of the same *birādarī*, very often between first cousins, and one important criterion is that the families should be compatible.

> In most cases the question of caste status in marriage does not arise explicitly because of the traditional Pakistani Muslim preference for marriage with first cousins. This stated preference is sometimes justified with reference to the Qur'ān, which permits first-cousin marriage, and the life of the Prophet Mohammed whose daughter Fatima was married to her cousin, the Prophet's nephew. It is also justified in terms of maintaining 'purity of the blood' and in this context the particular qualities of the family or caste are emphasised. In a society in which a dowry must be given by the girl's family when a daughter is married, the preference for first-cousin marriage is also important as a means of keeping property within the family.   (Shaw 1988: 98)

Alison Shaw investigated the extent to which younger members of the community, particularly those of the second generation, resented having their marriages arranged for them, and she found only a small amount of real dissent. In most cases, people felt that the system was good for them, and they preferred being part of the community which they seem to see as more caring and meaningful than the 'free' outside world. It seems from the more recent work of Fozia Tenvir, and Shaw herself, that this situation continues into the third generation, and families are less worried than they used to be about letting their daughters go to mixed schools. Girls whose outside marriages failed have proved a strong negative example, and although Pakistani boys sometimes have relationships with white girls from the wider community, they see these as playful, and argue that the girls don't mind, as their own sisters might.

This is one case of a relatively strong, well-defined ethnic community in a wider society, and it was chosen largely for the rich ethnography relating to the subject matter of this chapter. The First-hand Account 11.2 (overleaf) by a Jain student studying in the same city in 2006 presents a very different view, though compare this with Reynell's (1991) article listed below, and briefly referred to in the next section. For an alternative insight into the lives of some British families of immigrant origins, the novels by Zadie Smith (2000) and Monica Ali (2003 – see end of Chapter 14) are hard to beat!

Marriage

One of the reasons that Pakistani girls in Oxford prefer to marry within their own community is because they will be able to continue to count on the support of the wider *birādarī*. Marriage for them is more than a relationship between two people, and there may be reasons for making a match which goes beyond personal choice. They also observe the fragility of some of the unions made in wider British society, as divorce rates increase and remarriages complicate the lives of the children involved (see Simpson 1994). There are also religious differences, of course. Perhaps these alternative marriages don't seem very impressive.

It must be part of this chapter, then, to consider what exactly we mean when we talk about *marriage*. Let us start again by looking at the word in the English language, as an element in the *standard English family* we used as a model above. Something called marriage clearly played an important part in the construction of the *nuclear* unit, and it is 'marriage' which moves people from the family of their birth to a new one for procreation and continuing the lines of descent. However, what do people need to do in order to make this transition? And is it actually necessary for people to marry at all, if they simply give birth to children of their own?

First of all, there is a legal definition of marriage, and this will vary from one system to another, affecting the way that people are permitted to behave within any particular society. Inheritance rules are affected by the legal situation, and so may be the status of children. In some systems of legislation, it is only possible to have one legal spouse at a time, whereas in others polygamy is not only possible but sometimes a preferred arrangement. The laws with regard to divorce will indicate the possibilities for breaking a union once formed, and arrangements for children will also be part of the legal framework.

Polygamy – marriage involving more than one spouse, male or female

There are also often strong religious ideas about the state of marriage, and these may even be at odds with the evolving legal system. In a Christian church, for example, a couple makes a solemn undertaking to spend the rest of their lives together, through thick and through thin – 'in sickness and in health, until death us do part'. Not everyone gets married in church, but many of the couples getting divorced have done so, and even seek to do it again, an act which is actually permitted in some churches. Clearly there is a difference between the ideals expressed in the ceremony and the practice of real life. In other societies marriage may have little to do with religion, but it is not uncommon to find a discrepancy between ideals and practice.

This brings us to a third definition of marriage, namely the customary one. Here we enter the area of social control again. A couple wishing to marry is expected to comply with legal regulations, and they may choose to formalise their union with a religious ceremony, but it is also quite possible to set up a family without doing either of these things. It may not be the preferred arrangement of the parents of the couple concerned, but neighbours may well treat them in much the same way as they would people with a more conventional union. The term 'partner' has gained common currency in the English language for the relationship formed in such a situation, and it is also used for long-term homosexual relationships, although it is now possible in several countries for homosexuals to formalise their union with a marriage.

Marriage within Jain communities has traditionally been arranged with religious – and, often group – endogamy strongly being adhered to. That is, parents would not only prefer someone from the same sect, they would likely also choose someone from certain family lines that had shared origins and would be recognised as being part of the same 'group' (also known as caste, although without any hierarchical connotations). Marriage with kin or within a lineage would generally not be permitted and matches would usually be made between two families of similar socioeconomic standing.

First-hand account 11.2:
Ashini Kothari, Jain – on Marriage

You now find more of a mixture of approaches to marriage both from young people and their parents, which varies according to individuals, families, groups and communities! For instance, while arranged marriages and endogamy are still the norm in India, it is now more common to hear of cases to the contrary, especially in metropolitan cities such as Mumbai. Jain communities outside India are generally considered to be slowly changing their practices and attitudes although it varies greatly from one community to another. For example, the small Jain community in Antwerp, Belgium largely consists of first-generation migrants that originated from one town in Gujarat and who still regularly travel back to India. As a result, arranged and/or endogamous marriage is more common there than in England, for instance. In the case of the latter, not only is there a greater mix of different Jain groups and interaction with the host population, but many families spent a generation in Africa before moving to England, which could explain the greater changes and variances in their practices. Jain communities outside India often have a sense of shared identity, which may assume greater importance than the aforementioned 'groups' defined by family origins. Youth in overseas communities often share outlooks and backgrounds, which sometimes makes matches within them – arranged or otherwise – easier.

Even the way in which marriages are 'arranged' varies.

Belgium

Communities in India mostly have instances where the couple only meets for a handful of occasions before the engagement. But, in England, and even in communities in the USA, an 'arrangement' usually just entails families introducing a couple, and it is then largely the couple's prerogative as to how and whether they wish to pursue the relationship. It is often followed by dating for an extended period as the couple gets to know each other.

I think most young people in England view marriage as something which should be their choice and while most identify themselves as being part of the Jain community, decreasing numbers feel as though endogamy is vital. Both parents and young Jains tend to express a preference for spouses to have similar backgrounds (e.g. a preference for a Jain or Hindu over other religious groups), although this is stronger in the case of the former. Reasons for this preference among young Jains vary from parental or social pressure to personal choice. Of course, different families and individuals also differ in the extent of their preferences and there are plenty of cases where families' and individuals' wishes and views clash, which I think is greater now than ever before due to an uncomfortable blend of traditional and 'Westernised' ideas.

Ashini Kothari wrote this piece in 2006 while a student at Oxford University; she is a resident of Antwerp, Belgium.

Marriage for many people may be considered to be a union that should be entered into freely by a couple wishing to share a major part of their lives together, but this idea is by no means universal, and it is necessary to think carefully about what the institution means. It may, for example, be seen as something much closer to a political or an economic alliance, enabling the uniting of potentially hostile groups, or the consolidation of a vital means to trade. In rural Japan, the character used for a bride (or wife) is a combination of one for 'woman' and one for *ie*, or 'house', suggesting that the bride is seen as married to the house as a whole, not just to the young husband with whom she shares a bed. In some societies unions between ghosts, or between two women, are also quite possible, and it may certainly be thought less necessary for the couple to make choices than for social expectations to be fulfilled.

As was the case with kinship, *marriage* means different things in different societies, and in an article about the problems of defining marriage in *Rethinking Kinship and Marriage*, Peter Rivière even went so far as to write that 'marriage as an isolable phenomenon of study is a misleading illusion' (1971: 57). Again, he recommends, we must look at marriage as part of the wider society where it is found, at how it fits into wider systems of exchange and political allegiance, and then we can understand the role it plays in a particular case. Anthropologists have developed theory around the term *alliance* to examine some of the examples found in a way which does not imply underlying notions associated with the term *marriage*. In this final section, however, we will simply introduce and explain terms which have been used in describing arrangements in various societies, and try to give some idea of the variety that is possible. This will lay the groundwork for readers to understand any more specific ethnography they might find.

Endogamy, Exogamy and Incest

In most societies there are some limits, broadly agreed, about whom one may or may not marry. Rules of exogamy define groups *out of which* one should marry, and rules of endogamy define those *within which* one should marry. Rules of exogamy sometimes, but not always, coincide with rules of incest, in other words those who are prohibited for marriage are usually the same people with whom it would be inappropriate to have sexual relations. These groups vary from one society to another: they may include only the nuclear family, they may comprise a lineage to a certain distance, or even a whole clan sharing a name. The Chinese character for incest literally means 'confusion of relationships', and this is a nice expression of the way rules of incest and exogamy often actually help to define important groups in any particular society. However, they must be separated as concerned with sexual relations and marriage respectively.

exogamy – rules relating to marriage outside a particular group.

endogamy – rules relating to marriage within a particular group.

incest – sexual relations which are forbidden in any society because the partners are too closely related.

Anthropologists have pointed out that *marrying out* creates *alliances* between groups that may not otherwise have a great deal of contact, or whose contact may be hostile. Tylor even went so far as to suggest that people 'marry out or die out'. Others have written that in Africa people 'marry our enemies' in order to create peaceful ties, although in the tropical forest of South America, marriage is no insurance of peace and there are even people whose word for 'brother-in-law' is synonymous with that for 'enemy'. However, as was pointed out in the section on exchange, marriage is one means of maintaining *communication* between peoples, whether it be friendly or hostile.

Rules of endogamy, on the other hand, put an outer limit on the range of marriage partners. Even where there are few explicit rules, marriages may provoke disapproval if they cross lines of class, race, religion or nationality. We saw that members of the Pakistani community in Britain choose to arrange marriages with their own people, preferably cousins of a similar caste background. In the India subcontinent, there may be more explicit *caste endogamy* since members of different castes are often regarded as different kinds of people. At the same time there may be *village exogamy*, so the two categories are by no means mutually exclusive.

Marriage as Exchange – Dowry and Bridewealth

Another phenomenon found in India is hypergamy, which refers to the fact that those who receive a wife, the *wifetakers*, are regarded as superior to the *wifegivers*. This system must be seen in the context of the payment of dowry, which is wealth that travels with a bride to her new family. The Jains of Jaipur (northern India), a religious community concentrated mainly among business and trading castes, provide an example. According to Josephine Reynell (1991), the dowry here includes furniture, kitchen utensils and electrical goods to equip the bride's new home, as well as clothes and jewellery for the bride, and money for the bride's new-parents-in-law. The practice of religious and caste endogamy, as a way of maintaining control over economic resources, limits

hypergamy – a system of marriage in which a bride moves into a family that occupies a higher position in some locally accepted form of hierarchy.

dowry – wealth which travels with a bride to her new family.

Photograph 11.2 A Jain marriage ceremony, in Jaipur, northern India. The father of the bride (right) has formally handed his daughter over into the safekeeping of the groom and his family. The bride holds her hands over the right hand of the groom. Their right hands will be bound, symbolising their lifelong union (photograph courtesy of Josephine Reynell).

overall hierarchical difference, but a bride's parents would not eat with her new family after the marriage (Photograph 11.2 was taken at a Jain marriage ceremony; however see First-hand Account 11.2 on pp. 224–5 for a personal Jain view).

In other societies this system is reversed and *wife givers* will be seen as superior to *wife takers*, when the situation is described as hypogamy. In this case, it is more likely that goods called bridewealth, or brideprice, will be travelling in the opposite direction. Whenever imbalances of this sort occur, exchange must be *indirect*, or *generalised*, to use Lévi-Strauss's terms mentioned in Chapter 3; in other words, there must be at least three groups involved as people can't be seen as superior and inferior at the same time. A more straightforward exchange, where women move on a regular basis between two different groups (see below), was called by Lévi-Strauss *direct exchange*, and this can also refer to a situation where women are apparently being exchanged for *labour* or for bridewealth.

hypogamy – a system in which the bride's family is regarded as superior to that of the groom.

bridewealth (or **brideprice**) – goods or wealth travelling from a groom's family to that of his bride as part of the establishment and formalisation of continuing relations between their peoples.

Missionaries and other visitors from outside societies where such systems operated condemned these arrangements because they appeared to represent the purchase of women or, perhaps worse, the persuasion by the use of wealth to have women taken away. A deeper examination reveals much more significance, however, and bridewealth in different locations may also play one or more of several important roles. It is, for example, very likely to initiate or continue a series of exchanges which ensures long-term *communication* between the groups involved, who will of course both be related, as kin, to the children of any union set up.

Bridewealth may also play the important role of *validating* the marriage. In the absence of any other kind of legal contract, a couple setting up home without prior payments could well be seen to have an improper, illegitimate union. The payments also act as a kind of *security*. If a husband and his family treat the wife badly and she returns home, they will lose the payments they have made. Conversely, if the wife behaves badly, her husband may ask for a return of his payments. Since the bride's family may already have handed on the bridewealth to marry one of their menfolk, it is likely that they would put pressure on the woman to fit into her new home.

In Japan, there is no term for 'bridewealth', as such, but wealth in various forms is paid over by the groom's family in betrothal gifts which the bride uses in turn to prepare her *trousseau*, usually worth much more than the payments received. She receives goods from her own family and, like some cases of *dowry*, she takes these away again if the marriage breaks up, for they also represent a share of her family's inheritance. In families with no inheriting son, the initial payments may be made from the bride's family to that of the groom, who will join the house as potential successor. In both cases, as in situations in societies where a substantial dowry is paid over with a bride, the goods become part of the security of the new family.

Particularly in Africa, where bridewealth is often paid in cattle, the movement of animals may be seen as marking out a kind of map of human relationships. Bridewealth received for a daughter will be used for the wives of sons, and many relatives will make contributions to each other's weddings when they have livestock available in the knowledge that they will be able to draw on reciprocal support when they need it. Writing of the Nyakyusa of Malawi and Tanzania, Monica Wilson (1963) thus noted that cattle are continually driven down the paths of human relationships. Beattie suggested going a step further when he said, 'they tread out these paths' (1964: 125). The movement of wealth made in connection with marriage can clearly play roles which go way beyond the nuptial link being made.

Direct sister exchange (see Figure 11.5) is another type of marriage discussed by anthropologists as a way of describing long-term arrangements of *alliance* between two groups in which men who think of themselves as 'brothers' set up reciprocal links through their wives and sisters. In practice, the men involved probably share a lineage group, as described above, where the category 'brother' includes all males of the same generation. As the relationships continue through

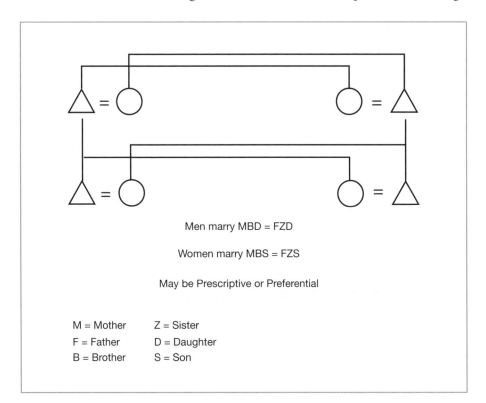

Men marry MBD = FZD

Women marry MBS = FZS

May be Prescriptive or Preferential

M = Mother   Z = Sister
F = Father   D = Daughter
B = Brother   S = Son

Figure 11.5   Direct (sister) exchange (for example, the Amba of Uganda)

the generations, a girl from a man's mother's lineage, a mother's 'brother's' daughter (MBD in the diagram) would be an appropriate partner, who would also be classified as a 'father's' sister's daughter (FZD).

Such a situation would be compatible with the system of exogamy which ensures communication between different groups of people, but it is a very male-oriented view and allows the women involved less say in the matter than they may in practice exercise. In Figure 11.5 I have also shown the relationships from the point of view of the wives. *Direct exchange* is found in situations where this type of alliance is *preferred*, perhaps to keep goods within a family group, but not necessarily *prescribed*, as would need to be the case for an interesting form of *indirect* exchange known as *matrilateral cross-cousin marriage*, where men *must* marry their mother's brother's daughters to make the system work (see Figure 11.6).

It is important again to remember that the triangles and circles here represent categories of people in particular relationships to one another. It will be noted that men in such a system move in one direction and women in the other, so direct exchange of sisters would not be possible. There may also be an element of hypergamy or hypogamy here, where the wife givers are considered superior or inferior to the wife takers, and this may have ramifications for the political sys-

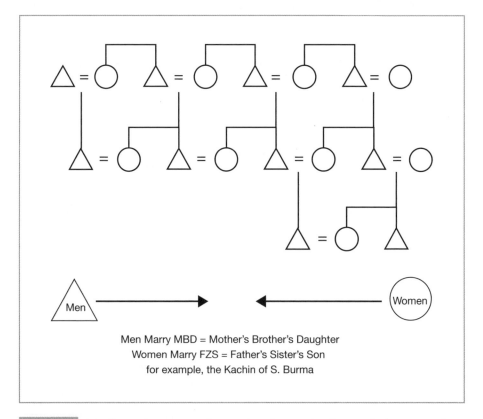

Men Marry MBD = Mother's Brother's Daughter
Women Marry FZS = Father's Sister's Son
for example, the Kachin of S. Burma

Figure 11.6 Matrilateral cross-cousin marriage (example of prescriptive system)

tem. An interesting example of this is the case of the Kachin people of southern Burma, described by Edmund Leach in *Political Systems of Highland Burma*. He writes:

> Much the most important set of relationships in any Kachin community are those which establish the mutual status relations between the various *htinggaw* groups that exist in that community. From the individual's point of view every *htinggaw* group within the community falls into one or other of four categories:
>
> (i) ... lineages which are treated as being of the same clan as Ego's own and are near enough related to form an exogamous group with Ego's ...
>
> (ii) *mayu ni* are lineages from which males of Ego's lineage have recently taken brides.
>
> (iii) *dama ni* are lineages into which females of Ego's lineage have recently married.
>
> (iv) .... lineages which are recognised as relatives .. but with which the relationship is distant or indefinite ...
>
> The essential feature of the system is that the [first] three categories ... are distinct. A man may not marry into his *dama*, a woman may not marry into her *mayu*. From an analytical point of view the system is one of matrilateral cross cousin marriage, but it needs to be stressed that a Kachin, in marrying a girl from his *mayu ni*, does not normally marry a true matrilateral cross cousin but only a classificatory cross cousin.
>
> (1954: 73–4)

The practicalities of such a system are discussed in great detail by Leach, who demonstrates in this now classic study an example both of the ingenious possibilities of structural analysis to make sense of social and political behaviour, and the way that such an abstract construct works in the practice of real-life relationships. Another extract, this time laying out more clearly the political elements of this system, also illustrates this point:

> This account of Laga village has brought out the fact that within the village the more permanent *mayu–dama* links serve to display the formal political status relations between different *htinggaw* lineage groups. In this formal system it is assumed that the *dama* are the political subordinates of the *mayu*; but let it be stressed that even within the village this subordination may be theoretical rather than actual. Any nominal inferiority can, in practice, be largely compensated by strategic marriages outside the village. (1954: 81)

Locality of Marriage Residence

Decisions about where a couple will live after they are married are very often decided by custom, or by a practical economic or political consideration, in a particular society. Anthropologists have terms to describe various arrangements. For example, where a man moves in with his wife's family, or into his wife's community, the marriage is said to be *matrilocal* (from the point of view of the next generation) or *uxorilocal* (from the Latin for 'wife'). If the woman moves to the man's former residence, the marriage is said to be *patrilocal* or *virilocal*. A completely new residence would be *neolocal*.

Factors like this may have very important ramifications for future relations, and again may play a part in the political system of the people concerned. In a society with patrilineal descent and patrilocal marriage, strong stable descent groups are likely to result, and these can form the basis of the political system, as is found among the Nuer. In Japan, during a period between the ninth and thirteenth centuries, there was a family known as the Fujiwaras who dominated the political scene through a continual series of matrilocal marriages with the imperial family, which for generations ensured that the child emperors grew up in a Fujiwara household. They were thus subject to the influence of their Fujiwara grandparents from an early age, and usually married into another Fujiwara household where they would be close to Fujiwara in-laws as they came to the throne. The Fujiwaras occupied a series of positions in the court, but the influence they exerted through marriage is widely acknowledged by historians of the period today.

Monogamy and Polygamy

So far we have talked little about forms of marriage that involve more than two partners. A system involving *one* person marrying *one* other is known as *monogamy*, where *mono* stands for 'one'. In a society where this is the law, if one of those partners wishes to marry someone else, they must first divorce their existing spouse. If a person thereby takes several spouses over a period of time, this is called serial monogamy. In some societies, however, it is perfectly acceptable for a man to maintain marriage to more than one wife (polygyny) or a woman to have more than one husband (polyandry). In either case, the system is described as *polygamy*, or multiple marriage.

> **polygyny** – marriage involving one man and more than one woman.

In some ostensibly monogamous societies, where it is illegal for people to have more than one spouse, it is nevertheless fairly institutionalised that a man may maintain more than one household, one with a legal wife, others with his mistresses. The *casa chica*, or 'small house' is a phenomenon of this sort found in Latin America, and the situation has also been well known in Japan. A man's wealth will determine his ability to do this, of course, as it would in

> **polyandry** – marriage involving one woman and more than one man.

a society that accepts polygamy, and his status will also be affected. In the case of the leaders of the tropical rain forest, discussed in the politics section, an abundance of wives were mentioned as a distinct advantage. The living arrangments for women in polygamous marriages, often in separate units with their children, may thus be rather similar to the 'single-parent families' we mentioned at the start of the chapter.

The Nayar and the Anderi, of India, are examples of peoples who practise polyandry. In the first case, women grow up and continue to live with their brothers, receiving visits from one 'husband' at a time. He leaves a spear at the door to deter any other who might think of calling while he is there. In the second case, one woman may be expected to take care of a whole group of brothers single-handedly, as a mechanism to avoid dividing up the family land. This will also have the effect of limiting the number of children they might collectively produce. Small wonder that polygyny is much more common!

Conclusion

This chapter has brushed rather cursorily over some of the abundance of work anthropologists have produced on the subject they call *kinship*, and the related one of *marriage* – it is probably one of the most widely studied fields in anthropology, and a selection of books on the subject have been listed below, both theoretical and ethnographic. David Schneider's (1980) influential symbolic analysis of American families conflicted with that proposed by Needham (outlined above), although both reacted to the important work of Lévi-Strauss that we mentioned briefly in Chapter 3. Carsten (2004) revisits some of the issues in a readable recent publication. Otherwise, the volume has abated somewhat, attention turning instead to the consequences of new forms of technology on family and reproduction. We have therefore focused on equipping the reader with a conceptual framework to make sense of other studies they may find. The textbook by Parkin (1997) and the reader he edited with Stone (2004) offer good sources of further depth for those who wish to pursue the subject.

Discussion Questions

1 If you draw up a family tree, anthropological style, of all your known relatives, how far back can you go? And with how many degrees of collateral relatives do you keep in touch? Does it matter where they live?

2 Do you have different ways of behaving with people in different positions of relationships to you? Can you identify categories here, or is this just a personal thing?

3 Are there any groups of people with whom you would be unhappy to marry, or to find your son or daughter marrying? Why? What are the boundaries of your social world?

References and Further Research

Books
Beattie, John (1964) *Other Cultures* (London: Routledge & Kegan Paul).
Carrithers, Michael and Humphrey, Caroline (eds), *The Assembly of Listeners: Jains in Society* (Cambridge: Cambridge University Press).

Carsten, J. (1997) *The Heat of the Hearth: The Process of Kinship in a Malay Fishing Community* (New York: Oxford University Press).

Carsten, Janet (2004) *After Kinship* (Cambridge: Cambridge University Press).

Edwards, Jeanette (2000) *Born and Bred: Idioms of Kinship and the New Reproductive Technologies in England* (Oxford: Oxford University Press).

Franklin, Sarah (1997) *Embodied Progress: A Cultural Account of Assisted Conception* (London: Routledge).

Goody, Jack and Tambiah, S. J. (1973) *Bridewealth and Dowry* (Cambridge: Cambridge University Press).

Holy, Ladislav (1996) *Anthropological Perspectives on Kinship* (London and Chicago: Pluto Press).

Howell, Signe (2006) *The Kinning of Foreigners: Transnational Adoption in a Global Perspective* (Oxford: Berghahn Books).

Leach, E. R. (1954) *Political Systems of Highland Burma* (London: Athlone).

Needham, Rodney (ed.) (1971) *Rethinking Kinship and Marriage* (London: Tavistock).

Parkin, Robert (1997) *Kinship: An Introduction to the Basic Concepts* (Oxford: Blackwell).

Parkin, Robert and Stone, Linda (2004) *Kinship and Family: An Anthropological Reader* (Oxford: Blackwell).

Scheper-Hughes, Nancy (1993) *Death without Weeping: The Violence of Everyday Life in Brazil* (Berkeley: University of California Press).

Schneider, David (1980) *American Kinship: A Cultural Account* (Chicago and London: University of Chicago Press).

Shaw, Alison (1988) *A Pakistani Community in Britain* (Oxford: Blackwell).

Shaw, Alison (2000) *Kinship and Continuity: Pakistani Families in Britain* (London: Routledge).

Strathern, Marilyn (1992) *Reproducing the Future: Anthropology, Kinship and the New Reproductive Technologies* (Manchester: Manchester University Press).

Wilson, Monica (1963) *Good Company: A Study of Nyakyusa Age-Villages* (Boston, Mass.: Beacon Press).

Articles

Abrahams, Ray (1986) 'Anthropology among One's Affines', *Anthropology Today*, 2(2): pp. 18–20.

Clarke, Morgan (2006) 'Islam, Kinship, and Reproductive Technology', *Anthropology Today*, 22(5): 17–21.

Keenan, Jeremy (2000) 'The Father's Friend: Returning to the Tuareg as an "Elder"'. *Anthropology Today*, 16(4): 7–11.

Reynell, Josephine (1991) 'Women and the Reproduction of the Jain Community', in Michael Carrithers and Caroline Humphrey (eds), *The Assembly of Listeners: Jains in Society* (Cambridge: Cambridge University Press).

Rivière, P. G. (1971) 'Marriage: A Reassessment', in Rodney Needham, *Rethinking Kinship and Marriage* (London: Tavistock) pp. 57–74.

Rivière, P. G. (1985) 'Unscrambling Parenthood: The Warnock Report', *Anthropology Today* 1(4): 2–7.

Sherif, Bahir (1999) 'Gender Contradictions in Families: Official v. Practical Representations among Upper Middle-Class Muslim Egyptians', *Anthropology Today*, 15(4): pp. 9–13.

Shore, Cris (1992) 'Virgin Births and Sterile Debates: Anthropology and the New Reproductive Technologies', *Current Anthropology*, 33: 295–314 (including comments).

Simpson, Bob (1994) 'Bringing the "Unclear" Family into Focus: Divorce and Re-marriage in Contemporary Britain', *Man*, 29: 831–51.

Simpson, Bob (2006) 'Scrambling Parenthood: English Kinship and the Prohibited Degrees of Affinity', *Anthropology Today*, 22(3): 3–6.

van Bremen, Jan (1998) 'Death Rites in Japan in the Twentieth Century', in Joy Hendry (ed.), *Interpreting Japanese Society*, 2nd edition (London: Routledge) pp. 131–44.

Novels

Achebe, Chinua (1962) *Things Fall Apart* (London: Heinemann) is a best-selling story of an Igbo family trying, but largely failing, to adapt to a British Nigeria.

Ariyoshi Sawako (1981) *The River Ki* (trans. by Mildred Tahara; Tokyo: Kodansha, 1981) is a moving tale about several generations of a Japanese family.

Ishiguro Kazuo (2005) *Never Let Me Go* (London: Faber & Faber) is a gripping, bitter-sweet story about growing up in the age of new technologies, which addresses the whole question of what it means to be human.

Jung Chang (1991) *Wild Swans* (London: HarperCollins) is the much-celebrated account of three generations of Chinese women who lived most actively through the tremendous changes of the Cultural Revolution.

Mistry, Rohinton (2002) *Family Matters* (London: Faber & Faber) is a moving tale of a Parsi family dealing with matters that touch on universal themes.

Smith, Zadie (2001) *White Teeth* (London: Hamish Hamilton) weaves a complicated tale of relations between families of a variety of origins living in North London.

Tanizaki, Junichiro (1993) *The Makioka Sisters* (London: Mandarin) is a novel which details the problems that arise for a Japanese family trying to arrange appropriate marriages for a group of four sisters.

Films

Secrets and Lies (directed by Mike Leigh, 1996) is a feature film illustrating problems which can arise when people reared in an adoptive family take steps to make contact with their parents of birth.

Strangers Abroad: Everything is Relatives (André Singer, 1985) is a film about the anthropologist W. H. R. Rivers, whose work we discussed in Chapter 1, focusing on his study of kinship and genealogy among the various people with whom he worked.

Under the Sun: The Dragon Bride (Joanna Head, 1993) depicts the preparations and marriage of a 16-year-old girl of the Nyinba people of Nepal to four brothers from another village. Personal interviews flesh out and illustrate this unusual example of fraternal polyandry.

Without Fathers or Husbands (Hua Cai, 26 minutes, 1995) tells of the Na, an ethnic group in south-east China, where all the members of each household are consanguineous relatives, their social organisation is matrilineal and their sexual life mainly takes the form of nocturnal visits of men to women.

Websites

http://www.geocities.com/Hollywood/Theater/2404/nepotism.htm – a long list of actors who have made it into 'showbiz' because of their famous parents.

http://www.umanitoba.ca/faculties/arts/anthropology/kintitle.html – an online interactive tutorial on kinship from the University of Manitoba, Canada.

http://www.preacherssons.com – a website about a male couple and their five sons adopted from foster care.

12

Economics and the Environment

Introduction

In the last two chapters we dipped our toes into some of the deeper issues anthropologists address, but we also glimpsed a little of the way an anthropological approach can contribute to an understanding of subjects of wider interest. In this chapter we take up this theme in reference to the contribution anthropologists can make, and have made, to the study of economics and the environment. While doing this, we will draw together elements of anthropological work that we have considered in previous chapters of the book, and demonstrate how a good understanding of economic life depends on an understanding of the systems of classification and notions of exchange that we introduced in Chapters 1 and 3.

environment – a broad term referring to surrounding conditions and circumstances that influence the life of a people, but that the people classify and use in different ways.

We will start with a very basic part of the study of any society, and draw up a fairly crude classification of social groups according to the means of subsistence. Most classic anthropological studies actually start out by describing the economic base of a particular people and the environment in which they live, for this is usually a highly influential part of social life. Even at the most basic level, the environment is socially constructed, however, and it is important for anthropology students to be aware that the big 'global' discourses about threats to the natural world reflect levels of technological achievement. We will return to that specific theme in Chapter 14, when we look at global issues more broadly, but in this chapter we will lay out some of the variety of possibilities.

Over the years anthropologists have learned a lot about social life by focusing on small groups, and those who live at a basic economic level provide interesting information which is not irrelevant in a more complex, multicultural world. In the end, one person can only operate socially within a limited number of family, friends and associates, and there are certain rules of behaviour which pervade life in these micro-level groups, wherever they are found. In Chapter 3 we discussed Sahlins' ideas about forms of generalised reciprocity, which he argued operate within the closest circles; in Chapter 9 we examined methods of social control effective in such groups; and in the last chapter, we looked at the specific example of the Pakistani *birādarī*. There we glimpsed the important idea, continually aided by developments in information technology, that groups geographically separate can also easily keep in touch.

Subsistence and Survival

Economics is first of all concerned with the means of *survival* and how this is achieved. It is concerned with the way food is produced, shelter is provided, and with other everyday activities essential to life. Exchange, and specifically that of a market, is a further development of economic life, made possible when subsistence is secure. Small-scale societies were divided into three types by early anthropologists making sense of the world they observed (for example, Forde 1934), and these divisions are still used to describe forms of basic economy of both isolated contemporary peoples and earlier forms of social life described by archaeologists, though evolutionary schemes and generalisations about social interaction have been severely challenged. The three types are: hunter–gatherers, pastoralists and agriculturalists.

Hunter-gatherers or 'gatherer-hunters'

People described in this way collect food from their immediate environment, and they have been characterised as picking or catching only as much as they could eat at any one time to avoid problems of storage or transport. They were said to be usually nomadic, since they must move about to avoid exhausting their supplies, and to seek foods when they are in season and abundant. They were also said to have little role specialisation, the chief division of labour being made along lines of age and gender, so that the healthy and capa-

nomadic – a term used to describe people who move about in the course of making a living rather than settling in one place.

ble collect for the very young and the very old and infirm, and, typically, men hunt, while women gather.

Economists had described this life as hard and difficult, but ethnographic material indicated that many such people only 'worked' for long enough to provide themselves with sustenance, leaving the rest of their lives to relax and enjoy each other's company. Marshall Sahlins thus described hunter–gatherers as the 'original affluent society':

> Hunters and gatherers have by force of circumstances an objectively low standard of living. But taken as their *objective*, and given their adequate means of production, all the people's material wants usually can easily be satisfied [a common understanding of 'affluence', Sahlins 1974: 1] ... The world's most primitive people have few possessions, *but they are not poor*. Poverty is not a certain small amount of goods, nor is it just a relation between means and ends; above all it is a relation between people. Poverty is a social status. As such it is an invention of civilization.   (Sahlins 1974: 36–7)

Sahlins' argument is worth following up, for he makes the interesting point that if people want no more than their food, and that is available, then they have all they desire. In other words, they have not been corrupted by the addictive and competitive traps of property ownership and capitalism. This idea became somewhat romanticised, however, using as a classic example the Ju/'hoan (also known as San Bushmen, see Barnard 2007 for a discussion of names) of the Kalahari Desert, whose warm and abundant surroundings made life comparatively rather easy. The feature film *The Gods Must Be Crazy*, cited below, illustrates this view when it tracks the events following the arrival of an empty Coca-Cola bottle into a Ju/'hoan camp, thrown carelessly out of the window of a small plane, but forthwith corrupting the otherwise innocent lives of these formerly apparently idyllically happy people. The subsequent fate of the Ju/'hoan people is something we will return to in the next chapter.

In practice, there are many and varied peoples in different parts of the world who have sustained themselves largely through hunting and gathering techniques, or 'gathering and hunting', as some feminists have argued they should be called, in deference to the female provision of gathering as the basis of their economy, with hunting supplementing the diet only for special or sporadic occasions. Some own property and store food, and others live very tough and difficult lives in regions much less hospitable than that of the continual African sunshine. They have a range of interesting sets of power relations and ideologies, and they also produce some highly skilled art and material culture.

Anthropologists of peoples who fall under the category of 'hunter–gathering', or 'gatherer–hunting', tend to meet and compare their findings, despite this diversity, and a very useful two-part collection (Ingold et al. 1988) justified this practice, as follows:

> In some ways hunter–gatherer societies have developed independently of other branches of social anthropology. Yet we believe that they are

not simply in tune with social anthropology more generally: they are the backbone of the discipline. They are often much more in touch with the essence of what it is to be human than are trends in virtually any other branch of the subject.   (Barnard and Woodburn 1988)

Examples of surviving hunters and gatherers, apart from the rather well known Ju/'hoan Bushmen and Mbuti Pygmy peoples of southern Africa, include several groups of Australian Aborigines, such as the Yolngu people whose art was discussed in Chapter 6, rain forest peoples, for example in Malaysia, and like those of South America whose politics we discussed in Chapter 10, and peoples like the Inuit and Cree who still make at least a part of their living by hunting in the harsh snowy climes of the extreme northern hemisphere. Some groups on the West Coast of North America used to challenge the original definition by having settlements as well as leading a largely hunter–gatherer life, and they also made beautiful artefacts. Among these are the Kwakwaka'wakw (formerly described as Kwakiutl), Tlingit and Haida, whom we considered in Chapter 3 as practising exchanges described as *potlatch*.

Many more people lived from hunting and gathering in the distant past, and they used to be seen as technologically the most primitive people (as Sahlins suggests above), but anthropologists who specialise in contemporary hunter–gathering peoples are keen to point out the social and cultural complexities that may go along with this means of subsistence, and argue that it is not necessarily possible to learn about ancient societies by looking at the modern ones. Few of the latter are now completely out of contact with the wider world, and they have anyway changed themselves over time, apart from adapting to technological change. A good collection about hunter–gatherers is to be found in Ingold et al. (1988).

Pastoralists

Pastoralist is the term used for people who live off the produce of herds of cattle, sheep, goats and so forth. They also generally need to move about to find fresh grazing for their animals, so they may be nomadic, but they could also be **transhumant**, that is, moving between fixed locations, as we saw in the case of the Nuer. The splendid tents (known as *yurts*) constructed and occupied by various nomadic peoples of Central Asia, and displayed in many ethnographic museums around the world, demonstrate the extent to which 'mobile homes' may be substantial and highly decorative. Some people in this part of the world now own houses in the towns, but at certain times of the year prefer to live in their *yurts*, even erecting them in their back yards when they are not in the desert because they prefer to sleep outside.

Some pastoralists satisfy almost all their requirements – food, shelter, clothes and fuel – from their animals, as well as finding aesthetic appreciation in them, as we saw in Coote's discussion of the Nilotic peoples, such as the Nuer and Dinka, in Chapter 6. They may also create semi-permanent relationships of exchange with their neighbours, for example giving cheese to secure grazing rights. An example of this type of situation is described in an excellent ethnography by John Campbell (1964) about the Sarakatsani, Greek shepherds whose view of the world also demonstrates a system of classification based on different degrees of trust, a scheme of relations rather similar to that outlined by Sahlins for his cycles of reciprocity (discussed in Chapter 3).

The greatest trust is with the family, but lesser degrees of trust are established with 'patrons' on whom the Sarakatsani depend for grazing, both sets distinguished from other outsiders. Campbell writes:

> Sarakatsani are deeply concerned about three things; sheep, children (particularly sons), and honour. It is a common feature of many pastoral peoples with simple material cultures that they are highly dependent on their physical environment and that the care of herds, the structure of the community, and its social values, form a coherent pattern of activities and sentiments which present few inconsistencies. The three concerns of the Sarakatsani are mutually implicated. The sheep support the life and prestige of the family, the sons serve the flocks and protect the honour of their parents and sisters, and the notion of honour presupposes physical and moral capacities that fit the shepherds for the hard and sometimes dangerous work of following and protecting their animals. (1964: 9)

Campbell goes on to present the social and spiritual life of these shepherds, within the wider Greek community, as totally constructed around the sheep who form the economic base of their lives. It is also an excellent example of another society where the values of honour and shame underpin the system of social control so that fear of gossip and ridicule are strong sanctions for compliant behaviour, as we saw in Chapter 9.

Agriculturalists

The earlier evolutionary economic arguments turned to the development of agriculture and horticulture as requiring a more sedentary lifestyle, and a longer-term investment in the land, which could then support larger populations. This, they argued, allowed a greater division of labour, specialisation became feasible, and a complex political system could be sustained, freeing some people from the needs of survival to rule, fight, judge and so forth. Differences may still be based on age and gender, but there could develop further possibilities for gaining status and more ways to develop an aptitude, for example for oratory, or divination.

A sedentary population is in a better position to accumulate surpluses, which allows the greater development of systems of *exchange*, it was argued, and as the extent of these spreads out from the immediate surrounding community, the beginnings of a *market economy* may be observed. As a society becomes more and more complex, any one individual is less likely to provide for his own survival directly, and more likely to be engaged in exchange and specialisation. Food is mostly purchased, and the wherewithal to purchase it is earned through specialist employment. It was from this point of perceived complexity that it seemed appropriate to apply and develop economic theory, and a branch of anthropology developed called Economic Anthropology (see, for example, Firth 1967).

In fact, people who grow crops may also move about, as we have seen in shifting agriculture, such as the *slash-and-burn* type of cultivation found in the tropical rain forest of South America, and the millet growing of the transhumant, predominantly pastoral, Nuer, and we have looked at some of the social implications of these systems in Chapters 8 and 10. We have also seen that property and exchange may characterise the lives of peoples in simpler economic circumstances, such as hunter–gathering and pastoralism. Thus the evolutionary economic argument is not particularly helpful, though we did see in Chapter 9 the greater effectiveness of certain social sanctions in a cooperative rice-growing community, than where people could easily move in and out. In the next two sections we will consider some of the contributions ethnographic studies have made and can still make to an understanding of economic ideas.

Property and Tenure

Important aspects of economic life are related to notions of *property* and *land tenure*, and anthropologists have gathered interesting material on these subjects. Ideas about the ownership of land have been variable throughout the world, with subtle differences eventually causing horrendous long-term problems between neighbouring and colonising peoples. Hunters and gatherers are dependent on using land as they need it, which is fine as long as there is abundant land available. Pastoralists, too, need to seek pasture for their animals and, if this is scarce, they may have to seek grazing rights. Even agriculturalists, such as those who cultivate by the slash-and-burn method, may just have expected to move around as they needed to, but such freedom has become rare in the modern world.

A scarcity of land for the people trying to use it leads to the development of rules, which may become more and more complex as the pressure increases. In some parts of Africa and North America, there was a concept described by anthropologists as usufruct, which granted rights to use land, but without overall ownership. The land may have been perceived of as belonging to a tribe, a lineage, to 'the Creator' or to a king, perhaps, and if it were not in use it would revert to a central pool. So long as a family used it, they could pass it on through the generations, but it was not seen as theirs in perpetuity. This was one of the areas of greatest misunderstanding and conflict between Europeans and Native Peoples in North America, where the latter granted rights to use land, which the former then thought they had purchased (see First-hand Account 12 overleaf).

usufruct – a term to describe ideas certain peoples hold about land which gives them the right to use it, but without implying outright ownership of it.

Throughout the colonised world, and particularly since the raising of local awareness during the United Nations' Year of Indigenous Peoples in 1993, problems such as these have become hot political issues. Anthropologists have had a

Indigenous peoples of Turtle Island (The Americas) value the sacredness of every rock, every tree, every river, and every blade of grass as imbued with life; with breath. When I was growing up in the Northern Boreal forests as a young Cree girl, I was always mindful of the aliveness of the ecosystem around us. Our parents, aunties and uncles taught us much about the interconnections we needed to sustain us and to keep us healthy and well. The plant life, from their roots to their leaves, provided much wealth for our food and medicinal and wellness needs. The animals gave their lives for our needs. We honoured them by offering Tobacco to the Creator as a sacred transaction. Our Elders tell us that the Tobacco is a sacred plant given by the Creator to our

First-hand account 12:

Laara Fitznor, Cree First Nation with German/ Scots ancestry – on Space-Place-Location and Sacredness

people to use for giving thanks and gratitude for the bounties of the Earth and Land. It was not meant to be misused like it is today by smoking as an addiction. When I was an adult learning about our ways I realised that this practice of using Tobacco as an offering was unique to our indigenous lifeways, and it was one of the practices threatened by the colonial experience so that many of our people no longer practise this activity. I learned that by engaging in this practice it reminds us to be ecologically minded and thankful for the health and wealth of the Earth/land.

I learned that engaging relationships that energise an eco-balance of all life forms across all space–place–location is an important goal for sustainability now and in the future. Our Elders tell us that everything was placed on earth by the Creator and that our Sacred Places are blueprints left by our wisdom keepers to engage our present living and to work to care for the earth for the mutual benefits of future generations to come. We were given a responsibility to 'look after' what was left for us to use in our daily lives. We are to be sustainable engagers of everything alive. A respected Indigenous American scholar, Greg Cajete, tells us that 'the land and the place we lived were in a perfect state... the real test of living was to establish a harmonious relationship

CANADA

Manitoba Province

with that perfect state was Nature – to understand it, to see it as the source of one's life and livelihood, and the source of one's essential well-being ... this nature-centred orientation helped individuals come to terms with the environment where they lived in a holistic way' (1994: 75). This ecological thinking calls us to give attention to space–place–location and the holistic engagement of people as an aspect of understanding our respective responsibilities to respect the spaces we use for our families and communities.

Our Elders tell us that people must recognise that we are primarily receivers of the gifts given by our Mother the Earth and there is a tenuous relationship that currently exists because of the colonial agenda of our recent past wherein the onslaught of land appropriation has damaged ongoing relationships between people and the land. Perhaps, how much has been robbed from our indigenous understanding of space-place-location of our lands might be measured by the minimal use of our lands as sacred places today. Much of our land has become a playground for use by people not from that place. The sense of spirituality and sacredness of lands tend to get lost in the translation of using the land for other uses, spurred by the 'the rapid transformation of the Earth by science and technology, and the ecological crises that has begun to unfold...' (ibid. 81).

For example, during the past few centuries the consequences of misusing and appropriating our sacred lands are showing their devastating effects on the environment. If tourism is a way for our indigenous populations to continue to sustain local economies our responsibility becomes clear to ensure that space–place–location finds its ecological centre and a 'spiritually integrated perception of Nature' (ibid). This kind of ecological thinking then moves us to become an integral part of sustaining the places where we live without adding more damage to the environment.

Reference
Cajete, Greg (1994) *Look to the Mountain: An Ecology of Indigenous Education* (Kivaki Press, 1994).

Laara Fitznor, originally from Wabowden, Manitoba, Canada, has a Doctor of Education Degree from the University of Toronto, and now teaches Aboriginal education at the University of Manitoba. Laara received an award recognizing her 'Environmental Education and Aboriginal Cultural Studies'.

role to play in helping Indigenous people translate their point of view into terms which could be understood by the wider authorities, and the Kayapo Indians of the Xingu Valley in Brazil were aided in this way, as we saw in Chapter 10. However, the rights of Indigenous peoples have become a global issue now, and the support of the United Nations in setting up standing committees has enabled considerable mutual support for people helping themselves to reclaim their lands. Hugh Brody's film *Time Immemorial* addresses these issues for the Nishga'a First Nation in the interior of British Columbia in Canada.

Important rules have developed about the inheritance of land, as we have already glimpsed in the section on kinship in the last chapter, and about keeping land within a family, as may be a consideration in the setting up of a marriage. If land is constantly divided between children, the area will become smaller and smaller, so there are usually institutionalised ways of avoiding this. The solution of the Anderi, where a group of brothers work together, marrying one wife between them, is rather unusual. In Japan, the *ie*, or 'house', was until postwar legal changes seen as owning the land, but only one person inherited the position of head of the house, with the right to cultivate the household property. Other children left to set up their own houses, or to marry into pre-existing ones. In Mexico, there is a dual system, with owned land, known as *huerta*, and village land which is leased to families to use, known as *ejido*. The latter reverts to the common pool if it is not cultivated.

Moveable property, on the other hand, may be exchanged, and passed on, and there may be separate inheritance rules for this, as was mentioned in the section on kinship. It may also be given as **tribute** to a leader, which helps to perpetuate a centralised political system, as we saw in Chapter 10. In societies without money or recognised currency, people would give away perishable goods as a kind of insurance for future needs. They trust that those who receive the goods will return the favour when they have a surplus. Similarly, the payment of tribute to a chief may be seen as a kind of investment, and chiefs have even been described as primitive bankers. Some of this form of exchange has economic aspects, then, but much of it is social, and it is difficult to draw a hard and fast line.

Market Economics

We discussed the social aspects of some simple market economies in Chapter 3, where we talked of the villages in Mexico and Guatemala which specialise in the production of specific goods, such as bread, pots, woollen garments, flowers and fireworks, and we suggested that the markets serve to maintain communication over a wide area and offer entertainment as well as providing for basic needs. This system works because people marry **endogamously** within their communities, passing on the skills required for their trade through the generations. The economic aspects of these markets are thus best understood within the context of social arrangements through time.

These endogamous villages were contrasted with those in Africa and elsewhere where rules of **exogamy** can be seen to ensure communication over particular cultural areas. In this case, women seem to become commodified as objects of exchange, at least according to some interpretations, but this idea was modified in the last chapter, where we saw that outsiders such as missionaries and colonial administrators misunderstood bridewealth transactions. In practice, they embodied important social elements like the validating of the union, the legitimising of offspring and the provision of security.

Anthropological studies of markets and exchange usually throw up social factors which economists are inclined to overlook, and this emphasis affects the principles of analysis too. The concept of value, related to their cherished laws of *supply and demand*, is an interesting aspect of economic theory to consider. It is usually associated with scarcity, and very often related to the degree of access to resources. It is no good offering gold to someone dying for lack of water in a desert, for example, but in global terms water is much more abundant than gold, and the latter has acquired a widely recognised exchange value. Once subsistence is secure, food too is assigned differential value. The avocado, a relatively luxurious fruit in British supermarkets, lies rotting in superabundance in Mexico. Apples, which often do the same in Britain, are highly prized in Japan, where an aubergine, or eggplant, again a less usual and therefore more valued part of the British diet, is regarded as a poor food.

Serving a 'high value' food, is a way to gain status and even a contemporary visit to palaces built and decorated by European monarchs during the periods of discovery and exploration of the New World (as far as they were concerned) illustrates some of the social reasons why they were prepared to make enormous investments of their resources in ships and sailors. The example of gold also demonstrates the idea of aesthetic value, and a consideration of the use of gold for the production of jewellery can lead us into its symbolic value. Wedding rings denote a social relationship which, as we have seen, may have a variety of particular connotations, and gold and silver are commonly used for gifts to mark rites of passage. The loss of such objects means more than a reduction in wealth.

The conversion of wealth into status was demonstrated forcibly in Chapter 3 by the case of the potlatch feasts, but another Mexican example illustrates a different element of constraint in this type of transfer. Here, fiestas are financed by one person known as a *mayordomo* who pays for the whole event, thus winning a position of respect and power within the community. So unpopular are those who gain wealth but fail to do this that people will bankrupt themselves for several years to put on a good show when their turn comes. George Foster's (1965) 'Theory of Limited Good' relates this practice to a collective idea that if one family gets too rich others believe they are being deprived. Financing a festival not only redistributes wealth, then, but also offers a means to avoid jealousy and bitterness.

We briefly discussed social ideas about money in Chapter 3, where we gave examples of how cash may be converted into a gift. The use of any type of currency requires a certain agreement about its value, and the locally symbolic nature of this value is immediately evident when we return from travelling abroad with a pocketful of foreign coins. Out of the country where they are recognised, they might as well be pebbles for all the use they are. A credit card, likewise, has little intrinsic value, but it has acquired a very useful global symbolic status. In the end, the global value of 'money' is determined in international markets in a system which looks remarkably like the barter that economists called 'primitive'. We also showed in Chapter 3 that barter may be imbued with morality, and the lack of a shared system of morality at a global level may be another factor that bothers critics of the contemporary capitalist world order.

In Sahlins' cycles of reciprocity, the generalised end of the continuum is the area of most social and moral implication, and thus another problem for Western economic theory when it assumes that people are always trying to *maximise their gains*. Even if the gains of prestige, power, status and divine benefits are added to material gains, there still remain the personal ties of that closest group, expressed in culturally specific notions like love, friendship and loyalty, even just a shared system of classification. At all levels of economics social factors play a part, and one of the reasons why foreigners doing business in Japan find themselves so well wined and dined is because their Japanese counterparts assign great value to making a business relationship a social one.

Anthropologists have now ploughed several ragged edges into the universalist furrows economists had previously presented as so straight and clear, and the use of words such as **commodity** and **consumption** abound in *their* recent discourse. An influential work entitled *The Social Life of Things: Commodities in Cultural Perspective* (Appadurai 1986) sought to shift attention from the forms of exchange and reciprocity, such as gift-giving, barter and trade, to the objects themselves, and how they are understood and appropriated in different ways, with different values and interpretations in the different situations in which they find themselves. We saw examples of this type of approach in the last section of Chapter 3.

An earlier influence was *The World of Goods: Towards an Anthropology of Consumption* (Douglas and Isherwood 1979), where an anthropologist and an economist together focused similar questions on the reasons behind the purchasing and acquisition of goods. The focus on **consumption** as a means to understanding social behaviour has since become popular amongst anthropologists, including not only the behaviour of shoppers in supermarkets and other retail outlets, but subjects formerly seen as ritual and symbolic, such as weddings. In Japan, a wedding package may be purchased in its entirety, including every detail of dress and bridal coiffure, ceremony and feast, through to the arrangement of a suitable honeymoon location – the consumption of all of which Ofra Goldstein-Gidoni has interpreted in the global marketplace as an expression of Japaneseness (1997).

Social Views of the Environment

We come back here to thinking about classification. In the early chapters we discussed anthropologists who classified themselves at the pinnacle of the developed world. At the time of this writing, the whole world's 'natural environment' is thought to be under threat from too much development, and the same people whom our forebears thought primitive are admired for their care and techniques of conservation. In practice, problems arise in thinking about the *environment* because of apparently incompatible views, and an anthropological approach can help to formulate less fiercely opposed alternatives. This, in turn, can help decision-making bodies to take account of all the people involved when they devise plans to make economically advantageous developments.

In a book entitled *Environmentalism: The View from Anthropology*, Kay Milton has collected together a series of articles which offer various contributions to the debate. She points out, in the introduction, that concerns with the preservation of the environment are by no means new in small-scale societies:

> The Australian Aborigine who avoids hunting animals on sacred sites, and performs ceremonies to ensure the continued existence of edible species, is, like the Greenpeace campaigner, implementing environmental responsibilities. The rubber-tappers of Amazonia, the Penan of Borneo, the subsistence farmers of northern India and many other communities have attempted to defend their traditional patterns of resource-use against what they see as the destructive consequences of large-scale commercial exploitation. (1993: 3)

Milton considers the advantages some local discussion and interpretation could have when governments and international NGOs (non-governmental organisations) formulate their environmental policies. An understanding of each other's motives and expectations would go a long way towards easing in changes perceived as globally important at a local level, but a greater understanding of local views might even offer an opportunity for a better system of conservation to be put into place. As Milton explains, ideas about the environment are constituted through discourse, and this draws on all kinds of ammunition depending on the point of view being advocated. Aboriginal people may be credited quite falsely with environmental concerns if it suits an argument for them to be so cited. On another occasion, the same people may be painted in a negative light for the same set of practices. Before we pursue this line of discussion, it is important that we try and see how complicated the issues may be.

In industrialised countries, for the most part, people are able to transcend environmental limitations, except in extremes of weather, such as snow, floods and excessively high wind, and even then they get upset when the forecasters don't warn about the problems in time, or the authorities don't react swiftly enough. Damage caused by environmental phenomena is something that appears on television, and the *tsunami* that caused havoc in South East Asia in late 2004 was particularly shocking to people in the rest of the world who watched chaos hit a normally idyllic holiday zone. Equally shocking was hurricane Katrina, which devastated New Orleans, a place with an international reputation for music and easy living in the heartland of the richest country in the world. Another shock was the stark contrast between technological achievement and the indiscriminate damage caused by the mighty earthquake which hit Kobe, Japan, in January 1995.

People in less highly industrialised regions live in much closer contact with the physical environment, and their view of the world may well reflect this intimacy. The various Inuit groups have a multitude of ways of dealing with the snow and ice in which they spend so much of the year, reflected in their words for different forms of it, and the Bedouin of the Sahara desert have a similar understanding of the sand. An anthropologist living amongst such people must consider environmental factors as a prime feature of their study, but novelists and film-makers have sometimes better captured the feel of a way of life so alien to a cosseted twentieth century city dweller. The novel by the Danish writer Peter Høeg, *Miss Smilla's Feeling for Snow*, presents a Greenlander's view of the snow, for example, and some passages of Michael Ondaatje's book *The English Patient* forcibly illustrate the importance in the desert of understanding different types of wind. Both of these works have now been made into films that well illustrate the environmental exigencies of life in these extreme circumstances, and an early anthropological film known as *Nanook of the North* makes clear the stark daily life of a traditional Inuit family.

Anthropologists must look at environmental conditions wherever they work, but they realise that the world view of the people they live with may involve quite different perceptions to those which they themselves classify as 'the environment'. The anthropologist must aim to unearth this view, and in Chapter 6, where we showed how perceptions of the landscape could be unlike anything familiar to proponents of Western, or even Eastern art, we began to approach the potential complexity of the problem. Another aspect of the subject is the way in which people place themselves in the context of their surroundings and, in this environmentally conscious contemporary world, the extent to which their ideology is reflected in practice.

In the opening of the book *Japanese Images of Nature*, the authors write:

> It is often claimed that the Japanese have a particular love for nature, a love often reflected in their art and material culture. But today equal notice is being given to the environmental degradation caused by the Japanese at home as well as abroad. How can these phenomena be reconciled? The aim of this volume is to address this question through an in-depth analysis of the human–nature relationship in Japan.   (Asquith and Kalland 1997: 1)

In the book, much attention is devoted to Japanese ideas which are translated as 'nature', demonstrating again the problems of definition, as well as conceptions of human interaction with the rest of the world.

In another article in Milton's book, developed further in a fascinating collection of his own essays entitled *The Perception of the Environment* (2000), Tim Ingold makes a point very apt in this context about our whole notion of the environment as a *global* phenomenon. To think of the world we live in as a *globe* implies a view taken from the outside, as opposed to an earlier (European) view of humankind being part of a series of spheres which surrounded as well as included human activity. We learn of the world at school in global terms, although few of us have actually seen more than a photograph of this version of our environment, and we also study maps which colour the land masses in nation states which represent a history of colonialism and voyages of discovery and exploration.

Ingold refers to an idea that this view represents a triumph of technology over cosmology which, in contrast,

> places the person at the centre of an ordered universe of meaningful relations.... and enjoins an understanding of these relations as a foundation for proper conduct towards the environment. (1993: 41)

Seeing the world as a globe puts human society '*outside* what is residually construed as the "physical world" and furnishes the means for the former's control over the latter' (ibid.). Ingold concedes, however, that each view contains the seeds of the other, and this is the basis of the approach taken up by some of the contributors to the Asquith and Kalland volume, mentioned above. Japanese often argue that they think of themselves as 'one with nature', an idea which they oppose to a Western desire to control it, although, in practice, the Japanese clearly make efforts to control natural forces too.

In an indigenous system of Indian thought, too, a person is seen as integrally connected with the cosmos. According to Tambiah:

> The Ayurvedic system we have in mind postulates that the constituents of nature and of man are the same, and that processes such as the ingestion of food and medicine and the excretion of bodily waste products are part and parcel of the flow of energies and potencies between man and nature. Physical illness is the result of imbalances that can be corrected by exchanges at various levels – by ingestion of the right substances and diet, by exposure to or protection from climatic conditions, by maintaining proper relations with other persons – family, kin, and the gods. (1990: 34)

It is important not to fall into the temptation of explaining the whole of social and political life in environmental terms, however. Several explanations of Japanese idiosyncratic 'character' seek causes in the rugged mountainous scenery, or the predominance of rice cultivation. There are mountains elsewhere, however, and plenty of people grow rice. It is important to avoid a *determinist* view. The physical environment undoubtedly limits the social arrangements a people are able to make, but it cannot be said to *determine* them. If it could, there would always be the same social system in the same environment and this is by no means the case. A glance at the variety of Mexican ethnography will illustrate the point, for there have been highly centralised, artistically and technologically advanced peoples living in precisely the area now populated with societies much more diffuse in political organisation, and much less developed in technological terms.

To take one environmental factor, one 'problem' for a people to solve, usually reveals a variety of solutions, and these will depend on cultural differences. Everyone needs water to live, and a shortage of water can be a serious issue. The hunter–gatherer and pastoralist people discussed in the previous section generally solve the problem by moving around, by seeking water sources to resolve their needs immediately. Their response to the 'problem' is the nomadic way of life, and the transhumance of people like the Nuer is a more stable possibility. Elsewhere, a long-term response to the same 'problem' may be achieved through the building of irrigation systems, which in turn involves a social organisation capable of maintaining and administering them, as well as sharing out the supplies. Rules of land ownership are then likely to characterise economic life, and access to water will very likely be regulated. Edmund Leach's book *Pul Eliya* (1961) is about the system of land ownership in a community in Sri Lanka, and it gives an abundance of detail about the social consequences of such a system.

The environment cannot be said to *determine* the social system because the environment is no objective reality. It is always categorised by the people who live in it and make use of it, according to their view of the world. One last example of different views, which has become a highly contentious international issue, involves the varying perceptions of the problems of *whale conservation* found in Japan and among members of different Western nations. According to a Japanese view, based on their own independent research – a view which is shared by Norwegians and Icelanders – there are enough whales to be harvested for consumption; indeed, if they are not harvested they will eat up food supplies for fish which could otherwise also have been caught to feed the Japanese population. Whale meat is a valuable source of protein, and the catching and preparation of whales are specialist occupations, which have been passed down through generations.

The predominant Western view, however, is that the whale population is threatened with extinction, and if the Japanese (and others) keep catching them, they will soon be no more. Many of the people who take this view have been brought up on stories about affable whales such as Moby Dick, and the tale of Jonah, and very few of them regard whale meat as part of their diet. Japanese commentators remark that if the whales were called 'cows' there would be no problem, and criticise the Western world for being sentimental. A very similar, but measured, anthropological view is presented by Niels Einarsson (in Milton's collection), who set out the case of Icelandic fisherman who were losing their entire livelihood for reasons seen locally as quite indefensible. A Norwegian anthropologist, Arne Kalland, even took a place on the International Whaling Commission to try and present a more objective viewpoint.

I have no idea whose scientific figures are more accurate, and this is not the place to take up the issue. A demonstration of differing perceptions is the aim at this point. The whaling issue emphasises the importance of seeing how the environment is classified by those who live in it, and also how views of the environment may be created through discourse about it. Greenpeace can be commended for its commitment to many important issues, but it can hardly be denied that it has made use of – nay, even exploited – the romanticism of the 'intelligent, singing' whale in attracting support. If these words are making the reader angry, then turn to consider the plight of the people around the world who rely on whales and other sea animals for their livelihood (see, for example, Barnes 1996 and Photograph 12.1).

Photograph 12.1   Villagers in Lamalera, Indonesia, divide up a whale they have hunted – a good source of protein (photograph courtesy of R.H. and R. Barnes).

Environmental Influence in Social Life

The environment does of course influence economic, political and ritual life in most parts of the world, although in industrial societies this relationship may very often be neglected, especially from the reciprocal point of view. However, as we have seen in the case of the whale, all apparently economic resources may not be regarded in the same way, and when a whale became trapped in the Thames estuary in 2006, no one mentioned its previous value as a huge source of food, oil and whale-boned corsets. Amongst Hindus, the cow is regarded as a sacred animal, and though perfectly edible in objective terms, it is forbidden for consumption by local custom. Cows wander rather freely in some parts of India, damaging crops and impeding traffic, possibly even competing with human beings for the limited resources available.

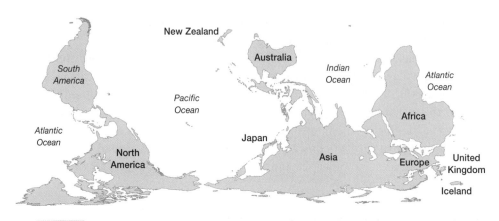

New Zealand

Australia

South
America

Indian
Ocean

Atlantic
Ocean

Pacific
Ocean

Atlantic
Ocean

Africa

Japan

North
America

Asia

Europe

United
Kingdom

Iceland

Map 12.1   A view of the world from the Southern hemisphere

As we have seen elsewhere in this book, it is also possible to point to relationships between the environment and political arrangements. In the first section of this chapter we saw that the choice of economic activity affects the possibilities for political development. Hunter–gatherers and pastoralists live in groups limited in size by the availability of food for themselves and, in the second case, their cattle, whereas sedentary agriculturalists are better able to develop larger populations and more complex political systems. The case of Nuer politics, sometimes called *fission/fusion politics*, is clearly influenced by the transhumance of their lives, since allegiances can be adjusted twice a year.

Environmental features also undoubtedly influence ritual and religious activity. Festivals are often associated with changes of seasons, planting and harvest, or the depths of winter and summer. Even where the agricultural cycle has been superseded by the wonders of technology for bringing goods to the supermarket, seasonal goods such as pumpkins, strawberries and sprouts are still drawn upon for celebrations. In Japan, where the land area is 90 per cent mountainous, mountains are the sites of religious shrines and pilgrimages, as well as often being regarded as mystical in particular ways. In a land where irrigation is important, water festivals are to be expected, and long spells of dry weather may still be punctuated with rain-making dances.

The very cosmology a people hold is often quite unintelligible without an understanding of attitudes to the environment, its limitations, and associations that have been created with it. Christmas in Europe and North America is inevitably associated with snow, for example, whereas the same feast in Australia is held in mid-summer. It is interesting the way that some of the symbolic associations have persisted through this inconvenient climatic difficulty, and in parts of Australia there is a 'seasonal Christmas' festival, probably largely a commercial venture, but allowing the use of northern symbols such as blazing fires and snowmen at the appropriate time of year.

A visit to the opposite hemisphere, or a completely different climate, is a good way to realise how environmentally orientated one's language is. For those of European stock who have grown up in Australia, New Zealand, or other southern climes, daily language contains some wonderful anomalies imported from a completely different ecosystem. The four seasons used in Australia are sometimes only illustrated by the deciduous trees planted by the colonisers and the agricultural cycles imposed by their farmers. Australian indigenous trees flower in the winter and the climate is very often rather warm, especially in the north. Map 12.1 illustrates a view of the world, from an Australian point of view.

Conclusion

In global parlance, too, we have adopted some originally directional words to take on meanings now quite inappropriate in orientation. The 'Far East', like the 'Middle East', was measured from the point of view of Europe, actually west from America, and north from Australia and New Zealand. 'The West' is an expression used to describe an amorphous collection of non-Eastern countries, now rather different from each other, but sharing the language which perpetuates these directional idiosyncrasies. I hope that this book, though it emanates from the original source of these misnomers, will have made way for a more equal and open sharing of different possibilities for seeing that world. In the next chapter we consider the increased likelihood of intercultural encounters that might offer an opportunity to express that awareness.

Discussion Questions

1 Consider what proportion of your life is spent securing your survival. How do you achieve this? On whom do you depend, and what do you offer in return? Now consider how much more time you spend working, and for what, or whom, are the extra benefits?

2 Under what circumstances would you give away your last food, when you yourself were still hungry? Would this be economically rational behaviour? If not, how would you explain it?

3 What for you is the epitome of 'nature'? Consider how much of this vision has actually been influenced by the intervention of human beings. Did they improve the vision you hold?

References and Further Research

Books
Appadurai Arjun (1986) *The Social Life of Things: Commodities in Cultural Perspective* (Cambridge: Cambridge University Press).
Asquith, Pamela and Kalland, Arne (1997) *Japanese Images of Nature: Cultural Perspectives* (London: Curzon Press).

Barnard, Alan (2007) *Anthropology and the Bushman* (Oxford and New York: Berg).

Barnes, R. H. (1996) *Sea Hunters of Indonesia: Fishers and Weavers of Lamalera* (Oxford: Clarendon Press).

Biesele, Megan, Hitchcock, Robert K. and Schweitzer, Peter P. (2000) *Hunters and Gatherers in the Modern World: Conflict, Resistance, and Self-Determination* (Oxford: Berghahn).

Campbell, J. K. (1964) *Honour, Family and Patronage* (Oxford: Clarendon Press).

Douglas, Mary and Isherwood, Baron (1979) *The World of Goods: Towards an Anthropology of Consumption* (London and New York: Routledge).

Firth, Raymond (ed.) (1967) *Themes in Economic Anthropology* (London: Tavistock Press).

Forde, Daryll (1934) *Habitat, Economy and Society* (London: Methuen).

Goldstein-Gidoni, Ofra (1997) *Packaged Japaneseness: Weddings, Business and Brides* (London: Curzon).

Humphrey, Caroline and Hugh-Jones, Stephen (1992) *Barter, Exchange and Value: An Anthropological Approach* (Cambridge: Cambridge University Press).

Ingold, Tim (2000) *The Perception of the Environment: Essays in Livelihood, Dwelling and Skill* (London: Routledge).

Ingold Tim, Riches, David and Woodburn, James (eds) (1988) *Hunter–Gatherers* (Oxford: Berg).

Koelewijn, Cees and Rivière, Peter (1987) *Oral Literature of the Trio Indians of Surinam* (Leiden: KITLV).

Leach, Edmund (1961) *Pul Eliya* (Cambridge: Cambridge University Press).

Mauss, Marcel (1979) *Seasonal Variations of the Eskimo* (London: Routledge & Kegan Paul).

Milton, Kay (ed.) (1993) *Environmentalism: The View from Anthropology* (London: Routledge).

Sahlins, Marshall (1974) *Stone Age Economics* (London: Tavistock).

Strang, Veronica (2004) *The Meaning of Water* (Oxford and New York: Berg).

Tambiah, Stanley Jeyaraja (1990) *Magic, Science, Religion, and the Scope of Rationality* (Cambridge: Cambridge University Press).

Articles

Barnard, Alan and Woodburn, James (1988) 'Property, Power and Ideology in Hunter-gathering Societies: An Introduction', in Tim Ingold et al., *Hunter–Gatherers* (Oxford: Berg), pp. 4–31.

Crook, Tony (2000) 'Length Matters: a Note on the GM Debate', *Anthropology Today*, 16(1): pp. 8–11.

Foster, George (1965) 'Peasant Society and the Image of Limited Good', *American Anthropologist* 67: 293–315.

Hill, Polly (1985) 'The Gullibility of Development Economists', *Anthropology Today*, 1(2): pp. 10–12.

Ingold, Tim (1993) 'Globes and Spheres: the Topology of Environmentalism', in Kay Milton (ed.), *Environmentalism: The View from Anthropology* (London: Routledge) pp. 31–42.

Kalland, Arne (1993) 'Whale Politics and Green Legitimacy: A Critique of the Anti-Whaling Campaign', *Anthropology Today*, 9(6): 3–7.

Richards, Caspian (2004) 'Grouse Shooting and Its Landscape', *Anthropology Today*, 20(4): 10–15.

Novels

Høeg, Peter (1994) *Miss Smilla's Feeling for Snow* (London: Fontana) is a novel that is set in the context of a Greenlander's immensely deep and detailed understanding of the qualities and characteristics that snow may have to tell a story.

Ondaatje, Michael (1992) *The English Patient* (London: Picador) contains passages that illustrate the importance for those who dwell in the desert of understanding the wind and its effects on their environment.

Sobel, Dava (1999) *Galileo's Daughter: A Drama of Science, Faith and Love* (London: Fourth Estate) brings to life the family story of the great astronomer and the force of resistance he encountered in early seventeenth-century views of the environment.

Films

Depending on Heaven (Peter Entell, 56 minutes, 1988), a film focusing on the Mongols living in the Inner Mongolia Autonomous Region of China.

The Emerald Forest (John Boorman, 1986) is a feature film about industrial threats to the life of an imaginary Indigenous people of the Amazonian tropical rain forest in which the young son of the chief engineer is captured and reared by the Indians.

Garden Days: A Village in Papua New Guinea (Ariane Lewis, Jon Jerstad and Gilbert Lewis, 25 minutes, 1988) shows domestic life in the Sepik area of Papua New Guinea, mainly from the women's point of view. It describes their everyday activities in the 'gardens' in order to produce the staple food (sago). The different stages of the preparation and cooking of sago are shown. The film closes with the puberty rite of a young girl.

The Gods Must Be Crazy (James Uys, 1980) is a somewhat overly dramatic feature film about the San Bushmen, now more properly known as the Ju/'hoan, of the Kalahari and the encounter of one of them with life in a neighbouring African war.

A Kalahari Family (John Marshall, 2002) is a five-part, six-hour series documenting 50 years in the lives of the Ju/'hoansi of southern Africa, from 1951 to 2000. These once independent hunter–gatherers experience dispossession, confinement to a homeland, and the chaos of war.

Medicine Man (John McTiernon, 1992) is a feature film, which stars Sean Connery as a researcher looking for pharmaceuticals in the Amazon rain forest, where he comes under the threat of loggers and rival researchers, all working to the detriment of the local Indigenous people.

Nanook of the North (Robert Flaherty, 1922), one of the earliest ethnographic films, depicts the life of an Inuit man and his family.

Ten Canoes (Rolf de Heer and the People of Ramingning), 2004 – a storytelling film set in Aboriginal Arnhemland, Australia, during a hunt for goose eggs.

Time Immemorial (Hugh Brody, 1991) is a moving film about the land claim of the Nishga'a people of British Columbia, Canada.

The Whale Hunters of Lamalera, Indonesia (John Blake and Robert Barnes, 51 minutes, 1988, 'Disappearing World Series'). The film vividly and carefully records the technical process involved in catching cetaceans and large fish, culminating in the catch itself.

Website

http://www.fieldtofactory.lse.ac.uk/ – film and ethnography of industrialisation in Chattisgarah, Central India.

http://www.drugnerd.com/archives/435/shamans-of-the-amazon-great-documentary/ – link to a film about environmental destruction in Amazonian Equador.

Tourism and the Intercultural Encounter

Cultural Difference for Recreation

An interesting thing has happened to cultural difference over the last few decades, for it has become part of the battery of interests and activities available for people to pursue during their leisure hours, and large numbers of individuals around the world, way beyond anthropologists, become involved. No longer is the intercultural encounter reserved for the intrepid explorer, the economic migrant or the curious anthropologist; it is now much more likely to be an expected part of normal life. This is the case whether you hail from a country that hosts a myriad of 'ethnic' restaurants, and sends out vast numbers of tourists to inspect the rest of the world, or whether you happen to live in one of the formerly relatively isolated places that the same tourists have 'discovered'. In this chapter we will examine both ends of the process, and some of the consequences that have emerged.

An early example of people exploring cultural difference for recreation was the use of food: going out to eat in Chinese, Indian, Mexican and Italian restaurants (and plenty more) has in many countries other than the host ones become a regular option for everyday as well as special occasions. It is often a relatively cheap way to engage in an experience that may seem quite exotic – though an Indian dish that has become one of the most popular 'British' foods in the country, chicken *tikka masala*, is said to have been designed to please the local British population. For residents of the source countries, for whom some of the foreign versions of their food may actually be quite strange, it is likely that the locals will also have the opportunity to enjoy exotic food, even if it is only the ubiquitous American fast fare with the Scottish name. There are local adaptations, even to the McDonalds menu and ethos, however, as an interesting anthropological collection on this subject soon made clear (Watson 1998).

With several days of free time to spend, those with the resources may choose to go further afield for their foreign experience, and a huge global industry has made it possible for such a venture to come quite cheap as well, certainly within Europe. It is now economically possible for large numbers of people to travel abroad, even if only for sunshine and sea air, but their arrival necessarily impacts on the experience of the local people, and this impact may be positive or negative. Visitors usually take an interest in some aspect of the cultural difference they encounter, and many local people benefit from the extra income that derives from the tourists enjoying their holidays, but there can also be problems. An area of interest to anthropologists, and others, is how locals react to being *on display*, and how far their presentations may be considered to be *authentic*.

Young travellers, who pack their worldly goods on their backs and set off to spend a year or more travelling around the world, may be surprised to know that this 'gap year' has become institutionalised only rather recently. When I took off in the late 1960s to try out life in a few other countries, even some of my peers were rather shocked, and my parents were worried that I would never settle down. Australians and New Zealanders I met on the way were ahead of the game, for visiting 'the continent' (of Europe) was already a popular thing for young people to do, and several were already spending time working abroad to finance their trips. Some of my contemporaries joined the 'hippie trail' through the now war-torn countries of Persia and Afghanistan, among others, and they probably contributed to the trend.

Now, according to returning students, backpackers vie with one another to find unusual locations to visit, and there to encounter 'real' people in their 'real homes', an experience which may not be as welcome to the local people as they might have imagined. At a conference I attended on international tourism in Indonesia, the nation that includes the so-called paradise island of Bali, several speakers mentioned the intrusion to local people of strangers tramping through their fields and villages, often inappropriately dressed, and behaving in a manner locally quite unacceptable (Nuryanti 1997). The backpacking visitors may be having a great experience, but thinking about how they appear to local people is another matter, and these informal encounters provide grist to the new anthropological mill of analysis.

An intriguing spin-off to the recreational interest in cultural difference that has been growing around the world is to be found in the use of culture as a theme for entertainment parks, and my own research for a while took this subject as a focus. Delving into the variety of possibilities to be found around the world, I came to the conclusion that museums, or at least the new, interactive versions of them, could be discussed in the same category as the more sophisticated theme parks I encountered. The museum is a product of the colonial world, housing collections of usually foreign material culture for research and posterity, but, like the findings of anthropologists, their treasures now attract an interest way beyond the educational. The implications of this popularisation of material culture provide another field of study, and another opportunity for a (relatively contained) intercultural encounter.

A last example of the popularisation of interest in travel and cultural difference is to be found in the television programmes that have been attracting large audiences. The first edition of this book included a list of films at the end of each chapter, mostly made by anthropologists, or at least with their help and consultation, and many had appeared on television. They were educational films for the most part, and some started their broadcasting lives as schools' programmes, but there was a wonderful period when anthropology reached prime-time viewing. Reality TV and house and garden makeovers now occupy many of these slots, but there has been a small resurgence of interest in cultural difference, though this time with more of an entertainment slant. *Tribe*, which documents the visits of one young British man to the homes of various isolated peoples, would seem to be a BBC version of foreign food and ethnic travel, and anthropologists are as yet not quite sure what to make of it (see the discussion in various issues of *Anthropology Today* following Caplan 2005). Michael Palin's encounters with local people where he wanders may be seen in the same vein and the globally distributed Discovery Channel is another example, which does use anthropological consultation. Film references are still to be found in this edition, but this is an explanation of why some may seem rather old.

The Study of Travel and Tourism

Travelling for pleasure is, of course, not new at all (see First-hand Account 13.1, on pp. 260–2, for example), and it is quite likely that all people everywhere have found ways of enjoying journeys that they might make, alongside any more practical reasons for their trips. They may well have enjoyed meeting new people along the way as well, for tales of journeys pepper the literature from most historical periods, and in the stories of many pre-literate peoples as well. Chaucer's *Canterbury Tales* is an example that we study in England, and *The Long Narrow Road to the Far North* is a classic work of the Japanese poet Basho. Polynesian peoples tell wonderful tales of the long, arduous boat journeys that they made across vast swathes of the Pacific Ocean, and the Six Nations of the Iroquoian peoples was founded upon the travels of a prophet they call the Peacemaker.

Photograph 13.1

The increase in sheer numbers of tourists makes it quite difficult to move around in some of the more popular tourist resorts as can be seen here at the Ponte della Paglia in Venice (photograph: Robert Davis and Garry Marvin).

Three major things have changed in the last couple of generations, however. First, it has become possible to travel large distances in a relatively short period of time, so visits to the other side of the world may be completed within a fortnight's summer holiday. Secondly, journeys such as these are within the economic means of increasingly large numbers of people, so the sheer volume of human bodies on the move has grown out of all proportion to those who travelled in the past (see Photograph 13.1). Thirdly, the propensity for people to make journeys simply in order to have fun and enjoy themselves has been met with an equally avid provision of entertainment for their edification–at least at first. The result of all this activity has attracted the attention of scholars in several fields–geography, economics, sociology, and, of course, anthropology. Indeed, a huge new disciplinary field of tourism has opened up, often to be found in Departments of Business and Marketing, to reflect the growing size of this huge global industry, as well as the economic possibilities for host communities.

Anthropologists were not the first to comment on this propensity for leisure travel; indeed, they were sometimes a little put out to find places where they had worked being 'invaded' by less well informed travellers. We have spoken of the way that anthropologists arriving in a relatively isolated area would be taken in, fed and accommodated, by no means unusual treatment for strangers anywhere–when they were few and far between. An anthropologist also expected to adapt to the ways of the people he or she encountered, and would gradually find ways to reciprocate the hospitality received. Tourists, on the other hand, very often expect to find at least some of the facilities they enjoy at home, even though they have travelled halfway round the world.

The title of an early anthropology book on the subject – *Hosts and Guests* (Smith 1977) – alludes to the relationship between peoples thrown into contact by this tourist phenomenon, at the same time as highlighting the old expectation broken. Tourists may bring the resources to pay for their expectations, but the often huge differential access to income between the visitors and the local people adds political and ethical dimensions to the relationship that has formed an

The investigation of tourism and intercultural encounter in Egypt has a long history which goes beyond recent decades. The unique features of Egypt encouraged a wide spectrum of people to visit and explore the country. One of these features, inter alia, is that Egypt hosts the oldest university in the world, Al-Azhar University (see www.alazhar.org), which allowed students from all over the world – since the tenth century – to visit, settle in and travel around the country.

By the end of the eighteenth century, the discovery of the Rosetta Stone opened the door, even more, for further exploration, tourism activities and cultural encounters – in particular, for archaeologists. However, more recently, in the mid-1970s, the political stability in the Middle East in general and in Egypt in particular witnessed the beginning of a new era for the tourism industry in Egypt.

First-hand account 13.1:
Ashraf Tageldeen, Egyptian – on Tourism and the Case of Cultural Encounter

Another perspective for looking at the cultural encounter in Egypt requires not only an exploration of Egyptian history but also Egypt's location and topography. Situated at the conjunction of three continents, Africa, Asia and Europe, Egypt has always been a passage and commercial route, more recently via the Suez Canal. This location created a sort of familiarity with foreigners being around, at least at the major cities and ports.

The landscape of Egypt influences and reflects the culture of the population and their readiness for cultural encounters and tourism because it dictates the economic patterns and activities of life. For instance, the west of the country is mainly desert with some oases and valleys, limited population and few historical sites. The east is mainly high land, with some unique seashore and natural sights but once again with very limited population. Lastly, the most populated area is the strip around the Nile Valley that used to be the land of pharaohs, where the ancient Egyptian civilisation thrived. Therefore, it should be stated that the Nile Valley strip was more open and more ready for cultural encounters with foreigners and tourists, in particular the north and the south of this strip.

Since the late 1970s, the focus of tourism activities in Egypt has mainly been on cultural tourism, i.e. visiting historical sites. In late 1980s, more opportunities were explored, including recreational types of tourism (in areas like Sharm El Sheikh and Hurghada) and adventure travel (such as mountain climbing in Sinai and safaris in the Western Desert), attracting a new kind of tourist. This opened the door for change in the local culture of the western and eastern population as a new economic opportunity became apparent.

In addition, the introduction of the new types of tourism created a sort of local migration of some professionals working in the tourism industry, which enhanced understanding and the cultural encounter between the local population and tourists. In the past, it was common to meet only tourists in historical sites and accommodation premises but nowadays it has become ordinary to meet tourists in the underground or in other venues of normal life. In 2006, Egypt had a record of 9.81 million visitors, with the ambition of reaching 14 million by 2011.

The sensitivity to local people and local culture has been tackled early on by travel agents organising tours and travel plans to Egypt. I can recall from my experience while working in the hotel industry that tourists (visiting Egypt via organised tours) used to have a short briefing from their tour guides about the local culture and other spiritual issues, for instance, the fasting month (Ramadan).

It can also be claimed that indigenous people in many places around the country were able to recognise the benefits of providing tourism-related services and products. In popular areas for tourism, a large number of families have inherited tourism-related professions and crafts. In line with this view, the Egyptian Ministry of Tourism is embarking on an awareness campaign to demonstrate the importance of tourism to local people, as tourism is related to almost 70 other industries in Egypt.

A reflection on how Egyptians provide their own account of cultural encounters can be found in various formats. For instance, the sound and light at the Pyramids, Salah Eddin Castle, and the Temple of Karnak in Luxor aim to reflect the identity and authenticity of Egypt, and the Pharaonic Village on the Nile provides a living museum for ancient Egypt, the objective being to provide a link and confirm the identity of the Egyptian civilisation.

Confirming the identity and the authenticity of the Egyptian civilisation to tourists can be seen as an impossible task to achieve, considering the changes in lifestyle and similarity of daily routine between local people in Egypt and tourists in their own countries. However, exploring local culture and enjoying contact and culture difference is an experience that tourists look forward to – something that can only be witnessed by sharing rather than by material culture in its traditional form.

Dr Ashraf Tageldeen is Lecturer in Tourism and Hotel Management at Alexandria University, Alexandria, Egypt

important focus of the study. When Smith's edited volume came out, in 1977, she reported that tourism was already one of the world's largest industries, pumping an estimated 80 billion US dollars into the world economy; economists and geographers were already busy analysing the effects.

The first edition of *Hosts and Guests* contains a wealth of small studies that examined the way that tourism was changing the lives of the people with whom the authors had been working, and a range of issues were raised about the impacts of the intercultural encounters that resulted. Some talked of the breakdown of the previous economy, others of the revitalisation of the local production of arts and crafts. Some presented the views of the local people affected, others sought to analyse the motives of the visitors. A second edition, some 20 years later (Smith 1989), was able to follow up with a longer-term evaluation, and place the earlier material in a broader, global context; and there is now a new book called *Hosts and Guests Revisited*, which set out to examine tourism in the twenty-first century (Smith and Brent 2001).

In the meantime, the field has become much more widely studied in anthropology, and there have been several books that focus on particular regions. *Coping with Tourists*, for example, is a volume to which Jeremy Boissevain (1996) invited contributions from anthropologists working in European tourist destinations. His own long-term work in Malta would have been incomplete without taking account of the burgeoning tourist trade there:

> The Maltese Islands had developed from a poor, insular backwater to a thriving, modern tourist destination whose inhabitants were themselves increasingly becoming tourists. If in the 1960s tourists were welcomed with pride and native hospitality, by the beginning of the 1990s the welcome seemed less enthusiastic. (1996: vii)

There is a detailed analysis of the Maltese case by Annabel Black (1996) in the same volume. Tourism is not new in Europe, of course, and the visitors are very often people who themselves receive tourists in their own home locations, but the sheer increase in numbers has brought about many changes, and Boissevain's book addresses the strategies used in Europe to cope with these changes.

Earlier anthropological studies tended to focus on the more stark interferences that the arrival of large numbers of strangers brought about in the areas where they had worked. Michael Hitchcock, for example, published a number of articles about tourism in South East Asia, addressing how this affected local ideas about ethnicity and identity (Hitchcock et al. 1993 and Hitchcock and Teague 2000 contain many references to this work). Numerous and well-organised tourist groups from Japan have become a common sight around the world, and Japanese anthropologist Shinji Yamashita has published in both Japanese and English, notably about the effects of tourism in Bali, but broadening his approach comparatively as well (e.g. Yamashita 2003).

Various theoretical approaches had actually already been advanced by sociologists and students of tourism, but it is interesting that some of these classical writers have gradually come around to realising things about travel and tourism that anthropologists were probably aware of earlier by force of their own experiences. For example, there is recently a resistance by scholars of tourism to dividing participants into visitors and those who are visited, looking instead at the mobile nature of the whole touristic venture (Rojek and Urry 1997; Sheller and Urry 2004). *Authenticity* has been a thorny subject, too, with early writers discussing how tourists were inadvertently destroying the very cultural authenticity they were seeking to visit, or encouraging people to reinvent themselves along the lines of tourist expectations and enjoyment. In the next sections of this chapter, we will examine some contributions anthropologists have made to these debates.

Play and Rites of Passage

An important early anthropological contributor to the subject was Nelson Graburn, whose work in both the Inuit Arctic and in Japan has raised an interesting range of issues over the years. A classic article of his (Graburn 1977, 1989, 2001) that appeared in all three editions of *Hosts and Guests* puts the activities of a tourist – or simply a traveller – in the broader context of anthropological theories about rites of passage. Thus travel is seen as marking a break in normal routines, a separation of the play of tourism from the usual life of work. This division he shows as parallel to that between the sacred aspects of festivals and the profane ones of the everyday life, therefore celebrated in some way by all people everywhere, as we saw in Chapter 4 (pp. 77ff.).

It is clearly possible to compare the travel associated with tourism with van Gennep's territorial rites of passage, as we intimated in discussing the routines associated with air travel. Before setting off, tourists also often make quite elaborate preparations, such as:

- buying special clothes
- preparing a selection of protective products

During their time away they:

- eat different food

- send back postcards
- buy presents to bring back, for friends and relatives,
- buy souvenirs for themselves.

The activities are thus marked in the same ways that were noted for ritual activities in Chapter 4, and some travellers even seek physical ordeals, such as:

- sleeping rough
- climbing mountains
- bungee-jumping etc.

Graburn also discusses the way that touristic breaks mark variations in the passage of time (referring to the Leach article we discussed in Chapter 4), as well as different stages in life, so that the 'gap year' may in this way be seen as another part of the attainment of adulthood, just as a period in the bush is for the Maasai and others.

Some aspects of tourism are specifically associated with the sacred, indeed pilgrimage journeys have many of the same qualities, and before the advent of cheap holidays a spiritual quest of this sort was a common goal of travel. In Japan, for example, whole communities would save up collectively to send small groups of members, in turn, to visit important shrines such as the site of remembrance of the founding ancestor Amaterasu in Ise; these trips were rare opportunities to enjoy travel during periods when other movement was forbidden. The Hajj, the pilgrimage journey made by Muslims to Mecca, is one of Islam's five essential pillars, said to have been taking place annually for over 1400 years. Preparations for, and the activities of, this journey bear many of the characteristics of a rite of passage, and a person who has completed it is said to be transformed for life (see Hammoudi 2005 for the personal account of a Moroccan anthropologist).

Graburn goes further, however, arguing:

> For Westerners who value individualism, self-reliance and the work ethic, tourism is the best kind of life for it is sacred in the sense of being exciting, renewing and inherently self-fulfilling. The tourist journey is a segment of our lives over which we have maximum control, and it is no wonder that tourists are disappointed when their chosen, self-indulgent fantasies don't turn out as planned.   (1977: 23)

This is not a new phenomenon, Graburn notes, for by the seventeenth-century, Europeans with the financial means were regularly travelling to visit historical sites, as well as for activities such as hunting and health, and in eighteenth-century Britain a Grand Tour of Europe became an essential rite of passage for aristocrats and other potential leaders. The provision of breaks for spiritual and physical renewal began to be provided more generally during the Industrial Revolution in England by philanthropic (and often religious) employers, and Thomas Cook, now a name well associated with mass tourism, was actually a Baptist minister whose first 'package' tour was part of a programme of social reform – taking a party to a temperance meeting (ibid. 25).

Now it is commonplace for tourists to seek refreshment and renewal–in a nutshell 're-creation' – when they travel, whether they choose history and culture as a focus, total relaxation in the sun, or 'natural' activities, like hunting and fishing, which might well have been the means of livelihood of their forebears, or of the local people in the places they visit. North Americans and other former colonials also sometimes display a yen for outback living as a way of bonding – perhaps between father and son, or a group of young people, even alone – and this experience can again take on the qualities of a rite of passage. It is ironic, and sometimes more seriously invasive, if there are local people whose land is taken over by the tourist industry so that outsiders can make a living off their traditional lands, and the case of the San Bushmen in Botswana is a notorious example of this problem, also found in the so-called wildernesses of America and Australia, for example.

We will return to the impact on local people of tourism in the next section, but in the meantime, the aim of our travellers can often simply be translated as *play* of one sort or another. Victor Turner drew up some parallels with the analysis of ritual activities in small-scale societies by identifying playful periods in the lives of members of larger, complex societies as liminoid, a development of the term *liminal*, used for the transition period in a rite of passage. He also used this term for theatrical performances, suggesting a sense of make-believe or fantasy, but he tended to continue with the idea of associating such a period with the sacred, and a good development of his argument is to be found in the book about pilgrimage published with his wife, Edith (Turner and Turner 1978).

> **liminoid** – a term proposed by Victor and Edith Turner to describe periods of play and other activities that have qualities of rites of passage and the **liminal**, but which may be less ritually (and religiously) important than many of the classic ones discussed.

For many other commentators, *play* is a quite secular activity, but it can nevertheless be separated rather clearly from the ordinary workaday life, and the characteristics of the liminal, or transition period of a rite of passage may well apply to people during play, especially when they are away from home. Tourists are outside of their usual social milieu, and therefore unconstrained by their normal rules of conduct, so they might well experience a sense of freedom and escape. Even on a trip to the seaside, people wear clothes that they would never don in the office, and in some European resorts, wild groups of noisy tourists have been known to create havoc among the local facilities – drinking too much, taking illegal drugs, and seeking to satisfy their sexual urges in any convenient location, however public it might be. These examples might be extremes, but in the next section, we will examine a variety of consequences for local people of the arrival of tourists.

Ecotourism and Sacred Places

While tourists are seeking renewal and perhaps spiritual fortification by 'playing', the story may be very different for residents of the locations where those tourists make their fun, as we have already mentioned in connection with groups whose lands have been designated as recreational parks. In some cases, local people may be hired for their knowledge of terrain or tracking and hunting techniques; in others, they have been barred from their own lands so that tourists can be more easily guided to observe and photograph the non-human animals that live there. In Africa and parts of South East Asia, especially, animals are often given priority over humans in conservation programmes, and the people who collect money from the tourists and other visitors are only rarely local residents, though the latter may be given some minor benefits to keep them from making too much fuss.

Two examples will serve to illustrate the point, and the first was partly recounted to me by a student taking the anthropology course at Oxford Brookes. He had grown up as a white resident of Botswana, where he had been employed during his school holidays as a guide for people he described as 'rich tourists' seeking to hunt big game. The land they used had previously been the source of all livelihood for the San Bushmen, who had been excluded by the Botswana government, in theory for the conservation of big animals, but in practice for tourism and, if the price is right, for hunting with guns. Survival International regularly publicised information about the plight of these San people, quite a number of whom had died in the resettlement camps in which the government had housed them. As this book goes to press, the high court in Botswana ruled that the government's eviction of the Bushmen was 'unlawful and unconstitutional', and that they have the right to live on their ancestral lands … so it will be interesting to see what happens next.

The second example is of a large park in Malaysia which was opened a few years ago precisely to display the natural resources the country can boast, as well as various forms of cultivation that have been developed and practised there. Visitors are encouraged to wander over a substantial area of land, or they may take a park bus from one to another of the special features that have been laid out for them. Monkeys swing freely in and out of the trees on either side of the pathways, occasionally swooping down to rob passing visitors neglectful of their sandwiches. It seems fun, unless a visitor takes enough interest in the section of the park map marked *Orang Asli* – or **Aboriginal** people – for those who used to occupy and live off this area of land are now confined to a cramped village in one small corner of it.

These examples may represent extreme-sounding cases, but the problem becomes more subtly controversial when the tourists' so-called spiritual experience of communing with nature and wildlife comes directly or indirectly into conflict with the spiritual life of people in the areas where they travel. In a book entitled *Is the Sacred for Sale?*, Alison Johnston (2006) examines the concept of ecotourism, which in theory has a positive ring to it because of its association

ecotourism – a term that has been used by tour operators to induce travellers to feel comfortable about activities that otherwise might seem to be compromising aspects of the environment, which indeed they still may, especially for local people whose lives are affected by the arrival of tourists.

with sustainability and respect, but in practice often literally destroys the lands and lives of the Indigenous people who are featured as part of it:

> Testimonies from Indigenous Peoples confirm that ecotourism is highly oversold as a concept. Most say that ecotourism proposals look little different in character than other industry ventures in their midst. Their experience is that the ecotourism industry profiteers off indigenous cultures, behind a mask of doing good. (Johnston 2006: 15)

Bristling with examples from locations around the world, the book examines a range of issues from the policies and directives of big international bodies such as the United Nations and NGOs to the desperate attempts of local people to confine and contain the interests of tourists that also bring much-needed income.

One famous sacred site discussed in some detail is Machu Picchu, still a sacred place to the Quechua-speaking peoples of Peru but now also designated as a World Heritage site by the United Nations and an archaeological Inca ruin by the Peruvian government. The annual gate receipts of some six million dollars constitute only a fraction of the overall benefit to Peru of the industry brought by this tourist magnet, but most Quechua people cannot even afford the 20 dollar entrance fee, and on Sunday, when they can enter free, they have no chance of maintaining the silence that used to mark their respect for the ancestral presence there (Johnston 2006: 127). The other famous site that gets attention is Uluru – or Ayers Rock – in Australia, advertised as a site sacred to the Anangu people, who have occupied that land for some 60,000 years, and who now do officially share in the running of this designated World Heritage Area. Unfortunately their message – that the rock should not be climbed – is ignored by a large percentage of the visitors (ibid. 129–30).

This kind of exploitation is being gradually turned around in some parts of the world, and during my own research in North America and the Pacific, I was able to witness and talk to people who were reclaiming their own representations alongside a renewed use of their lands (Hendry 2005). In New Zealand, for example, there are several places where the representations of Māori culture are entirely in the hands of Māori people, and they make the rules (see First-hand account 13.2. Indeed, there are some Māori entrepreneurs who have started to make a good living out of their tours for tourists, who seem to appreciate first-hand attention, and are quite willing to go along with requests to make Māori greetings, and respect requests to stay off certain parts of the land (see Photograph 13.2). In Vanuatu, as well, an independent country that banned outside anthropologists for a period, and where local fieldworkers are employed to record customary practices, some tours have been created especially so that tourists may learn what ni-Vanuatu people wish to present.

It is quite rare to find places where the actual Indigenous people are making much of a living out of tourism, however, for their priority to respect and protect their own land and sacred sites conflicts with what seems to appeal to outsiders, namely to find out about precisely what the Indigenous people are trying to con-

Māori cultural tourism offers individuals an understanding of 'the unique set of values and behaviours of Māori through which they seek to foster a sense of oneness and unity with the world' (Royal 2002: 30). This is particularly important given the view of many Māori and others that 'the world and humanity as a whole has to make some kind of quantum paradigm shift towards a fundamental unity' (ibid. 44). This shift is required to address the social and environmental challenges the world needs to face in order to overcome the 'crisis of sustainability' (Cajete 2005). Tourism, as the largest vehicle for human connectedness, can participate in achieving sustainability – and Māori cultural tourism can be at the forefront of this as a global leader.

First-hand account 13.2:
Chellie Spiller, Māori – on Principles that Help Guide the Actions of Sustainable Māori Cultural Tourism Businesses

Many Māori entrepreneurs draw upon *mātauranga* and *mōhiotanga* (which is rendered as *knowledge* and *wisdom* and the insights contained therein) to develop sustainable models of business. Thus, Māori cultural tourism businesses are guided by principles such as: *Whakapapa* – an ordering principle that encompasses human genealogies and the evolution of the Universe; *Wairuatanga* – spiritual knowledge; *Kotahitanga* – respect for individual differences and the desire to reach consensus, unity and solidarity; *Kaitiakitanga* – setting a high value on stewardship or guardianship of the environment; *Manaakitanga* – demonstrating caring, sharing and hospitality; *Whanaungatanga* – acknowledging the importance of bonds of kinship that exist within and between *whanau* (family), *hapu* (clan) and *iwi* (tribe) and building and encouraging a wide range of stakeholder relationships; and *Tau utuutu*, often referred to as the principle of reciprocity – giving back or replacing what is received. Several of these principles are expanded upon below with references from field research.

Māori businesses can incorporate *wairuatanga* (spirituality) as a guiding principle. Henare (2001) describes this as a respect for life and the physical, intellectual, emotional and spiritual well-being of things and people. It is to remember, at all times, the 'spirit'

Aotearoa **New Zealand**

of people, and of the endeavour in which they participate with others and it is also to acknowledge the forces that are greater than human endeavours. A leading tour guide sees the principle of spirituality as being at the heart of the experience offered to cultural tourists:

> I make it a spiritual experience, I make it a memorable experience, I make them feel at home, I make them feel part of my family. The spirituality part of their experience starts from the beginning... with a prayer, grace, karakia... from there – once we enter into the forest, it just entwines it in a different atmosphere ... you just get more ... it just gets stronger ...

Manaakitanga (hospitality) guides Kaupapa Māori cultural tourism organisations to welcome visitors and show them fitting hospitality: in *manaakitanga* 'to be is to give' (Shirres 1997: 119). *Manaakitanga* is to care for the *mana* of others and the 'real sign of a person's *mana* and *tapu* is not that person's power to destroy other people, but that person's power to *manaaki*, to protect and look after people' (ibid. 47). The CEO of a case-company explains this:

> It's about, once again, the authentic experience. I keep using that word but it's about people being committed to serving someone else, *tangata whenua* (Māori) serving *manuhiri* (visitors). Genuinely. Hospitality. That they really want another person to enter their world to be entertained, to be informed. We want them to see what their life is like in that connection to the land, in their *Whakapapa* (genealogy), in their role in the history of this place.

The concept of 'sacred ecology' (Cajete in Royal 2002: 29) represents 'unification of the human community with the natural world' and is of uppermost concern for Māori. 'I believe', says Marsden (in Royal 2002: 3), 'that whilst colonisation is a reality for so-called "indigenous" peoples, the ontological and epistemological concern of unification with the world is a better place for us to meet'. This is reflected in a CEO's aspiration for their clients:

> [what I want people to leave with is to] take back that Māori people are a gift to the world, really that we still have what some cultures have lost in terms of oneness, a linking together, a feeling of belonging to each other and the world.

Following on from this is the principle of *Kaitiakitanga* that indicates stewardship or guardianship of the environment. Many Māori cultural tourism enterprises realise they are in a unique position to 'teach' visitors about living in harmony with the environment, and in doing so they are contributing to global awareness of living with respect for the environment. This principle is described by Henare (2001) as caring for and nurturing all aspects of the environment, physical, intellectual, emotional and spiritual. It is also to act as, and be seen to act as, guardians of the resources that Māori are entrusted to care for. Henare observes that this need not be impossibly altruistic but can act as a guideline for organisational development and activity. A research participant CEO highlighted this imperative and the opportunity for its achievement:

> [we want to] send people in touch with themselves and their environment, you can't help not being aware of the environment when you are here.

Chellie wrote this piece in 2007 while a PhD student at the University of Auckland Business School. See the end of this chapter for full references for Cajete (2005), Royal (2002) and Shirres (1997), and Chapter 3 for Henare (2001).

serve. A wonderful show of dinner, dancing and story-telling put on by Coast Salish people at the top of Grouse Mountain in Vancouver, Canada, was poorly attended when I was there, and later I heard it had closed down. In Brantford, Ontario, the Aboriginal tourist office works with the local Ontario office to publicise their attractions, but an Aboriginal person I met who was working in the tourist industry there had given up that job because she was unable to make a decent living.

Photograph 13.2

Greeting for visitors at the Māori Arts and Crafts Institute in Thermal Valley, Rotorua, New Zealand (photograph, Joy Hendry, courtesy New Zealand Māori Arts and Crafts Institute).

Elsewhere, Indigenous people have more or less closed off their sacred sites, and especially their events, because large numbers of tourists with cameras completely devalue the occasion. The Hopi, for example, whose well-known Kachina dolls represent spiritual beings powerful in their world view, may allow visitors to watch the dances when the spirits appear, but they have banned photography. In Johnston's book there is a sign reproduced that clearly bans 'outside white visitors' altogether from a Hopi village 'because of your failure to obey the laws of our tribe' (Johnston 2006: 251). As Johnston points out, among many Indigenous Peoples the word 'sacred' is fundamentally synonymous with the idea of 'sustainability', for the way to sustain the Earth is through respecting its Creator and its spiritual power (ibid. 250).

Performance, Identity and Authenticity

How then to proceed? So far, we have assumed that there can be people called tourists, and those formerly called hosts, who received them in their territory. However, these terms are far from clear-cut, and another good collection of papers by anthropologists (Abram et al. 1997) sets out to examine and discuss some of the variations, and their implications. So-called tourists, for example, may be residents, even if temporary, in a place foreign to them, others may even have chosen to live there, or anyway be there primarily for work. On the other hand, some of the contributors to their book examine the 'community' that the tourists are visiting, and discuss ways in which local people perform cultural difference, often specifically for the benefit of visitors (see also Coleman and Crang 2002). In both cases, the editors argue, an important issue is one of identity, and how this is constructed and differentiated from another such identity.

I mentioned in the last section that tourists to Vanuatu may learn what ni-Vanuatu people wish to present, and a short description of one example will raise the various themes of this section. In Port Vila, visitors may buy a ticket to visit a place called Ekasup Cultural Village. At the appointed time, they board a bus that transports them to the edge of a nearby forest, where they are asked to continue on foot. As they approach the place of the presentation, a man dressed in the very skimpy garments that used to be worn in this land jumps out and challenges the party to identify itself, just as he would have done in precolonial times when strangers passed close by. The leader of the tour knows how to respond, and once they have been 'approved' the visitors continue to a reconstituted 'village', where details of life in the bush are explained and demonstrated.

identity – ideas about oneself and one's social allegiances that usually reflect birth and upbringing, but may also include an element of choice, especially in response to the global dissemination of goods and cultural ideas, and the increased movement of people within this globalised world.

As well as the guide, there are people recreating the life of the past, just as if they had had no contact with the industrialised world of electricity and mobile phones, and families with children simultaneously pass on their heritage as they entertain the tourists. On one level, this situation may be compared with displays of *heritage* around the world, as we will see shortly. For the tourists, their visit to Vanuatu has been enhanced by a display of life as it was before they had access to such a situation, and they may or may not find this recreation 'authentic', especially if they catch sight of some of the 'villagers' in town later, dressed like everyone else in jeans and T-shirts. On another level, however, these people are reconfirming their own identity as ni-Vanuatu people by recreating life as it used to be before outsiders – not unlike many of the tourists who now come to look– came and colonised their lands.

In the situation we have described, people in Vanuatu are *performing* their past for the benefit of the tourists, and, at the same time, they are confirming their own identity by putting on this performance. It may not be the pristine past those tourists may seek, but without change they would know nothing of it, and the crucial fact is that the people who are performing it have chosen to do it themselves. In many other situations around the world, big multinational enterprises build the hotels and other tourist facilities and expect to pick up the profits. If local people are engaged to display aspects of their culture – dancing shows are a popular example, or stalls of local handicrafts laid out in the hotel lobbies – they receive only a small proportion of the takings, and they may be strictly limited in what they can present. The tourists, on the other hand, can relax in comfortable, relatively safe surroundings, so they may prefer this kind of arrangement if they have the resources.

Abram's own article, in the book we referred to above (Abram et al. 1997), examines the *performance* of history in the Auverne in rural France in various situations and in the presence of varying degrees of outsider. Again, music and dancing are common activities, and the choice of clothes now not often seen in everyday life may mark an occasion for representation of characteristics of the locality. Abram argues that there is a difference between presentations to total touristic outsiders, who need 'explicit labelling and framing of events', and those which draw in local people, or visitors from nearby communities, for whom some of the knowledge and experience is shared. In either case, the performance is also an opportunity for the expression of identity, and the making and selling of postcards and souvenirs to tourists and other visitors is a means to maintain valued practices and continuity with the past.

In these cases, then, the presence of visitors actually encourages the definition and redefinition of local identity, rather than destroying it, as others had previously argued. Another article (by Kohn 1997) in the same book looks at the way that visitors themselves may absorb more and more local identity by participating over a period of years in the activities of an island in the Inner Hebrides of Scotland, even if they only spend their summers there, and some of those with the strongest 'natural' claims to local identity – like birth and language – may work away for many years in the city. A parallel case, set in a magical spot in Mallorca now marketed as the place where Chopin and Georges Sand stayed, though actually only for a few months, is analysed by Waldren, both in this volume (Abram et al. 1997), and in a book entitled *Insiders and Outsiders – Paradise and Reality in Mallorca* (Waldren 1996), a great ethnography on the subject.

All these examples illustrate the flexible and dynamic nature of identity, always defined through difference and in contrast to something else, here embodied – even if unconsciously – in the presence of tourists and other relative outsiders taking an interest in it. For visitors to imagine some pristine 'authentic' situation that existed before they arrived and 'discovered' another people, however, is an arrogant way of thinking about cultural difference. It also irritates the people who are accused of inauthenticity because they have changed over the years. Of course they have changed, they have undoubtedly always been changing, and that these new arrivals should expect the world to change only when they arrive, albeit with a wealth of high-tech tools and toys, sadly misunderstands and undervalues millennia of local knowledge and experience.

Theme Parks, Museums and Material Culture

Sharon Macdonald (1997) extrapolates some of these ideas a little further by recounting the tale of a pair of young Gaelic speakers who set up a heritage centre called Aros in the island of Skye, just off the coast of Scotland. This, they say, is for local people, to conserve *their cultural heritage*, as well as to present it to tourists. Such an idea seems only to develop those we have been discussing already, but the venture is not necessarily popular within the community, and it has encountered some opposition. Crucially, however, Macdonald argues that the work it brings allows these young people to stay there, rather than needing to go off and seek work in the city, so in this case the possibility of bringing visitors is actually enabling them to conserve and continue their own heritage.

The idea of putting cultural heritage on display is not a new one, and museums have been doing it for a long time, if only by using collections of objects from far-flung places as evidence of travel, and of the extent of imperial power. In countries that became part of such an empire, it was an important exercise to erect a museum which laid out examples of the material culture of the people who had formerly lived there. This was partly an exercise in *conservation*, for as the fruits of the Industrial Revolution were dispersed throughout the world, the wherewithal for preindustrial craft production often became redundant, but it was also a kind of record of peoples who were either eliminated, or thought to be dying out. For the same reasons, examples of such materials were carried home and stored, or displayed in ethnographic museums.

In fact, many of the descendants of those people have survived and are now choosing to emphasise and represent (by themselves) those earlier identities, so for them museums may still carry the negative connotations of such untimely and unpleasant predictions. Probably partly in response to this, many more lively and active forms of cultural display have appeared around the world, some still called museums, but perhaps with modern work alongside the older objects, or houses laid out in the open air. Others have contrasting names such as culture or heritage centres – one is the Box of Treasures we discussed in Chapter 3 – serving the purpose of enabling local people to retrieve and celebrate a selected identity for themselves, at the same time as offering a contained version of their cultural features for their visitors. Some sites of cultural display – often in this case of others, rather than selves – may even be called theme parks.

In the book *The Orient Strikes Back: A Global View of Cultural Display* (2000) I examined examples of cultural display found in different parts of the world, from the ethnographic and other museums found in Europe, through the development of World Fairs and Exhibitions that spread around the world, to Disneyland and other kinds of theme parks that became popular, first in America, and then beyond. My initial interest had been aroused by an abundance of such so-called theme parks in Japan, which chose to build replicas and representations of the major attractions of several foreign countries, thus enabling visitors to spend a day or more imagining themselves abroad without all the hassle and inconvenience of actually going there! Investigating beyond Japan, but still in East Asia, I found many other kinds of impressive displays of cultural difference, much more sophisticated than American-style theme parks, but engaging forms of representation, such as replica and reconstruction, that are not usually approved of in museums.

In a book that has become a classic in tourism studies, sociologist Dean McCannell (1976) suggested that the separation of cultural artefacts from their original context, and the interest of others in visiting such representations, was an important characteristic of *modernity*. The artificial conservation and reconstruction of the premodern is a characteristic of the modern, he argued, and the interest of those who feel they have lost their traditional cultural forms in others who they think still have them is a search for *authenticity* in a world that was rapidly losing it. For those who became bothered by such interest in their 'backstage' lives, it was necessary to create a way to satisfy the visitors, and preferably benefit from their interest, so, McCannell argues, tourist spaces began to 'stage authenticity'.

The creation of copies of things, or the reconstruction of trips that might be dangerous in real life (such as the Jungle Cruise in Disneyland), have in fact been interpreted as *postmodern*, and McCannell himself argues in a later edition of his book that the social arrangements he described in the 1970s became out of date as his book went to press – if the founding claims of postmodernism are taken seriously (1999: 1). In the same way that I commented above about authenticity, however, I suggest that it is another form of Western arrogance to classify the behaviour of people around the world according to our divisions of recent time and 'development' towards our ways of doing things as signs of 'modernity', or 'postmodernity'. I predict that these descriptions will enter the historical list of expressing ways of thinking – such as 'primitive' and 'pre-logical – that we began to draw up as characteristic of the early anthropologists in Chapter 1 of this book.

Conclusion

As anthropologists, I suggest that we still need to look at local situations in their own context, and within their own systems of rationality, and my interpretation of the Japanese theme parks included not only the global picture – which clearly influenced the Japanese choice of words to describe their *tema paku* (or theme parks) – but also prior Japanese ideas about display and learning. These include a very positive attitude to copying, as a good way to learn and pass on skills, and also as a way to ensure the continuity of things which might otherwise eventually disappear. The idea of reconstructing something from the past is also seen positively, and several parks in Japan represent historical periods of importance, just as they now do elsewhere, in fact. A reconstruction of Shakespeare's birthplace is found in one Japanese park (see Photograph 13.3), which admits that it is a 'copy' of the 'real place' in Stratford-upon-Avon, but claims greater *authenticity* as it is more like it would have been when the Bard himself lived in it!

This Japanese version of the 'New Place', Shakespeare's later home in Maruyama, Japan, has been built according to historical accounts of building techniques in England at the time.

Museums and collections of material culture, even humble souvenirs (see Hitchcock and Teague 2000 for an interesting set of articles on this subject), have for some centuries marked the interest of travellers, explorers and colonial settlers – and of course anthropologists – in the unusual 'other' people they encountered in parts of the world they visited. More recently, craft centres have provided places where people may sit and make their characteristic materials for the visiting tourists, and miles and miles of shops, street markets – even emporia – offer goods for sale to the growing numbers of curious visitors, though often with overheads collected by entrepreneurial outsiders. The newer culture centres, where local people are able to design and present themselves as they see fit, and even use methods that might shock some of the foreign visitors, are a relatively new way that culture may be *shared* rather than *consumed*, and here I suggest that a more satisfactory intercultural encounter may be secured wherever one may travel.

1   Have you spent time travelling abroad? How much do you think your visits impacted on the lives of the local people? Did they benefit from your visit, or do you think your behaviour could have been annoying, at least to some of them? If the latter, do you have any ideas about how the situation could be rectified?

2   Have you had the experience of tourists, or other foreigners arriving in your place of residence, or in a place that you regard as special or sacred? If so, how well do you think they behaved? If not, try to imagine a scenario where the visitors are quite noisy and numerous. What are the limits of toleration in a situation such as this?

3   Now consider how you behave when foreign visitors come to stay in your home. Do you change anything about your usual way of life? If you are asked to show the visitors around, where would you take them and what would you show them? Would the visitors get an 'authentic' experience?

References and Future Research

Books

Abram, Simone, Waldren, Jacqueline and Macleod, Donald V. L. (1997) *Tourists and Tourism: Identifying with People and Places* (Oxford and New York: Berg).

Boissevain, Jeremy (1996) *Coping with Tourists: European Reactions to Mass Tourism* (Oxford: Berghahn).

Coleman, Simon and Crang, Mike (2002) *Tourism: Between Place and Performance* (Oxford: Berghahn).

Crick, Malcolm (1994) *Resplendent Sites, Discordant Voices: Sri Lankans and International Tourism* (Switzerland: Harwood).

Davis, Robert and Marvin, Garry (2004) *Venice, the Tourist Maze* (Berkeley, Los Angeles and London: University of California Press).

Harrison, Julia (2003) *Being a Tourist: Finding Meaning in Pleasure Travel* (Vancouver: University of British Columbia Press).

Hendry, Joy (2000) *The Orient Strikes Back: A Global View of Cultural Display* (Oxford: Berg).

Hendry, Joy (2005) *Reclaiming Culture: Indigenous People and Self Representation* (New York: Palgrave).

Hitchcock, Michael, King, Victor T. and Parnwell, Michael J. G. (eds) (1993) *Tourism in South-east Asia* (London: Routledge).

Hitchcock, Michael and Teague, Ken (eds) (2000) *Souvenirs: The Material Culture of Tourism* (Aldershot: Ashgate).

Johnston, Alison M. (2006) *Is the Sacred for Sale? Tourism and Indigenous Peoples* (London: Earthscan).

MacClancy, Jeremy (1992) *Consuming Culture* (London: Chapmans).

MacDonald, Sharon (1997) *Reimagining Culture: Histories, Identities, and the Gaelic Renaissance* (Oxford: Berg).

McCannell, Dean (1976) *The Tourist* (New York: Schocken Books; 2nd edn Berkeley, Los Angeles and London: University of California Press, 1999).

Nuryanti, Wiendu (1997) *Tourism and Heritage Management* (Yogyakarta: Gadjah Mada University Press).

Rojek, Chris and Urry, John (eds) (1997) *Touring Cultures: Transformations of Travel and Theory* (London and New York: Routledge).

Royal, C. (2002) *Indigenous Worldviews – A Comparative Study*, a Report on Research in Progress, prepared 21 February 2002.

Sheller, Mimi and Urry, John (eds) (2004) *Tourism Mobilities: Places to Play, Places in Play* (London and New York: Routledge).

Shirres, M. (1997) *Te Tangata: The Human Person* (Auckland: Accent Publications).

Smith, Valene L. (ed.) (1977) *Hosts and Guests: The Anthropology of Tourism* (Philadelphia: University of Pennsylvania Press; also Oxford: Blackwell, 1978; and 2nd edn, Philadelphia: University of Pennsylvania Press, 1989)

Smith, Valene L. and Brent, Maryann (eds) (2001) *Hosts and Guests Revisited: Tourism Issues of the 21st Century* (New York: Cognizant Communication).

Turner, Victor and Turner, Edith (1978) *Image and Pilgrimage in Christian Culture: Anthropological Perspectives* (Oxford: Basil Blackwell).

Urry, John (1990) *The Tourist Gaze: Leisure and Travel in Contemporary Societies* (London: Sage).

Waldren, Jacqueline (1996) *Insiders and Outsiders: Paradise and Reality in Mallorca* (Oxford: Berghahn Books).

Watson, James L. (ed.) (1998) *Golden Arches East: McDonalds in East Asia* (Stanford, Calif.: Stanford University Press).

Yamashita, Shinji (2003) *Bali and Beyond: Explorations in the Anthropology of Tourism* (Oxford: Berg).

Articles

Adler, Judith (1985) 'Youth on the Road: Reflections on the History of Tramping', *Annals of Tourism Research*, 12: 335–54.

Anthropology and Tourism Special Issue (2004) *Anthropology Today*, 20(3).

Black, Annabel (1996) 'Negotiating the Tourist Gaze: the Example of Malta', in Jeremy Boissevain, *Coping with Tourists* (Oxford: Berghahn), pp. 112–42.

Cajete, G. (2005) *Indigenous Science: A Foundational Paradigm for Sustainable Economic Development*, in 'Te Ara Matariki: Pathway to New Beginnings' Conference, 20–1 June 2005, Centre for Māori Innovation and Development, Rotorua.

Caplan, Pat (2005) 'In Search of the Exotic: a Discussion of the BBC2 Series *Tribe*', *Anthropology Today*,. 21(2): 3–7, and discussion in several subsequent issues of *Anthropology Today*, including 22(4) and 23(2).

Eindhoven, Myrna, Bakker, Laurens and Persoon, Gerard A. (2007) 'Intruders in Sacred Territory: How Dutch Anthropologists Deal with Popular Mediation of Their Science'. *Anthropology Today*, 23(1): 8–12.

Fish, Adam and Evershed, Sarah (2006) 'Anthropologist Responding to Anthropological Television: A Response to Caplan, Hughes-Freeland and Singer', *Anthropology Today*, 22(4): 22–5. .

Graburn, Nelson (2001) 'Tourism: The Sacred Journey', in V. Smith, *Hosts and Guests* (1977, 1989) and V. Smith and M. Brent, *Hosts and Guests Revisited* (2001).

Holtorf, Cornelius (2007) 'What Does What I'm Doing Mean To You: a Response to the Recent Discussion on Tribe', *Anthropology Today*, 23(2): 18–20.

Kohn, Tamara (1997) 'Island Involvement and the Evolving Tourist', in Abram, Simone, Jacqueline Waldren and Donald V. L. Macleod, *Tourists and Tourism* (Oxford: Berg), pp. 13–28.

Macdonald, Sharon (1997) 'A People's Story: Heritage, Identity and Authenticity', in Chris Rojck and John Urry, *Touring Cultures* (London and New York: Routledge), pp. 155–75.

Moore, Alexander (1980) 'Walt Disney World: Bounded Ritual, Space and the Playful Pilgrimage Center', in *Anthropological Quarterly*, 53(4): 207–18.

Pellow, Deborah (1986) 'An American Teachers' Strike in China: Misreading Cultural Codes', *Anthropology Today*, 2(4): 3–5.

Russell, Andrew (1997 'Miss World Comes to India', *Anthropology Today*, 13(4): 12–14.

Selwyn, Tom (2001) 'Bosnia-Hercegovina, Tourists, Anthropologists', *Anthropology Today*, 17(5): 1–2.

Russell, Andrew (1997 'Miss World Comes to India', *Anthropology Today*, 13 (4): 12–14.

Selwyn, Tom (2001) 'Bosnia-Hercegovina, Tourists, Anthropologists', *Anthropology Today*, 17 5: 1–2.

Novels and Other Books of Interest

Garland, Alex (1997) *The Beach* (London: Penguin Books, 1997) is a page-turning mystery novel set among young travellers in Thailand.

Hammoudi, Abdellah (2006) *A Season in Mecca: Narrative of a Pilgrimage* (translated from the French by Pascale Ghazaleh, Cambridge: Polity Press), recounts the decision and journey of a young Moroccan anthropologist to join the Muslim Hajj.

Heldke, Lisa (2003) *Exotic Appetites: ruminations of a food adventurer* (New York and London: Routledge) is an amusing account of the huge variety of food the cosmopolitan world now has available to enjoy and consume.

Films

The Beach, a feature film starring Leonardo DiCaprio, based on Alex Garland's novel about backpackers, listed above.

Cannibal Tours (Dennis O'Rourke, 1988). The film follows a number of Europeans and Americans as they travel from village to village throughout the Sepik River area in Papua New Guinea, driving hard bargains for local handcrafted items, paying to view formerly sacred ceremonies and taking photographs of every aspect of 'primitive' life. The tourists unwittingly reveal an unattractive and pervasive ethnocentrism to O'Rourke's cameras.

Condors and Bulls Brought on Stage (Andre Affentranger, 41 minutes, 2003, student film). A bull-fight, in which a condor is tied on the back of a bull, in the South-Peruvian Andes is visited year by year by photographers and film teams from all over the world in order to document this event for a foreign audience. This film, shot during two years of anthropological fieldwork, focuses on these visitors from abroad and argues that the idealisation of other cultures as a kind of market strategy, can well be interpreted as a form of visual colonisation.

Culture Show (Rong Li, 36 minutes, 2003). In a remote Sani village, local leaders and ordinary people interact with anthropologists, television journalists and other Sani groups to create a picture of a traditional life that tourists find attractive.

80 Days, *Pole to Pole*, *Himalaya*, *Sahara* and *Full Circle* document Michael Palin's intercultural encounters with people around the world (see website below).

Global Villages (Tamar Gordon, USA, 61 mins) Global villages are theme parks in China and Japan that show imagined cultures. (RAI Festival 2005 submission.)

Harpoons and Heartache (Bessie Morris, 1998, 30 minutes, student film, Granada Centre for Visual Anthropology). An exploration of the relationships between female tourists and local Greek men, focusing on the personal story of Vassilis, a young bartender in the tourist resort of Hania, Crete. These relationships are often said to be exploitative, but who is exploiting whom?

Hippie Massala (Damaris Luethi and Ulrich Grossenbacher, 2006, 93 minutes). From the mid-1960s onwards thousands of Western hippies and 'flower children' moved to India in search of an alternative lifestyle, spiritual enlightenment and drug experimentation. Most returned after a few months or years, but some stayed forever.

Holy Man and Fools (Michael Yorke, 2005, 61 minutes). Uma Giri, a Swedish woman, has become a Hindi nun. She is one of the few Western women to be accepted into the most radical order of wandering Hindu ascetics. The film follows her and 29-year-old yogi Vasidhit giri on an 18-day pilgrimage into the High Himalaya.

A Kalahari Family: Part 5, Death by Myth (John Marshall). Shows the impact of a tourism project on Kalahari Bushmen in Namibia.

Lost in Translation (Sofia Coppola, 2003) is a feature film set in Tokyo about two Americans who are there for different reasons but find themselves doing things together. It appealed to foreigners, but went down very badly in Japan – a useful exercise would be to try and work out why this was the case.

Tribe is a somewhat controversial BBC film series, which employs anthropological researchers, but focuses as much on the presenter Bruce Parry as on the people he visits in each film (see website below).

Walking Pilgrims: Arukihenro (Tommi Mendel, 2006, 73 minutes – student film). For over a thousand years, the Shikoku Henro pilgrimage has connected 88 sacred places along a circular route of 875 miles around Shikoku, Japan's fourth largest island. Shot over a period of nine months and based on ethnographic survey methods, this film reveals in an intimate manner the motives, aims and desires of modern Japanese people as they follow this Buddhist pilgrimage.

Websites

http://coombs.anu.edu.au/Biblio/biblio_tourism1.html – a bibliography for the anthropology of tourism.

http://www.anthrobase.com/Txt/M/Mollerup_Paulsen_Simonsen_01.htm – online paper on interactions between tourists and salespeople in Egypt.

http://www.bbc.co.uk/tribe/ – the website for the BBC series *Tribe*, provides access to further information about the peoples concerned, as well as an opportunity to see the films.

http://www.palinstravels.co.uk/ – lists Michael Palin's various films and provides links to further detail, new programmes, etc.

Transnationalism, Globalisation and Beyond

Anthropology for the Future

transnationalism
– a word used in the social sciences to refer to the phenomenon, made possible by advances in technology, of large numbers of people whose family and other close connections transcend national boundaries.

The subject we set out to describe at the start of this book has been transformed in several ways over the century or so of its existence, and in this last chapter we look towards the future. The first twelve chapters of this book demonstrated the way that understanding the different subjects that anthropologists study is ultimately dependent on seeing links between them in any one society, wherever that society might be. In the last chapter and this one, however, we are examining ways in which new technologies have enlarged our perspectives, our methods and our potential roles, though not our basic approach to that deeper understanding we have always sought among people with whom we work.

The conditions described in the last chapter to account for the huge tourism industry and related aspects of the recreational interest in cultural difference have brought about many other consequences in the contemporary world. First, fast and relatively cheap transport attracts many movers beyond the tourists, and as large numbers of people travel around the world, anthropologists have followed them to gain an understanding of what they are doing and why. Some of the movers are part of the huge development of multinational corporations which have permeated the world at large with an apparently shared culture of Coca-Cola, sushi and brand-name trainers, to name but a few of the material objects that have travelled in their wake. In local contexts, however, this 'global culture' of *consumption* is interpreted and used in quite different ways, despite the apparent similarities, as we began to see in Chapter 13 and will consider further below.

Another big change has been in the opportunities for people who move to keep in touch with those who stay behind, indeed, for instantaneous and quite cheap communication between people in widely separated places. Internet and mobile telephone technology have introduced completely new forms of communication and cultural sharing that have also provided grist to the anthropological mill. To keep abreast of the social and cultural consequences of these technological developments, anthropologists have had to devise and discuss new forms of research that allow them adequately to follow up their new interests, and in another section of this chapter, we will take a look at some of the ways they have been doing this.

Thirdly, and most importantly for the future of our subject and the global world, anthropologists have potentially helpful roles to play in this new arena. As intercultural encounters become commonplace, but are still often troublesome, those who can understand and explain cultural difference could be out there using their training and knowledge to alert people in positions of power about how to avoid problems that may arise. This kind of work is needed at the local level to enable people of different origins to live side by side, but at the global level too, where another aspect of the new technologies that have been developed is that they have the potential to destroy us all. More slowly, but evidently quite surely, this is happening already, and some of the Indigenous people with whom we have long worked have also been aware at the local level of big problems that the so-called 'developed' world has been blindly ignoring. In the last section of this chapter we will examine some of the ways in which anthropologists can and do make positive contributions to the intercultural understanding that the global world so sorely needs, and we will look ahead to how these contributions could develop in the future.

People on the Move and Transnational Connections

In this new world of heightened people movement, there are many reasons for setting out that go beyond the pleasure trips we examined in the last chapter. For example, a large number of movers are economic migrants – people who seek to improve their standard of living, or their general lifestyle, by finding a new home away from their place of birth. This phenomenon is not new in itself, indeed people have been moving around in this way since time immemorial, but in the last couple of decades it has become much easier for migrants to maintain links with their home base. Thus young people will set off to find more lucrative work than they can gain at home, possibly only for a temporary period in the first instance, and they will send much of the new-found wealth – which may be relatively little in the places they settle – back to their families. Others may settle down and start a new life.

Another set of people on the move are those who have been forced out of their homelands because of invasions, wars, famine, and other natural disasters such as earthquakes and *tsunami*. These kinds of events have also always scattered migrants, and refugees have been a subject of anthropological study for some time. A growing phenomenon in Europe has been the sheer number of people who are choosing to settle in the countries that had formerly colonised their own. Thus the focus of an anthropological study about a particular people may now quite easily be moved from Africa to France, from India to England, or from Indonesia to Holland, and residents of my own home town of Oxford include Dinka people whom we discussed in Chapters 1, 6 and 10 as living in (the now war-torn) Southern Sudan (see websites).

Again, technology has made it possible for people on the move to keep in touch with each other, and also for people who have built separate, new communities in lands far from those of their heritage to re-establish contact with their homelands. The resulting movement of goods and capital is of interest to economists, of course, but for anthropologists the transnational connections that have been set up have formed a whole new area of study. A good introduction to the subject is a book by Ulf Hannerz (1996), which is actually a collection of essays and lectures he gave as he worked on and developed the study of this subject. His style is easy to follow, and he recounts cases around the world that will be recognisable and understandable to a wide range of readers. He writes:

transnational connections – links between families and other social and ethnic groups that are scattered across different nations but which, with modern technology, may be maintained at quite a high level of frequency and intensity.

diaspora – a term, taken from the Greek, for a group of people scattered geographically but still sharing a common identity, usually ethnic or perhaps religious.

> this is a time when transnational connections are becoming increasingly varied and pervasive, with large or small implications for human life and culture. People move about across national boundary lines, for different reasons: in the Swedish village, because for someone an earlier way of life elsewhere has been destroyed, in a part of Germany no longer German, or for someone else because the pay in Canada is better. The technologies of mobility have changed and a growing range of media reach across borders to make claims on our senses. (1996: 4)

Another phenomenon that has formed a focus of anthropological attention has been the increased development among scattered peoples of a kind of shared cultural identity, known after the Greek as diaspora, but also used to refer to groups bound by other criteria, such as religion. The Jewish situation was an early example of this. Now many people around the world grow up in one country, but maintain an important part of their identity as part of another one, or at least as part of another people who in turn form part of another one, and it is interesting to see how much is conserved, and how much changes in the new locations. Steven Vertovec (2000) examines the different meanings that have been assigned to this word, as well as presenting a detailed case, in a book that focuses on another long-standing example, namely the Hindu diaspora.

More locally – and, ironically, often quite tragically – people are nowadays sometimes displaced in the interests of large global policies like the conservation of biodiversity. A book edited by Dawn Chatty and Marcus Colchester (2002) brings together a wealth of research on this subject; in a nutshell, ideas about wildlife conservation and the general protection of the environment have led to the setting aside of lands which were formerly the means of livelihood for mobile Indigenous people, as illustrated by the cases mentioned in the last chapter in the context of so-called ecotourism. Always marginalised, these peoples are often now excluded from their own ancestral lands, and this subject of human–wildlife conflict has become another focus for anthropologists, bringing together primatologists, as well as biological and social anthropologists.

Another interesting set of travellers are the Indigenous people themselves, however, for there is a huge, global movement of people reclaiming their lands and various other rights, with the help of NGOs and international bodies like the United Nations, which has several standing committees to discuss their issues. They find all sorts of reasons for visiting each other, offering support, comparing situations, and doing something they call 'cultural exchanges' (Hendry 2005, especially chapter 5). Thus, members of many First Nations I worked with in Canada knew more about the Ainu – as fellow Indigenous People – than they knew about the rest of Japan. This is ironic, because the Japanese government does not officially recognise that status for Ainu people, though the financial support it offers for 'cultural preservation' enables many Ainu to travel abroad as dancers or artists.

First Nations – an expression chosen by Native peoples of Canada to express their prior status within that nation; it is now officially accepted in various contexts such as the First Nations Assembly, the First Nations University, First Nations' art and so forth.

Globalisation of Business, Objects and Ideas

Technology has actually made communication between widely separated parts of the world so quick and easy that people do not even need to meet each other in order to carry out quite productive relationships. My last book, for example, was commissioned and marketed in New York, where the cover was also designed, but with art work made in Canada. It was mostly written in Scotland, but based on fieldwork carried out in Canada, Japan, and a number of other countries. The copy-editing and book production were very skilfully carried out in India. Finally, the finished book was distributed from Virginia, USA. A minor glitch occurred when a set of proofs was temporarily diverted by being sent to Scotland, USA, but even that was quickly remedied. During the whole procedure I met none of the people involved in the production process!

This kind of scattered business forms the economic base of a phenomenon now described as globalisation, and the constant movement of people, things, ideas and encoded messages around the globe provides the impetus for the title. The notion is ultimately a by-product of the way of thinking described by Tim Ingold (explained in Chapter 12), and those who think globally can make a lot of money, largely because of the huge differential in costs and local wages, as we saw for tourism. This phenomenon is not new either, of course, except for the speed of the transport and communication, and European colonial expansion into all corners of the earth built a framework for what has ensued – often upon or against prior colonial endeavours. A preliminary definition of 'globalisation', proposed in a very useful anthropological reader on the subject, is 'the intensification of global interconnectedness' (Inda and Rosaldo 2002).

globalisation – a term used in different ways in different disciplines to describe the consequences and increased global connectedness associated with the new intensified movement of people, things, ideas and encoded messages around the globe in a way made possible by a huge surge in technological competence.

Inda and Rosaldo go on to discuss some of the deeper implications, because this intensification of communication is largely brought about by the possibilities for speedy contact, and the subsequent 'shrinking' of our social constructions of the world whether we move about in it or not.

> Yes, space is shrinking. The pace of life is speeding up. The time taken to do things is becoming progressively shorter. The world, in short, is witnessing the intensification of the compression of time and space. (2002: 7)

In other words, our notions of time and space have been profoundly affected by the fact that we can maintain those previously named 'face-to-face' relationships with people in geographically distant locations, and even perhaps see their faces as we speak through computers or into our mobile phones. Not everyone is moving in this new global world, but those who stay put are increasingly affected by the movements of others, and their worlds invaded at the very least by the consumer goods that are also available a thousand miles away.

It is a mistake to assume that the same things found in different places will operate, or be understood, in the same way, however, as we found for theme parks in the last chapter. In other disciplines, scholars who have taken a broad overview of this phenomenon of globalisation have been predicting a decline in cultural difference and a general Americanisation of the world, noting that America is now the big spreading colonial power because of its economic wealth. Anthropologists, on the other hand, are particularly good at demonstrating the importance of understanding local differences, and their reports may be very different. It is important to remember that the focus of anthropological study is ultimately people, and how they think and behave, even in this world of technological wizardry, still varies greatly.

My colleague Mitch Sedgwick, for example, has focused for many years on the organisation of Japanese companies, but he has carried out extensive fieldwork in Thailand and France, as well as in Japan. His findings demonstrate two major departures from the theories of Americanisation, for he is able to describe detailed ways in which Japanese companies have developed quite distinctive work patterns, though they may have followed America's lead in expanding into a global market, and at the same time, he can show how those Japanese work patterns have had to be adapted to local differences in Thailand and France. The reactions of the Thai and French employees of these Japanese companies have also greatly informed his understanding of global business (Sedgwick 2000, 2007).

Japan has also been playing a leading role in disseminating popular culture, as well as the means to consume it, and young people around the world share the experience of enjoying *manga* (comics) and *anime* (cartoons) created by Miyazaki Hayao and his team, as well as a great variety of video games and the exploits of their characters. The now almost taken-for-granted portability of entertainment, information, and the ability to communicate with friends, family and business, was largely pioneered in Japan and, according to a former PhD student of mine, builds rather well on historical aspects of Japanese material culture. Phil Sawkins (2007) examined mobile phone use for his thesis, and identified several significant differences in the way people use these instruments in different cultural groups.

携帯電話の通話はご遠慮ください

Photograph 14.1

Mobile phone use in Japan is much more likely to be text-based than spoken, especially on trains. This sign politely asks users to refrain from speaking on them (photograph Phil Sawkins).

To give just one example, there is a notable difference in different countries in the extent to which people use the speaking facility on their phones in public, some being quite happy to air all sorts of business, and even personal anguish, in front of the whole restaurant or train carriage, others being more reticent. In Japan, a lot of people use their mobile machines on the train, but they are doing it silently, sending and receiving text messages and e-mails rather than speaking out loud, and an incoming phone call usually has the recipient rushing to the end of the carriage to avoid the irritated stares of fellow passengers (Photograph 14.1). Sawkins has argued that this cultural difference affects the technological development, so that Japan was years ahead in prioritising the use of the 'phone's' screen, and he links the clever use of text-messaging in Japan to the influence of short, pithy poetry such as *haiku* and *tanka* (ibid.).

Nevertheless, the spread of popular culture still gives a superficial feeling of sameness in cities around the world, as large advertisements announce the presence of familiar brand names, and music emerging from loudspeakers in hotels and restaurants may often be quite recognisable. Indeed, travellers can quite easily strike up companionship, possibly leading to longer-term friendships, through shared interests in fashion, world music, sports, and perhaps dancing styles. As we discussed in Chapter 5, people symbolise things about themselves in the clothes they wear, and the way they behave, and global cultural forms are emerging all the time, especially amongst young people travelling around before they decide to settle down somewhere. Indeed, this travelling may be influential in the way they ultimately form an identity for themselves.

Identity formation is another area of interest to anthropologists, and ease of travel and communication offers new opportunities for people to choose an identity that differs from that of their parents, already a phenomenon common in the UK, as we also discussed in Chapter 5 of this book (see First-hand Account 14.1 opposite for an example of the possibilities for one person). There is evidence to suggest that when people are sent to work abroad, especially if the period is limited, their use of markers of cultural identity from their own background may actually increase in daily life, but an interesting aspect of the global dissemination of goods, people and ideas seems to be a general resurgence of efforts by people at all levels to consider their identity, and very often to seek cultural associations to help mark their place in this world of shifting boundaries. A book by Gordon Mathews (2000) entitled *Global Culture, Individual Identity: Searching for Home in the Cultural Supermarket* examines precisely this issue, and one set of examples is taken from a group of jazz musicians, born and usually resident in Japan, but making different choices about whether to emphasise their identity as Japanese, or go for the influence of the music they perform.

My work with Indigenous people offers another example of this phenomenon, as many of them have faced choices about whether to express themselves as Ainu, Mohawks or whatever First Nation they can lay claim to through a parent, or even just a grandparent, or whether to try to assimilate to the wider society. Often

My name is Wong Si Lam. 'Wong' is my family name and 'Si Lam' are my given names. 'Wong Si Lam' is my Chinese name in Portuguese. I have been better known as 'Selina' instead of 'Si Lam' since I entered a Catholic English secondary school when I was 12 years old.

I was born in Macau, a former Portuguese colony. I am not pure Chinese because my grandmother was Indonesian. When I finished my junior secondary education in 1996, my family immigrated to Vancouver, Canada, because of the fear of the Chinese government. Soon after I received my Canadian citizenship, my brother and I came to England to study. I just received my MA award in the Social Anthropology of Japan this year.

First-hand account 14.1:

Wong Si Lam – on Transnational Identity

I always find it difficult to tell people who I am. Macanese? Definitely. Chinese? Yes, I think so. Portuguese? That is my nationality. Canadian? That is my nationality too. In fact, mine is not a special case at all in Macau and Hong Kong because we all went through similar situations. However, it is quite interesting to the people who 'have a country' or directly belong to a country. To me, and many people of both of these former colonies, the cities are where we belong – not Portugal, England or China.

We, the Macanese, have our own unique culture, which is not Chinese or Portuguese, but a combination of both. Because of the modern technology that makes communication between peoples from around the world possible, there are other cultural infusions that have taken place in Macau as well, such as Japanese and Korean culture. Such cultural infusions, however, have not weakened the cultural uniqueness of Macau. Although the Chinese are ashamed of their political weakness in the past and the Portuguese are so ashamed of their aggressiveness that they have removed some of the historical architecture in Macau, many of the beautiful buildings and sites still remain to remind us, the Macanese, the reasons why we have such a unique culture that makes us Macanese. In 2005, many such architectures have become World Heritage sites.

they, or their forebears, have experienced considerable discrimination, so giving in to the policies of assimilation imposed by many colonial, or formerly colonial, governments was an easy option that they may well have thought preferable for their children to grow up in. However, these days there is considerable support for Indigenous people in the world at large, and artists in particular may find that their careers are helped by emphasising Native origins, as I discuss in *Reclaiming Culture* (Hendry 2005).

In Canada, especially, some of the young people I talked to found the choice of a First Nation identity much more fulfilling than the broader Canadian one. Their determination to learn about their ancestors, and perhaps to learn a language that their parents have lost, seems to give them a real purpose in life, and sometimes they would criticise their age mates in the general high schools they attend for lacking any serious intentions in their studies. At a conference on language revival that I attended, I was deeply impressed by the speeches made – in English – by several school leavers (aged around 17 years) who had chosen to learn their native languages, virtually from scratch. They had also done well in the English medium, and they were extremely articulate, pronouncing that they 'knew who they were' and what they wanted to pass on to their children. I found similar sentiments expressed in several other countries by those who claim 'first' status there.

For these people, as well as for ethnic groups that have been struggling as minorities in the nations which, through circumstances beyond their control, virtually swallowed them up, globalisation has been a very positive phenomenon. The rapid dissemination of knowledge from beyond their own localities has brought awareness of shared situations that has, in turn, led to cooperation and mutual support, which has been enabled by the greater travel possibilities for visits and meetings. Mobile phone technology has reached more areas than land lines in some parts of the world (see the photograph in 'First-hand Account 6' for rural Tanzania), and the internet has been made available very widely among peoples formerly rather isolated. Type any tribal name into a search engine, and there will usually be a wealth of information, often written by the people themselves, though anthropologists may feature as well.

Indigenous political movements have also sometimes been quite dramatic, and the Zapatista movement that came to a head in Chiapas, Mexico, on New Year's Eve of 1994 has been reported widely in the world press. An excellent anthropological account of this movement and its place in the wider scheme of things has been published by June Nash, an anthropologist with long-term experience in Mexico and elsewhere. Her book, entitled *Mayan Visions: The Quest for Autonomy in an Age of Globalisation* (2001) looks to a future she calls 'pluricultural' in which a 'transnational civil society … cultivates multicultural coexistence' (ibid. 254). The election in early 2006 of an Indigenous president for Bolivia added a valuable plank to this vision for the renewal of some of the ancient peoples whose worlds were threatened.

New Themes and Methods for Anthropology

In this new world of movement, communication and self-representation, the field has also opened up considerably for anthropologists, who have been rethinking their approach. It has already been mentioned that our **informants** have now become **collaborators**, and the first-person voices in this book acknowledge the authority of people speaking for themselves. Although it is still as important as ever that anthropologists seek to gain a deep understanding of how others think, we must acknowledge that the people we work with may already know a lot more about the rest of the world than they did in the past. In my own first long-term fieldwork location, in rural Japan in 1975–6, I was the only foreigner that many local people had seen, but a student of mine who worked in the same area 20 years later had several foreign friends, and he has met people he worked with in the area in several other countries.

> **field** – the site of research for an anthropologist, very often a single bounded location for a lengthy period of time, but recently also involving multiple sites, or movement alongside people or other themes of interest.

The kind of anthropological research required to make the studies described above – and for many of those referred to in the last chapter – has by its very nature to be carried out in ways that differ from those we described in the first, introductory chapter of this book. Researchers have to be much more mobile than they used to be in order to observe global movements and to follow people on the move, and a new type of anthropological research has become known as multi-sited ethnography. George Marcus (1995), who proposed the phrase, talked of following connections and associations, and he discussed various ways of structuring the process: for example by following the people, following the thing, following the metaphor, the plot or story, the life or biography, or perhaps following a conflict:

> **multi-sited ethnography** – a term proposed by George Marcus to discuss anthropological research that involves more than one **field** site, possibly because people are moving, but also to follow objects, events and themes that move between and occupy distinct locations in a world linked by easy travel and instantaneous communication across the globe.

> Multi-sited research is designed around chains, paths, threads, conjunctions, or juxtapositions of locations in which the ethnographer establishes some form of literal, physical presence, with an explicit, posited logic of association or connection among sites that in fact defines the argument of the ethnography. (1995: 05)

Following people has probably been the most abundant in terms of research projects, and the transnational connections we talked of above would offer just such paths for anthropologists to pursue. In the global world, many people's lives are literally divided between their places and countries of birth and origin, and other places where they choose to work, and as they and their families travel between at least two sites in this way, an anthropologist wishing to understand how they are living would also need to move. An early example, mentioned by

Marcus, was the study of Mexicans moving regularly across the US border and back, and in Oaxaca a few years ago I was told that half the income of the state came from California, so it would be very incomplete to carry out a study there that did not take these movements into account.

Following a 'thing' has been another interesting line of research, as objects made in one place for one purpose may be acquired by someone quite unexpected and taken to another place where they are given a completely different value. Museums are full of such things, and some of them are now being requested for repatriation by people who claim they were stolen, or obtained under false pretences. Laura Peers (2003), at the Pitt Rivers Museum in Oxford, regularly works with people in Canada on just such a mission. I also have a PhD student, Leonor Leiria, who carried out fieldwork in museums in Europe looking at the way that precious lacquer boxes brought from Japan in the sixteenth century have been cherished, but reassigned roles and values over the centuries (see Photograph 14.2). Some came back with human relics inside them which have apparently been dusted away as though worthless (Leiria 2006). A good anthropological book on this subject is entitled *The Social Life of Things* by Arjun Appadurai (1986).

In my research on parks that represent cultural difference, I was literally following a theme, trying to work out possible influences on my main focus of Japanese parks, but at the same time looking to see what the local meaning would be. I also thought quite a bit about how and whether the work I was doing, running from one place to another in a full circumlocution of the world, could still be called anthropology (Hendry 2003). I decided that our strength as anthropologists lies precisely in pursuing a serious depth in the different ways that similar things are perceived and understood locally – something along the lines of the handkerchiefs we discussed in Chapter 1, when thinking about souvenirs and systems of classification. This is impossible unless we can draw on good relationships with people who know well the different locations we visit, so our network of collaborators also needs to be broadened.

The papers included in Eriksen's (2003) edited volume on *Globalisation* together illustrate a variety of ways in which anthropologists have adjusted to

Photograph 14.2

A lacquerware chest brought from Japan in the sixteenth century and now in the Mosteiro de Arouca in Portugal (photograph: Leonor Leiria, with permission of Arouca Monastery).

doing research in this new world of easy, speedy contact. First, as Eriksen himself points out in the introduction, anthropologists may simply be caught up with movement because the people they have chosen to work with move:

> when Karen Fog Olwig describes the creation of place among migrants from Nevis in far flung places in the USA and Europe, it is not necessarily because she is interested in movement as such, but because she is committed to a long-term ethnographic project dealing with Nevisians, whose social worlds cannot be physically encircled by the shores of Nevis itself. (2003: 5)

Hannerz (2003), on the other hand, points out in the same volume that one may well do multi-sited ethnography in the same physical location, say a city, where representatives of a number of different groups or networks may be located, or may simply meet as both parties pass through. His own work with foreign correspondents is his chief example here, but he cites several other cases of work which he describes as beyond place, or *translocal*.

Another interesting paper in Eriksen's volume reports on research which was very local, in that it was carried out in Trinidad, but that made its focus the use of the internet, a subject matter that could hardly be more global in extent. Miller and Slater (2004) again raise the idea of research beyond place: 'Where is one going – literally – in internet research?' they ask. 'Is sitting in one place and surfing to sites constructed on the other side of the planet a form of single-sited research or a form of multi-sited research?' Either way, their report of internet communication between people from Trinidad – or Trinis – in 40 different countries brings clear evidence that the internet allows people to express and exchange ideas in a way that they understand because of that shared heritage, and which actually enables the continuation of that heritage across the global stage!

My student Phil Sawkins, mentioned above for his work on the use of mobile phones in Japan, agonised for some time about his methodology, and about which aspects of living in the phone-infested country that Japan has become could be regarded as fieldwork. The answer was actually that almost anywhere could be fieldwork, as people were using phones around him wherever he went, and he could – as the name of the Japanese company DoCoMo literally suggests – be contacted anywhere, and, if he kept his phone switched on 24/7 in the Japanese way, anytime! Indeed, his fieldwork continued well into the thesis writing period, for communication no longer stops when the anthropologist returns home, and some of his best ideas have been suggested by Japanese living in Europe.

An interesting new theme arising in anthropology that has been made possible by computers and other technological advances paradoxically takes us back in time to follow up interests that were held by some of our anthropological ancestors. This is the work of Harvey Whitehouse and others that I referred to in Chapter 7, but see the First-hand Account 14.2 overleaf for a more detailed explanation of how this has come about, and how it brings us back into contact with other disciplines from which we had grown apart.

The future of anthropology may lie in the contributions it can make to answering major questions about the causes, origins and potential of human nature, society, history and cultural innovation. What features of human thinking and behaviour are universal and why? What are the causes of cultural variation? Why does history sometimes seem to repeat itself?

Many such questions were posed by the intellectual founders of the discipline: Frazer, Tylor, Spencer, Marx, Durkheim and Freud, among others. Enchanted by the idea that societies evolve,

First-hand account 14.2:
Harvey Whitehouse – on the Future

they nevertheless lacked the tools to build up a plausible account of those evolutionary processes and were subsequently castigated by generations of anthropologists for producing theories that were either unverifiable or, if rendered in a testable form, patently false. The apparent failure of early explanatory ambitions in the field, together with growing anxiety about the association between those ambitions and imperial colonial projects, brought grand theoretical aspirations almost to the brink of extinction. This lamentable descent began with a shift away from why-type questions towards how-type questions. Instead of asking about causes and origins (why societies and cultures are the way they are), anthropologists increasingly restricted themselves to problems of function and structure (how sociocultural systems fit together).

Almost unobserved, however, some of anthropology's neighbours had been making some startling discoveries. After a long period in the theoretical wilderness, owing to the dominance of behaviourism (a largely sterile view of humanity that on principle ignored mental activity and focused exclusively on its outcomes), scientific psychology suddenly underwent a revolution. The invention of computers led, by the middle of the twentieth century, to radically new models of information processing which, taken together with advances in biology and the neurosciences, opened up a new window on the human mind and brain and its evolutionary history. The emerging cognitive sciences suddenly made it possible to address more persuasively than ever before the big questions that had led to the establishment of anthropology in the first place.

By now, unfortunately, relatively few anthropologists were listening any more. For several decades those pursuing big questions about human nature have been working in such fields as developmental psychology, primatology, experimental economics, cognitive archaeology, and co-evolutionary theory, largely without the help of their (at times grumbling) neighbours in anthropology. The implications of this work for the findings of social anthropology, and (equally importantly) the implications of ethnography for the cognitive sciences, have (on the whole, though not entirely) been somewhat neglected. The future, I suspect, may be rather different.

What is increasingly hard to ignore is that there are now a multitude of well-supported hypotheses in the cognitive sciences concerning the naturalness of many features of human thinking and behaviour. These features are natural in the sense that they emerge in much the same way in all normal human beings (barring pathology – itself often a valuable source of insight into natural cognition), irrespective of differing cultural contexts, and without the need for deliberate instruction or training. Natural cognition shapes and constrains sociocultural systems even if, reciprocally, at least some of those features of cognition are also 'tuned' by cultural environments. It is no longer intellectually defensible, for instance, to claim that the basic psychological differences between men and women are exclusively the effects of varying sociocultural, political or economic institutions. Many of the contrasts we observe in male and female psychology are rooted in biology (e.g. testosterone levels during foetal brain development) and patterns of gender difference arising from this are similarly apparent in all human populations. A key question for the anthropological study of gender must now be not whether but *how* historically constituted sociocultural environments impact on (and are in turn shaped and constrained by) the expression of natural gender differences. Just as feminist scholarship has begun seriously to grapple with and contribute to the discoveries of evolutionary sciences and experimental psychology, so too must anthropology. And this is true across all the traditional domains of anthropological research.

In my own area of specialist interest, the anthropology of religion, there can be little doubt that natural features of cognition contribute to the content and salience of beliefs in the afterlife, in supernatural beings, in the efficacy and meaning of ritual, in patterns of deference, myth-making, and notions of the sacred. Religious thinking and behaviour is underwritten by a mass of complex evolved psychology producing striking continuities across time and space despite the presence also of interesting differences. It so happens that my own research focuses most heavily on the causes of religious *variation*, in particular the differences obtaining between small cohesive cults and much larger (regional and global) religious traditions. But understanding variation also requires a firm grasp of natural cognition; in this case (I would argue) it requires knowledge of creative and analogical thinking, on the one hand, and systems of learning and memory, on the other. The nature of human minds is similarly vital for an understanding of economic behaviour, the world of politics, and patterns of kinship, marriage and descent (to take some of anthropology's traditional heartland subject areas) as well as more fashionable areas of research, for instance the study of performance, art and display or of intellectual property rights.

Over the course of the twentieth century, anthropology became 'mindblind' but more generally the discipline developed a kind of biological myopia. The future of anthropology lies in the development of much sharper vision in these areas. Anthropology not only needs to be informed by major discoveries in neighbouring fields but it can and should be a major player in making those discoveries. It remains one of the broadest of all the human sciences and its emphasis on cross-cultural comparison based on long-term ethnographic research makes it also the most informed discipline on questions of cross-cultural recurrence and variability. These are valuable traits, our discipline's abiding legacy to future generations.

Harvey Whitehouse is Professor of Social Anthropology at Oxford University.

The Value of Anthropology in our Future World

Anthropologists have many valuable roles to play in this world of increased intercultural encounter and rapid communication; indeed I would argue that the subject is crucial if the world is to be rebuilt in a peaceful and sustainable fashion. However, although governments around the world seek advice from economists on a regular basis, anthropologists who influence big policy decisions are still rather few and far between. At the time of the destruction of the twin towers of the World Trade Center in New York, for example, many of us were wringing our hands at the lack of understanding that underpinned the action and subsequent reactions, but it seems that few were invited officially to comment. A little book of essays, which came out a few years later, gives a taste of some of the deeper issues (Kapferer 2004).

There would, however, seem to be a gradual realisation that detailed advice about cultural difference is becoming essential in many spheres, and anthropologists are at last making some impact in some of them. The arenas of big business and finance, for example, until recently resisted our insistence on **cultural relativism** in the mistaken belief that the world was converging towards the kind of global homogenisation mentioned above. The so-called 'tiger economies' have illustrated forcibly that it is possible to contribute successfully to world markets, however, with many of their cultural differences still firmly in place, as Sedgwick and others have shown. Likewise, the oil barons of the Middle East retain their own distinctive views of the world. Anthropologists are now called upon not only to help companies set up outlets in foreign countries, but also to understand their own corporate culture from a social point of view.

Another important role that anthropologists have played for some time is to help the people with whom they have worked to defend their territories against the incursions of businesses, large and small, whose industries plunder the land and its produce that have sustained them for centuries. In the last chapter we considered the case of tourism, in Chapter 10 that of oil prospecting in the rain forests of South America. The rise of indigenous political movements mentioned above is often related to land issues, but also sometimes to intellectual property rights and protecting valuable indigenous knowledge that is sought, without proper recompense, by pharmaceutical companies. In some cases, anthropologists are standing aside now to let people represent themselves, but an anthropologist who did a lot of work in this area was Darrell Posey (see Posey 2004 for a selection of his work).

A growing role for those with anthropological training is a direct by-product of the phenomenon of globalisation, where increasing numbers of people travel outside their own home territories, individuals grow up in one place and settle in another, and children are born and raised in a mixture of cultural arenas. Schools around the world are realising the advantages of employing teachers who understand the plurality of backgrounds of the members of their multicultural classes, and a degree that includes combination of education and anthropology prepares students well for this role. At a local level, anthropologists can help schools reach the children of isolated or itinerant groups – even in Oxford, some of my ex-students play such roles in building good relations with Travellers/Gypsies, for example.

Health workers, carers and counsellors are also taking time and trouble to find out about the variety of attitudes and beliefs which exist amongst their patients and other clients, so that these may be taken into consideration in the treatment and advice they offer. Medical anthropology is a thriving branch of the subject, and many universities now offer one-year courses to train health professionals in the contribution the subject may make to their work, as well as opening their eyes to the values of indigenous methods of coping with ill health. Anthropologists have also had an important contribution to make to world health programmes, especially, for example, where the administration of inoculations may offend local cultural values, or there is local resistance to the treatment of sexually transmitted diseases like HIV/AIDS. For some of the possible complexity in communication in such a situation see Lambert (2001).

Anthropologists are also employed to advise on the realisation of development projects, whose administrators have gradually come to appreciate the advantages of taking into consideration the views of the people they are aiming to help before imposing expensive projects on recipients whose unwillingness has rendered them useless and wasteful. There have been some classic cases of misunderstanding, dotting the underdeveloped 'third' world with crumbling constructions, rusting machinery, and local boycotting of perfectly good health measures, simply because the people they were designed for were neither consulted, nor their views taken into consideration. Indeed, a series of books have been published recently about the advisability of incorporating local or indigenous knowledge into the so-called development plans, especially where practice that worked prior to colonisation may actually have been more successful in resisting the vagaries of local conditions. Bicker et al. (2004) is an accessible collection of essays on the subject.

The application of anthropology is not new, but sometimes the subject has become associated with endeavour which is now politically unacceptable at a local level. Some early anthropologists were expected to help colonial administrators rule the peoples in their charge, for example, so they set out to understand the customs, language and political systems of Aboriginal or tribal people in order that their compatriots could subdue them. Anthropologists also adopted a role of advocacy, helping the people they knew so well to represent their own interests comprehensibly to the outside world, but local people have also complained about feeling patronised and diminished by such help, so the aid situation is not without complications.

A very useful book on the subject of applied anthropology, including the reservations that people may have about it at both an academic level and in practice on the ground, is a volume edited by Sarah Pink (2006), which includes essays by a number of practitioners, some quite long-term. It opens with a section on the history and development of applied anthropology, attends to the applications of anthropology in industry, and examines the relationships between anthropology and the public sector. The final section includes an assessment of the role of anthropology in the media, including changes in its presence on television, and its usefulness in law. Roles in these last two arenas have been played by many of us over the years, when we are asked to advise people making television programmes where we have worked, or to act as expert advisees in legal cases involving people from our fieldwork zones.

Nevertheless, and despite all these contributions, there are those who argue that anthropologists need to make more effort to put ourselves and our knowledge into the public arena. Thomas Hylland Eriksen (2006) takes an uncompromising stand in his book *Engaging Anthropology: The Case for a Public Presence*, which he opens as follows:

> Anthropology should have changed the world, yet the subject is almost invisible in the public sphere outside the academy. This is puzzling, since a wide range of urgent issues of great social importance are being raised by anthropologists in original and authoritative ways. Anthropologists should have been at the forefront of public debate about multiculturalism and nationalism, the human aspects of information technology, poverty and economic globalization, human rights issues and questions of collective and individual identification in the Western world.
>
> But somehow the anthropologists fail to get their message across.
> (2006:1)

Eriksen writes from Norway, where anthropologists are assigned a role of high value among intellectuals, something we still need to assert in Britain, although our colleagues in Japan do better, I think. In general, he is right, though; we could and should make more of an impact, especially in situations where interethnic relations have broken down, and politicians without enough briefing about local ways of thinking make disastrous decisions that lead to the tearing apart of countries with a rich, proud history. We are not in a position to wave a magic wand, of course, and there is a limit to the value of mutual understanding in resolving disputes, but some of the roles we examined in Chapter 9 could be usefully applied in helping those who involve themselves in resolving such difficulties.

Conclusion

Some of the indigenous people with whom we have worked over the years claim that they were living in harmony with the land before European colonisers arrived and began telling them what to do (see First-hand Account 12 on pp. 242–3, for example). These ideas resonate quite well with those of activists in movements that are described – in Western ways of thinking – as 'environmental' and 'conservationist'. If we, the anthropologists, have become tarred with the brushwork of those of our forebears who took over the lands of such people and destroyed their means of livelihood, then maybe we need not only to listen to what they have to say, but to share that knowledge more broadly. That would be another good future for anthropology … perhaps you, the reader, can carry it forward?

Discussion Questions

1 Do you think about your own identity? How do you define it? Is it based on your parentage, your birthplace or where you live? Is it based on your occupation, or your taste in music? And does it vary depending on where you are and who you are talking to? Try comparing your ideas with those of your parents or grandparents.

2 If you look at the First-hand Accounts in this chapter you will see that they have no ethnic identity alongside the name of the writer. This is unlike those of all the other chapters, and there is a reason for this. Can you work out what it is, and also think about problems that might arise with the others? See first-hand account 12, for a hint ... look at the heading, and then compare it with the way the writer describes her upbringing. The book edited by Cohen (1982) on the reading list for Chapter 5 might help.

3 OK, so now you've finished the book ... how are you going to put your anthropological knowledge into practice? Have a look at the 'discover anthropology' website below for some ideas!

References and Further Research

Books

Appadurai, Arjun (1986) *The Social Life of Things: Commodities in Cultural Perspective* (Cambridge: Cambridge University Press).

Bicker, Alan, Sillitoe, Paul and Pottier, Johan (2004) *Development and Local Knowledge* (London and New York: Routledge).

Chatty, Dawn and Colchester, Marcus (eds) (2002) *Conservation and Mobile Indigenous People* (Oxford: Berghahn).

Collier, J. and Ong, A. (2004) *Global Assemblages: Technology, Politics and Ethics as Anthropological Problems* (Berkley, Calif.: University of California Press).

Edelman, Marc and Hangerud, Angelique (2005) *The Anthropology of Development and Globalization* (Oxford: Blackwell).

Eriksen, Thomas Hylland (ed.) (2003) *Globalisation: Studies in Anthropology* (London and Sterling, Vir.: Pluto Press).

Eriksen, Thomas Hylland (2006) *Engaging Anthropology: The Case for a Public Presence* (Oxford & New York: Berg, 2006).

Friedman, Jonathan (1994) *Cultural Identity and Global Process* (London: Sage).

Friedman, Kajsa Ekholm and Friedman, Jonathan (2005) *Global Anthropology* (Oxford: Altamira Press).

Hannerz, Ulf (1996) *Transnational Connections: Culture, People, Places* (London and New York: Routledge).

Hendry, Joy (2005) *Reclaiming Culture: Indigenous People and Self Representation* (New York: Palgrave).

Howes, David (ed.) (1996) *Cross-Cultural Consumption: Global Markets, Local Realities* (London: Routledge).

Inda, Jonathan Xavier and Rosaldo, Renato (eds) (2002) *The Anthropology of Globalisation: A Reader* (Oxford: Blackwell Publishing).

Kapferer, Bruce (2004) *The World Trade Center and Global Crisis* (Oxford: Berghahn).

Mathews, Gordon (2000) *Global Culture, Individual Identity: Searching for Home in the Cultural Supermarket* (London and New York: Routledge).

Miller, Daniel and Slater, Don (2004) *The Internet: An Ethnographic Approach* (Oxford: Berg, 2004)

Nash, June (2001) *Mayan Visions: The Quest for Autonomy in an Age of Globalisation* (London and New York: Routledge).

Peers, Laura (2003) *Museums and Source Communities: A Reader* (London: Routledge).

Pink, Sarah (ed.) (2006) *Applications of Anthropology: Professional Anthropology in the Twenty-first Century* (Oxford: Berghahn Books).

Posey, Darrell (2004) *Indigenous Knowledge and Ethics: A Darrell Posey Reader*, edited by Kristina Plenderleith (New York and London: Routledge).

Rapport, N. and Dawson, A.(1998) *Migrants of Identity: Perceptions of Home in World of Movement* (Oxford: Berg).

Sawkins, Phil. (2007) '(Not) only Connect – Investigating the Place of the Mobile Phone in Japanese Lives', PhD Oxford Brookes University.

Sedgwick, Mitchell W. (2007) *Globalisation and Japanese Organisational Culture: An Ethnography of a Japanese Corporation in France* (London: Routledge Curzon).

Vertovec, Steven (2007) *The Hindu Diaspora: Comparative Patterns* (London: Routledge).

Wilk, Richard (2006) *Home Cooking in the Global Village: Caribbean Food from Buccaneers to Ecotourists* (Oxford: Berg).

van Willigen, John (1993) *Applied Anthropology: An Introduction* (Westport, Conn. and London: Bergin and Garvey).

Yamashita, S. and Eades, J. S. (2002) *Globalization in Southeast Asia: Local, National and Transnational Perspectives* (Oxford: Berghahn).

Zolberg, Aristide R. and Benda, Peter M. (2001) *Global Migrants, Global Refugees* (Oxford: Berghahn).

Articles

Hendry, Joy (2003) 'An Ethnographer in the Global Arena: Globography Perhaps?', *Global Networks*, 3 (4).

Hannerz, Ulf (2003) 'Several Sites in One', in T. H. Eriksen, *Globalisation* (London and Sterling, VA: Pluto Press), pp. 18–38.

Lambert, Helen (2001) 'Not Talking about Sex in India: Indirection and the Communication of Bodily Intention', in Joy Hendry and C. W. Watson (eds), *An Anthropology of Indirect Communication* (London and New York: Routledge).

Leiria, Leonor (2006) 'Time Signature in *Namban* Lacquerware: Tangible Forms of Storing Remembrance', *Bulletin of Portuguese/Japanese Studies* 12: 21–38.

Marcus, George E. (1995) 'Ethnography in/of the World System: the Emergence of Multi-sited Ethnography', *Annual Review of Anthropology*, 24: 95–117.

Sedgwick, Mitchell W. (2000) 'The Globalizations of Japanese Managers', in H. Befu, J. S. Eades and T. Gill (eds), *Globalization and Social Change in Contemporary Japan* (Melbourne: TransPacific Press).

Novels and other Books of Interest

Ali, Monica (2003) *Brick Lane* (London: Doubleday) is a compelling novel set in a Bangladeshi community living in the East End of London through the world shocks of the 9/11 destruction of the towers of the World Trade Center.

Bryson, Bill (1996) *Notes from a Small Island* (London: Black Swan) – an amusing and affectionate account of the American writer on his travels around the UK.

Films

Amir (John Baily, 52 minutes, 1986) in which Amir, an Afghan refugee in Pakistan, tells his story through music. His work with other musicians and his precarious existence as a refugee are at the centre of the film.

A Kabul Music Diary (John Baily, 52 minutes 2003) in which ethnomusicologist John Baily returns to Kabul to see what is happening in the world of music one year after the defeat of the Taliban. Implicitly, the film identifies some of the dilemmas facing those seeking to help Afghans rebuild their music culture.

Calcutta Calling (Andre Hörmann, 16 minutes, 2006) is a film about Indian call centres, which at the time of making employed approximately 350,000 people to maintain contact between Western companies and their customers.

Reclaiming the Forest (Paul Henley and George Drion, 39 minutes, 1987) shows the potential conflict between the interests of Aboriginal peoples and the responsibility of nation states to implement ecologically sound policies in tropical forest areas.

Scenes of Resistance (Alejandra Navarro-Smith, 30 minutes, 2000), a student film from the Granada Centre for Visual Anthropology that presents a series of portraits of life in a Zapatista community in Chiapas, southern Mexico, and presents their own views of the fight against misrepresentation and oppression.

The Most Admired Man (Julia Berg, 29 minutes, 2002, a student film from the Granada Centre for Visual Anthropology), mythologised as the Daoist physician from the Jade Dragon Mountain, Dr Ho receives hundreds of visitors and tourists in search of the 'Real China' every year. But what lies behind the doctor and his fame?

Websites

http://www.courses.fas.harvard.edu/~anth1610/articles/escobar.pdf – Harvard University. Chapter by Arturo Escobar on anthropology and cyberculture.

http://www.discoveranthropology.org.uk/ – a great website full of ideas and information put out by the Royal Anthropological Institute in London, UK.

http://www.anthropologistabouttown.blogspot.com/ – a good website for residents and visitors to the UK about doing things with anthropological interest to them.

http://news.myspace.com/science/anthropology – lists recent anthropological news stories and blogs.

www.sil.si.edu/SILPublications/Anthropology-K12/ is designed specifically for US primary and secondary students/teachers.

http://www.exiledwriters.co.uk/projects.shtml

http://freddymacha.blogspot.com/2007/08/and-now_13.html – links to a website that features a performance about Darfur of the Sudanese ethnomusicologist Ahmed Rahman, when he was invited to perform at the Human Rights Centre in East London in 2007. As this book goes to press, Rahman is in the process of completing an interactive DVD about the peoples of Sudan and their music and culture. Look out for it!

Map of Peoples and Places

GREENLAND

ICELAND

Tlingit

NUNAVUT

Inuit (Eskimo)

Nishga'a

Cree

Haida Kwakwaka'wakw
Haida Gwaii Coast Salish
Vancouver

Crow

Pipestone
Crow *Chicago*
Brantford
Haudenosaunee

Plains

Alcatraz

Navajo Zuni *Waco*
Hopi

Aztecs

Maya

Zapotec

Guatemala

ATLANTIC
OCEAN

• *Bermuda*

Hawaii

• *Nevis*

Trinidad
Yaruro Akawaio
Trio

Yanomamo
Piro
Kayapo Mehinacu

Samoa

Polynesia

Machu Picchu
Inca
Quechua
Aymara

Akwe Shavante
Nambikwara

Rio de Janeiro

World Map Peoples and places mentioned in this book

Lewis
Skye
Manx
Antwerp
Auverne
Venice
Mallorca
Sarakatsani
Marrakesh Malta Cyprus
Bedouin
Alexandria
Dervishes
Swat Pathans *Kabul*
Jerusalem
Kirghis *Jhelum*
Mecca
Mumbai
Nuer Nuba Bodi
Fulani
Tiv
Mende Wodaabe Dinka
Bella
Shilluk
Azande
Mursi
Lagos
Amba
Lugbara
Nandi Rendille
Pygmy
Nyakyusa Masai
Mafia Is.
Ndembu
Barotse
KALAHARI
DESERT BaVenda
Ju/'hoan
Zulu
Cape Town

Kalasha
Islamabad
Na
Gujar
Newar
Nyinba
Yakha
Anderi Sani
Tamil Nadu
Nayar
Kerala *Andaman
Pul Eliya Is.*
Kachin *Macao*

Tungus

MONGOLIA

Beijing
Ainu

Tokyo

PACIFIC
OCEAN

MALAYSIA
Penan

Abelam
Mini Wahgi
Kawelka Kwoma
Lau
Bali Flores TORRES Solomon Is.
STRAITS
Trobriand Is. *Vanuatu*
Yolngu *Fiji*
Arunta
Anangu
*Uluru
(Ayers Rock)*

Maori

Tasmanians

INDIAN
OCEAN

Malagasy

© MAPS IN MINUTES™ 2008

Glossary

Aboriginal refers to the first status of **Indigenous** peoples around the world, used by explorers and travellers who arrived in their lands. Its negative connotations in the English language made it an unacceptable term in many countries for years, though it was still used in Australia. Now it has become a preferred term again by some of the people themselves (e.g. Aboriginal Peoples Television Network in Canada).

acephalus (literally, 'headless') **political system** – a system without any easily recognisable head or system of hierarchy. See Chapter 10 for various types.

aesthetics – strictly speaking, a branch of philosophy concerned with beauty and the physical ability to recognise it.

age grade – divisions of society through which people pass, and which may determine various roles, particularly ritual and perhaps political, during the course of a lifetime. They are found quite commonly in Africa, but also to a lesser extent in Japan and other Asian countries.

age set – a term used to describe a group of people who share a social position that cuts across kin ties. It is based on their birth within a particular period and they are therefore approximately the same age. Members of such a group share certain obligations to one another, and usually pass through age grades together.

animism – the attribution of souls or a spiritual existence to animals, plants and other natural objects, such as mountains and rocks, thought by early anthropologists to be an early stage of religion, a theory now shown to have no supporting evidence.

applied anthropology – using knowledge gained through the academic study of anthropology out in the public arena, usually to the benefit of people there.

bridewealth (or **brideprice**) – goods or wealth travelling from a groom's family to that of his bride as part of the establishment and formalisation of continuing relations between their peoples.

ceremonial dialogue – a way of transacting formal negotiations between villages for many peoples in the rain forests of Latin America, used for resolving disputes and potential disputes, as well as for trade and to arrange marriages.

classification – a system of organisation of people, places and things shared by all human beings, but in ways that differ in different societies, which therefore forms a subject of interest to anthropologists.

collaborators – a term used recently in anthropology to describe those with whom we work, who collaborate in our research, to replace the less equal-sounding term **informant**.

collective representations – symbols understood and used for communication between members of a particular social group (after Durkheim).

commodity – this word is used to describe articles designated an economic value, usually for the purpose of trade, and it may be applied to people and inanimate objects as well, if such an economic value is assigned.

conspicuous consumption – the ostentatious consuming of food, drink or other goods interpreted (initially by Veblen) as a way of demonstrating wealth, or laying claim to a wealthy group or society.

cosmology – broad ideas and explanations that people have about the world in which they live and their place in that world

couvade – a practice in some societies in South America where the father of a baby goes through a series of rites parallel to those undergone by the mother as a way of expressing and confirming his paternity.

cross-cousins – are the offspring of siblings of opposite sex.

cultural relativism – a term devised by Franz Boas to explain that as cultures are based on different ideas about the world, they can only be properly understood in terms of their own standards and values. The phrase has been misunderstood to deny human universals, and to suggest that cultures cannot change.

descent – **unilineal descent groups** – groups of people related on the basis of lineal descent from a common ancestor. See also **lineage**.

diaspora – a term, taken from the Greek, for a group of people scattered geographically but still sharing a common identity, usually ethnic or perhaps religious.

diviner – a person thought to have powers to explain the past, anticipate the future and to advise about related decisions, such as causes of illness, marriage partners and travel plans.

dowry – wealth which travels with a bride to her new family.

ecotourism – a term that has been used by tour operators to induce travellers to feel comfortable about activities that otherwise might seem to be compromising aspects of the environment, which indeed they still may, especially for local people whose lives are affected by the arrival of tourists.

endogamy – rules relating to marriage within a particular group.

environment – a broad term referring to surrounding conditions and circumstances that influence the life of a people, but that the people classify and use in different ways.

ephebism – displaying and admiring nubile bodies in their physical and sexual prime, although how the ideal body is conceptualised will vary from culture to culture.

ethnography – literally, writings about a particular 'ethnic' group of people, the descriptive part of what anthropologists provide in their reports of fieldwork. The term is also used in other disciplines to describe research methods that resemble those of anthropologists.

exchange, direct/ indirect, restricted/ generalised – words used to describe types of social interaction between individuals or groups, ranging from gift giving to marriage.

exogamy – rules relating to marriage outside a particular group.

field – the site of research for an anthropologist, very often a single bounded location for a lengthy period of time, but recently also involving multiple sites, or movement alongside people or other themes of interest.

fieldwork – carrying out practical investigations necessary to a particular study chosen by an anthropologist.

First Nations – an expression chosen by Native peoples of Canada to express their prior status within that nation; it is now officially accepted in various contexts such as the First Nations Assembly, the First Nations University, First Nations' art and so forth.

functionalism – a word used to describe theories that explain social behaviour in terms of the way it appears to respond to the needs of members of that society, as advocated by Bronislaw Malinowski and his followers.

gender – a term of classification used to refer to conceptions of male and female, or masculinity and femininity in any society, and 'gender studies' refers to research and teaching that makes this distinction its primary focus.

genitor – a term devised by anthropologists to describe the genetic father of a child, when this might be distinguished from a social parent, who would be named **pater**.

ghost marriage – a marriage arranged posthumously to ensure lineal continuity and thus perhaps care of the soul of the dead in the afterlife.

globalisation – a term used in different ways in different disciplines to describe the consequences and increased global connectedness associated with the new intensified movement of people, things, ideas and encoded messages around the globe in a way made possible by a huge surge in technological competence.

hypergamy – a system of marriage in which a bride moves into a family that occupies a higher position in some locally accepted form of hierarchy.

hypogamy – a system in which the bride's family is regarded as superior to that of the groom.

identity – ideas about oneself and one's social allegiances that usually reflect birth and upbringing, but may also include an element of choice, especially in response to the global dissemination of goods and cultural ideas, and the increased movement of people within this globalised world.

incest – sexual relations which are forbidden in any society because the partners are too closely related.

Indigenous People – a term adopted collectively by those, also called **Aboriginal** or **First Nations**, whose territories have become subsumed into nations built around them, and who are seeking various 'rights' through international bodies like the United Nations.

informants – the word used for members of the society under study by anthropologists.

inheritance – rules for passing on status, roles, goods and membership in particular social groups from one generation to the next.

initiate – a person joining a new stage of life, typically learning in order to be an effective member, sometimes through certain trials and ordeals.

kingship – a centralised system of hierarchy, not necessarily responsible for political activity, in which the holders of high rank have a status and authority that were compared by European anthropologists with their own systems of monarchy.

kinship – a term used by anthropologists to describe sets of relationships considered primary in any society, also called *family* and *relations*, but demonstrating huge variety in different societies in practice.

lateral relations – the term used to describe relatives who are connected through siblings, distinguished in many languages in the next generation (i.e. for the children of siblings) as **matrilateral** or **patrilateral** in order to mark important kin divisions in a society.

liminality – a term used by anthropologists to describe something separate from, or on the periphery of the wider society; thus used to describe those set apart during the period of transition in a rite of passage, or a people marginalised in a particular social situation.

liminoid – a term proposed by Victor and Edith Turner to describe periods of play and other activities that have qualities of rites of passage and the **liminal**, but which may be less ritually (and religiously) important than many of the classic ones discussed.

lineage – a group of relatives based on **lineal** connections.

lineal relatives – individuals related along a line which can be traced through the generations; see also **patrilineal** and **matrilineal** relatives.

matrilateral relatives – those in the same generation related through the mother's family.

monotheism – a belief system that holds that there is only one God.

multi-sited ethnography – a term proposed by George Marcus to discuss anthropological research that involves more than one **field** site, possibly because people are moving, but also to follow objects, events and themes that move between and occupy distinct locations in a world linked by easy travel and instantaneous communication across the globe.

mythology – a term used by anthropologists to describe the study of myths, bodies of stories held by a people about themselves and their origins, described by Malinowski as a codification of belief, which acted as a charter for ritual, justifying rites, ceremonies and social and moral rules.

nomadic - a term used to describe people who move about in the course of making a living rather than settling in one place.

norms - aspects of expected behaviour that people learn as they grow up within social groups, and which provoke some kind of reaction from those groups if transgressed.

nuclear family - a basic unit of parents and children, as defined by English language usage.

objets d'art - literally, an object with artistic value, but used here in French to suggest the way that people in the world of very expensive art create a language of their own to make decisions about what (and who) may and may not qualify for inclusion.

parallel-cousins - are the offspring of siblings of the same sex, male or female.

participant observation - a method used by anthropologists to learn about a people and their activities by observing at the same time as participating in their lives.

pater - a term devised by anthropologists to describe a man who plays the social role of father to a child when this needs to be distinguished from a genetic parent, who would be named **genitor**.

patrilateral relatives - those in the same generation, but related through the father.

pollution/ purity - a pair of terms used by anthropologists to describe institutionalised ideas about dirt and cleanliness in any particular society, especially where these have connotations with notions of spiritual power.

polyandry - marriage involving one woman and more than one man.

Polygamy - marriage involving more than one spouse, male or female

polygyny - marriage involving one man and more than one woman.

polytheism - a belief system that holds that there are multiple gods.

primogeniture - indicates a special role of inheritance for an eldest son.

profane - see under **sacred/profane**.

public symbols - are those shared by members of a particular social group, usually meaningful to all members of that group, though possibly in different ways.

reciprocity - a return for something given, often part of a continuing arrangement expressing social relations, and analysed by Marshall Sahlins into three types: generalised, balanced and negative.

rites of passage - rites that celebrate and protect the move of an individual or a social group from one 'class' or social category to another.

ritual - behaviour prescribed by society in which individuals have little choice about their actions; sometimes having reference to beliefs in mystical beings or powers.

sacerdotal, a term meaning 'priestly', used by anthropologists to refer to the role of communicating with higher powers, such as gods and spirits, often played alongside the more mundane **governmental** role in a system of dual leadership or authority.

sacred/ profane - this dichotomy is used by anthropologists to describe a variety of distinctions made between things, people and events that are set apart (sacred) from everyday life (profane), though the deeper meanings vary between societies, some of which have no such distinction, and they always require further study.

sanction - a reaction on the part of a society or of a considerable number of its members to a mode of behaviour which is thereby approved (positive sanctions) or disapproved (negative sanctions).

segmentary system - An abstraction of a social and political system, first described by Evans-Pritchard for the Nuer people of the Southern Sudan, as a 'set of structural relations between territorial segments'.

shaman - a person thought to have the power to communicate with the spirit world, perhaps by travelling there or receiving a spirit into his or her body, and also sometimes to influence and control the activities of those spirits.

social control - mechanisms within a society that act to constrain members of that society to behave within a range of acceptable norms.

social facts - the proper materials, which 'exist outside the individual and exercise constraint', to be collected by sociologists and anthropologists, as advocated by Emile Durkheim.

Social structure – a way of describing the make-up of the features of a society in order to devise general theories that could be applied to specific cases, but also allow cross-cultural comparison.

socialisation – the inculcation into a child of a society's systems of classification and ways of behaving so that it is converted from a biological being into a social one. The term may also be used for adults acquiring a new set of social rules and mores.

sorcery – ideas about the use of medicines and other occult powers, usually for evil ends, and the ways in which these are passed on from one practitioner to another.

soteriology – a term used to refer to ideas about salvation in any particular system of cosmology, notably in the religious traditions that are based on written scriptures, where they form part of a broad moral system.

spirit mediumship – an engagement with the spirit world where communication is thought to be voluntary so that the medium makes deliberate efforts to call spirits into the presence of gathered company, although he/or she may have limited control.

spirit possession – an engagement with the spirit world distinguished from others (by Raymond Firth) as largely involuntary, though some (like Lewis) interpret possession as invited – either way, a spirit is thought to express itself through a human being, causing the latter to engage in extraordinary behaviour.

structural functionalism – a theory of expla-nation of social behaviour which examines the way that components of a particular society functioned to maintain the **social structure**. It was developed by Radcliffe-Brown and applied for a while by his followers.

structuralism – a method, originally developed in linguistics, of analysing elements of social phenomena for their meaning in displaying the framework of society as a set of structural relations which express a universal human capacity to classify and construct such systems of thought.

symbol – a thing regarded as typifying, representing or recalling something else by possession of analogous qualities or by asso-ciation in fact or in thought (*Concise Oxford Dictionary*, 1958). Symbols are particularly significant in the interpretation of rituals, but also as the visible features of invisible aspects of social organisation.

syncretism – the coexistence of cosmological systems which can still be identified as distinct, although in practice may become quite intermingled.

taboo – something prohibited, usually for reasons associated with a wider system of clas-sification, perhaps related to ideas of pollution, or with notions of the **sacred** in any society.

total phenomenon – a social phenomenon that is found to involve all areas of life in a particular society. The term was chosen by Marcel Mauss in the case of *le don* – translated as gift or 'prestation' – which he saw involving simultaneous expressions of a 'religious, legal, moral and economic' nature.

totem – thought by some early anthropologists to be a sacred symbol, which represented a specific part of society known as a clan, but eventually discovered to have more complex meanings, which were different in Australia and in North America.

totemism – a term used by Émile Durkheim to describe what he thought was the earliest form of religion, which brought together the wor-ship of ancestors with the notion of a **totem** to represent the clan to which they belonged.

transhumant – a type of lifestyle spent between two distinct locations, usually related to annual changes in the climate, such as dry and wet, or hot and cold seasons.

translation – for anthropologists, this practice involves much more than finding an equivalent word in a different language; gaining an understanding behind the meaning of words and phrases, is an important part of anthropological work.

transnational connections – links between families and other social and ethnic groups that are scattered across different nations but which, with modern technology, may be maintained at quite a high level of frequency and intensity.

transnationalism – a word used in the social sciences to refer to the phenomenon, made possible by advances in technology, of large numbers of people whose family and other close connections transcend national boundaries.

tribute – goods or other forms of wealth paid to a central person or body, which shows recogni-tion of that body, and enables the central body to administer the public funds made available on their behalf.

usufruct – a term to describe ideas certain peoples hold about land which gives them the right to use it, but without implying outright ownership of it.

witchcraft – ideas about psychic powers thought to be held by certain people, and the associated practices held to harness them, or sometimes to oppose them.

wizardry – beliefs which people have about the capabilities and activities of others and the action which they take to avoid attacks or to counter them when they believe they have occurred (Middleton).

Index of Authors and Film-Makers

Brenneis, Donald van, 202–3
Brent, Maryann, 262, 277
Brody, Hugh, 255
Brown, Peter, 157
Bryson, Bill, 299
Burridge, Kenelm, 147

Cajete, Gregory, 268, 269, 277
Callaway, Helen, 29
Campbell, John, 240, 254
Cannadine, David, 91
Caplan, Lionel, 148
Caplan, Pat, 31, 33, 173,
    181–2, 185, 258, 277
Carey, Peter, 128
Carsten, Janet, 233
Chagnon, Napoleon, 64, 72
Charsley, Simon, 107-8
Chatty, Dawn, 283, 298
Chaucer, Geoffrey, 258
Chevalier, Tracy, 128
Clarke, Morgan, 234
Clavell, James, 205
Clifford, James, 29, 33
Cohen, Abner, 185
Cohen, Anthony, 104–5, 108
Colchester, Marcus, 283, 298
Coleman, Simon, 271, 276
Collier, J., 298
Colson, Audrey, 158–9, 168
Comte, Auguste, 9
Condorcet, M.J.A.N.C.,
    Marquis de, 9
Cook, Captain, 38, 111
Cooper, Matthew, 3
Coote, Jeremy, 112–13, 115,
    121, 123, 127, 239
Coppet, Daniel de, 53, 75, 91
Coppola, Sofia, 279
Cornwall, Andrea, 32, 33
Cowan, Jane K., 177
Crang, Mike, 271, 276
Crick, Malcolm, 276
Crook, Tony, 254
Crow Dog, Mary, 145, 148
Curling, Chris, 92, 206
Cushing, Frank Hamilton, 25

D'Alisera, JoAnn, 91
Darwin, Charles, 10, 137
Davies, Charlotte, 14
Davis, Robert, 45
Dawson, A., 299
de Heer, Rolf, 255
Deliege, R., 42
Desjarlais, R., 185
Diamant, Anita, 41, 49
Douglas, Mary, 12, 42–4, 152,
    157, 167, 246, 254

Drion, George, 300
Dumont, Louis, 42, 59
Dunbar, Robin, 136
Durkheim, Emile, 11–12, 21,
    24–8, 30, 33, 133–7, 147,
    292
Durrell, Lawrence, 34

Eades, J.S., 299
Eco, Umberto, 148
Edelman, Marc, 298
Edwards, Jeanette, 109
Edwards, Walter, 86, 91
Einarsson, Niels, 250
Eindhoven, Myrna, 277
Eliade, Mircea, 168
Endo, Shusaku, 148
Engelke, Matthew, 148
Entell, Peter, 255
Erikson, Thomas Hyland, 290,
    297
Escobar, Arturo, 300
Evans-Pritchard, Edward, 12,
    133–4, 147, 150–5, 169,
    188, 197–200, 201, 204
Evershed, Sarah, 277
Ezzy, Douglas, 167

Faris, J.C., 112, 127
Fassin, Didier, 49
Ferguson, Adam, 9
Ferguson, R.B., 191, 204
Firth, Raymond, 56, 57, 99,
    159, 241, 254
Fish, Adam, 277
Fitznor, Laara, 242–3
Flaherty, Robert, 255
Folly, Anne Laure, 169
Ford, Hiroko, 82–3
Forde, Daryll, 237, 254
Forge, Anthony, 117, 128
Forster, E.M., 15
Fortes, M., 188, 204
Foster, Robert J., 71
Foster, George, 245, 254
Franklin, Sarah, 209, 234
Frazer, Sir James, 131–2, 292
Freud, Sigmund, 292
Friedman, Jonathan, 298
Friedman, Kajsa Ekholm, 298
Fruzzetti, Lina, 128
Fukuda, Curt, 45, 140, 162
Fukuzawa, Yukichi, 44

Gaborieau, Marc, 49
Gaetz, Stephen, 181–2, 185
Ganly, Mick, 46
Gardner, Robert, 109
Garland, Alex, 278

Geissler, Wenzel, 91
Gell, Alfred, 33, 98, 108, 115,
    123, 127
Gellner, David, 160, 167
Gennep, Arnold van, 77–90
    passim
Gibb, Robert, 185
Glass, Aaron, 72
Gledhill, John, 189, 204
Gluckman, Max, 181, 185
Godelier, Maurice, 189, 204
Goldschmidt, Walter Foster,
    185
Goldstein-Gidoni, Ofra, 5,
    246, 254
Gombrich, Richard, 130, 147
Goody, Jack, 234
Gordon, Tamar 278
Gow, Peter, 114, 127
Graburn, Nelson, 263–4, 277
Greer, Germaine, 31
Gregor, Thomas, 186
Grossenbacker, Ulrich, 278
Gulik, Robert van, 186
Gullestad, Marianne, 32
Gulliver, Philip, 181–2

Haley, Shawn D., 140, 162
Halverson, J., 48
Hammermesh, Mira, 49
Hammoudi, Abdellah, 148
Hangerud, Angelique, 298
Hannerz, Ulf, 282, 291, 298,
    299
Hardman, Charlotte, 160, 168
Hardy, Robin, 92
Harrison, Julia, 276
Hart, Keith, 15
Hawkins, Richard, 92
Hayne, Katie, 125
Head, Joanna, 92, 235
Heald, Suzette, 92
Heldke, Lisa, 278
Heller, Joseph, 205
Henare, Manuka, 56, 268, 270
Henckel von Donnersmarek,
    Florian, 186
Hendry, Joy, 15, 49, 69, 70, 91,
    166, 168, 175, 267, 274,
    276, 288, 298, 299
Henley, Paul, 300
Hernandez White, Maria
    Guadalupe, 60–1, 161
Hertz, R., 33
Herzfeld, Michael, 177, 199
Hiatt, Les, 92
Hill, Polly, 254
Hillerman, Tony, 148
Hirsch, Eric, 114, 127

Ouzo, Mario, 186
Owen, Chris, 169

Pamuk, Orhan, 34
Parkin, Robert, 233
Parnwell, Michael J.G., 276
Parry, Jonathan, 57, 59, 67
Pasini, Carlos, 186
Peers, Laura, 290, 299
Pellow, Deborah, 277
Pink, Sarah, 8, 296
Pitt-Rivers, Julian, 175, 177, 185
Posey, Daryll, 295, 299
Pottier, Johan, 298
Price, Simon, 91
Prince, Ruth, 91

Quigley, Declan, 42, 49

Radcliffe-Brown, 10–11, 12, 49, 137, 142, 147, 172–7, 180, 185
Raheja, Gloria Goodwin, 59, 71
Ranapiri, Tamati, 56
Rand, Ayn, 205
Rapport, N., 299
Raymattja Marika, 124–5
Reader, Ian, 146
Redfield, Robert, 29
Reynell, Josephine, 224, 227–8, 234
Richards, Caspian, 254
Riches, David, 168, 239, 254
Rival, Laura, 196, 205
Rivers, W.H.R., 22–3, 34
Rivière, Peter, 156, 168, 208, 209, 225–6, 334
Roberts, Simon, 172–3, 178–80, 185
Rochlin, S., 148
Rojek, Chris, 263, 277
Rosaldo, Michelle Z., 31, 34
Rosaldo, Renato, 284, 298
Royal, C., 268–9, 277
Rubenstein, Robert, 185
Russell, Andrew, 278
Ryle, John, 169

Sahlins, Marshall, 56, 57, 64–6, 71, 237, 238, 240, 246, 254
Saint-Simon, C.H. de R., Comte de, 9
Sawkins, Phil, 285–6, 291, 299
Scheper-Hughes, Nancy, 128
Schnedier, Arnd, 128
Schneider, David, 233, 234
Schrift, Alan D., 57

Schweitzer, Peter, 254
Sedgwick, Mitchell, 285, 295, 299
Selim, Monique, 185
Selwyn, Tom, 278
Seneviratne, H.L., 205
Shahrani, Nazif, 186
Shaw, Alison, 219–24, 234
Shaw, Rosalind, 166, 167
Sheller, Mimi, 263, 277
Shelton, Anthony, 112, 115, 121, 123, 127
Sherif, Bahira, 234
Shinoda, Masahiro, 109
Shirres, M., 269–70, 277
Shore, Bradd, 38, 49
Shore, Cris, 188, 205, 209, 235
Sillitoe, Paul, 298
Silverberg, James, 185
Simon, Andrea, 148
Simpson, Anthony, 109
Simpson, Bob, 224, 235
Singer, André, 148, 169, 235
Slater, Don, 291, 299
Smith, Adam, 9
Smith, Valene, 259, 262, 277
Smith, Zadie, 224, 235
Sobel, Dava, 255
Solomons, Natasha, 34
Spencer, Herbert, 10, 133–4, 292
Spencer, Paul, 200, 205
Sperscheinder, Werner, 15
Spiller, Chellie, 268–9
Sprenger, Guido, 91
Steinbeck, John, 72
Steiner, Franz, 38, 49
Stephen, Lynn, 203
Stewart, Charles, 166, 167, 168
Stewart, Pamela, 157
Stone, Oliver, 206
Strang, Veronica, 254
Strathern, Andrew, 72, 157, 185, 205
Strathern, Marilyn, 209, 234
Suttles, Gerald D., 199
Sutton, David, 177
Sykes, Karen, 7

Tageldeen, Ashraf, 260–2
Taje, Merinto, 194–5
Tambiah, S.J., 131, 147, 234, 249, 254
Tan, Amy, 15
Tanizaki, Junichiro, 235
Tartt, Donna, 91
Tati, Jacques, 143
Tayler, Donald, 2, 15
Taylor, Drew Hayden, 15

Taylor, Lucien, 128
Teague, Ken, 263, 275, 276
Tenvir, Fozia, 224
Thomas, Keith, 155–6, 168
Thomas, Nicholas, 67–8, 71
Thompson, E.P., 176, 185
Todd, Harry, 185
Trollope, Joanna, 148
Tuchtenhagen, Ruth, 91
Tuladhar-Douglas, Bhawana, 163–5
Turner, Edith, 265, 277
Turner, Terence, 206
Turner, Victor, 76, 91, 105–6, 109, 265
Tylor, Edward, 12, 119, 130, 131, 133–4, 147, 226, 292

Urry, John, 263, 277

van Willigen, John, 299
Vertovec, Steven, 283
Vincent, Joan, 189

Waldren, Jacqueline, 273, 276, 277
Warner, Sylvia Townsend, 169
Wasan, David, 72
Watson, C.W., 299
Watson, James L., 257, 277
Webber, Jonathan, 148
Weiner, Annette, 57, 67, 71, 203
Wendt, Albert, 72
Whisson, Michael G., 15
Whitehouse, Harvey, 136, 291–4
Wilk, Richard, 299
Willis, Roy, 168
Williamson, Margaret H., 116,128
Wilson, Monica, 200, 205, 229, 234
Winter, E.H., 152, 156, 168
Wong Si Lam, 28–9, 287
Woodburn, James, 239, 254
Woodhead, Leslie, 49–50, 206
Worsley, Peter, 143–6

Yamashita, Shinji, 263, 277
Yellowtail, Thomas, 148
Yorke, Michael, 279
Young, Michael, 180, 185

Zolberg, Aristide R., 299

Index of Peoples and Places

This list is made up of categories that may be used to identify groups of people who share ideas by virtue of membership in those groups. The **world map**, on pp.302–3 gives the approximate locations of **peoples** and **places** which may be defined geographically, but national boundaries, anyway less relevant sometimes than a notion of shared identity, have not been marked. However, further geographical information is included below.

Bedouin (Sahara Desert), 248
Beijing, 19
Belgium, 189
Bella (West Africa – Liberia), 97
Bermuda, 2
Birmingham, 2
Bodi (Ethiopia), 206
Bolivia, 196, 288
Boston, 210
Botswana, 265, 266
Bragar, 175
Brahmins, 42
Brantford, Ontario, 270
Brazil, 156, 186, 191, 196, 244
Brighton, 2
Britain, 2, 10–11, 19, 36–7, 42, 44–6, 53, 55, 84, 89, 99, 103, 104, 144, 160, 189, 203, 212, 226, 245, 297
British, 96, 106, 108, 125, 174–5, 209, 224, 257
British Columbia, 58
Bruges (Belgium), 60
Brussels, 19
Buddhists, 144
Bushmen *see* Ju/'hoan

California, 290
Cameroon, 186
Canada, 55, 84, 90, 103, 135, 178, 283, 287, 288
Cape Town, 10
Cape York Peninsula, 92
Central Asia, 239
Chiapas (Mexico), 288, 300
Chicago, 11, 199
China, 27, 28, 90, 113, 120, 186, 278
Chinese, 40, 186, 235
Chinook, 55
Christians, 80, 89, 106, 142, 145, 155; Armenian, 96; Protestants, 96, 105, 106; Roman Catholics, 87, 105, 107, 133, 142
Church Hanborough, 8
Coast Salish. 270
Colonial Williamsburg, 90
Cree, 239
Crow, 148
Cyprus, 235
Czech Republic, 8

Dervishes (Kurdistan), 148
Devon (England), 105
Dinka (Southern Sudan), 23, 112–13, 199, 239, 298

East Asia, 274
Egypt, 260–2
Ekasup Cultural Village, 271
England, 42, 88–9, 96–7, 106, 155–6, 157, 175–6, 219, 258, 282
English, 23, 88
Equador, 169
Eskimo *see* Inuit
Europe, 10, 37, 43, 87, 95, 103, 113, 114, 120, 135, 145, 151, 161, 180, 253, 282
Europeans, 21, 53, 67, 104, 125, 144, 188, 189, 241, 245, 249, 264, 278, 284

Fiji, 38, 143
First Nations, 283, 286, 288, **283**
Flores (Indonesia), 109
Florida, 248
France, 9, 11, 36, 87, 103, 177, 282, 285
Fulani, Bororo (West Africa), 97, 128

Germany, 90
Gisu, 92
Glasgow (Scotland), 105, 107
Göttingen, 16
Greece, 31, 32, 176, 199
Greeks, 126, 240
Greek Cypriots, 235
Greenland, 248
Grouse Mountain, Vancouver, 270
Guatemala, 62–3, 244
Gujars (North India), 59

Haida, 55, 120
Haida Gwaii, 119, 120
Hampton Gay (Oxford), 175
Haudenosaunee, Six Nations of the, 203, 206
Hawaii, 90
Hebrews, 217
Hindus, 39–40, 88, 251, 279, 283
Holland, 90; *see also* Netherlands
Hong Kong, 28–9, 40–1
Hopi, 271

Iceland, 250
Inca, 267
India, 36–7, 42, 58–9, 190, 226, 233, 247, 249, 251, 282, 300
Indian sub-continent, 226–7

Indonesia, 251, 282
Inner Hebrides (Scotland), 272
Inuit (Eskimo), 178, 179–80, 239, 248, 255, 263
Iraq, 177, 182
Ireland, 181–2; Northern, 105
Irish, 175, 181
Iroquoian, 206, 258; *see also* Haudenosaunee
Ise, 264
Islamabad, 219
Israel, 103
Israelites, 140
Italy, 87
Ivory Coast, 128

Jain, 222–3, 224, 227
Jakarta, 90
Japan, 4, 18, 19, 25, 44, 51–2, 68–70, 82–3, 85–7, 89–90, 98–9, 102, 120–1, 137, 166, 171–4, 177–8, 183–4, 191–2, 200–3, 232, 244, 246, 252, 264, 274, 275, 278, 283, 285, 286, 289, 291; historical, 37, 101, 103–4, 107, 166, 174, 196
Japanese, 11, 22, 27, 41–2, 62, 79–80, 111, 112, 113, 120–1, 142–3, 159, 160, 173–4, 249, 250
Japanese, 96
Jerusalem, 96
Jews, 11, 40, 81, 84, 88, 96–7, 283
Jhelum (Pakistan), 148
Ju/'hoan (Southern Africa), 238, 255

Kabul (Afghanistan), 300
Kathmandu, 162, 163–4, 167
Kawelka (New Guinea), 72, 206
Kayapo (Xingu, Brazil), 196, 206, 244
Kenya, 83, 97, 181
Kerala, 109
Kobe, Japan, 248
Kurdistan, 148
Kwakiutl (British Columbia), 55, 118, 239; *see also* Kwakwaka'wakw
Kwakwaka'wakw, 58
Kwegu (Ethiopia), 206
Kwoma (Sepik River, Papua New Guinea), 115–18, 126

Lagos (Nigeria), 181
Lalitpur, 167

General Index

Coca-Cola, 238
cognition, 293–4
coins, 89
collaborators, **5**, 7, 289
collective representations, 30, 108, **115**, 245
colonial: administrators, 190, 244; authorities, 196, 288; endeavour, 68, 188; influence, 102; rule, 187–8
colonies, 39, 190
colonization, 22, 158, 190, 241, 252
colour(s), 25–8; animals, 112; of clothes, 76, 87, 94–5, 107; of skin, 42
'coming of age', 84
commerce, 59, 247, 252
commodity, **110**, **246**; women as, 244
communication, 20, 25, 51–2, 54, **62–4**, 102, 108, 120, 122, 180, 191, 226, 228–9, 244, 281, 284; cheap, 281; cut off, 174; indirect, 177, 203; intensification of, 284; intercultural, 69; new forms of, 281; non-verbal, 69, 202; subtlety of, 120; with spiritual world, 41, 157–9; symbolic, 94–5
community, 52, 54, 64, 80, 86, 96–8, 105, 115, 117, 137–8, 172, 173, 176, 180, 192–3, 197, 271; Aboriginal, 111; affairs, 201; British, 221; Chinese, 186; Greek, 240; isolated, 237; Mexican, 245; moral, 133, 142; Pakistani, 219–24; performing, 271; religious, 226; socioeconomic, 62; Sri Lankan, 250; structure of, 240; values, 156
companies, 118, 173; pharmaceutical, 295; transnational, 196
comparison, 129, 151–2, 178, 191, 220
compensation payments, 65, 177
competition, 29, 55, 106, 121, 176, 179, 238, 251
computers, 291, 292
copying, 275
conception, 208–10
Concise Oxford Dictionary, 94
condolence, 68, 87
confinement, 80, 83

conflict, 29, 137, 142; ritualization of, 179–80
confrontation, 191, 202–3
Confucianism, 18, 166, 167
confusion, 145, 160, 208, 220
consciousness, 152
conservation, 160, 247
consumption, 111, **246**, 250–1, 281; **conspicuous**, **55**
contest, 68, 102; Inuit song, 180
context, 68, 106–7, 111, 136, 143, 146, 181–2, 188, 191, 195, 203, 233, 249
cooking, 31, 51
co-operation, 29, 136, 173–4, 183, 193, 200
corruption, 61
Cortez, Hernando, 190
cosmology, 111, **130**, 138, 150–1, **158**, 160–2, 249, 250, 252
cosmopolitan society, 110, 111, 120, 170
court, 156, 170, 189, 232; Aztec, 190; of inquiry, 154; of law, 173, 180–1
courtesy, 120
couvade, **81**
Coventry, sending to, 174
coxcomb, 97, 99
craft centres, revitalization of, 273, 275
creativity, 113, 126, 220
Creator, the, 271
credit, 64; card, 246
crime, 5–6, 144, 181
cross-cousins, **218**
cults, **142–6**; Branch Davidian, 146; 'cargo', 143; of the dead, 141
cultural: blinkers, 209; difference, 256–8, 273; encounter, 260–1; exchange, 283; preservation, 283; reciprocity, 113; **relativism**, 11, 23–32 *passim*, 36, 70, 93, 110, 295; systems, 182
culture, 112, 135, 137, 141, 273–4; centres, 275; end of, 190; global, 90; heroes, 117; material, 258, 262, 273–5; popular, 285–6; shock, 42; as theme for leisure, 98–0
currency, 19, 67, 244
custom(s), 2, 19, 22, 30, 36–7, 41, 51–2, 75–6, 86, 89, 98,

99, 103, 174–5, 182, 225, 231, 251

dân (or *dana*), 58
dance, 53, 88–9, 106, 179, 183, 272; 'La Danza', 183
danger, 6, 21, 42–3, 47, 73, 79–80, 105, 132, 137, 156, 200, 203, 239
data, 105–6
Day of the Dead, 161, 162
death, 21–3, 41–2, 47, 52, 77, 92, 94, 141–2, 146, 166, 174, 179, 181, 183, 207, 213, 225; brain, 22; days, 159; of a king, 84; premature, 208; symbolic, 78, 86
debt, 155
deception, 53, 177; social, 69
decision-making, 181–2, 191, 193, 200, 212, 221, 231, 247
decorations, 173, 240
defence, 200
deference, 218
definition, 35–6, 93, 123, 130–3, 135, 150, 157, 224, 239, 248
democratization, 191
demography, 29, 196
dependence, 59, 188, 189, 219
descent, 189, **197**, **216–18**, 225; groups, 216–17, 232
desert, 239, 245, 248
destiny, 153; *karmic*, 59
destruction, 55, 190, 247
determinism, 250
development, 21; hyper-, 23; threat of, 247
Devil, the, 183
diaspora, **282–3**
diet, 140, 177, 192, 238, 249–50
diffusion theory, 12
diplomacy, 177
dirt, 21, 38, 43–6, 155
disaster, 140, 154, 190, 201, 248; natural, 282
discipline, 183
discourse, 191, 246–7, 250; universe of, 122
disgust, 18, 36–45, 99, 112
displacement of people, 283
display, 86, 99, 112, 115, 117–19, 121, 123, 125, 176, 183; cultural, 273–4; heritage, 273; people on, 19
dispute, 92, 112–15, 172–3, **178**, 181, 197; resolution,

flags, 95, 104
flowers, 244
folk tales, 22, 118
food, 3, 5, 22, 31, 37, 44, 78–80, 93, 106, 117, 120, 177, 220, 240, 252, 263; collecting, 237; cooked, 195; differential value of, 245; exotic, 257; sacred, 107, 133; ingestion of, 249; perishable, 103, 244; production, 237; taboos, 40–3
forensic: experts, 158; skill, 195
forest: rain see tropical rainforest
forgery, 126
formal pretence, 53
formality, 68, 76, 89, 104, 225
franchise, 190
frankness, 177
freedom, 241
French: Revolution, 135; wine, 177
friends, 17, 20, 52, 79, 86, 88, 107, 171, 176, 220
friendship, 45, 51, 62, 246
function, 62, 123, 126, 135
functional: explanation, 142; role, 142, 156, 200
functionalism, 10, 136–8
funerals, 23, 73, 76, 78, 87, 166, 181, 219
future, 280–1, 288, 292–7

galleries, 112, 121, 125, 126
gap year, 257, 264
garden(s), 113, 116, 117; of Eden, 111; gloves, 125–6
gathering, 238–9; see also hunter-gatherers
gender, 4, 19, 30–2, 37, 40, 45, 89, 92, 106, 115, 122, 142–3, 201, 216, 217, 220–1, 237–8, 241
genealogical: links, 24, 212; vocabulary, 212
genealogy, 208, 212
Genesis, Book of, 43, 106, 137, 142
generation, 3, 19, 23, 30, 64, 101, 106, 128, 133, 212, 214–15, 217–24, 244
generosity, 62, 143, 193
genetrix, 209
genetic material, 209
genitor, 208–9, 212
geomancy, 27

gestation, period of, 208
ghost(s), 134, 150, 159, 177; dance, 142
gift(s), 3, 18–19, 51–61, 69–70, 73, 77–8, 4, 102–3, 121, 246; exchange, 75, 93, 102, 219, 221; 'free', 59; of money, 86; wrapping of, 121, 202
global, 110, 246; community, 66; discourse, 237, 253; homogenisation, 295; interconnectedness, 284; market place, 69, 246; phenomenon, 249
globalization, 283–8, 290–1, 295
God, 40, 43, 76, 80, 134–5, 143, 156; acts of, 153, 174; creation of, 197; wrath of, 155, 174, 177
godparents, 80
gods, 47, 76, 131, 134, 141, 146, 161–2, 190–1, 195, 238, 249
gold, 245
gossip, 173, 240
government, 191, 202, 241, 247
Grand Tour, 264
graves, 87, 162
Greenpeace, 247, 251
greetings, 37, 52, 62, 64, 69–70, 75, 88, 94, 103–4
group membership, 212, 216, 217
Guadalupe, Lady/Virgin of, 60, 142, 162

hair, 82, 95, 97–102, 131, 175; style, 99, 121–2, 246
Hajj, 264
hand-binding ceremony, 86
handbags, 96
handkerchiefs, 17–19
handshakes, 79, 88, 103
harmony, 173, 195, 202–3
hau, 56, 57
head, 102, 189; butting, 179; gear, 96–7, 104; painting, 83; shaving, 99, 100; skin-, 99
headdress, 97–8, 121
healing, 140, 159
health, 112, 123, 166, 189, 225, 295–6
heaven, 142, 158, 177
hegemony, 68; Western, 125
Heisenberg uncertainty

principle, 29
hell, 142, 171, 177
herding, 112, 217, 239
heritage, 68, 118, 272, 273; centres, 273, 274; World sites, 267, 287
hermeneutics, 56–7
hierarchical: difference, 228; order, 55, 118, 157; organisation, 112, 117, 188
hierarchy, 190, 196, 202–3
Hinduism, 131, 164–5
Hippie trail, 257
historians, 150, 155, 232
historical records, 175
historical sites, 260–1, 262, 264
history, 8–13, 22, 53, 62, 89, 112, 146, 151, 155–6, 166–7, 174; colonial, 113, 190, 249; influence of, 43; of thought, 132
HIV/AIDS, 140, 296
htinggaw group, 231
Hogmanay, 88–9
holidays, 52, 87, 90, 248
holiness, 43
home, 30–2, 45, 65, 80, 115, 120, 221; mobile, 239
honeymoon, 86, 246
honour, 54, 176, 240; killings, 172
horoscopes, 28
horticulture, 173
hospital, 81
hospitality, 79
hostility, 155, 176, 225–6
hotel industry, 261, 272
house(s), 41–2, 4, 47, 66, 69, 74, 80, 86, 105, 166, 175–6, 183; building, 159, 166, 221; burning, 174–5; ceremonial men's, 115–17, 126; Japanese, 74, 79, 87, 174, 225, 244; Jewish, 79; long-, 193; plan, 220; Victorian, 220; warming, 52; work, 30–1, 221, 223
household, 208, 232; altar, 86, 106; property, 244
huerta, 244
human: mind, 140; nature of, 209; organization, 193; relations with nature, 249; rights, 297
humanism, 135, 141
humanity, 268
hunter-gatherers, 237–9, 241, 249–50, 252

hunting, 25, 141, 156, 193, 217, 239
hygiene, 43–4, 46
hypergamy, 227, 231
hypogamy, 228, 231

iconography, 119
identity, 89, 217, **271–3**; formation, 286, 288; transnational, 287
ideal, 195–7, 102; and practice, 225
ideology, 59, 94, 95, 104, 106, 182, 208, 239, 249
idiosyncrasy, 2, 70, 172
illness, 22–3, 40, 54, 138, 144, 154, 156, 157–7, 166, 177, 190, 225, 249
imperial/governmental system, 196
in vitro fertilization, 208
incense, 87
incest, 140, **226**
Indian religions, 143
indigenous: art, 111; categories, 150–1; ideas, 130, 133; knowledge, 266, 273; law, 188; **people, 4**, 68, 95, 111, 143, 181, 191, 241, 261, 267, 281, 283, 270–1, 286, 288, 297; political movements, 285, 295; practice, 162
individual, 2, 52, 62, 75, 82, 89, 104–5, 134–6, 154, 171, 191, 193, 201, 231
individualism, 95
individuality, 96, 99, 105
Industrial Revolution, 264, 273
industrialized: society, 158, 173, 181, 248, 251; world, 191, 200, 213
influence, 68, 183, 246
informants, 4, 7, 28, 106, 115, 160, 220, 289
inheritance, 151, 211–12, **214–16**, 218, 228, 244
inhibitions, 47
initiate, 200
initiation, 77, 81–5, 88–9, 92, 99, 117, 151
injury, 146, 175, 179
insurance, 244
intercultural encounter, 68, 70
international NGOs, 247
International Whaling Commission, 250
internet, the, 14, 281, 288

interpretation, 2, 8, 42, 59, 67–8, 69, 77, 93–5, 103–8, 111, 115, 118, 123, 135, 145, 146, 159, 182, 188, 201, 244, 246–7
interregnum, 74
insh'Allah, 154
inside/outside distinction, 44, 156–7
Irish Queen, 95
irrigation, 249–50, 252
Islam, 130, 141, 153–4, 177, 220–4, 264

Japanese Garden Society, 13
Japaneseness, 246
jealousy, 151, 152, 154–5, 245
Jesus Christ, 40, 88, 107, 133, 142
jewellery, 97, 215, 218, 245
Joan of Arc, 157
Job, 155
Jonah, 250
'joy-riding', 84
Judaism, 130, 141
judgement, 117, 122, 172, 181
judges, 170, 177–8, 180–1
jury, 180–1
justice system, 143–4, 180–1

Kachina dolls, 271
Kataragama, 169
kidnapping, 86
kin, 42, 198, 211, 220, 228, 249; diagrams, 213–14; terms, 217
king, 39, 77, 85, 152, 190, 244; **-ship, 188**, 190; of Mercia, 174
kinship, 31, 66, 114, 204, **207–23**, 225, 233, 244; systems, typologies of, 211
kissing, 37, 79, 88, 103
knowledge, 2, 8, 53, 70, 107, 117, 118, 123, 124, 130, 132, 140; local, 266, 273; second-hand, 130; types of, 13
kosher, 40
kula, 54–5, 123

labour, 55; division of, 62, 81, 238, 240
Lady Godiva, 174
land, 55, 173, 193, 295; ancestral, 144; appropriation, 265–6; claims, 9; investment in, 241; ownership, 59, 250–1; scarcity of, 244; tenure,

244–5
landscape, 113–14, 248
language, 3–5, 10, 20–1, 52, 93, 95, 104, 112, 120, 221, 252–3, 288; British English, 48; Dinka, 112; English, 3, 20, 25–6, 38, 80, 95, 133, 137, 150, 170, 174, 207, 209, 213, 217, 224; formal, 203; groups, 202; Japanese, 26, 62, 166, 225; Kachin, 48; manipulation of, 203; Nahuatl, 215; Nuer, 112; Punjabi, 220; revival, 288; Sinhala, 131; taboos, 45, 47; unspoken, 188, 202; Urdu, 220; Welsh, 26; Zande, 150
laughter, 176, 191
law(s), 9, 30, 37, 38, 143, 170–84 *passim*, 187, 225, 232; dietary, 40, 43; Islamic, 182; of nature, 132; poor, 157; of social life, 8–10; Tanzanian, 182; tribal, 83
lawyers, 170, 173
leaders, 181–3, **191–6**, 232, 244; charismatic, 145; cultural, 56; qualities of, 193–4
leadership, 62, 188, 191–6, 252
learning, 2, 7, 19–20, 45–6, 126, 170, 172, 200, 207, 249
legal: changes, 241; contract, 228; definition, 234–5; ideas, 209; system, 84, 141, 170, 187, 208, 215
legend, 54, 190, 217
legitimacy, 209, 244
leisure parks, 258
Lent, 89
letters, 62
Leviticus, Book of, 43
lies, 4, 176–7, 207; white, 177
life, 21–3, 32, 47, 104, 139–40; crises, 207; explanations of, 130; stages of, 52, 81, 99; support machines, 22
liminality, 78, 79, 80, 86, 89, 142
liminoid, 265
lineage, 65–6, 82, 106, 190, **197–8**, 201, 217, 231, 241; authority, 143; groups, 143, 226, 230; membership, 212
linguistics *see* language
listening, 5
logic, 21–4, 132, 141, 153, 192, 209, 213
London School of Economics,

10
long-term study, 183–4
'loud shouting', 176
love, 5–6, 225, 246, 249
loyalty, 59, 191, 246
luck, 153

magic, 25, 55, 121, **131–3**, 138, 157, 162; black, 152; counter, 155; eco-, 155; types of, 131
magico-religious beliefs, 78, **131**
make-up, 112
mana, 38, 54–5, 67, 102
manga, 285
managerial organization, 192–3
mangu, 150
manipulation, 111, 151, 182, 188, 202
mantras, 165
maps, 114, 228, 249
marginality, 115, 196
mariachis, 60
market, 63, 66, 95, 237, 245; day, 63; economy, 240, 245; super, 64, 245-6, 252; world, 246
marketing strategy, 70
marriage, 30, 52, 76–7, 115, 142, 166–7, 184, 201, **221–32**, 244; alliance, 202; arranged, 5–6, 64, 195, 219, 222, 224, 226; arrangements, 55, 65, 174; Boston, 210; breakdown, 86, 181; classes, 24; cousin, 223, 226; **ghost, 212**, 217, 225; homosexual, 225; **locality, 232–3**; love, 5–6; matrilateral cross cousin, 230–1; preferential/ prescriptive, 230; predicition, 106; rites, 85–7; and social control, 171; strategic, 231; suitability for, 27, 159; validating, 228, 244
masculinity, 32
masks, 117–18, 183
masquerade, 89
mate/toa, 22–3
mater, 209
material, 67; artefacts, 67–8; culture, 23, 58, 68, 120, 239, 249; gains, 246; goods, 5, 17, 53, 55, 65, 67, 145–6, 162, 177, 219, 228, 230, 238, 244, 246; help, 221;

raw, 14; rewards, 173; wants, 238; *see also* objects
matrilaterality, **218**, 220
matrilineality, **214**, 217
mayordomia, 245
mayu-dama, 231
meaning, 3, 12, 17, 20, 68, 69–70, 94, 102, 105, 107, 112, 117–18, 121–2, 140, 182, 229, 253
media, 87, 89, 103, 105, 248
mediation, 141, 180, 195
medicine, 4, 25, 173, 249; East Asian, 140; evil use of, 151–2
memorials, 158, 166, 217
menstruation, 40–1, 46
mentality, 21, 23–4
metaphysics, 56–7
meteorological phenomena, 24
methodology, 291
Mezuzah, 79
migration, 281–3
military: assistance, 53; might, 99
millenarian movements, 143–4
ministry, 138
misdemeanor, 155, 179–81
misfortune, 27, 142, 159, 177, 180, 217; explanations of, 142, 153–4, 158
missionaries, 23, 157, 162, 28, 244
misunderstanding, 221, 241
mobile (cell) phones, 285–6, 288, 291
mobility, 282
Moby Dick, 250
Mockerdy, 46
'mods' and 'rockers', 99
models, 66, 80, 213, 221, 253
modernity, 274
modernization, 144, 191, 241
moieties, 24
monarchy, 196, 245
money, 66–7, 86, 201, 219; earning, 221
monogamy, **232–3**; serial, 232
monotheism, 9, 135
monsters, 142
moral: capacities, 240; condition, 99; dogma, 177; implications, 64–5, 246; regeneration, 145; system, 67, 94, 136, 141–2, 150, 156–7, 171, 183, 189
morality, 117, 166, 182, 246

Mother Earth, 243
mothers' day, 60
motherhood, 80–1, 106, 208
mourning, 87, 137
mudyi tree, 106
multi-cited ethnography, **289–90**
multicultural worlds, 160, 212–13, 218
mura hachibu, 174
murder, 146, 157, 177
museums, 68, 104, 115, 119, 125; 258, 273–4, 275; ethnographic, 239; negative attitudes to, 273–4; Western, 126
music, 123
mwali, 54
mystical: attack, 153, 159; beings, 76
mysticism, 106–7, 140, 169
myth, 23, 116, 117, 123, 190; of Asdiwal, 142
mythology, 99, 112, 123, **137–40**, 217

name(s), 126, 132, 158, 200, 215, 217, 226
national: anthem, 104; costume, 96–7
nationalism, 297
nationality, 95, 226
'natural', 20, 45, 208; causes, 153; disaster, 282; resources, 160
nature, 25, 31, 131, 141–2, 248; control of, 249; harmony with, 266; worship, 160
negotiation, 120, 180–1, 195–6
neighbours, 70, 85, 103, 145, 171, 225; operation of, 51, 174, 212, 240; good opinion of, 155–6, 173; problems with, 21, 151, 175, 244; understanding, 29, 213, 220–1
nepotism, 212
networks, 291
neurosciences, 292
new reproductive technologies, **207–10**
New Year, 77, 88
NGOs, 267, 283
nirvana, 133, 177
noble savage, 111
nomads, **237**, 239, 249
normative effect, 171; of shamanism, 158; of witchcraft, 155, 157

profane, **38**, 79

prohibition, 38, 41

property, 53, 55, 212, 215, 224, 241–4; intellectual, 294, 295; moveable, 244

prophesies, 146

Prophet Mohammed, 223

prosperity, 121, 177, 190

protection, 41, 59, 78, 80, 122, 156, 160, 189, 201, 250; self, 156

psychiatry, 94

psychology, 9, 94, 133–4, 138

puberty, 81, 83; rites, 106

public: duty, 212; funds, 189; harangue, 179–80; life, 30; mockery, 175–6, 177; opinion, 152, 159; place, 37

puja, 163–4

punishment, 143–4, 170, 173, 181

punks, 99, 101, 122

purdah, 220

purification, 41

purity, 38, **41–8**, 58, 190; of blood, 223

quarrel, 103, 179

Qur'an, 137, 141, 233

Rabin, Yitzhak, 103

race, 31, 226

racial discrimination, 36

radio programmes, 28–9

rain-making dances, 252

Raj Quartet, 42, 190

rank, 39, 55, 65, 104

rationality, 119, 144, 158, 181

reciprocity, 59, **64–7**, 102, 143, 156, 177–8, 191, 229, 240, 246, 251; **balanced, 65–6; generalized, 65, 66; negative**, 64, **65–7**

reconstruction, 274, 275

Reformation, 156

regulations, 37; legal, 11, 30, 53; moral, 11, 30, 53

rehabilitation, 170

relationships, 5, 6, 41, 231; adaption of, 220; expression of, 52–3, 54, 62; map of, 228–9; rejection of, 62; representation of, 107; symbolizing, 102–4

relatives, 21, 23, 24, 43, 52, 79, 88, 108, 176, 208-9, 219–24, 237

religion, 25, 41, 47, 55, 94, 99, 106, 123, 125, 126, 161,

227, 283, 293–4; **definition of, 130–2**; explanations of, 136–46; as a moral system, 141–2, 177; origin of, 9, 133–6; world, 59, 141

religious: activities, 143, 166, 195, 252; beliefs, 9, 59, 76, 154, 212; differences, 224; faiths, 12, 40, 107, 136; groups, 95; ideas, 209, 225; life, 217; movements, 144; orders, 95; practice, 133, 166; rites, 70, 136; service, 76; systems, 127, 183

remarriage, 213, 221–2

Renaissance, 114

renewal, 274, 265

repatriation, 290

replication, 126

representation, 32, 94, 107, 111, 114, 123, 126, 179, 196, 198; self, 276

reproduction, 208, 233

reputation, 68, 156, 172, 176

residence, 66, 207, 212, 216, 231–2

resistance, 181; to oppression, 146

resources, 55, 105, 112, 219; access to, 245; investment of, 245; scarcity of, 22, 245, 251; use, 247; waste of, 73

respect, 76, 122, 160, 176, 200, 218, 220, 245

responsibility, 41, 203, 247

restaurants, 256

retribution, 172, 177

revenge, 156

rhetoric, 182, 196

rice, 173, 240, 249

ridicule, 173, 176, 240

rights, 38, 59, 84, 209–10, 214–15, 217; grazing, 239, 241

rites, 2, 76, 135, 137, 155, 160, 217; **expressive, 140; of passage**, 77–90, 93, 106, 140, 245, 263–5; **instrumental, 140**

ritual, 23, 26, 48, 53, **73–90**, 93, 106–7, 122–3, 140, 159, 197, 200, 217, 246, 252; bureaucratic, 79; behaviour, 75–6; charter for, 137; cleansing, 177; of crossing threshold, 79–80, 87; experts, 162; precautions, 132; of purification, 41, 43; support, 189; symbols, 106

rivalry, 99; factional, 157

role(s), 117, 121, 133, 159, 174, 180, 201, 213, 225, 228, 241; expressive, 142, 156, 166; gender, 30–1, 115; instrumental, 156; reversal, 89, 183; specialization, 238; symbolic, 196

Romeo and Juliet, 179

Rosetta Stone, 260

'rough music', 176

routine, 73, 87, 248; break from, 87–90; technological, 132

Royal Anthropological Institute, 300

rubbish, 44, 51

ruler, 190

rules, 37, 43–5, 52, 66, 76, 137, 172, 182; dietary, 24, 40; of etiquette, 203; infringement of, 144, 177; **inheritance, 214**, 225, 241–2; lack of, 84, 86; of land ownership, 241, 250; marriage, 226

sacerdotal, **190**, 196

sacred, **38**, 43–4, 79, 120, 133, 135, 144, 264; cow, 40, 42, 47, 251; sites, 247

sacredness, 242–3

sacrifice, 43, 134; human, 22, 190–1

saint's day, 161, 162

Sakyamuni Buddha, 165

salvation, 143; personal, 133

same-sex parentage, 210–11

samurai, 101, 104, 108

sanctions, 37, 53, 64, 83, **172–8**, 180, 182, 241

sanctity, 41

scarring, 83, 116

school, 52, 77, 160, 220, 249, 295; mates, 66

science, **130–3**, 134, 137–8, 158; indigenous, 277

scientific: developments, 208; discovery, 160; figures, 250; ideas, 209; technology, 252

sculpture, 158–9, 171; Yena, 117–20

séance, 158–9, 171

seasonal goods, 252–3

seasons, 25, 88; change of, 77, 87, 252; cycle of, 89

seclusion, 80–1

secrecy, 84, 111, 207

secret societies, 84

secular activities, 75, 106–7
secularization, 144
security, 79, 228, 244
segment, 197–9
segmentary system, 196–9,
   220
self: dual, 134; esteem, 176,
   211; interest, 183, 201;
   reliance, 196
serenatas, 60–1
sexual: access, 200; 'feeding',
   209; maturity, 83, 117; potency, 116; prime, 112; relations, 226; transgression,
   175; urges, 265
sexuality, 31, 89, 99–100
sexually transmitted diseases,
   296
shamanism, 151, **158–60,** 171,
   177, 184, 196
shame, 176, 180, 240
sheep, 240
shelter, 240
shepherds, 240
Sherlock Holmes, 186
shining, 112, 121, 123
Sinto, 86, 107, 131, 166, 167
shoes, 44, 73–5, 79
shopping, 246
shrine, 123, 137, 143, 252;
   visit, 80, 86, 166
siblings, 218, 240, 242
sign, 79, **94–5**
silence, 5, 62
sin, 58
singing, 104, 175, 179, 250
skills, 55, 63, 97, 117, 125–6,
   151–2, 179, 195, 201, 203,
   244
slash and burn cultivation,
   192–5, 241
slavery, 39, 55, 98
social: anti, 83–4; behaviour,
   134, 231; change, 136, 145,
   157, 160, 162; cohesions,
   136, 156; constraint, 12, 30,
   136, 171, 182, 221;
   construct, 207–8; context,
   203; **control,** 144, **170–84,**
   187, 225, 237, 241;
   differentiation, 32, 39;
   distance, 64–6; **facts,** 11,
   30, **136, 137–8;** integrity,
   137; organization, 95, 142,
   198, 249–50; reform, 264;
   relations, 41, 48, 52, 62,
   114, 176, 182–3, 191, 207;
   rules, 14, 183; **structure,**
   10, 136, 157, 199; tensions,

154–5, 159
socialization, 20, 136
society, 6; anonymous, 173;
   complex, 20, 137, 159, 172;
   creation of, 134;
   democratic, 201; small-
   scale, 53, 77–8, 127, 144,
   171, 173, 181, 237, 247;
   state, 62; Zande, 152–3
sociologists, 144
sociology, 9–12, 134–6
songs, 104, 123, 124
sorcery, 150–3, 157, 180, 191
soteriology, 141
soul, 22, 41, 87, 134, 158
soulava, 54
sounds, 114
Southern hemisphere, 252–3
souvenirs, 17–19, 110–11, 275
space: division of, 25–6, 142;
   notions of, 114; shrinking
   of, 284; *see also*
   classification
specialization, 62, 64, 70, 105,
   133, 240
speculation, 134, 136
spells, 131, 151
spirit(s), 117, 158, 169, 189;
   control over, 159; favour
   with, 55; **medium, 159,**
   176; **possession, 152–3,**
   159–60, 171; world, 41,
   117, 126, 157; wrath of, 177
spiritual: beings, 130, 266;
   forces, 54–5; healing, 111;
   life, 160, 240; meaning,
   111; notions of, 113, 134;
   quests, 264; value, 115, 134
spirituality, 56, 269
sports, 63, 179–80, 199
standard: of behaviour, 172,
   221; of living, 145, 238
statistical surveys, 6
status, 19, 39, 54, 58–60, 66,
   82, 99–104, 117, 118–22,
   160, 173, 193, 213, 232,
   238, 240, 245–6; **ascribed**
   and achieved, 201–2; caste,
   224; change of, 52, 77; level
   of, 95, 142; relations, 231;
   symbol, 120
stories, 116–17, 118, 124, 139,
   175–6
strangers, 15, 20–1, 37, 62, 70,
   79
strategy, 160
streakers, 37
structural: analysis, 136–41,
   156, 231; **functionalism,**

10, **137;** inversion, 156;
   overview, 202; system, 201
structuralism, 12, 140–3
structure, 56, 106, 115–16,
   117, 166, 181
students, 8, 29, 37, 83, 99, 143,
   145, 150, 158, 160, 176
subsistence, 192, 237, 239, 245;
   farmers, 247
success, 173, 193, 201
succession, 84, 228
Suez Canal, 260
suicide, 99, 146, 172
suit of armour, 104, 157
supernatural, 118, 134;
   agencies, 180
superstition, 107, 131, 166
Supreme Being, 150
surrogacy, 208
survival, 174, 177, 237, 240
Survival International, 266
suspicion, 37, 42, 212
sustainability, 267, 268, 271
symbolism, 90, **93–108,** 115,
   121, 123, 183, 246, 252
symbols, 109; ban-the-bomb,
   104; bodily, 95–102, 110;
   group, 104–5;
   manipulating, 102, 105;
   private/public, 94–5, 102;
   sacred, 135
syncretism, 160–7

taboo, **38–41,** 43, 73, 106, 131,
   142, 176
tabu, 38, 55
tagba boz, 179
Taman Mini Indonesia Indah,
   90
Taoism, 26, 166
taonga, 55, 57, 67
'tarring and feathering', 175
taste, 11, 19, 96, 122–4
tattooing, 84, 97–9, 112, 202
tax, 189; return, 30
teaching, 144, 19, 144, 161,
   183, 219–20
technological: achievement,
   25, 27, 248; change, 239;
   development, 21, 122, 249;
   routine, 76; superstate, 26
technology, 135, 192–3, 208,
   233, 282; information, 237
telephone calls, 62, 79
television, 248, 258;
   anthropology on, 296;
   taboo on watching, 41
temple, 41, 43, 79, 137, 159
terminology, 108, 112, 151–3,

213–15, 217–18
text messaging, 286
theatre, 89, 123, 145
theft, 55, 65, 84, 157–8
theme parks, 89–90, 273–5, 290
theory, 79, 29, 42, 59, 67, 77, 79, 88, 102, 131–2, 133–40, 151, 153; of kinship, 209; of witchcraft, 155–7
Theory of Limited Good, 245
Thomas Cook, 264
thought: modes of, 115; mythical, 141; scientific, 132; systems of, 29, 150; theories of, 132
time, 23, 26–7, 30, 64–5, 89, 142; divisions of, 26; investment of, 112, 173; notions of, 114; passage of, 77, 87–90; and space, 284, 294; waste of, 73
titles, 173, 214
tobacco, 242
tolerance, 160, 172, 195
Tonantzin, 162
tools, 192–3
total phenomenon, 53
totem, 118, 135; poles, 118–19, 121, 135
totemism, 135, 139
tour: guides, 261, 269; package, 264
tourism, 17, 90, 95, 111, 257, 258–76, 280–1, 295; cultural, 261, 268–70; industry, 260, 267; see also ecotourism
trade, 57, 121, 64–6, 195, 226, 244, 246
tradition: European, 114; Judaeo-Christian, 130,143
training, 84, 133, 158; anthropological, 203; child, 74
trances, 134, 158
transactionalism, 202
transcendental experience, 130
transhumance, 239–40, 250, 253
transition, 78–9, 84, 88
translation, 6, 20, 21, 24, 129, 203, 217, 220, 280–98; dictionary, 3
translocal, 291
transnational connections, 282, 289
transnationalism, 287, 280

travel, 17, 21, 36, 54, 70, 200–1, 258-63, 286, 295; agents, 261; ethnic, 258; railway, 175
travellers, 23, 68, 111, 126; tales, 9
treaties, 65, 103; peace, 25
trials, 181; witch, 155–6, 169
tribe, 23, 54, 65–6, 83, 197–201
tribute, 189, 244; as investment, 244
trickster, 141
tropical rain forest, 114, 186, 188, 192–6, 226, 232, 240, 252, 255
trousseau, 228
trust, 67, 244
Turkish carpets, 120

umpires, 180–1
uniform, 104, 191–2
unilineal descent groups, 216–17
underworld, 158
United Nations: standing committees, 244; Year of Indigenous Peoples, 241
universality, 124, 245
university, 52, 221; degree conferment, 103; of Oxford, 130; Oxford Brookes, 157; 'rag week', 83
upbringing, 19, 21, 124
Upper Canada Village, 90
usufruct, 241

value(s), 10–11, 56, 69–70, 106, 110–11, 122–3, 181–3, 203, 240, 261, 268, 268, 280, 290, 296; concepts of, 245; contested, 123, 181; economic, 17, 72; esoteric, 111; 'gentlemanly', 181; moral, 144; nutritional, 192; socioeconomic, 22; symbolic, 245–6; system, 5, 176–7
variation, 264, 271
vengeance, 172, 179
victim, 152, 156, 176
Victoria and Albert Museum, 118
video games, 285
village, 63, 65–6, 86, 115, 156, 173, 176, 179, 183, 197–9, 231; autonomy, 192; meetings, 174
violence, 65, 99, 104, 181;

interpersonal, 178–80, 181
virginity, 107
vito, 175

wake, 87
war, 53, 64, 104, 116, 141, 157, 172, 217; First World, 179; religious, 151; Second World, 107, 131, 191
Warnock report, 208-9
warriors, 200
water: shortage, 250; supply, 173–4, 181, 245
wealth, 53–5, 61, 65–6, 97, 112, 118, 121, 176, 183, 212, 229, 232
wedding(s), 27, 37, 73, 76, 85–7, 107–8, 166, 228-9, 246; cake, 107–8; rings, 245
West Side Story, 179
Western society, 27, 30–2, 62, 96, 103, 115, 123, 154, 208, 250, 253
whale, 251; conservation, 250
'wilderness', 265
Windows of the World, 90
winter solstice, 88
witchcraft, 131, 150–7, 161, 169, 180, 184; coven, 157; roles of, 153–7, 171
witchdoctor, 159
wizardry, 152
women's: liberation, 30, 32; studies, 31
work, 30, 52, 88, 183, 238; mates, 42, 173; patterns, 285; retirement from, 200
world: ancient, 160; creation of, 88, 130; as globe, 249; high-tech, 112; New, 245; views, 115, 137, 160, 248, 250, 253
World Trade Centre, 295, 299
worship, 43, 106, 137; ancestor, 134, 143; nature, 160; rites of, 135
wrapping, 67–70, 73, 75, 102, 120–2; of the body, 202; paper, 69; social, 69; of space and time, 202–3
writing, 29

yin and yang, 26, 159
Yirritja and Dhuwa, 124–5
youth, 88, 99, 112, 182, 200; club, 181; groups, 201
yurts, 239

Zapatista movement, 288, 300